New Public Leadersh

MW00651197

Most leadership literature stems from and focuses on the private sector, emphasizing personal qualities that bind leaders and followers to a shared purpose. As the authors of *New Public Leadership* argue, if these shared purposes do not build trust and legitimacy in public institutions, such traditional leadership tropes fall short of the standard demanded by contemporary public servants. For 20 years the authors have been developing a leadership education and training framework specifically designed to encourage public service professionals to 'lead from where they sit.' This book presents that comprehensive, integrated and practical leadership framework, grounded in the uniqueness of public legal missions, culture, history and values.

The authors explore three key elements of leadership success: 1) an understanding of our public service *context*, including the history, the values and the institutions that comprise our leadership setting, 2) a set of tools designed to help leaders initiate collective action in wicked challenge settings and 3) tools to support sound judgment, enabling leaders to do the right thing in the right circumstances for the right reasons. The authors further provide readers with a basic understanding of democratic institutions, encouraging them to work within and across multiple vertical and horizontal systems of authority. The book is organized into four parts, each of which is accompanied by a Master Case that provides the reader with an opportunity to apply the principles and leadership tools discussed in the text to practice. To further reinforce the practice-centered approach to leadership knowledge and skills, the authors have developed the accompanying EMERGE Public Leadership Performance Platform, complete with exercises, available online. Written specifically with the practicing public manager in mind, this book arms public servants with a large repertoire of leadership skills, designed to accommodate changing public values and conflicting priorities at all levels of our public organizations.

Douglas F. Morgan is Professor Emeritus of Public Administration in the Hatfield School of Government at Portland State University, USA.

Marcus D. Ingle is Professor of Public Administration and Director of the EMPA Program and Global Studies Concentration in the Hatfield School of Government's Department of Public Administration at Portland State University, USA.

Craig W. Shinn is Professor Emeritus of Public Administration in the Hatfield School of Government at Portland State University, USA.

"This book is a 'must read.' It confronts readers with the complex reality that effective, ethical leading for the public good is an honor and privilege but also an unprecedented challenge... The authors provide practical advice about improving public leadership using an artful blend of theory and their own decades of experience working hand-in-hand with public leaders."

J. Steven Ott, *University of Utah, USA*

"The deep respect the authors show for the critical and deeply honorable action of public leadership, and the grounding they provide in the historical, political, and moral context, ensures that the book will have an enduring impact on students, scholars, and practitioners who will, each in their own way, become the leaders their fellow citizens need."

Brian J. Cook, *Virginia Tech, USA*

Our problem is not the lack of knowing; it is the lack of doing. Most people know far more than they think they do.

(Mark O. Hatfield)

We dedicate this book to those who have chosen a life of public service even though it has lost much of its fashion and high place of honor. We are particularly indebted to the thousands of experienced practitioners we have taught over the last many decades. Their prudence and practical understanding of what is needed to make democracy work in the thousands of local government and nonprofit organizations across the diverse American landscape is the single inspiration and guiding focus of this book. We have sought to capture what they have taught us and to render this accessible to their successors. We believe the well-being of our systems of democratic governance depends upon capturing the wisdom of our practitioners and passing it on to a public sector workforce that is undergoing a major succession turnover in leadership. We thank our students for all that we have learned, but hold only ourselves responsible for any failings or mistakes in this work.

Contents

Contributors

Douglas F. Morgan is Professor Emeritus of Public Administration in the Hatfield School of Government at Portland State University. He has held a variety of administrative leadership positions at the University of Illinois, Springfield, Lewis and Clark College and at Portland State University where he served as Director of the Executive Leadership Institute, the Executive Master of Public Administration Program and Chair of the Public Administration Division. He has held a variety of public positions, both elected and appointed. His research interests focus on the role career public administrators play in ensuring effective and responsive systems of local democratic governance. He is co-author of *New Public Governance* with Brian Cook (M.E. Sharpe, 2014), of *Foundations of Public Service*, 2nd ed. (M.E. Sharpe, 2013) and *Budgeting for Local Governments and Communities* (M.E. Sharpe, 2014). His work has appeared in the *Handbook of Administrative Ethics, Oregon Politics and Government, The International Encyclopedia of Public Policy and Administration, Public Administration Review, Administration & Society* and *Administrative Theory & Practice*.

Marcus D. Ingle is Professor of Public Administration and Director of International Public Service in the Mark O. Hatfield School of Government at Portland State University. He has served as lead for the Global Leadership and Management Specialization and Acting Director of the Center for Public Service. He has worked in more than 80 countries in administrative leadership positions for the U.S. Agency for International Development, the World Bank Group, the University of Maryland and Booz-Allen Hamilton. His research, training and technical assistance activities focus on complex and dynamic public challenges that can be addressed through leadership and management approaches. His co-authored articles have appeared in *Public Administration and Development* and *The International Journal of Public Administration*. He earned his BA in Political Science from the University of California, Riverside, his MPA. from the University of Washington, and his PhD in Social Science from the Maxwell School, Syracuse University.

Craig W. Shinn is Emeritus Professor of Public Administration. He has served as Director of the Executive Masters Degree Program, the Public Administration and Policy Doctoral Program and the Masters in Public Policy in the Hatfield School of Government at Portland State University and the program lead for natural resource and management leadership and technical assistance programs in the Hatfield School's Center for Public Service. He served as Chair of the Public Administration Division. He earned his BA from the University of Maine in Forestry and Forest Management, his MPA from Lewis and Clark College and his PhD in Forest Management (Sociology and Policy) from the University of Washington. He has served on numerous natural resource advisory boards and task forces for Oregon State natural resource agencies and has consulted widely at local, state, regional, national and international levels of society. His research, training and technical assistance activities focus on "conciliatory practices" that can improve natural resource policy and administration. He is a co-author of *Foundations of Public Service*, 2nd ed. (M.E. Sharpe, 2013). His articles have appeared in *Administrative Theory & Praxis* and *The Journal of Public Affairs Education.*

Preface

This book is the product of the authors' collective experience of both leading public organizations and teaching practitioners and aspiring public servants how they can become more effective leaders from where each of us sits. We have had the good fortune of holding faculty appointments in the Hatfield School of Government's Center for Public Service, which functions as a major university portal for public service agencies in the Pacific Northwest region, seeking various kinds of assistance in dealing with leadership challenges. The authors have worked closely as colleagues over the past 20 years in using the lessons we have learned from our agency training experience to design a leadership focused curriculum for our Executive Master of Public Administration (EMPA) program. Our EMPA cohorts and the specially designed agency leadership programs we have developed have served as the "testing ground" for our EMERGE leadership framework and the accompanying tools in this book.

An increasingly common characteristic of agencies requesting our help is their desire to prepare their leaders for challenges they have not faced before. We noticed that beginning in the late 1980s and continuing through the next decades, agencies requested our assistance in developing the capacity of their middle managers and senior leaders to deal more effectively with the following combination of concerns:

- The resources being allocated to fund the missions of public organizations have not been sufficient to meet legal mandates. Tax limitations locally and budget constraints at the state and national levels are forcing "hard choices" on agency leaders as they are asked to make greater use of volunteers, contract out services and find other cheaper ways to achieve their mission.
- The framework for dealing with public challenges has been shifting away from an expertise-centered mindset to a co-production approach. Instead of thinking about building, curing, solving, there is a new emphasis on prevention, assets, restoration, all of

which require collaboration and shared governance with community partners and multiple public agencies and jurisdictions.

- Public challenges have become more "wicked" as natural resource managers, public safety officers, educators, social workers, etc. are being called upon to address issues for which science and politics do not have clear answers. Public officials dealing with watershed management, wildlife restoration, homelessness, poverty, racism, educational performance etc. do not have a firm body of knowledge and set of best practices that tell them what they should do when mediating competing political, ethical and scientific claims. In short, our public servants are not well equipped to embrace this growing complexity and moral conflict in ways that enable them to turn these conditions into leadership opportunities.
- Public agencies are experiencing a technology and information revolution they do not know how to manage and keep secure.
- Large numbers of public officials in leadership roles are expected to retire within the next decade with no clear succession plans in place to replace them.

As we pooled our practical experience and our knowledge of the research on public sector leadership, we soon realized that it was not adequate to the task at hand. So we decided to expand our pool of knowledge and form co-production teams with our agency sponsors who had asked us to design leadership development programs for a newly emerging world of wicked problems. We agreed to co-design the content and co-deliver these programs to agency participants as one integrated academic/practitioner team. We deliberately choose leadership development opportunities that were six to nine months in length, so that we could invest heavily in the co-production activities and learn deeply from the experience. Most of these programs have been offered for agencies as diverse as cities, counties, state agencies and large federal agencies like the Army Corps of Engineers, the Bureau of Land Management, the U.S. Forest Service and the Bonneville Power Administration. It was a "learning by doing" experience for all of us with many good training designs left on the cutting room floor because they did not meet the "relevance" test of our agency co-designers and co-producers. Most of our leadership development programs target mid-managers, have a long history and are supported by a strong advisory board of regional executives.

The most important thing we have learned from this experience is the need to ground leadership in the uniqueness of public legal missions, culture, history and values. This stands in contrast to the generic leadership literature, most of which comes out of the private sector, which emphasizes personal qualities and transactional functions that bind leaders and followers to a shared purpose. Shared purposes that make people feel good, work harder and be more effective are all well and good, but if these purposes do not build trust and legitimacy in public institutions, leadership falls short of the standard we have set for ourselves in this book. History is filled with examples of leaders who successfully rallied support for a common vision, which was then used to undermine and destroy their citizens' precious political institutions. As Abraham Lincoln warned, the greatest threat to American democracy will come from those who like a Caesar, a Napoleon, an Alexander see no distinction in "adding story to story, upon the monuments of fame, erected to the memory of others." Their distinction will be found in establishing a new order that obliterates the memory of the past (Lincoln, "Lyceum speech," 1838). Our goal is to strengthen the foundations of public service leadership by expanding its stewardship to include the 90,057 local jurisdictions that employ nearly two thirds of the public service workforce in the United States.

Two features of our work have helped us appreciate the significance and uniqueness of public sector leadership, one domestic and the other international. On the domestic front, we have benefited immeasurably from the deep and broad experience of mid-career professionals from a multitude of jurisdictions, sectors and types of organizations. They have actively contributed to our learning via co-production in partnership with pre-service students who are equipped with their own sense of purpose in each generation of learners—aggressive learning with a demand that we deliver theoretically significant and robustly practical knowledge. Together, they have prompted us to think deeply about why public leadership is different and why it matters.

Our appreciation of the uniqueness of public service leadership has been further strengthened by our multidisciplinary work and extensive engagement with more than 40 PhD students and over 200 EMPA students. They have absorbed the best we have to offer, rigorously tested our ideas, enabled us to better connect theory and practice and in the process profoundly advanced our learning. This multidisciplinary work has reminded us that public service leadership, unlike most disciplines, is an integrative and organic activity that both requires and presupposes an understanding of the whole, especially of the moral ends of leadership action. Most disciplines are "means-entered." By that we mean they are focused on "how" you get from point A to point B, not whether "B" is a morally worthy end.

An important phase of our learning through the co-production process we have used has been our work abroad, especially in Japan, Vietnam and China. We have had the opportunity over a decade of working on management development with local government officials in Japan (funded by the Tokyo Foundation), redesign of the leadership curriculum for the Ho Chi Minh National Academy of Politics and Administration (funded by The Ford Foundation) and a government performance and leadership improvement partnership with Lanzhou University School of

Management in Lanzhou, China. This international experience has helped us better understand how to integrate the unique values, culture and institutional environment into ones leadership framework so that it can guide and inform leadership initiatives from where we sit.

We are ourselves practicing leaders—all having built nontraditional pracacademic careers where we have always served in public office, held positions on boards and commissions, carried a significant managerial portfolio from deanships and directorships to program and project leadership. This provides us with tacit understanding as well as the vantage of full academic lives. You will know us by our students—who are exemplary public service leaders—we are grateful for what we have been able to impart, what we have been able to co-learn and profoundly fortunate in what these leaders have shared with us.

Acknowledgments

Our approach to "leading from where we sit" is grounded in the work of scholars and distinguished practitioners who take seriously the uniqueness of public service and the fragility of public institutions. We owe a deep debt of gratitude to a small core of public administration colleagues—among them Herbert Storing, Kent Kirwan, David Schaefer, John Rohr, David Rosenbloom, Phillip Cooper, Brian Cook and Larry Terry—all of whom have placed the U.S. Constitution at the center of public service education and training.

We have drawn heavily from other scholars such as Stephen Elkin and Karol Soltan, Camilla Stivers, Paul Van Riper, Leonard White, Dwight Waldo, Philip Selznick, Richard Scott, Theda Skocpol, Hugh Helco, Eleanor, Vincent Ostrom and Pat Ingraham.

We wish also to acknowledge our appreciation for the work of William Scott and David Hart, Richard Stillman, Terry Cooper, Michael Spicer, Daniel Kemmis, Walter Powell, Paul DiMaggio and Carmen Sirianni, who have sharpened our thinking about the historical and institutional forces that shape public service leadership roles. We also want to recognize the contributions of professional colleagues in the U.S. and Vietnam who collaborated with us on developing the EMERGE Leadership Approach. These include Dr. Kristen Magis, Dr. Ngo Huy Duc, Dr. Bui Phuong Duh and Dr. Dang Van Huan. Finally, we want to acknowledge scholars writing on public leadership from whom we have generously drawn for this monograph: Joseph Nye, James Kouzes and Richard Posner, Mathew Fairholm, Richard Hames and Barbara Crosby and John Bryson.

Colleagueship is rare in the academy. Most academic institutions are governed by the instrumental mindset of bureaucracies and faculty unions where rules prevail over relationships. Our experience has been fortunately different. And we wish to acknowledge our Center for Public Service Director, Phil Keisling, our Assistant Director, Dr. Masami Nishishiba and the Center staff who have created an environment where intellectually worthy ideas and projects are always the first and most important priority.

We are grateful for the role models of reflective practice that have been provided to us by such exemplary public leaders as Charles Cameron (retired county administrator), Deb Whitall (U.S. Forest Service), Davis Moriuchi (Army Corps of Engineers), Don Bohn (active county administrator), Elaine Zielinski (Bureau of Land Management), Dan Vizzini (retired city administrator), Jean Thorne (state administrator), Gary Larson (retired U.S. Forest Service), Rick Mogren (retired Army Corps of Engineers), Scott Lazenby (city manager) and numerous others who have been splendid teachers. This book is intended to cultivate all of the public service qualities their careers embody.

Finally, we wish to acknowledge the significant editing and formatting work that has gone into this text. We wish to thank Jason Normand, Master of Public Policy, who co-developed the EMERGE Public Leadership Performance Platform with Tools and Practices as elaborated in Chapters 9 and 11 of this volume. We are especially grateful to Rebecca Craven, PhD candidate in Portland State University's Public Affairs and Policy Program, for the exceptional and sustained work on this manuscript. Her work went far beyond what most graduate students are called upon to do when assisting with book editing. Ms. Craven performed the role of a professional book editor, which enabled us to bring a much-belated manuscript across the finish line without sacrifices in quality. We also want to thank the exceptional work of our Taylor & Francis team, Misha Kydd and Laura Stearns.

Part I

Foundations of Public Service Leadership

Master Case: The Angry Library Patron

Cheryl Miller was quietly working on her monthly administrative report to her supervisor as she was doing double duty at the library circulation desk when she was suddenly confronted by an angry father dragging a six-year-old child by the hand.

"Why is this kind of book on the children's bookshelves? It clearly is unfit reading and should be removed immediately to another section of the library."

This is not what you, the children's librarian at a local branch library, need to hear at this time of day. Two of your clerks failed to appear for work today because of icy road conditions. That did not seem to stop the hoards of school kids who flocked to the library to pass the time of day. As a result of having to work without a break checking out books all day at the circulation desk, you will have to spend the evening completing your budget request for the next fiscal year in order to meet the 8:00 a.m. deadline set by your library director. As a professional children's librarian, you deeply resent the endless administrative work that takes you away from what you most enjoy and have been best prepared to carry out: selecting and recommending good literature to children and their parents. You've been having second thoughts about whether you are really cut out for your current position. There is just too much time spent on keeping track of time cards, doing budget preparation, undertaking personnel evaluations and responding to patrons' complaints. As you think about what it might be like to work in a larger library system where you could make more use of the knowledge and skills for which you have been trained, you are suddenly jolted into the reality of this training by a distraught parent who insists that he, not you, should make the choices about the suitability of children's library selections.

You notice that the book in question is a copy of Maurice Sendak's *In the Night Kitchen*, one of the most popular children's stories of the past four decades and a 1971 Caldecott Honor Book. You've dealt with this kind of situation before, so you politely give your standardized response:

"We encourage parents to help their children select material that is appropriate to their interests and level of reading skill. Could I help you find a more suitable book?"

"That's not the point. Both the nudity and bizarre images in this book make it unsuitable reading for any kids under 10. I want it removed from the children's section of the collection to the juvenile section."

As the line of patrons waiting to check out books begins to build, you see that your efforts are not going to prevail. So you resort to another technique that has usually worked in the past. You give the angry patron a form to put his objections in writing, which usually ends the matter.

That did not happen in this case. The following week the director of the library hands you the following letter from the angry patron, Charles Jones, with a request to draft a response that can be sent out under the library director's signature. She gives you a sample letter that was mailed last week to another library patron who had a complaint about the appropriateness of having the *The Joy of Gay Sex* in the library collection.

Case Supporting Materials

Patron's Complaint Form for Library Materials
Your Name: Charles Jones
Your Address: 2004 SW Happy Lane
Title: In the Night Kitchen
Author: Maurice Sendak

1   What do you find objectionable about the material? (Please be specific and cite pages, etc.)
    Specifically, the nudity of male genitals and the fanciful and unrealistic images.
2   Why do you object to the material?
    The nudity is not suitable for young children who will have access to this material in the library, especially when reading books unsupervised after school or on weekends.
      Many of the images frighten young children and encourage an unhealthy attitude toward the unreal and supernatural.
3   Did you read the material in its entirety?
    Yes.
4   What do you believe is the theme of the material?
    Magic is responsible for producing the things we most like in life, i.e., cake.

5   Do you think that people who want to read this material should be able to find it in the Library?
Not paid for by public tax dollars.

6   Do you think groups or other members of the community should have the right to keep you from having access to materials you want if they disapprove of your viewpoint?
Yes, especially when books like this are harmful to others.

7   Do you believe that parents have the right and responsibility for guiding their own children's reading and deciding what limits, if any, they place upon it?
Yes, of course, but they need the help of professionals and adults; especially when they cannot be supervised by their parents.

8   Do you think other people should be able to tell you what you or your children should or should not read?
Yes. This happens all the time. Schools and libraries don't have money to buy everything. They have to make choices. This is what we pay our professional librarians and teachers to do. Some parents either do not pay attention to what their children are reading or do not understand the kind of harm that some books can have on the development of their children. That is why we trust professionals like you to assist us.

9   Are you usually able to find what you want in the Library? If not, what materials would you like to be able to find in the Library collection?
Yes.

Date: June 26, 2002
Signature: Charles Jones

> Happy Valley Regional Library
> 2404 Happy Valley Road
> Happy Valley
> LIBRARIES to be proud of!

Draft Letter to Library Patron
June 9, 1991
Dear _____:
Thank you for expressing your opinion of the book *The Joy of Gay Sex* by Dr. Charles Silverstein and Edmund White. The Library's Selection Review Committee has reviewed the material and the issues you have raised.

As you have noted, the book is an illustrated manual on adult male homosexual practices. You have asked that the book be removed from the collection because it provides information on sexual practices that may result in the transmission of the AIDS virus.

The Joy of Gay Sex was published prior to the identification of the AIDS virus and, therefore, does not mention it specifically. However, it does include a section on the dangers of sexually transmitted diseases and the importance of practicing "safe sex". It also recommends frequent medical examinations. Finally, when discussing potentially dangerous sexual practices, the authors provide explicit information on possible harm.

The Joy of Gay Sex has been in the library's collection for over ten years. It has been useful to a variety of people in our community. It continues to be an important book for male homosexuals. They recommend that it be read along with more recently published materials on the prevention of AIDS.

In addition, this book has frequently been used by people seeking information on male homosexual lifestyles. A recent article published in both the *Conservative Review* (February 1990) and the *Journal of the American Family Association* (April 1990) offers an example of how this book has been used by people who are not homosexuals. Writing in opposition to the homosexual rights movement, the author, Gary Bullert, highly recommends *The Joy of Gay Sex* as one of the two best sources on homosexual lifestyles.

American democracy is dependent upon a free flow of ideas, many of which conflict with each other. The library's responsibility is to provide information on as many points of view as possible. For example, we believe that those groups who strongly oppose homosexuality, like the American Family Association, as well as practicing male homosexuals and people who wish to inform themselves in order to make up their own minds should all have access to information about homosexual lifestyles and practices in their public library: *The Joy of Gay Sex* continues to fill this need. We have, therefore, decided to retain it in the collection.

The Happy Valley Regional Library, which serves three counties and 13 cities, has a number of books on AIDS and we will continue to add new titles as they become available. If there are titles you would like to recommend, we will be happy to consider them for inclusion in the collection.

We appreciate the concern that prompted you to express your opinion. The issues you raised are serious.

We are pleased that you usually find what you want in the library.
Sincerely,
Constance Harmony
Library Director

Happy Valley Regional Library
2404 Happy Valley Road
Happy Valley
LIBRARIES to be proud of!

Case Analysis

What should Cheryl Miller do under the circumstances described above? She clearly has a variety of leadership opportunities, but which path she takes depends on how she "sizes up" and balances her multiple and maybe conflicting responsibilities. There is first her responsibility to ensure the efficient and effective delivery of the services outlined in the Happy Valley Regional Library's organizational mission. Second, there are her personal values and an assessment of the degree to which they are in alignment with the mission of the organization and/or the application of that mission to the circumstances at hand. Third, she is a trained professional librarian with a specialized body of knowledge and skills. Additionally, in this case, there is a fourth responsibility: to act in a manner that is consistent with the larger structure of constitutional procedures and values within which one works.

As a member of a hierarchical organization Cheryl must necessarily consider the impact of her response on other standard operating procedures and on the efficiency of the organization as a whole. How can she write a response that can be used in other similar circumstances? How might her response encourage or discourage other similar communications from angry parents? How much time and energy should be spent on this assignment at the expense of other activities that will improve the quality and amount of service to patrons in the local community? Is Mr. Jones's letter part of an organized campaign by a local organization to obtain greater community control over the purchase of and access to library materials? The kinds of questions that Cheryl raises, and how such questions are answered, are influenced first by what will best contribute to the efficient and effective running of the organization, and second by the understanding she has of her personal, professional and larger stewardship roles.

Cheryl has previously found herself in an uncomfortable position responding to teenage requests for appropriate reading material on birth control. Her personal religious views are very much opposed to making this material available, especially when the parents are not involved in the process. However, since the library has a policy of allowing children and teenagers to check out materials without the consent of their parents, her personal views have not had an opportunity to influence the administration of policy. In the case at hand, her personal views very much have an opportunity to shape the tone and structure of her response to Mr. Jones, the angry parent.

In some ways this may be the perfect opportunity for Cheryl to use her discretionary leadership authority to encourage the library staff and governing board to revisit the library's existing policy. The patron's complaint can serve as a foil for her own personal views. However, she is given pause in taking this course of action because of the duty she has to the library profession whose code of ethics commits its members to "resist all efforts to censor library resources," to "distinguish between our personal convictions and professional duties and ... not allow our personal beliefs to interfere with fair representation of the aims of our institutions or the provision of access to their information resources."

In the final analysis, this case also implicates larger values of the American constitutional system of government. There is, first of all, some requirement to be responsive to the needs of those you serve. But what does responsiveness require in this case? What are the terms upon which discourse between Cheryl Miller and Charles Jones should take place? The complaint provides a unique educational opportunity for members of the library staff to engage citizens on issues that go to the very heart of our democratic system of government. Where should we draw the line between parental authority and public organizational responsibility? Yes, parents need the help of public organizations in carrying out their parental roles, but how far should this help go? Should it stop with the advice from professional librarians about the contents of a given book and the appropriateness of that content to the intellectual and social maturity of the potential reader? Even to be this minimally responsive requires an intimate knowledge of each individual client. In this respect, librarians must function as teachers, psychologists, members of the clergy, therapists and others who administer to the needs of the public. But this kind of intimate familiarity with those being served is neither necessary nor possible.

It is not possible because organizations are constructed around abstractions. Cheryl functions in an organizational environment that has some notion of the average child, the typical parent, the presumed standards of acceptability within the local community, and so on. Books are purchased, collections are developed and levels of service are defined based on considerations that abstract from the needs of this or that particular patron or client. This necessity for abstraction is made into a virtue, especially in the public sector, where organizations like libraries are purposely created to meet the needs of citizens, not simply individuals. Thus, by starting with the need for a librarian to be responsive opens up larger questions about the nature of the community and the relationship of the library to its citizens.

These larger questions are troublesome for Cheryl Miller. She has thought about the possibility of other groups and individuals objecting to the choices the library has made about its collection and the access to it. She has wondered what might happen if the appointed library board is pulled into the debate by Mr. Jones. Given the existing membership on the board, Cheryl believes this would likely lead to a change in the existing library policy, making access more restrictive than it has been in the past. While this would bring the world more into conformance with her personal views, would it be a good thing for the library, for the community? Since the members of the Regional Library Board are appointed by the County Board of Commissioners in three separate counties, how adequately do the appointed Board members reflect the sentiment of the community? Even if they did, to what extent should minority views be held subservient to a dominant local majority that restricts the freedom to read either by placing limits on what is purchased and/or who can obtain access to it? These questions trouble Cheryl as she ponders her assigned task to respond to Mr. Jones's letter.

In the chapters that follow, we will explore these issues in much greater detail. Chapter 2 explores the multiple levels of leadership and the kinds of knowledge and skills needed to lead oneself, lead groups and teams, lead organizations and lead within the larger political community. Knowing what competency you possess to undertake these different kinds of leadership roles is a necessary first step in assessing your leadership possibilities. In Chapter 3 we focus on what it means to think and act organizationally. Since organizations are human artifacts, like a good anthropologist, it is hard to experience a "good leadership find" if you don't know what you should be looking for. In Chapter 4 we expand the organizational lens to include the larger polity within which organizations reside. As the Library Case makes clear, public leaders can't successfully do their work inside their organizations without understanding the external legal and political landscape. For example, the regional library is governed by a complex arrangement among three counties with more than a dozen community libraries in the system, each of which has its own advisory board of friends. Like Charlotte's Web, it is hard to alter a strand in the web without setting the entire web in motion. Finally, we end Part I with a discussion in Chapter 6 of the moral values that should guide public service leadership. As the Library Case illustrates, we carry around a tangle of personal, professional, organization and public service values without being very clear about where one ends and the other begins. By the end of Chapter 5, each of us should be in a better position to assess what Cheryl Miller should do, and to justify our choice in terms of the core democratic values that guide our administrative work as stewards of our many and varied American systems of democratic governance.

1 Public Service Leadership
Discovering Opportunities to Make a Difference from Where We Sit

Vignette 1: Amanda McDonald, recently appointed Assistant Clerk for the City of Concord (population 15,621), was struck by the absence of the use of social media by city administrators and the five elected members of council. This was particularly surprising given the regular personal use of such media by both members of council and fellow administrators. Amanda believed strongly in the need for public agencies to use all forms of media to cultivate higher and more informed levels of civic engagement by citizens and improve public service responsiveness, but she had no formal authority to take such initiative. After multiple informal conversations with her supervisor, fellow employees, the City Manager and a couple of council members, she was convinced that there was interest in exploring the development of a social media policy. She took it upon herself to lead the exploration process into possible policies after being given the OK by both her supervisor and the City Manager. She started with a literature review and a survey of best practices. She prepared a summary of her findings, which she provided to her supervisor and the City Manager. These initial steps ultimately resulted in the adoption of a social media policy by the City Council nine months later, after considerable additional research, multiple internal conversations and debate among all managers and supervisors and external vetting with the council and members of the community.

Vignette 2: Cheryl Miller, children's librarian for the Happy Valley Regional Library, was quietly working on her monthly administrative report, while also doing double duty as the circulation librarian at the front desk, when she was suddenly confronted by an angry father dragging a six-year-old child by the hand (see Master Case of this volume for more detail). "Why is this kind of book on the children's bookshelves? It clearly is unfit reading and should be removed immediately to another section of the library." Cheryl noticed that the book in question was a copy of Maurice Sendak's *In the Night Kitchen*, one of the most popular children's stories in the past four decades and a 1971 Caldecott Honor Book. While she thought the father's judgment was misplaced, for some time she had been considering whether the library's existing policies governing children's free access to the library's full reading collection should be re-visited. She personally favored a policy that requires separation of adult and children's reading material and parental supervision of children who wish to check out books classified as "adult". This case provided her with an opportunity to align the values of the organization with those that she believed are more professionally appropriate as a children's librarian and, she believed, more in tune with the values of the larger community.

Vignette 3: After completing an employee orientation program by the agency for which he had just been hired, Gerald Smith was left disappointed by the legal and technical focus of the experience. There was little information about the history, vision and mission of the organization and no opportunity to have "face-time" with those in charge of the various programs and departments. He left knowing little about the organizational structure and linkages with other organizations or the executives in charge. He was left feeling that he was just a small cog in a larger machine that was expected to merely learn all of the rules and regulations that were the primary focus of the orientation. He wanted to change that, but how? Fast forward two years, and as a result of Gerald's initiative, perseverance, *savoir faire*, and perhaps good luck, the agency's employee orientation program received the International City-County Manager's (ICCMA) annual Program Excellence Award.

Vignette 4: As the Assistant County Administrator for a large suburban county, Dale Bright pondered how his county could best deal with the widening gap between growing service expectations of citizens and the financial capacity to pay for these services. The county had become a bedroom community filled with residents with "urban-level" service expectations but with "rural-level" willingness and capacity to pay for these public services. In addition, the county's minority and low-income population was rapidly growing, placing an ever-higher demand on health, housing, public safety and other human services. Dale recalled the project he had completed nearly 15 years earlier for his master's degree on a co-production model of service delivery that expanded the service providers to include the nonprofit, public and private sector partners in a community consortium of coordinated resource providers. This kind of initiative was part of neither the responsibilities of Dale's role, nor the county's mission and strategic plan. Using the template from his master's degree and counsel from his former university professors, Dale crafted a strategy that ultimately resulted in a community-wide envisioning process and the creation of a new 501(c)(3) that served as the holding company for social service needs and coordination in the county for all social service providers, including churches, nonprofit social service agencies, the county and private sector organizations.

Leading from Where We Sit

The opening vignettes capture some common themes that serve as the focal point for this book's focus on our EMERGE leadership approach:

- Regardless of where we sit, public servants have the opportunity to take initiative to improve the common good.
- Leadership opportunities do not always align with our official role responsibilities.
- Leadership initiative requires the application of the right tools for the leadership challenge.
- Leadership practices, such as taking the initiative to improve the common good, can be deliberately cultivated through a combination of knowledge, skills and competencies.
- Public service leadership requires an understanding of the unique role of public institutions and their interface with multiple entities in the public, nonprofit, for-profit and civil society sectors.
- Public service leadership, like other practices, is a learned craft, but differs from other crafts because of the need for expertise in the moral ends of collective action.
- The growth of "wicked challenges", diverse value conflicts in society and declining trust in public institutions require the new leadership tools and practices that we call EMERGE Polity Leadership.

This book has been prompted by three major influences on our lives that have coalesced over the past two decades to hone the three goals of this book. First, we have been struck by the multiple forces of balkanization that have resulted in a loss of civic discourse and the polarization of our communities into physical and metaphorical walled cities. Our capacity to even talk about a shared public interest has become much more difficult at a time when the need has become ever greater. In the face of this experience our first goal is to provide leaders with the mindset, tools and practices that will enable them to bridge these divides.

A second and reinforcing influence arises from our more than 100 years of collective learning through our teaching, researching and practicing leadership. We have observed the consistent tendency of career public servants everywhere to undervalue the opportunities they have to undertake leadership initiatives to improve the public good by bridging various socio-economic, religious, cultural, gender, generational and other divides. America's career public service is at all levels a powerful yet underutilized institutional force for the common good. While there is great danger in a public service that is untethered to political accountability and core regime and constitutional values, we believe the greater danger is a timid and negative mindset that causes our career public servants to act like sheep and to assume they are part of the problem, rather than part of the solution to the challenges that plague our communities. While the general public may often view and treat our career public service as "sheep in wolves" clothing, this mindset is not good for democracy. The recent flow of politics at the national level has reminded us that in many ways our public service, along with our courts, are the junkyard dogs of our democratic institutions and public problem-solving processes. An important goal of this book is to create this "junkyard dog" mindset by providing our career public servants with the confidence, knowledge and tools to lead from where they sit.

Finally, we have also been struck by the increasing "messiness" of leadership challenges. A third goal is to arm our readers with the leadership practices to face this messiness by providing them with the mindset and tools to untangle the complex web of leadership challenges into pathways for action. The title of our book, *New Public Leadership: Making A Difference from Where We Sit*, reflects our three goals.

We use the term emerge in several different ways throughout the book. Sometimes we use the term as an adjective, as in *emergent* leadership challenges, to capture the uncertain and unsettled nature of a set of leadership conditions. Sometimes we use the term emerge to describe a particular genre of challenges that in the literature have come to be known as "wicked" challenges, which are different than simple or complex challenges (see especially Chapter 8). More particularly we use the term emerge to describe our approach to leadership and leadership development in this book. This approach puts a bright light on three elements of leadership success. The first is an understanding of our public service *context*, including the history, the values and the institutions that comprise our leadership setting (Chapters 3–6). The second is a set of tools (Chapters 9 and 11) designed to help leaders "size up" and initiate collective action in wicked challenge settings. Third is an understanding and set of tools that accelerate the development of prudential judgment, which enables leaders to do the right thing in the right circumstances for the right reasons (especially Chapter 12 and accompanying tools in Chapter 11). Our approach assumes that leaders "make sense out of messes" and that "messiness" is becoming more the routine than the exception because of the growth of complex interdependence and the uniqueness of public service leadership.

The Leadership Challenge of Increased Complexity and Interdependence

One of the central themes of this book is the need for leaders to make sense out of messes in ways that inspire collective action for the common good. This "sense-making" has grown in importance and difficulty as a result of increased political, social, global and technological complexity. An important first step in making sense out of what is going on for followers requires sorting and ordering leadership challenges and opportunities, a kind of leadership triage activity.

Leadership challenges and opportunities never appear in neat bundles that enable leaders quickly to match the challenge or opportunity with the appropriate set of leadership practices. But some challenges and opportunities on their face seem much simpler than others. Take, for example, the case of 911 responders in a mass shooting, a condition that is initially chaotic. The opening vignettes seem to present much tamer leadership challenges, but just how tame? This requires public service leaders to "size up" the challenges and opportunities. Changing a library's reading access policy for underage readers (Vignette 2) or altering the structure of social service delivery to underserved populations (Vignette 4) may seem much more difficult than creating an organizational social media policy (Vignette 1) or a new employee orientation program (Vignette 4). But first appearances may be deceiving. The process of "unpacking" the dimensions of a leadership challenge, including who has what resources, who has what authority, who cares, what it will cost and similar kinds of first order questions, may produce some surprises. It may turn out that redesigning social service delivery in the community is hard and complicated, but it may not be as complex as changing a library's reading access policy or creating a social media policy, both of which have the potential for raising issues of censorship, the right to privacy, free speech, parental control, religious freedom and similar concerns that quicken the moral pulse of the community.

The Uniqueness of Public Service Leadership

There has been an enormous growth in leadership books over the past several decades, as the idea that "leaders matter" has replaced an earlier emphasis on the art and science of organization design and development. Most of these books make the generic assumption that good leadership principles and practices can be applied across sectors and organizational settings. This assumption is quite reasonable, given that the majority of books share the basic principles of humanistic social psychology: human beings are willing to follow those who can meet their needs. But as leadership systems expand beyond one's work group, program or department to include the needs of the larger organization, community groups, stakeholders and other jurisdictions, the craft of leadership in the public sector becomes more complex. These conditions require a combination of new leadership practices that can accommodate the growing social complexity and diversity of moral views within which leadership action occurs.

But public service leadership is not simply measured by the capacity of leaders to accommodate increasing social complexity and moral diversity. It is about taking collective action, which occurs at the group, organization and larger community levels. The majority of leadership books written to date emphasize the importance of attending to the personal needs of the leader as well as the needs of followers. We review this body of literature in more detail in Chapters 2 and 3. Our conclusion is that these books do not adequately address the "action" and "moral" dimensions of leadership when moving from one level of public service leadership to another, whether from the group to the organization or from the organization to the community level of engagement.

While we do not take issue with the assumptions of social psychology that dominate the current literature on leadership, we argue that public service leadership deserves special treatment for three reasons. First, public service leaders act within defined legal structures of authority that simultaneously constrain and create leadership opportunities. To be successful, leaders need to have an intimate, practical understanding of the nature of the dynamic system of governance within which they operate. This system establishes a structure of authority that creates the cultural norms for how things get done. Violation of these norms erodes the conditions for gaining the support of potential followers.

A second distinguishing characteristic is that public service leaders must be cognizant of the constellation of democratic values promoted by the legal structures and processes within which they operate. These values create norms for *what should get done*, just as the processes and structures norm expectations of *how things get done*. Public service leaders have moral responsibility for promoting and preserving the collective values that have acquired authoritative status through law, history and public institutions. But this role is especially problematic because public values are constantly in a state of contention and flux. To be successful, leaders need robust enabling conditions and lots of help from followers. This creates a third distinguishing characteristic of public service leadership.

Public service leaders need to be armed with a large repertoire of leadership practices to accommodate changing public values and conflicting priorities at various levels of our public organizations. For example, how do the street-level librarians in Vignette 2 work with middle managers, senior leaders and the community to decide how best to reconcile the conflict between the circulation of an award-winning book and those who believe it is unfit reading for children? Together, first line managers and middle managers in all of the opening vignettes shape the meaning of the public interest on a daily basis as much as department heads, chief executive officers and elected officials. While the roles of these various public servants are quite different, their influence in shaping the public interest is equally pervasive. This kind of discretion throughout all levels of a private business organization may be viewed as building a "culture of empowerment" that improves organizational performance, but it is never defended as an essential condition for promoting the public interest.

The unique structures of legal authority and the core political values that these structures are intended to serve create a fourth distinguishing feature of public service leadership. An overall goal of this book is to provide our readers with a basic understanding of these democratic intuitions. We believe this understanding will enable our leaders to work within and across multiple vertical and horizontal systems of authority in ways that leverage and align co-producers of the public good in the public, private, nonprofit and civil society sectors of our local communities. We call this "polity leadership," a regime-centered focus that emphasizes the cooperative, collaborative and intersectoral competencies that separate public service leaders from their private sector counterparts. Unlike the public sector, the private sector is rewarded for keeping secrets, protecting its brand and hiding its plans from its competitors. We illustrate the more collaborative-centered model of the public sector in Exhibit 1.1. The exhibit calls attention to the alignment role that public service leaders play in identifying, leveraging and facilitating mutual cooperation among multiple partners in the co-production of the public good. In keeping with our regime-centered focus to public service leadership, the contextual framework for this book is the American political system. However, we draw on our extensive leadership development work with public officials in foreign countries to extend the argument to other political systems in Chapter 2.

Leadership for High-Performance Governance

Alignment of Partners; Co-Production of the Public Good

Exhibit 1.1 Leadership for High-Performance Government

Public Service Leadership as a Passion Flower

We find passion flowers a useful metaphor for capturing what we wish to convey with our EMERGE leadership approach. The passion flower is noted for its beauty, complexity and the unique regenerative conditions necessary for pollinating offspring. In the passion flower, the pollen is not at the tip of the stamen, as is the case in most flowers, but at the tip of the five anthers that emanate from the stamen. The flower consists of ten brightly colored petals that serve as attractors for hummingbirds, bats and bumble bees whose large proboscis is needed to break through the complexity of the inner portion of the flower to collect the nectar and in the process release the generative pollen. The regenerative potential of the inner complexity of the passion flower is not easily released, which is a fitting metaphor for the unique complexity of public service leadership. We argue that leaders are pollinators, like the bumble bees, bats and hummingbirds for the passion flower. But to be successful they need to understand where to find the pollen that is deeply imbedded in the inner wheelhouse of the passion flower in order to release the germinating pollen that is needed to spawn collective action. Leaders are the ones who can find the pollen that enables others to see new possibilities, infuse passion into these possibilities, courageously champion these new possibilities, and know how to transform these possibilities into organizational and institutional legacies that can endure over time. Successful leaders have to align with and/or break through institutional, legal and historical inertia and find ways of using the generative bounties these sources provide to spawn new initiatives that require fertile ground to take root.

Another characteristic of the passion flower that we find useful is the very large numbers of species that are in existence around the globe. There are over 530 species, each of which is a product of the long history of contextual conditions that have produced its uniqueness. Transplanting species from one context to another does not work without a long process of hybridization grounded in a basic set of generative guidelines. This is a useful reminder for those who wish to transfer leadership varieties from the private sector to public organizations or to transfer public varieties of leadership from one part of the world to another. In Chapter 2 we draw from our experience of working in more than 80 foreign countries to discuss the transferability of generic leadership principles and the additional steps necessary to put these principles to work in the unique contextual setting of a given place to produce results that last.

The Prudential Wheelhouse that Guides Collective Action: The Limits of the Passion Flower Metaphor

The passion flower represents an intricate process for germinating new possibilities. But the process is structured to occur without insight, without prudence and without human judgment. This is where human beings are different from flowers in ways that have significant implications for leadership. Human beings consciously hold values and can use these values within limits to undertake intentional collective action with others to improve the human condition or make it worse (Haidt, 2013). Humans also have a clear sense of the present and can connect that sense to both the past and future. This enables human beings to think and act historically and institutionally through time, using history and institutions as resources to improve or worsen the public good. Finally, human beings are advanced inventers and creators of new tools and technologies. From a leadership point of view human beings can use their foresight, curiosity and most of all prudential wisdom, to take advantage of new ideas and technologies to create new "right answers" and mobilize resources to take advantage of windows of opportunity to bring these new possibilities to fruition. In doing so, leaders produce collective action that alters the human condition.

The Organization and Design of the Book

We have organized the following chapters into four parts, the first of which focuses on the Foundations of Public Service Leadership. Part II focuses on Identifying Leadership Opportunities. Part III provides the reader with the knowledge and tools for Taking Leadership Action. The final chapter is its own part and serves as an integrative conclusion for the book. Each of the parts is accompanied by a Master Case that provides the reader with an opportunity to see how the principles and leadership tools discussed in the text can be applied to practice. To further reinforce our practice-centered approach to the acquisition of leadership knowledge and skills, we have developed an accompanying *EMERGE Leadership Platform* that is available online at www.pdx.edu/cps/NewPublicLeadershipBook. In Chapters 8, 9 and 11, we will direct the reader to this website to complete various leadership exercises. These exercises allow for practice using various leadership tools and are a critical step in the process of acquiring prudential judgment, which is the distinctive virtue for successful leadership in the public sector.

2   Leadership Theory and Action

Public and private management are fundamentally alike in all unimportant respects.

> Wallace Sayre (1958, 102–105)

...Sayre's assertion is not supported by the empirical evidence. Therefore, the injunction that public managers can learn useful lessons from private managers is worthy of serious, but cautious, consideration.

> George Boyne (2002, 98)

[A] government must be fitted to a nation, as much as a coat to the individual; and consequently, that what may be good at Philadelphia may be bad at Paris, and ridiculous at Petersburgh.

> Alexander Hamilton (1975/1787–1789, 404)

[The] globalization of public administration has highlighted the parochial nature of much of the literature, which was written to apply to one nation or to a small group of similar countries. When literature that was designed for the West or for Europe is applied to non-Western nations, it rarely fits well, exaggerating the tension between theory and practice.

> Welch, Erch, and Wilson Wang (1998, 40)

The opening epigraphs capture the on-going debate about the transferability of leadership theories, principles and practices from the private sector to the public sector, and from one country to another. In this chapter we review the major theories that seek to explain leadership success in different arenas. We conclude from this review that there are common motivational principles and techniques that are applicable to leaders in all kinds of organizational and contextual settings. But what is held in common is overshadowed by the governance roles and responsibilities of public sector employees at all levels of public organizations, as well as by the contextual settings where leadership action occurs. We review the theories that support this conclusion as well as the theories that provide the rationale for our particular focus on the competencies needed to lead in highly dynamic and even chaotic conditions, which we call EMERGE polity leadership.

Leadership Theories and their Inadequacies[1]

An extensive literature exists on leaders and leadership.[2] It draws from a variety of professions, including public administration, business administration, education and social work, and from academic disciplines such as history, political science, psychology, social psychology, sociology and anthropology. It is hard to consolidate, summarize or distill this diverse literature around any single theme or principle. For our purposes, we have organized this literature around individual, group and organizational levels of analysis. We do this for two reasons: first, the literature lends itself to this kind of analysis; second, in our own leadership development work with practitioners, we have found that the knowledge, skills and competencies needed for these varying levels of leadership are quite different. After reviewing the leadership theories associated with the individual, group and organizational levels, we show how this collective body of literature is relevant to our focus on governance and polity leadership. We conclude the chapter with a discussion of the leadership theory that supports our particular emphasis on leading public institutions.

Trait-Based and Individual-Centered Theories

Leadership theory has focused from the very beginning on the unique qualities of individuals who assume the responsibility of leading. Advocates of this popular approach look for traits or characteristics that distinguish leaders from followers (Yukl, 1981; Boyatzis, 1982; Kirkpatrick and Locke, 1991). Until recently these traits have been associated with the "great person" approach to leadership, emphasizing distinctive qualities in settings traditionally dominated by men. People are fascinated with the qualities they believe make great leaders, especially those who shaped our own history, whether they are presidents such as George Washington, Abraham Lincoln, and Franklin Delano Roosevelt, or successful entrepreneurs such as Andrew Carnegie and Bill Gates. Charisma, courage, energy, wisdom, and other traits have been identified as a basis for distinguishing these leaders from their followers. More recent research has explored traits among women, such as compassion, emotion, affinity, and other qualities that yield a distinctive "relational" approach to leadership (Regan and Brooks, 1995; Gilligan, 1993). An accompanying literature summarizes individual characteristics of women leaders (cf. Helgesen, 1990; Farrel, 1996; Martin, 1996; Rosenthal, 1998; Fisher, 1999).[3] However, as appealing as these studies of male and female leaders may be, individual trait theories fall short of explaining leadership success.

One individual-centered approach to leadership that we have found extremely useful focuses on strengths rather than traits. This approach assumes that our minds and experiences are wired in quite different ways and that leadership success requires obtaining a better understanding of our own wiring and the wiring of others (Brooks, 2013; also see our discussion in Chapter 12 of the neuroscience of moral leadership). Rath and Conchie (2017/2008) have developed a validated strengths-based leadership assessment instrument that organizes individual leadership strengths into four domains (executing, influencing, relationship building and strategic thinking) with between six and nine subthemes for each domain. The assessment instrument uses the subtheme components to generate a score for each leadership domain. The instrument assumes that every member of a group has a unique and complex combination of strengths that, once known, can be used by leaders to get the appropriate combination of traits for the leadership challenge at hand. Unlike classic trait theory, Rath and Conchie do not assume that there are a set of superior traits associated with leaders, but instead, there are a combination of traits among both leaders and followers that need to be mobilized and organized to address the situation at hand. In short, they use a trait-based approach to support group- and contextually based leadership theories.

Overall, the weaknesses of trait-based theory has pushed researchers to shift their unit of analysis away from individuals to groups. For example, analysis of trait-based studies and their supporting literature have found no clear distinction between leaders and non-leaders in terms of the many dozens of traits explored (House and Aditya, 1997; Kirkpatrick and Locke, 1991). Little consistency and predictability can be found in relating any given trait to successful leadership (Jennings, 1961). Recent research using bundled personality characteristics suggests that some traits are related to leader emergence, but they are not reliable in predicting leader success (Judge et al., 2002).

One group of scholars has focused attention on the dynamics that occur within small group settings, while another group has focused on the larger external factors that shape what counts for "good leadership." Together, these group- and contingency-based theories have helped to broaden the leadership lens to focus on those factors that are distinctive to successful leadership in the public sector. An analysis of this broadening focus of leadership follows.

Group-Centered Theories

Sociologists have taken the lead in focusing attention on the dynamics of leadership within group settings. For example, Guy Swanson (1970) observed that when people find themselves in groups, they engage in formative social processes that are interpretive and deliberative in nature. Leaders emerge through the group's search for substantive meaning and direction. Leaders test ideas in relationship to group members. Group members associate themselves with the people who are expressing ideas that resonate with them. The intricate dance between leader and follower builds the shared meaning of the group and inculcates a sense of purpose from which specific goals emerge. This social process matures as leader-expressed meanings and actions become vested in the group as a whole. The group-formation literature underscores the interaction necessary for groups to take ownership of expressed values, and how work roles are sorted out and defined over time (Wilson, 2002; Yukl, 2012; see also Chapter 11). The process is interactive and recursive, meaning that leadership roles are redefined and reassigned as group values evolve and group solidarity ebbs and flows.

Group theory introduces another level of sophistication through its attention to ideas and meanings, as well as roles. Leadership does not depend entirely upon manipulation of psychological needs or individuals' management styles. Leaders emerge, evolve and devolve within groups over time, in part due to the normative saliency of their ideas and their ability to inculcate or cultivate shared meaning. As shared meaning coalesces, work roles develop that define expectations and appropriate relations among members. People grow or adapt to the defined roles, which in turn shape attitudes and norms about proper leadership. Good leadership is defined in large measure by the content of, and relationships among, institutional roles. These aspects of group theory embrace the idea that leadership functions exist in many group roles, there are multiple leaders, and intergroup dynamics have as much of a formative influence on groups as internal dynamics.

Group theories have had an important influence on our thinking about organizations. For example, some organizational sociologists describe complex organizations as conglomerations of workgroups that evolve around common means as well as purposes (Weick, 1979). Organizations engender patterned relationships that constitute structures, within which there is order and role definition. The complexity arising from the development of these multiple patterns of relationships within organizations is now known as contingency leadership theory.

Contingency Theories

In the 1950s and 1960s, social psychologists began to focus on leadership as a manifestation of group functions and dynamics in corporate organizations (McGregor, 1960; Hersey and Blanchard, 1981, Hersey, 1977; Hersey, Blanchard, and Johnson, 2001; Blake and Mouton,

1964). Their research found that effective leadership depends upon an appropriate match between organization or group conditions and leadership style (Fiedler, 1967; Fiedler and Garcia, 1987; House, 1971, 1996; House and Mitchell, 1974; Vroom and Yetton, 1973). Blake and Mouton (1964) developed a popular leadership grid along two primary dimensions, one focusing on "concern for task" and the other on "concern for people." The grid, presented in Exhibit 2.1, displays a range from one to nine along each dimension, reflecting how varying degrees of concern for task and concern for people yield different leadership styles.

William Reddin (1970, 41–47) refined the grid into quadrants that yield four basic leadership styles: supporting, coaching, delegating and autocratic. These styles emphasize the importance of "sizing up" what is most appropriate to the needs of a given group before determining what type of leadership will be most effective. We use the term "sizing up" throughout the rest of the book as a short-hand for the complicated set of skills that enable a leader to figure out "what is going on" in a given setting. It can include the group dynamics at work in a given team; it can include the contextual factors and their implications for defining both the limits and possibilities for action. It is analogous to the skill of a good quarterback who can read the defenses, call the right play and make a perfect pass to a tight end.

A variety of contingency models exist in the literature. All follow the same basic logic and strongly resemble each other. They improve on

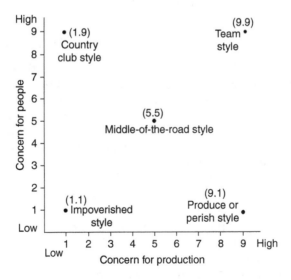

Exhibit 2.1 Small Group Leadership: Blake-Mouton Grid

trait and group theory approaches by suggesting that leadership can, at least to some extent, be trained and adapted to varying circumstances to enhance effectiveness. For example, emergency conditions may call for more directive, task-oriented leadership, while leading a problem-solving team through an emergent, poorly defined and long-term situation may require more attention to relationships and process skills. In a public sector marked by frequently conflicting values, both of these skillsets are especially important.

However, the inadequacies of the contingency model are evident in its exclusive focus on workgroups and organizations with simple superior/subordinate relationships. It presumes a single, formal leader, or at least a clear hierarchy of formal leaders within a single organization. Such assumptions should not be made—especially in public service contexts where subordinates often have multiple superiors and many workgroups have collegial membership across several organizations. Moreover, legal authority and personnel protections in public life are likely diffused among subordinates as well as supervisory positions. The absence of clear hierarchy and multiple legal obligations means that subordinates bring more independence to the table than is presumed in the corporate contexts of contingency models. Contingency theorists are likely to claim that their models still apply but must be tailored to the differing circumstances of each sector. While there is some merit in this argument, contingency theorists consistently ignore sectoral differences in favor of a workgroup model based in generic social-psychological theory. Philip Selznick (1957, 1949) built on these insights to fashion an institutional approach to leadership that recognizes the significance of the organization as the unit of analysis.

Organizational and Institution-Centered Leadership Theories

Selznick begins with the organization as his unit of analysis. He argues that leadership at organizational levels is a process of weaving and co-opting narrower group interests into a broader organizational community of mutual interests and common vision. His classic study of the Tennessee Valley Authority (TVA) (Selznick, 1949) illustrates how federal officials bargained, cajoled and co-opted a diverse array of community and business leaders into long-term collaboration with the TVA to bring electricity to the valley, control flooding and promote economic development of a rural and economically impoverished region. Selznick emphasizes that leadership in this context is an institution-building process that transforms instrumental group and organizational agendas into larger communities of shared meaning, capacity and purpose (see Chapter 4 for further development of this argument). He describes how institutionalization emerged over time through a gradual and successive process of tying the work of the TVA more deeply to the partners in the region. This type of leadership presumes a sense of the whole, a sense of proportion and a sense of how disparate groups and interests in the institution's environment can be knitted together.

Selznick's work has been criticized for its preoccupation with the co-optative nature of leadership of large-scale, conservative and monolithic institutions of the post-World War II era. Although this critique has merit, his work represents an important precursor to "new institutionalism," a school of sociologically oriented scholars who, in the 1980s, rejuvenated the focus on institutions as the primary unit of analysis of leadership studies. These scholars emphasize the fluid, interpretive, adaptive and dynamic nature of institutions (cf. Douglas, 1986; Elkin and Soltan, 1993; Powell and DiMaggio, 1991). Selznick's pioneering work and the new institutionalism that followed drew attention to the unique characteristics of public institutions where powers are intentionally diffused and shared.

Leading Public Institutions

Since the mid-1970s, a number of scholars have focused their attention on the uniqueness of the public sector and the implications this may have for the exercise of leadership. One of the more influential theorists, Burns (2012/1978), developed a leadership dichotomy that adapted much of the previous literature for use in political settings. He posited that leaders typically adopt one of two general methods of leading. Many leaders use a "transactional" approach that relies on a sense of reciprocity or exchange between leaders and followers. Politicians, for example, make campaign promises to constituents in exchange for their votes. While this is a common approach to leadership, it lacks much in the way of synergy needed to cultivate and sustain a common vision or shared sense of the public interest.

For Burns, the more attractive type of leadership is "transformational," which he defines as the ability to raise the consciousness of followers regarding common and higher values that transform mere aggregations of interests into a shared commitment to a larger common good (Burns, 2012/1978, 141–254). This kind of leadership changes people, affects their outlook on individual and collective life, and draws them together with a new identity and shared meaning. For all its claims, however, Burns' work rejuvenates an individual level of analysis, as evidenced in his biographical treatments of exemplary transformational leaders, and fuses it with the modern social-psychological literature. It is an appealing fusion, but from a normative and constitutional perspective, it creates the potential specter of demagogues—leaders with immense charisma who manipulate the social-psychological dimensions of motivation through charm, information technology and propaganda to consolidate power toward their own ends. Communities of "true believers" who construct a solidarity of shared meaning may be transformative, but they may not be very interested in, or respectful of, the constitutional system of governance and the competing values it seeks to hold in dynamic balance. We believe Burns' emphasis on the social-psychological dynamic of leadership gives insufficient attention to institutions, norms and structures that are inherent to America's constitutional system of governance.

Another popular author, Jeffrey Luke (1998), developed the concept of "catalytic" leadership. Luke argues that successful leadership results from the proper timing of speech and actions that catalyze others to employ resources and information and use of their formal and informal position power for collaboratively determined purposes. Control over formal authority, resources or information is less important than being able to make sense out of the complexities of a community or policy subsystem, and having a sense of proper timing of one's actions. In Luke's catalytic model, effective leaders identify critical points for action by thinking strategically, cultivating key relationships among powerholders and operational groups, and maintaining constancy of purpose that inspires others by leading from passion and strength to achieve appropriate ends.

> With catalytic leadership, individuals and groups convene multiple stakeholder groups, and facilitate and mediate agreement around tough issues. We live in a complex world of interconnections in which take-charge leaders are less successful than individuals and groups who provide the spark or catalyst that truly makes a difference.
>
> Luke (1998, 4)

Implicit in Luke's approach is the idea that leadership is not necessarily a matter of constant effort, repeated exhortation and monitoring by leaders. Rather, effective leaders know how to wait—how to time words and actions for full rhetorical effect. They sense when groups are more or less ready to hear a message, engage in meaningful discourse, reach consensus and act. This kind of leadership helps cultivate conditions of trust and interaction that lead to fruitful communication and discourse about things that matter to everyone involved. It also respects followers for their own judgments as political actors who bring their own contributions to the effort (Green and Zinke, 1993).

John Carver's work (1990) has also made an important contribution to our thinking about the distinctiveness of public leadership. Carver focuses on the challenge of leading in a world of shifting coalitions and rapid organizational change. In the nonprofit world, for example, leaders often run organizations that depend on shared commitments and causes among staff, volunteers and partners whose organizational identities are tenuous at best. Their host organization may radically change in scale of operation as well as in its linkages to related nonprofit organizations and public agencies. Leaders must maintain constancy of the mission in the face of severe organizational instability. Preparing employees, whether paid or volunteer, for such conditions presents a leadership challenge in its own right. For example, a local community and educational services nonprofit recently experienced severe cutbacks in a critical service due to reductions in federal grant funding. Two paid staff positions were threatened as a result. The director of the nonprofit had prepared the employees well in advance for this contingency, and worked with them to find alternative funding from a local organization to continue their services with some modifications. This included converting the staff members to employees of the paying organization, while retaining them at the same site to preserve service integration.

Finally, Crosby and Bryson have synthesized the work of a generation of scholars and reflective practitioners on leading in public organizational and community settings where no single person is in charge. They argue that the conditions of modern life require "a new understanding of power" (2005, 17) whereby agencies, organizations and other entities must learn to share resources, authority and activities to meet common goals. Achieving coordinated action requires a variety of leadership capabilities. From their research, Crosby and Bryson derived the following list of capabilities (2005, 34–35):

- Understanding the social, political and economic givens as well as potentialities;
- Understanding and deploying personal assets on behalf of beneficial change;
- Building effective workgroups;
- Nurturing humane and effective organizations;
- Creating and communicating shared meaning/vision in forums;
- Making and implementing decisions in legislative, executive and administrative arenas;
- Sanctioning conduct and adjudicating disputes in courts;
- Coordinating leadership tasks over the course of the policy change cycle.

No leader possesses the entire list. Rather, these capabilities are exercised by "a number of people leading at different times and in varying ways over the course of a policy change effort" (Crosby and Bryson, 2005, 36) and one might add all change efforts, even those designed to align organizations and behaviors with existing policy goals. Crosby and Bryson's essential point is that leadership in all of its dimensions is itself a collaborative enterprise. We characterize the methods and techniques they and their colleagues use in this enterprise as matters of conciliatory practice, because they are designed to win accord—to move from hostility or distrust to agreement, even if only for a short time. Our conciliatory practice model draws from the individual, group and organizational levels of leadership theory discussed earlier in the chapter. When these theories are applied within larger community leadership networks, the unique characteristics and values of the social, legal, historical and economic setting become extremely important for public servants engaged in leadership work.

Theories Especially Relevant to EMERGE Polity Leadership

Leading from where we sit requires an understanding of the strengths and limitations of each of the individual, group, organization and institution (community) levels of theory we have reviewed above. In this section we review additional theories that are especially relevant to our emphasis on the governance role of public service leaders during times of "wicked challenges:" regime theory, social change theory and the social construction of reality, chaos and adaptive systems theory, and the neuroscience of the brain and its implications for prudential judgment and the art of reflective practice. Together these theories provide foundational support for our thematic focus on the polity legal principles, values and framework that create trust and build leadership legitimacy; the tools for leading in wicked challenge settings; leading organizations in times of change; using conciliatory practices to build community agreement; and the virtue of prudence, which we argue separates public sector leaders from their private sector counterparts.

Regime Theory: Leadership as Governance

Regime theory focuses on the organic wholeness of a political system to explain leadership behaviors and their policy outcomes. This includes the history, culture, geopolitical setting, formal structures of authority and all of the relevant contextual and contingent conditions that give a community its unique moral identity. This focus highlights the limits to the transferability of principles and governance principles and leadership practices from one contextual setting to another (Rohr, 1989; Morgan et al., 2013/2008; Ozawa, 2005; Elkin and Soltan, 1993; Johnson, 2002; Stone, 1993; Leo, 1997, 1998; Lauria, 1997). We may be able to transfer administrative functions and systems from one cultural setting to another, but the results will not necessarily be the same because of the political values that arbitrate the conflicting moral purposes built into these systems. For example, the conflict between efficiency and equity in the United States neither has the same meaning nor will be resolved in the same way in China.

The significance of regime theory surfaced over the last two decades in the development and implementation of the New Public Management

Movement. This movement has swept across the globe and purports to improve government performance by reducing the size of government, contracting out for services, decentralizing, adopting management improvement systems and becoming more customer-service-oriented (Hood, 1991; OECD, 2003). This movement assumed that there were universal principles of good government, leadership and administration that stand independently of the political values, ideologies and historical traditions of the community that is seeking to make changes. But the implementation of this movement has resulted in the discovery that a new set of "conciliatory" leadership skills is needed to help negotiate the various conflicting political values that come into play, particularly at the local level (Brookes and Grint, 2010; Micheli and Neely, 2010).

A similar discovery has been made in implementing the Local Government Autonomy Movement (United Nations, 2006). Over the last decade the countries of Japan (Muramatsu, Iqbal, and Kume, 2001; Nishishiba, Ingle, Tsukamoto, and Kobayashi, 2006), South Korea (Shair-Rosenfield, Hooghe, Kenan, and Marks, 2014), India (Stepan, Linz, and Yadav, 2011), Indonesia (Fadzil and Nyoto, 2011) and Great Britain (Osborne, 2010) have undertaken major initiatives to grant greater autonomy to local governing units throughout the nation state. In East Asian countries the motivation to decentralize governance and increase local autonomy has been prompted by the desire to foster growth and reduce poverty by assigning:

> state powers, responsibilities and resources to sub-national authorities and to private and civil society agencies under various forms of contract, partnership or principal-agent relationship ... To this scale of governance is pinned the hopes of better service delivery and private enterprise promotion, and increasingly the sub national scale is seen as the site for the exercise of new forms of participation and citizenship emerging throughout the region.
>
> (Westcott, 2003, 20; also see Wescott, 1999; Chan, Sin, and Williams, 2016)

An additional reason to decentralize decision-making is to foster foreign domestic investment (FDI). In countries such as Vietnam, increasing FDI has become a core leadership mindset with the goal of creating ownership by local leaders of their economic well-being rather than looking up in the leadership hierarchy and depending on government largess from the central government (World Bank, 2013).

Whatever the cause, decentralization shifts performance away from a single-minded focus on universally transferable values like efficiency, effectiveness and customer satisfaction, to a focus on achieving and sustaining local agreements between and across structures of authority (Bao, Wang, Larsen, and Morgan, 2013; Osborne, 2010; Crosby and

Bryson, 2005; Morgan et al., 2013/2008; see Chapter 12; Osborne, 2010; Koliba, Meek, and Zia, 2011). The leadership competencies needed to succeed in in a given leadership setting (individual, group, organizational, community) require an understanding of the salient values at play and how these values are a product of the larger processes of social construction.

The Social Construction of Values: Leadership as Conciliatory Practice

If leadership success depends heavily on knowing the regime-specific sources of value conflicts that arise within a given political setting, knowing where these values come from and how they change over time also becomes an important component of leadership success. We draw heavily from the work of Berger and Luckman (1967) to understand how this process of change occurs through time.

Berger and Luckman's central argument is that the social interaction of individuals and groups produce concepts and mental representations of what is acceptable in various role relationships (i.e., being a member of a family, a student, a teacher, a lawyer, a legislator, a governor, a politician, a church member, a judge, etc.). These role relationships are in a constant process of change, but at any given moment in time these roles become habituated and acquire institutionalized recognition in the more formal and official structures of social, economic, cultural, political and legal authority. Together these socially created roles provide the frameworks for making meaning out of all social interactions and social institutions, thus resulting in the social construction of reality.

In Exhibit 2.2 we provide a summary representation of this process of social construction and the implications for managing and leading public organizations. Exhibit 2.2 has several important leadership implications for our discussion in the chapters that follow.

Leadership Principles and Practices Can't Easily be Transferred Across Settings Without Contextual Adaptation

Exhibit 2.2 emphasizes the social conditions and contexts within which leadership activities take place. These conditions determine the extent to which leadership models and principles are transferrable. For example, "servant leadership" has become a popular model in western countries over the past decade. But comparative research suggests "that servant leadership is best applied in a culture with low power distance, low to moderate individualism, low to moderate masculinity, low uncertainty avoidance and a moderate to high long-term orientation" (Hannay, 2009, 1). As Alexander Hamilton observed, "what may be good at Philadelphia may be bad at Paris, and ridiculous at Petersburgh" (Hamilton, 1975/1787-1789, 404).

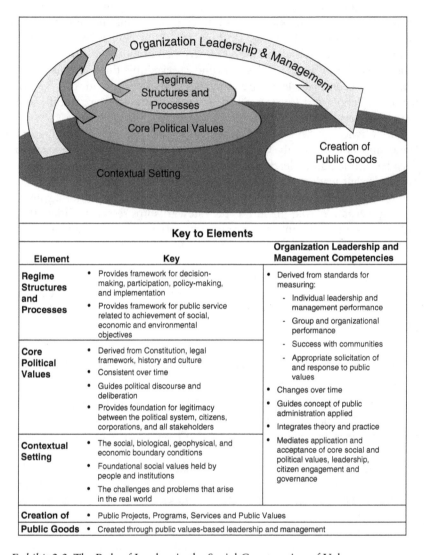

Key to Elements

Element	Key	Organization Leadership and Management Competencies

Regime Structures and Processes	• Provides framework for decision-making, participation, policy-making, and implementation
	• Provides framework for public service related to achievement of social, economic and environmental objectives
		• Derived from standards for measuring:
		  - Individual leadership and management performance
		  - Group and organizational performance
		  - Success with communities
		  - Appropriate solicitation of and response to public values

Core Political Values	• Derived from Constitution, legal framework, history and culture • Consistent over time • Guides political discourse and deliberation • Provides foundation for legitimacy between the political system, citizens, corporations, and all stakeholders	• Changes over time • Guides concept of public administration applied • Integrates theory and practice
Contextual Setting	• The social, biological, geophysical, and economic boundary conditions • Foundational social values held by people and institutions • The challenges and problems that arise in the real world	• Mediates application and acceptance of core social and political values, leadership, citizen engagement and governance
Creation of Public Goods	• Public Projects, Programs, Services and Public Values • Created through public values-based leadership and management	

Exhibit 2.2 The Role of Leaders in the Social Construction of Value

Public Service Leaders Are Important Participants in the Creation of Social Meaning

One of the explicit goals of this book is to convince every public service leader to see themselves, regardless of their position, as a moral agent of creating meaning regarding the common good. Even in their narrowly instrumental roles of implementing the classical management functions captured by the acronym POSDCORB (planning, organizing, staffing, directing, coordinating, reporting and budgeting), public servants are engaged in meaning-making activities. They are giving meaning to what "good" planning, organizing, staffing, etc. look like, even when they claim that their activities are merely instrumental means to ends that are established by others. But as the ends served by these instrumental practices become unclear, are contested, or get lost in the fog of memory, Berger and Luckman's theory takes on even more significance for public service leaders.

But a whole new body of leadership practice, called conciliatory leadership (see especially Chapter 10), has emerged over the past two decades. Conciliatory leadership takes into account the unique governance role that leaders play in creating collective agreement regarding the common good, especially when there appears to be no common ground. This governance role includes the stewardship responsibilities that public servants have in partnership with other governing agents (i.e., citizens, organizations, jurisdictions and sectoral actors) in "getting to yes" (Fisher, Ury, and Patton, 2002). This emerging body of conciliatory-centered leadership theory marries regime theory with Berger and Luckman's theory on the social construction of reality and provides the theoretical foundation for our discussion of conciliatory leadership practices in the chapters to follow.

Complex Adaptive Systems Theory: Leadership as "Wicked Challenge" Management

In this book we highlight the role of leaders in addressing "wicked challenges," which by definition have no permanent fix, solution or resolution (see especially Chapter 8). These challenges sit alongside those that are quite simple and routine and for which there are proven leadership practices. In between the wicked and the tame are complicated challenges that call for different combinations of leadership practices. The theories that help us make sense out of tame and complicated challenges are already well integrated into our scientific- and professionally based approaches to problem-solving and in the education and training of our professional practitioners in all fields of endeavor. These theories and their application constitute what we normally call "best practices." Taken together these bodies of knowledge and practice have given rise to high levels of organizational homogeneity, predictability and consistency, or what DiMaggio and Powell have described as isomorphism (DiMaggio and Powell, 1983).

But wicked challenges require us to draw from a different body of theory that help us understand how the interactions among the parts of complex systems can reciprocally interact to produce widely unexpected and surprising outcomes. Typical examples of complex adaptive systems include the global economic network of relationships regionally, nationally and locally; an ecosystem's relationship to the larger bio-sphere; the impact of brain functioning on our immune system; and the internet and cyberspace, which is composed, collaborated and managed by a complex mix of human and computer interactions. The "science of surprises," more commonly known as Complex Adaptive Systems Theory (CAST) provides the theoretical framework for our focus on the leadership competencies to address wicked challenges in ways that advance the common good (Page, 2010, 2007; Lichtenstein et al., 2006; Uhl-Bien, Russ, and McKelvey, 2007).

CAST seeks to understand the whole; for example, the patterned flight of a flock of birds or the foraging behavior of an ant or bee colony. It turns out that what explains the behavior of the whole is not to be found in having a leader, but in having organized followers who act in concert because each individual member of the group follows a set of internally held patterns of behavior. For an entertaining picture of the phenomena see the first follower video (Sivers, 2015). In this video we see how CAST shifts the leadership focus away from conformance to pre-determined scripts, structures, processes and rules to patterns of cohering behavior. The CAST approach to leadership can be illustrated by the simple question: "Where should we build our sidewalks?" Rather than relying on tried and true scripted formulas, CAST empha-sizes a "wait-and-see" approach to identify the patterns created by where pedestrians naturally walk before engaging in construction.

How does one become good in identifying cohering patterns? And more importantly, how does one cultivate the capacity to assemble these patterns into collective action that advances the common good? Answers to these questions require leaders to connect the world of facts with the world of values. It requires bridging the divide between the fact world of science and the value world of philosophy. It requires con-necting the executive and moral reasoning functions of the brain. As it turns out, neuroscience is helping us better understand where this leadership competency comes from and how we can become better at integrating the world of facts with the world of values to create an integrated and communally shared moral order.

Prudential Judgment and Neuroscience of the Brain: Leadership as Statecraft

At any given moment in time public leaders are confronted with moral tensions that are inherently part of the public good. To make the leadership challenge even harder, these tensions have been institutiona-lized into the processes and structures of authority for which leaders have stewardship responsibility. This produces multiple moral orders that need to be held in tension. An important goal of this book is to have our public service leaders take personal responsibility for "owning" this problematic, not to assume that good leadership is measured by resolving the moral tensions of public life. As a well-known Lincoln scholar has observed, one of the lessons from Lincoln's presidency is for leaders "to find the zone ... [between competing values] which advances the public good" writ large without demeaning the value of any of the component parts; "For this task there is no formula; for the wise statesman there is no substitute" (Jaffa, 1959, 377). Our aspiration is for public service leaders to view their work as "statecraft," but where do we turn for guidance on theories of statecraft?

At the heart of statecraft is the virtue of prudence, which is the ability to "size up" what is morally possible in the mix of competing values and to squeeze all of the public good that one can out of the moment without jeopardizing the possibility of achieving an even greater good when circumstances become more propitious. Prudence involves more than just having good practical judgement, which would make prudence equivalent to the kind of practical insight that makes for good cabinet makers, carpenters, plumbers and organic gardeners. Prudence is also more than a skill. It is a moral virtue that is grounded in the love of the republic, the regime, the larger political order, not for its instrumental value, but as an end in itself. It is a virtue that comes from the experience of leading for the common good, which is what makes public service leadership distinctly different than other kinds of leadership (Nonaka, 2010; Aristotle, 1947/c/340 BCE, 6.5–6.12).

We draw from the neuroscience of the brain to help us understand where prudence comes from and how it can be cultivated. As it turns out, creativity, meaning making, moral judgment and innovative thinking are located in a different circuit than the one that controls executive decision-making (see Exhibit 12.1 in Chapter 12). When the prefrontal cortex is in high gear to perform executive decision-making, it shuts down the part of the brain that is the repository of information needed for creativity, imagination and ethical decision-making (Levitin, 2014). The challenge in getting access to this imaginative storehouse is to activate the quiet, mind-wandering part of the brain, which is a low energy and quiet state (Rock, 2009, 212). For this reason, we place significant emphasis on the "art of reflective" practice throughout our discussions in the chapters to follow. The purpose is not simply to capture the lessons learned from practice but to cultivate the faculty of prudential judgment, an issue we discuss in much greater detail in our concluding chapter.

Conclusion

Leadership in American public life is intentionally frustrated by diffusion of powers among many public officials and multiple sectors of society. It is intentionally weakened out of fear for its excesses. Ironically, this condition sometimes provokes intense desire for just what we fear most—the charismatic leader who charms us with articulate and emotional pleas, who supplies winning ideas and achievements that fascinate us and who makes clever use of technology to entertain and confuse us. We have had many such leaders, some achieving fame well beyond their generation, most often for leading the American people through the most trying circumstances. Others achieved more notoriety than fame, and they remind us of the perils and fickleness of relying on charismatic leadership in public life. The American Founders taught us the wisdom of taking precautions against the free play of such leaders. They established a system of governance that encourages us to rely on more modest types of leadership.

Much of the leadership theory we have reviewed in this chapter is of this modest sort. It focuses on leadership of groups for more routine matters of task effectiveness, concern for maturation and professional development within organizations, conciliatory practices designed to draw citizens into public discourse and engagement, and the stewardship roles of subordinate career officials. We have focused on shared leadership in shared-power contexts, first because this is the kind of leadership that is most amenable to responsible exercise, and second because it is the kind of leadership increasingly needed in daily life—for the maintenance of regular affairs, for our education as citizens, and for the preservation of our public institutions in an increasingly fragmented world.

Notes

1 We wish to thank Routledge for their permission to use material for this section from Morgan, Green, Shinn, and Robinson, *Foundations of Public Service*, 2nd edition, 2013/2008, 357–64.
2 Literature related to leadership is extensive. Several of the social science disciplines have handbooks published periodically with a section on leadership. These are good places to start for a systematic review of leadership.
3 While there is an early literature on women who lead, much of the research and theory development has occurred in the last 25 years. The literature cited in this section provides examples, but it is not comprehensive. Applied areas such as health and nonprofit leadership have developed a related literature. Similarly, there is a literature building for both public- and private-sector leadership related to women. Also, since the early 1990s, a number of centers for the study and promotion of women in leadership have been created. For example, the National Education for Women's Leadership of Oregon (NEW Leadership Oregon) is a Hatfield School of Government program run by the school's Center for Women's Leadership and associated with a Rutgers-based national network of such programs.

3   Leadership in Organizations

Every organized human activity—from the making of pots to the placing of a man on the moon—gives rise to two fundamental and opposing requirements: the division of labor into various tasks to be performed, and the coordination of these tasks to accomplish the activity. The structure of the organization can be defined simply as the sum total of the ways in which it divides its labor into distinct tasks and then achieves coordination among them.

Henry Mintzberg (1983, 2)

To see these organizations as moral agents—as participants in the moral order; as potential objects of moral concern—we may draw some insight from the sociology of institutions. A strategic focus is the transformation of organizations into institutions and into agencies of community.

Selznick (1992, 231)

Many of the questions that both analysts and members of organizations confront are fundamentally *political*. That is, they have to do with making choices, allocating benefits and burdens, generating commitment and legitimacy, and coping with conflict, complexity, and uncertainty. This in turn suggests that one approach to understanding organizations is to conceive of them as political systems, or *polities*, that develop structures for channeling political dynamics and performing political tasks.

Hult and Walcott (1990, 5)

Our leadership focus in this text occurs within and through the aegis of public organizations. While contracting with private and nonprofit organizations to provide public services has increased over the last two decades, most services are still predominately provided by or through government entities that are responsible for results. Both the functions these organizations provide and the image we have of what they are and should be conditions our thinking about the possibilities for leadership action. For these reasons, we review the most common images of organizations and discuss the leadership implications for each image. We then discuss the differences between public and private organizations and the implications of these differences for leadership. Finally, we discuss the consequences of these differences for leading change within public organizations.

Images of Organizations: Consequences for Leadership[1]

The opening epigraphs capture the four core images of the role of leaders in organizations. Mintzberg's emphasis on organizing the division of labor to accomplish the goals of the organization focuses on the role of leaders in intentionally creating social collectivities that have explicit purposes and relatively discrete boundaries. In this sense organizations are clearly designed as instruments—a means to ends. This gives rise to the image of "organizations as machines."[2] Minzberg's emphasis on coordinating the division of labor calls attention to the relationship-based and value-centered set of transformational activities that give meaning to employees and the larger organization. Over time this constellation of values and relationships take on a life of their own and produce organizational practices, policies, and procedures that create an organizational culture. This culture defines ways of living together and determines appropriate and inappropriate means for achieving ends. This view gives rise to the image of "organizations as organisms."

When the expressive moral values of an organization go beyond providing a cohering moral framework for its members and become integral to a community's self-identity, organizations become institutions. The Green Bay Packers have acquired this status for the citizens of Green Bay, Wisconsin. We probably all have our favorite homegrown examples of organizations that have become, in the words of Selznik, agencies of community. When organizations acquire this status, they become morally embedded agents of both producing and defining the larger community good. "Organizations as institutions" thus calls attention to the political skills needed for playing this community-building leadership role.

Finally, Hult and Wolcott think of "organizations as polities" to capture the distinctive legal and political nature of our formal public organizations. The difference between organizations as institutions and organizations as polities is that the latter are the legally constituted forum within which we continue the larger on-going societal debates regarding the purposes and priorities that our political institutions are charged to implement. While political skills are needed in leading institutions like the Green Bay Packers, a much broader and more statesman-like set of political skills are needed by those exercising polity leadership. At the end of our discussion of each of the four images of organizations, we will provide a summary of the leadership practices that are associated with each.

Organizations as Machine: Leaders as Managers of Work Structures and Process

> The effect of the division of labor, in the general business of society, will be more easily understood, by considering in what manner it operates in some particular manufactures ... To take an example, therefore, from a very trifling manufacture; but one in which the division of labor has been very often taken notice of, the trade of pin-maker; a workman not educated to this business nor acquainted with the use of the machinery employed in it, could scarce, perhaps, with his utmost industry, make one pin in a day, and certainly could not make twenty. But in the way in which this business is now carried on, not only the whole work is a peculiar trade, but it is divided into a number of branches, of which the greater parts are likewise peculiar trades. One man draws out the wire, another straightens it, a third cuts it, a fourth points it, a fifth grinds it at the top for receiving the head; to make the head requires two or three distinct operations; to put it on is a peculiar business, to whiten the pins is another; it is even a trade by itself to put them into paper; and the important business of making a pin is, in this manner, divided into about eighteen distinct operations, which, in some manufactories, are all performed by distinct hands, though in others the same man will sometimes perform two or three of them. I have seen a small manufactory of this kind where ten men only were employed, and where some of them consequently performed two or three distinct operations ... They could, when they exerted themselves make about twelve pounds of pins in a day. There are in a pound upwards of four thousand pins of a middling size. Those ten persons, therefore, could make among them upwards of forty-eight thousand pins in a day. Each person, therefore, making a tenth part of forty-eight thousand pins, might be considered as making four thousand eight hundred pins in a day. But if they had all wrought separately and independently, and without any of them having been educated to this particular business, they certainly could not each of them have made twenty, perhaps not one pin in a day; that is, certainly not the two hundred and fortieth, perhaps not the four thousand eight hundredth part of what they are at present capable of performing, in consequence of a proper division and combination of their different operations.
>
> Smith (1799, 3)

Smith's classic study of the pin factory captures the four core leadership elements that comprise the machine metaphor: organizations are designed to achieve specific ends; there is a "best way" to organize work to accomplish these ends; efficiency is maximized through the division and specialization of labor; and workers can be incentivized to increase performance through external rewards. We elaborate further on each of these core elements in the following sections.

Organizations Are Created to Achieve Specific Goals Related to Production

One of the core beliefs that separates modernity from the pre-modern period (pre- and post-15th century respectively) is confidence that scientific knowledge can be used to control and improve the human condition. Modernity rejects the assumption that we are born into a world that pre-determines our status or our fate. We now accept the view that humans can make and remake the world to suit our image of "the good." The development of organizational theory is dominated by this single-minded confidence in the capacity of leaders to control the conditions for successful achievement of organizational goals. The modern godfather of this view is Max Weber.

In the 1890s, Weber,[3] a German sociologist, studied the emergence of modern, rational organizations around the world. Through these studies, he abstracted from organizational practices the following characteristics which he believed most logically fit a "legal-rational" structure:[4]

- Fixed division of labor by official function
- Offices ordered in a hierarchy
- Reliance on expertise, skills, and experience as the basis for selection
- Formalized rules that govern performance, including reliance on extensive written records of administrative acts, decisions, and rules
- Separation of organizational property and resources from personal property and resources
- Resources of the organization are free from outside control
- Employment is viewed as a career and compensation is sufficient for livelihood

All of these characteristics that comprise Weber's idealized legal-rational model serve to standardize behavior in the organization. By controlling the means of action, leaders can control the achievement of organizational goals.

ONE-BEST WAY TO ORGANIZE.

Another core assumption of the machine image is that there is one best way to design an organizational machine. By relying on the collection of empirical data, careful analysis, and employee feedback, advocates of the scientific study of organizations believe that the best way can be found for structuring work within organizations. Frederick Taylor's *Principles of Scientific Management* (1911) stands as one of the most prominent American works representing this view. Taylor enthusiastically advocated the use of time and motion studies to optimize the work of employees. In one of his shop studies, he pointed out that every person shoveling coal had an optimal shovel size that would help maximize daily output over a day's labor. He surrounded workers with functional foreman, who would study every aspect of an employee's work process and look for ways to improve on the efficiency of effort and motion. He believed that all types of work at every level of organization would eventually benefit from this concentrated, systematic analysis.

Taylor's contributions anticipate the rise of systems analysis and operations research, out of which emerged commonly known managerial techniques such as Critical Path Method (CPM) and Program Evaluation Review Technique (PERT), and more recent approaches that include Six Sigma, Dashboards, LEAN, Agile Management, Total Quality Management (TQM) and other process-improvement systems.[5]

Efficiency Is Maximized through the Division and Specialization of Labor

Finding the "one best way" is defended because it maximizes the achievement of the goals of the organization (effectiveness) at the least cost (efficiency). Weber defended the legal-rational bureaucratic model because it created better outcomes, as was the case for Frederick Taylor's scientific approach to management. The traditional organization relied on the personal loyalty and other intimate ties between employees, their employers, families, clans, and their communities. Weber argued that efficiency is gained by replacing this loyalty-centered system with one that relies on specialization, standardization, and formalization of administrative work (Weber 1946/1924, 1968/1924). Both Weber and Taylor argued that organizations designed on this model create uniformity of organizational action by "purging particularism" (Perrow, 1986). Trained expertise ensures competency in each office, and the hierarchical nature of the relationship among offices provides a chain of authority for purposes of control, as well as formal pathways of communication for coordination among offices. Oversight is made easier through written rules and standard operating procedures (SOPs) that provide substitutes for individual judgment. When this structure is combined with a systematic focus on using data to improve work processes, organizations achieve increases in both effectiveness and efficiency.

Workers Need to Be Motivated by Tight Supervision

The machine metaphor is based on the assumptions that workers generally dislike work, lack ambition, are self-centered and thus uninterested in organizational goals, are resistant to change, and prefer to be led rather than to take the lead (McGregor, 1960). Accordingly, management must closely supervise and control workers lest they substitute their own interests and values for those of the organization. When these assumptions began to be called into question through the systematic gathering of data and analysis, it changed the organizational metaphor from that of machine to that of social organism. At the heart of this change is the discovery that workers are motivated by more than just external rewards and punishments.

While there have been variations of the "machine metaphor" (see especially Rainey's division into three sub-schools: the rational/legal, scientific management, and administrative management schools, 2014, 46–47), they all share a pessimistic view of human nature, which assumes that rewards in the workplace are more important than relationships. The discovery of the human side of management has transformed our approach to designing and managing public organizations.

Organizations as Social Organism: Leaders as "Managers of People"

The social organism metaphor recognizes that organizations are not simply paper constructs or the product of engineers. They are filled with people who are more than just a bundle of self-interests. Employees care about shared moral purposes; they want to be members of a moral community. As a consequence, employees may at times respond better to praise and attention from bosses and peers than they respond to the promise of external rewards or threats of external punishment. They may sacrifice a lot for the sake of being part of a larger common cause. The major study that triggered a more systematic focus on the "human side" of organizations was the product of a set of scientific experiments, beginning in the early 1930s, that were aimed simply at improving worker efficiency at the Hawthorne plants of the Western Electric Company in Chicago (Roethlisberger and Dickson, 1939; Mayo, 1933). These studies gave rise to what has become known as the "human relations" school of management.

The most cited Hawthorne study, called the Illumination Study, examined the impact on work output of electrical relay assembly groups by varying the extent of lighting in their work rooms. The controlled experiment showed that the group experiencing variations in lighting (from extremely bright to almost dark) increased productivity regardless of the direction of the variation. Curiously, the study also indicated that production among the control groups, where there was no change in lighting, also showed increases. Light intensity, therefore, could not explain the difference. The scientists decided that what did explain the difference was the attention paid to each group by the researchers, rather than the effect of light intensity. This finding has been labeled the "Hawthorne Effect" in social science research. For organization and leadership theory, it added an additional layer of complexity in creating efficient, productive, and healthy organizations. In addition to thinking of motivation primarily as a personal economic or physical issue, motivation now included a broad array of social-psychological phenomenon.[6]

In his classic work, *The Human Side of Enterprise* (1960), McGregor captures the heart of the human relations approach to leading organizations with his Theory Y approach to leadership. In sharp contrast to the Theory X assumptions of the machine metaphor, Theory Y assumes that workers have a broad scale of needs that include desires for inclusion, esteem, and fulfilling work. The genius of his dichotomy lies in the self-fulfilling nature of the assumptions. Workers become indolent and resistive to management when treated in a negative, Theory X fashion. Instead, by adopting Theory Y assumptions that workers possess intrinsic motivation to work and to identify with organizational goals, managers can remove barriers and release more potential for self-motivated accomplishments. Workers will adopt organizational objectives and labor steadfastly to achieve them. Leaders must provide the proper conditions for this to occur, which means less emphasis is placed on direct supervision, direction, and control, and more is placed on indirect, coordinative, and facilitative functions. Employee work can be made more challenging (job enrichment), and more responsibilities can be delegated to them without much supervision.

The human relations school has spawned two distinct bodies of literature, which highlight different sets of leadership practices for obtaining maximum employee motivation. One body focuses on the role of leaders in creating the kind of culture that builds employee ownership of the mission and work of the organization. The other emphasizes the need for diversity in leadership styles and calls attention to the need for more diverse types of managerial roles and practices than offered by traditional theory. Our discussion of trait theory in the previous chapter reminds us that neither leaders nor followers are a natural product of ingrained traits. The workplace is a social setting that shapes values and behavior through the creation and transmission of culture.

Creating and Managing Culture

Since the 1980s there has been a growing body of literature devoted to the concept of organizational culture as a useful framework for explaining the dynamics of organizational design and behavior (Sergiovanni and Corbally, 1984; Schein, 1985; Sathe, 1985; Morgan, 1986; Ott, 1989). Borrowing from the sociology of professions, research on organizational socialization, and from work on political symbolism and interpretivism,[7] this literature views organizations as systems of highly ingrained, taken-for-granted assumptions, values, and symbols that affect behavior in largely unconscious ways. Organizational culture provides premises, parameters, norms, and expectations that unconsciously guide or induce people to prefer one method over another, to make certain kinds of decisions over others, and to choose certain groups over others in organizational life. Attention is drawn to shared meanings and assumptions, mental models, established rules of the game, organizational climate, guiding metaphors, and integrating symbols (Schein, 1993). These are phenomena of human belief, interpretation, and values that structure organizational relationships and define appropriate means as well as ends. Every organization displays a collage of these phenomena that define the lived experience of organizational life. They define expectations of what constitutes good work or good management in organizational contexts. They define the proper ways of acting and interacting in the organizational community. They also constitute interpretive systems for determining what is real, what is believed, and what is significant about organizational activities and the environment (Daft, 1992, 1984; Mogren, 2011).

Aligning Leadership with Tasks

Another body of human-relations research has emphasized the variety of leadership behaviors that are needed to accommodate the diverse patterns of relationships within and among working groups inside organizations (cf. Fiedler, 1967; Hersey and Blanchard, 1977; Vroom and Yetton, 1973). Other theorists have broadened attention to include the interrelation of group-based social systems with the nature of tasks and functions to be carried out. This focus has heightened the role of leaders in integrating individuals and groups with roles, structures, tasks, and technologies in order to achieve organizational goals (Argyris, 1964; Trist, 1981). This focus has also increased the importance of facilitative and participatory practices and laid the foundation for the development of contingency theories of leadership in organizations.

Organizations as Contingency: Leaders as "Managers of Institutions"

The evolving contingency focus of the human relations side of leadership set the stage for viewing organizations as greatly influenced by their external environment. By the end of the 1980s, organizational efficiency and effectiveness were viewed as the product of multiple contingent factors and depended on the ability of leaders to transform these factors into a set of actions that give meaning to the participants. But this began to change when the unit of analysis was shifted from an internal focus on the organization to the interface of the organization with actors in the external environment. This change opened the door to viewing organizations as institutional and moral agents embedded in the larger community.

In the 1950s and 1960s, starting in England at the Tavistock Institute of Human Relations, organizational scholars began focusing on empirical studies of organizations as "socio-technical systems." These scholars viewed the technical aspects of organizations, including structure, job design, and task technology, as being interdependent with social aspects such as motivation, group dynamics, and leadership. As borne out in many subsequent studies, a change in technical features of production, such as increased automation, would change peer relationships among workers that could lead to changes in their attitudes toward performance (Gibson, Shinn, and Locklear, 1990). Likewise, changes in social or peer relations may affect the ways tasks are perceived and performed. Furthermore, the relationships among these factors are affected by the organization's interaction with its environment (Emery, 1959; Emery and Trist, 1965; Trist, 1981). Studies of these factors concluded that the idea of a single, best organizational design had to be abandoned in favor of a contingency approach. For example, a more mechanical, Weberian-styled bureaucracy may work in a stable environment where there is a clear mission and little uncertainty about the tasks to be accomplished, but it would be inappropriate in most other conditions, especially those settings that are characterized by high uncertainty, rapid change, and powerful forces that threaten survival (Emery and Trist, 1965). The view that organizations are the product of contingency-based leadership calls attention to adaptive leadership practices that include: managing the interface with the external environment, creating and leading in multiple structures of authority, and using flexible strategies for resolving conflict (Eoyang and Holladay, 2013; Wheatley, 2000).

Managing the Interface with the External Environment

James D. Thompson's 1967 book, *Organizations in Action,* was the first major scholarly work devoted to the contingent nature of organizations and the implications for leadership. Thompson presented organizations as "open" rather than "closed" systems. Drawing from the field of organizational sociology, Thompson illustrated the need for an institutional-level perspective through which leaders focus on imminent and emerging conditions in the environment of their organization. This kind of leadership work requires diplomacy, cooptation, cutting deals, and cultivating multilateral relationships with potential partners, competitors, regulators, clients, media, and suppliers (Burns and Stalker, 1961; Selznick, 1957; Thompson, 1967). Leaders working at the interface of the organization and the external environment must anticipate trends, scan for threats, span boundaries, adapt to changes in the environment, and take advantage of opportunities to build on the organization's domain.

The external focus of the metaphor of organizations as institutions has important implications for leadership at various levels of the organization. For example, middle managers become translators, mediators, and buffers between the strategic apex of the organization and those doing the work on the front line. Middle managers must translate the implications of strategic information, decisions, and policy changes for street-level operations (the technical core of the organization), and likewise inform strategic managers about the needs and capacities of the technical core in light of environmental factors. They must also mediate conflicts and tensions arising from the internal need for stability and control, and the strategic demands for flexibility and adaptation in response to external changes. Then, through various coping tactics, they must buffer and smooth the rates and extent of change that impact various parts of the organization. According to Thompson, middle managers perform these functions through capacity-building, which entails developing a consistent supply of materials and human resources and providing support functions across coordinating subunits, and through boundary-spanning activities that organize and reorganize the governance structures within the organization to meet new contingencies (Thompson, 1967, Chap. 3).

Thompson and many subsequent theorists drive home the point that leadership is not a uniform activity nor is it clearly separable from management. Leadership practices vary dramatically across all levels and functions of organizational life. Thus, it is not uncommon for a technical core manager to be promoted into a middle-management position and experience great difficulty adjusting to its tasks and orientation. The same is true for middle managers who are promoted into strategic roles. The leadership tasks and perspectives ingrained at one level of management may actually inhibit the ability to understand and exercise leadership management roles at other levels. As mentioned earlier, this phenomenon is referred to as "trained incapacity" (cf. Merton, 1940), and it requires substantial reorientation and training to overcome.

Contingent Structures for Getting the Job Done

The contingency model emphasizes the need for varying structural designs in order for leaders to cope with the myriad tasks and functions of an organization. Different kinds of tasks face different kinds of challenges, depending on the type and extent of uncertainty involved. Complex tasks with lots of uncertainty as to expectations and/or outcomes require highly interactive, collegial structures (reflecting "reciprocal interdependence"), as illustrated by medical teams working in an emergency room or SWAT teams dealing with a threatening situation. Tasks with more certainty and fairly stable rates of change can be handled more efficiently through hierarchical, linear, and specialized structures. For example, a nonprofit food pantry may assemble meals on an assembly line in which tasks are sequentially interdependent. The work at one stage is dependent on work done at the prior stage. In other cases, the work may involve multiple lines delivering the same kinds of products or services, as illustrated at a motor vehicle licensing office. The staff depends on a common pool of resources ("pooled interdependence") but provides multiple avenues for accessing them (see Thompson, 1967 for further in-depth discussion of these structures).

Other important dimensions of organizational work involve task variety and task analyzability (Perrow, 1986). Low task variety allows workers to focus their efforts on narrowly defined problems, such as how to place test monitors on well heads for purposes of assessing pollution levels. High task variety requires broad training that enables workers to adjust quickly to many different kinds of challenges. Social workers handling family services cases rely on a range of skills and concepts, and they may have to interact with other professionals to render effective aid to their clients. Task analyzability refers to the ability to assess and solve problems in a timely fashion. Low analyzability requires more intensive and interactive work, as exhibited in teaching special education students and case-management work carried out by social services agencies. High analyzability enables standardization of work processes, as exemplified in various benefits determination processes and dispersal functions carried out by government agencies.

As task structures develop, they must be linked and integrated into the broader organization through various methods of coordination and control. These include more complex approaches involving mutual adjustment among organizational colleagues and different levels of management, as well as simpler approaches such as supervisory or expert-based direction (Mintzberg, 1979). Here again, middle managers play a crucial role in developing and operationalizing the working relationships among subunits. As they carry out this work, they also develop compliance mechanisms for monitoring performance and enforcing standards (Gross and Etzioni, 1985). The sources of compliance are both internal and external. Typical internal mechanisms include accounting and auditing procedures, standard operating procedures, program objectives, job descriptions, performance evaluations, and consensus building. External controls may include legislative and/or executive oversight, imposed competition with rival organizations, budgetary conditions and restrictions, and procedural regulation. There are also unobtrusive control mechanisms (e.g., shared vision, organizational culture, generational values, etc.) that may actually play more powerfully on employees than direct mechanisms.

Herbert Simon (1947) noted that those who set the premises or parameters of decisions exert tremendous control over those who must make the decisions. This idea has been popularized by Pirsig in his book, *Zen and the Art of Motorcyle Maintenance* (2006): she who defines the "system" controls the subsequent action. Thus, the way new employees are trained, the organizational vocabulary they learn, and the workgroup processes to which they are socialized exert a general but very powerful problem- and process-defining influence on their thought and behavior. Andrew Dunsire's (1979) empirical studies of employee behavior revealed that these unobtrusive factors more effectively guide and structure behavior than monitoring and supervision.

Organization Conflict and Controversy

In keeping with contingency theory's view that context matters, conflict and controversy are not always treated as bad things, nor should they be handled in the same way when they arise. Consider the conflict among engineers over the best design for developing a manufacturing production line. This kind of conflict is likely best solved by developing a traditional matrix that lists the criteria, then rank orders and/or weights their importance before collecting data to assess the alternative models. Contrast that with resolving a controversy among team members who are in disagreement about whether each member of the team is "pulling their weight." Neither the standards for measuring success nor the methodology used to "get to yes" will likely be the same (Fisher, Ury, and Patton, 2002). Success for members of the dysfunctional team is much more dependent on a reconciliation process grounded in emotions and feelings than is likely to be the case for reaching a decision on which engineering design is best for the new production line. Just as form needs to follow function, so is often the case for managing organizational conflict.

In Exhibit 3.1 we provide a graphic summary of the four images of organizations discussed above and the leadership implications of each. These leadership roles are not mutually exclusive, but additive. This is what makes leadership so interesting, but at the same time so difficult. This is also why leaders need to know their own strengths and surround themselves with a team of co-leaders that possess the complementary strengths needed to get the work of the entire organization done well.

What Is Uniquely Different about Leadership in Public Organizations?

In Chapter 2 we introduced regime theory to emphasize that public organizations reflect the unique values and characteristics of the particular political system that creates them. This may seem too obvious to warrant the kind of attention we give this idea in Chapters 4–6, but we do so because of our belief that regime values, history and institutions play a significant role in shaping public service leadership opportunities and in defining the conditions for their success. The early days of the Trump presidency indicate what happens when this kind of leadership knowledge is lacking: promises get made that can't be fulfilled because of the need of approval of other governing partners; institutional history and purpose gets confused with personal power, loyalty and friendship; the role of a public office can't easily be separated from one's persona; and citizen trust in governing institutions and processes are continually eroded (Brooks, 2013; Friedman, 2017). In this section we specifically focus on theories that treat organizations as political systems and the consequences that this focus has for leadership.

Political Goals Are Often Unclear and Contested: Why Public Service Leaders Satisfice

Establishing goals for any organization is always problematic because they are guesses about the desired future condition an organization seeks to obtain (Gross and Etzioni, 1985). Even in organizations with a rather simple goal of selling bottled water, goals are multiple and often competing. For example, some goals will be related to the policy outcome, in this example delivering water. Other goals will relate to the maintenance of the organization itself. The expectation is that the water supplier will maintain the facilities, records and staff competency to meet the over-arching goal of making a profit from selling safe bottled water. It is likely that the water supplier will adopt goals associated with meeting safe drinking water standards set by the federal government and perhaps others set at state or local levels. Clearly such a matrix of goals is not established without value trade-offs, i.e. politics. This suggests that within all political organizations goal setting is a

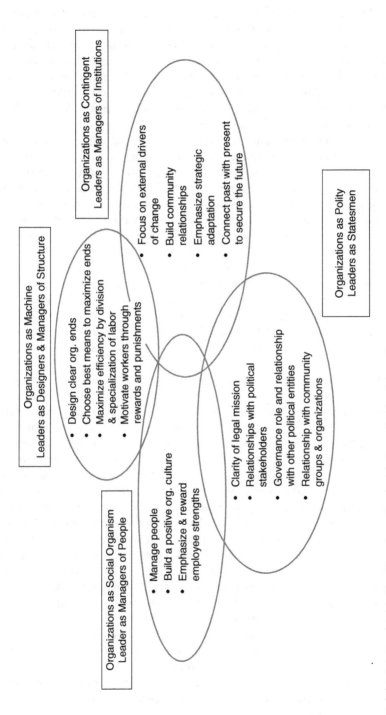

Organizations as Contingent
Leaders as Managers of Institutions

- Focus on external drivers
  of change
- Build community
  relationships
- Emphasize strategic
  adaptation
- Connect past with present
  to secure the future

Organizations as Machine
Leaders as Designers & Managers of Structure

- Design clear org. ends
- Choose best means to maximize ends
- Maximize efficiency by division
  & specialization of labor
- Motivate workers through
  rewards and punishments

Organizations as Polity
Leaders as Statesmen

Organizations as Social Organism
Leader as Managers of People

- Manage people
- Build a positive org. culture
- Emphasize & reward
  employee strengths

- Clarity of legal mission
- Relationships with political
  stakeholders
- Governance role and relationship
  with other political entities
- Relationship with community
  groups & organizations

Exhibit 3.1 Leadership Practices Associated with Organization Metaphors

political activity in which decision outcomes are determined by agreement among members of the dominant coalition in the organization and limited by external policy and the need to maintain legitimacy. This simple notion serves as the basis for those who argue that we need to take a political approach to understanding and leading organizations. Doing so highlights the development, location and maintenance of power, which is in this case the authority to set goals (Simon, 1947; Cyert and March, 1963; Olsen, 2001).[8]

A focus on power and authority has far-reaching leadership consequences for public sector organizations where power and authority are distributed both horizontally and vertically. We can illustrate this by extending the bottled water example in the previous paragraph to the goal of delivering safe water by a local water district. The water district can't restrict its goal to delivering affordable and safe drinking water. It has to consider the impact of taking and selling water on the environment, neighboring jurisdictions in the water supply business, the priorities of its elected governing board and the views of its ratepayers. While the water entity may not have to worry about turning a profit, leaders have to deal with "fuzzy and ambiguous" goals like "being a model employer," being good neighbors, being good stewards of the environment, affordability, fairness, and numerous other goals that cannot be reduced to an empirically accessible standard (Stone, 1997).

Another factor that further complicates the goal-setting function of leadership in public sector organizations is the accretion of goals over time. Examples include elementary schools that have taken on community health and social service functions and utility districts that have moved beyond electricity or telephone services to include a variety of energy conservation and communication services. A current trend in human services is to bundle services into "super departments" to improve the coordination among programs serving different target populations. State and local emergency managers face an enormous organizational design challenge because of federal policies adding terrorism response to the list of natural and social emergencies historically assigned to first responders. Local police departments are pulled in different directions by the federal government's desire to enlist their resources in the enforcement of federal immigration laws. New purposes add complexity, which strains existing designs. Adding to the strain are declining resources, dramatic demographic turnover in executive ranks, and changing sentiments in society about how public services should be delivered. These internal and external pressures create real tensions and trade-offs in organizational design. These tensions increase the tendency for public service leaders to "satisfice" rather than follow a more "maximizing strategy" that is typically used by their private sector counterparts.

Herbert Simon was the first organizational theorist to argue that few organizational decisions are ever optimal in nature. Rather, they are bounded by limitations of knowledge, experience, habit and capacity, and therefore require managers to make decisions that are just satisfactory and sufficient for the moment. He coined the term *satisficing* to character-ize such decisions (Simon, 1947, 38–41; also see Cyert and March, 1963). When Simon's basic idea is applied to public organizations, it has some far-reaching political consequences for the role of leaders.

Charles Lindblom (1959, 1965) drew from the pluralist political model (see Chapters 4 and 5 for a more detailed discussion) to argue that the multiple and fuzzy goals of public sector organizations require leaders to make decisions that allow their agencies and programs to adapt incrementally, rather than rely on a rational-comprehensive analytic approach commonly advocated in the traditional management literature. In their limited capacities, according to Lindblom, agency and program leaders must rely on existing patterns of resource alloca-tion and status quo operations, and they must adapt slowly at the margins (described as "successive limited comparisons") in response to external pressures. Leaders of public organizations adopt a variety of political tactics and games to finesse these marginal adjustments. Aaron Wildavsky, another highly influential political scientist, employed this framework in his classic work *The Politics of the Budgetary Process* (1964) to describe the variety of games played by federal agency officials to win favorable budgetary decisions through congressional and executive branch politics. He also later illustrated the usefulness of the approach in explaining how policy analysis works in practice (Wildavsky, 1979).

Political Goals Are Often in Conflict: Why Public Service Leaders Educate, Mediate and Conciliate

The goals of public organizations are often in conflict. This is an extension of our argument in the previous section that goals are often vague and ambiguous. But more often than not, goals are also both in conflict and built into the mission of public organizations because legislative bodies are unable or unwilling to resolve value conflicts among stakeholders. When this happens leaders of public organizations are stuck with the conflicting missions given to them by courts, legisla-tive bodies and executive branch leaders.

Take for example the common legislative mandate given to our natural resource agencies to carry out their mission to meet the test of "multiple use." This leaves organizational leaders with the challenge of figuring out how to reconcile the commercial value of these resources with the values of recreation, sustainable development, protecting the environment, and others (see the Mt. Hood Stewardship Master Case for Part II). Similarly, take the case of federal school funding, which may require school site councils or community action programs to provide opportunities for "maximum feasible participation" of stakeholders (Blumenthal, 1969). Organizational leaders are left to figure out what this requirement means within the dynamics of their local political setting.

When faced with such value conflicts, what should our public leaders do? We have no formulaic answer. But we do believe they have a moral responsibility as stewards of the public trust to be knowledgeable and worthy agents of owning these tensions. At a minimum, ownership means not shunning, hiding or burying the conflict. More proactively, it may often mean using conflict as an opportunity to engage the community in a discussion that educates and facilitates a conciliatory and temporary resolution. For example, in the Master Case of the Angry Library Patron, rather than fearing an organizational or community debate over the appropriateness of Madonna's *Sex* (1992) to be owned and circulated by local libraries, leaders may well embrace the debate as an opportunity to educate both employees and the community on the library's conflicting missions, and especially the legal obligations of public institutions to protect first amendment rights (see Chapter 5 for a discussion of what this ownership means and what it looks like in practice). Our emphasis in this book is on the development of this kind of conciliatory leadership knowledge, skills and practices, both because it is an inherent part of our system of democratic governance and also because it is a growing need.

Serving Many Bosses: Why Public Leaders Face Multiple Standards of Accountability

Who are the bosses of our public service leaders? Is it the chief executive of their respective jurisdictions (i.e., the mayor, city manager, etc.)? Or is it the elected representative body that provides them with the money and legal authority to do their work? Or is it the courts that ultimately draw authoritative lines regarding the limits of leadership discretion? Or is it the taxpayers that provide the funding? Or is it the clients who receive the services? Or is it the citizens at large for whom they work? Or is it the constitution and laws to which they swear allegiance? The answer to all of these questions is, "Yes!" The answer is that our public service leaders exercise "power over" while at the same time exercising "power with." At times, we want our organizational leaders to be the instrumental agents of elected legislative bodies, always "on tap" and never "on top." At other times we believe they have an affirmative moral obligation to anticipate the problems that need to be fixed and to take a proactive role in nipping problems in the bud before they ever reach public attention. Running effective programs, managing resources efficiently, being responsive to citizens, faithfully executing the will of the legislative body, protecting the rights of citizens and clients, being innovative, fair and transparent, all produce an accountability framework that is far more complex than the case for measuring the success of leaders in private sector organizations.

Structures of Public Authority are Morally Complex: Why Public Leaders Are "Bureaucratic"

The polity metaphor shines a bright light on the structures of authority within which public leaders carry out their work. These structures, while quite variable, share in common the need for specific legal authority before leaders can take leadership action. This need to comply with legal authority is often mistaken by citizens, clients and customers as "being bureaucratic." Consider Exhibit 3.2, a useful summary by Hult and Walcott (1990) of the types of governance structures of public authority identified through their study of public organizations.

Each governance structure listed in Exhibit 3.2 is the product of a legal decision in which organizational citizens work out matters such as issues of power allocation, "the extent and nature of members' participation in organizational decision making, and the bases of the political system's legitimacy" (Hult and Walcott, 1990, 113–14). These legal structures and norms produce widely varying roles and responsibilities and governing relationships among the participants in the system (Hult and Walcott, Chap. 8). Hult and Wolcott refer to the work of designing and running public organizational structures as *organization policy* (139), which calls attention to the citizen- v. customer-centered focus of public organizations that separates these organizations from their private sector counterparts.

Another closely linked difference between public and private sector organizations is the complexity of the network governance relationships that exist in the public sector environment. Different network structures are used to knit organizational subunits together and to link a public organization to other organizations in its environment. Because these linkages operate within a rule of law framework they require leaders in public organization to transcend the concern for instrumental control that is so prominent in the field of organization theory (Etzioni, 1975; Mintzberg, 1983; cf. Thompson, 1967) and rely more on decisions based in compromise, tradition, habit, rules, chance, intuition and competing forms of advocacy (Stone, 1997, 233–56). These differences can clearly be seen in the way in which we think about strategic leadership in public organizations.

Exhibit 3.2 Governance Structures and Networks

Governance Structures

- Hierarchical structures—top-down control, information up the chain, focus on rules and accountability, determinate ends and means
- Adjudicative structures—designed for recurring disputes of win/lose or right/wrong type, with rules of procedure to present views before a neutral decision-maker
- Adversarial structures—permits advocacy of more than two points of view before a neutral party
- Collegial-competitive structures—legislative or deliberative bodies, reflecting multiple interests, no neutral decision-maker
- Collegial-consensual structures—emphasizes agreement on the merits rather than by compromise, multiple revision of proposals, brainstorming, eliciting opinions
- Collegial-mediative structures—tactical maneuvering of interests, logrolling politics, clarification of positions, facilitation by mediators
- Market structures—undirected interplay of individual groups, minimal coercion, unspecified ends other than self-interest

Governance Networks

- Bureaucratic—standardized reporting, hierarchical authority
- Team—collaboration and collegiality, strong membership ties
- Decentralized—interactive, competitive, mutual adjustment
- Confrontational—intermittent clashes, limited participants, arbitrative
- Bargaining—rule-structured compromise and negotiation, votes and vetoes
- Consultative—conveying multiple types of expertise to decision-makers
- Appeals—reconsideration of decisions by other bodies via hearings and reviews
- Hybrid—networks embedded within networks, transformation of forms over time

Source: Hult and Walcott (1990, 33–47 and 96–109).

Strategic Leadership of Organizations

Over the past two decades strategic leadership of organizations has become a growth industry, resulting in the production of thousands of articles and monographs that now sit alongside the plethora of management-centered literature published in the 1960s and 1970s. There are two characteristics of this strategic leadership literature that help us answer the questions, why and why now? First, most of the focus on strategic leadership has come out of the private sector, as businesses have been pressured to remain competitive in an increasingly globalized economy. Second, there has been a decided shift away from associating strategic leadership with what happens by executives at the "strategic apex" of organizations, and instead towards viewing strategic leadership as a set of personal leadership qualities or practices that enable individuals at all levels of an organization to enlist the support of followers in doing what they should be doing tomorrow rather than what they are currently doing today (for example, see Hughes, Beatty, and Dinwoodie, 2014; Adair, 2010; Fulmer, Stumpf, and Bleak, 2009). In short, the concept of strategic leadership has been democratized and de-bureaucratized.

What remains at the heart of strategic leadership, whether applied to public- or private-sector organizations, or to the individual or organizational levels of analysis, is a focus on the alignment of the organizational mission and vision with future drivers of change. This focus draws heavily from the metaphor of organizations as contingent with leaders playing a central role in ensuring the future relevance of the organization based on past and current history. Strategic leadership provides an opportunity to ask, "What adjustments does our organization, program, work unit, etc. need to make in order to take into account current drivers of change?" As the term strategy implies, thinking about future goals is extremely important. And it is important for both private- and public-sector leaders, but for different reasons. Private and nonprofit sector leaders have to think and act strategically to make sure they have future customers, donors and clients who want their products and services. Public sector leaders need to think and act strategically to keep and build trust with citizens through the governance role they perform in our various systems of democratic governance. How successfully this strategic trust-building role is performed is measured partly by process criteria and partly by outcomes. Both dimensions are exercises in keeping public sector organizations morally tethered to the citizens they serve, an issue we deal with in greater detail in Chapters 5–7. As a result, strategic leadership of organizations in the public sector is less of a straight-line activity between leaders and followers than is the case for leaders in the private sector. A private sector organizational leader has the freedom to brand and rebrand as long as the profit-margins continue to meet investor expectations. But strategically rebranding in the public sector is not so clear and not so easy because leaders are legally constrained.

Let's take the example of a local sewage treatment district that has an obligation to produce effluent discharges into the local river that meet specific standards under the Clean Water Act. How does a sewage treatment organization take advantage of growing environmental concerns by its community stakeholders? Any kind of strategic transformation must be carried out within the constraints of the organization's legally prescribed mission and the mutual expectations of a network of other local districts, cities and counties that are competing for resources from the same limited revenue base. Strategic leadership in this kind of environment requires much more cooperation and reliance on conciliatory leadership practices (see Chapter 10) than is the case for leaders in the private and nonprofit sectors. Over a 20-year period leaders of the local sewer district in question transformed its name to "Clean Water Services" with the mission to "advance watershed restoration, resource recovery and organizational excellence through innovative strategies and to promote scientific research, education and environmental protection activities that benefit watersheds around the world" (see Clean Water Services, 2017). Most private business would not remain competitive if it took 20 years to alter their mission in order to address major new drivers of change.

There is another difference between strategic leadership in the public and nonprofit sectors. Government exists in part to address issues that the private sector won't or can't deal with very effectively. For example, while there is a robust private sector market to address drug addiction, mental health and other maladies, these individual-focused treatment programs require paying customers and do not seek to address the underlying political, economic and social conditions that may cause these individual maladies to rise or fall. And there are other issues like building infrastructure, preserving natural resources for future generations and educating students for careers and citizenship that the private and nonprofit sectors cannot do alone because the risks are too uncertain and/or the returns too nebulous and far off into the future. By taking on responsibility for dealing with future tragedies of the commons (Hardin, 1968), most public organizations are by their very nature are created to achieve strategic ends. Unlike employees in private sector businesses, public servants at every level of the organization are important participants in defining the strategic ends of the organization. Private businesses try to take their competitors by surprise as they secretly guard their strategic goals from employees, customers and competitors. In the public sector, strategic goals are publicly memorialized in law with a web of accountability and transparency requirements. For these reasons managing change in public organizations is both hard and less urgent than is the case for private sector organizations.

Leadership v. Management

Most of the literature on leading in organizations that we have reviewed so far is couched in terms of managerial control, efficiency and task effectiveness. Even when dealing with the human relations side of the organization, the advice to managers is: "Pay attention to your employees' social-psychological needs and they will work harder for you." In the end, as Henry Mintzberg (1983, 2) suggests, getting the job done is largely an organizational function of opposing tasks: "the division of labor into various tasks to be performed, and the coordination of these tasks to accomplish the activity." This view led to Drucker's famous aphorism that "leaders do the right thing and managers do the thing right" (Drucker, 2001). This belief is reflected in Fairholm's observation that:

> Management embodies the more reasoned, scientific, position-based approach to organizational engagement, such as setting and maintaining organization structure, dealing with complexity, solving organizational problems, making transactions between leader and those being lead and ensuring control and prediction. Leadership embodies the more relationship-based, values-laden, developmental aspect of the work we do in organizations, such as changing the organizational contexts, transforming leader and those being led, setting and aligning organization vision and group action, and ensuring individuals a voice so that they grow into productive, proactive and self-led followers (Burns, 1978; Kotter, 1990; Taylor, 1911; Urwick, 1944; Zaleznik, 1977; Ackerman, 1985; Rosener, 1990).
>
> (see Mathew Fairholm, 2013, endnote 1, 588)

We think Fairholm's distinction makes heuristic sense, especially in characterizing the differences between the institutional and polity models of leadership on the one hand, and the machine and social organism models on the other. But even leading machine-like and social organism activities requires an on-going interdependent back and forth movement between left and right brain work, and between doing management and leadership work. The left brain, or executive function, is associated with the management activities of creating order and control, while the right brain is associated with the kinds of value-centered and meaning-making activities described by Fairholm (see Chapter 12 for further discussion of the role of neuroscience in leadership success). But the executive tasks like setting and maintaining organization structure, dealing with complexity and solving organizational problems, require us to ask "why" questions, "when" questions and "fit" questions; all of this necessitates tapping into the interpretive reservoir lodged in the right brain. Consider the seemingly simply management task of deciding how to organize work flow and creating appropriate job descriptions. The popular view treats these activities as management functions because the end is about seeking greater control and predictability. But these control-focused goals cannot be achieved without interpreting data to figure out the right structure and flow that fits the circumstances at hand. Once created, putting this structure in place requires managers to answer all of the questions usually associated with leadership: How do we make sure the change aligns with the organization's strategic goals? How do we develop and roll out our change initiative so that employees feel a sense of ownership? How do we make sure the change is affordable and doable? These are leadership questions that managers are required to consider long before they jump-start a management change initiative. Once a new management system is in place and begins to be treated as a routine, then we agree that thinking of this maintenance role in management terms makes sense. But most of the management literature we have reviewed in this chapter focuses on changing the status quo to make organizations better. Making something better is a change-management activity usually associated with the role of leaders. For these reasons we are not big fans of drawing bright line distinctions between being a leader and being a manger. The latter requires an abundance of leadership skills and the former can't be done without understanding what "good" management looks like and the conditions needed for its success. Both leadership and management are more than a bundle of tools; they are practices that require continuous application over time to acquire the prudential judgment to know the right thing to do in the circumstances at hand.

Leading Change in Public Organizations

There is a large and growing body of literature on leading change in organizations. We found more than 63 books and nearly 52,500 articles published in *JSTOR*[9] between 1980 and 2017. Most of these articles are focused on change in private sector organizations (see especially Henderson, Gulati, and Tushman, 2016; Tushman and O'Reilly, 2013). The globalization of the economy has incentivized the need for leaders in the private sector to create nimble organizations that engage in continuous innovation in order to be competitive. This push to innovate and to be entrepreneurial, however, has had an important impact on public organizations. In fact, the New Public Management Movement that has swept the globe since the 1990s has been influenced by the desire to make public organizations more innovative and entrepreneurial (see our discussion at the end of Chapter 7). But public organizations are most often not created to innovate, but to ensure predictable, fair, legally accountable, responsive and continuous provision of public services and goods within the boundaries created by law. Still, there is the need to constantly re-examine why and how well our public organizations are achieving their legally assigned missions. Leaders and managers at every level of the organization are in the best position to ask both of these "why" and "how" questions and come up with improvements. The trust and legitimacy of most of our public organizations are linked to their capacity for creatively adapting to change. Being successful in doing this through time is part of what enables them to acquire institutional status (Selznick, 1949, 1992). In the sections that follow, we identify core principles for leading change from where we sit.

Organizational Metaphors: Some Key Diagnostic Questions for Leading Change

Organizations help structure and define where we sit. But the desire to lead change is almost always driven by a sense that things are not working well, and that we can do better. This sense of a gap between what is and what could be, a sense of discontent, is an essential precondition for all change. One principle for leading from where we sit is being comfortable with this discontent, but seeking conditions which foster this awareness. This is why fostering "essential tension" (Kuhn, 1977), structured disagreement, creativity and dissent within a work group, team or organizational unit is a good thing. However, for this tension to be functional it needs to be aimed at the larger enterprise, the common good and the organization's role in furthering that good. With this caveat in mind in Exhibit 3.3 we draw from our previous discussion of the various organizational metaphors to provide a check-list of key diagnostic questions you can ask to help gain perspective and initiate change.

Exhibit 3.3 Diagnostic Questions for Initiating Change From Where We Sit

Machine Metaphor Questions

1   What changes are needed in existing structures and processes?
2   What are the budget implications of these changes?
3   Whose expertise is needed?
4   Who has formal authority to make the desired changes?
5   What rules are barriers to change?

Social Organism Metaphor Questions

1   How will the change impact employees?
2   How will the change impact the organizational culture?
3   Is the culture a barrier to change or can it be used to leverage change?
4   What are the implications of the change for the informal relations within the organization?
5   How can the informal relationships be used to leverage change?

Institutional Metaphor Questions

1   How does the change affect external stakeholders, organizations and community groups?
2   How can these community entities be used to leverage change?
3   What are the implications of the change for other departments and organizational units?
4   How can these departments and organizational units be used to leverage change?

Polity Metaphor Questions

1   Will the change alter existing structures of political authority?
2   Will the change require the political support of the governing body? Other jurisdictions?
3   What community networks are impacted by the change?
4   How can community networks be used to leverage change?
5   Can the change be framed as a moral benefit to the community writ large?
6   What do followers need in the existing context?
7   How will we balance multiple leadership and management roles?
8   How do we balance conflicting legal mandates and moral purposes?

Core Principles for Leading Change from Where We Sit

In Chapters 9 and 11 we introduce a number of tools which can be used to foster successful change. These tools rest on some common principles, which include: being self-aware of where you sit, creating a culture of change, seeking continous learning, embracing multiple perspectives, stiring the pot, setting up "skunk works," managing the tensions, stimulating attractors, identifying emergence and supporting such change.

Self-awareness of where you sit is the starting point for managing change. The role(s) you fill in the organization determines what you see and what is possible. Things look different, and the points of leverage you have near at hand are different as your organizational role changes. Are you part of the front line staff, or a middle manager? Are you a senior staff providing advice to those in excutive roles or are you in an excutive role? Does your authority come from your techincal expertise or a critical staff support role you fill for the organization? Knowing where you sit is a first step in leading change.

Much of the current literature emphasizes the importance of *creating a culture of change and innovation.*[10] This is important for dealing with a permanent state of indeterminacy, a condition where the future cannot be known with enough certainty to employ traditional rational decision-making techniques like SWOT analysis and strategic planning. This is an issue we specifically address in greater detail in Chapters 9 and 11, where we provide some practical leadership tools for addressing these emergent kinds of leadership challenges.

A third principle is *embracing multiple perspectives.* Rather than assuming we as individuals can see and know the nature of the challenges the organization is facing, leaders need the assistance of others in sizing up the situation. Well-known leadership techniques like brainstorming and more recent experience with crowd sourcing draw on the basic idea that tapping into the collective intelligence of groups generates a larger pool of innovative ideas than relying on single individuals or a smaller group of insiders. Research on innovation suggests that one of the most important leadership practices for generating creativity in the workplace is to construct the network of formal and informal space among and between potential followers so that the system as a whole encourages individuals to generate new ideas, freely engage in dialogical exchanges between roles, across bureaucratic and legal boundaries and to take collective ownership for addressing challenges (Lichtenstein, Uhl-Bien, Marion, Seers, and Orton, 2007, 5; also see Lichtenstein and Plowman, 2009; Hazy, Goldstein, and Lichtenstein, 2007).

Part of leadership is not only embracing multiple perspectives but activating conditions for individuals and groups to "see things differently." This we call *stiring the pot.* Open discussions across organizational boundaries, both vertically and horizontally are some ways to stir the pot. Large group discussion methods, fish-bowl gatherings and dialogical approaches that are democratic, interactive and multidirectional are some proven techniques. "Walking around," ensuring diversity and inclusion in work groups, and listening to "outlying" voices all aid in embracing multiple perspectives and creating conditions for stiring the pot. Closely related to "stiring the pot" is creating the space for change to be initiated. One classic structural approach is to *facilitate skunk works,* separate temporary or semi-permanent working groups set apart from the normal flow of work where there is the real posibility of different solutions to emerge.

A challenge for leaders who are fostering change and innovation as suggested in these first few principles is ensuring that the change is functional to the underlying why and how of the organization. This means that leaders need to *watch the pot, and not let the pot boil over.* The risk of stirring the pot and encouraging a large diverse group to participate in sizing up a challenge or identifying potential leadership opportunities is that the process becomes a Tower of Babel, or worse, an unguided missile of dissent. It is therefore important for leaders to set limits to what is relevant to the dialogical process of sizing up leadership challenges and opportunities. In Chapter 9 we continue this discussion by drawing on the literature dealing with change management and the solicitation of stakeholder prticiaption (see especially Lichtenstein and Plowman, 2009; International Association of Public Participation, 2004).

Lichtenstein and his research associates have discovered that the group process for making sense out of leadership challenges and opportunities reaches a point when ideas begin to resonate with small groups of people at first and then gain momentum with an enlarging circle of followers. They call this stage of the process *the attractor phase* because, like honey to a bee, it gives structure and coherence to the process of making sense out of muddles. From the attractor stage, where part of the organization is moving in a new direction, leaders need to attend to the whole. We call this principle, *managing the conditions and monitoring emergence or keeping your focus on the hive.*

At the end of the day, not everyone in an organizational setting can or should be engaged in sizing up leadership challenges and opportunities. And it is especially the case that this cannot constitute the bulk of a public service leader's time. A highly respected local government executive, and former undersecretary of the Environmental Protection Agency (EPA), once observed in one of our leadership training programs that the secret to success in managing change in an emergent setting is to make certain the current work is getting done exceptionally well. He used the analogy of trying to change the direction of a large oil tanker about to hit a reef. You don't want those stoking the furnace to worry about being on the bridge trying to decide what to do. When there is a need for a creative change in direction, he observed that the leadership team needs to identify about 20 percent of the affected organization who are able and willing to help "size up" what is going on. There will always be about 20 percent of the organization who will oppose any innovation or change, regardless of the leader or the circumstances. The other 60 percent of the organization needs to work successfully on carrying out the current mission of the organization.

We have not found a research study which identifies the ideal number of leaders and followers needed to distill a leadership challenge and opportunity into sufficient clarity for action. But we do know from our experience and a review of a three-year Gallup study that followers have a choice in whether or not to follow (Rath and Conchie, 2009, 92–91, 251–56; Fairholm, 2013), as well as a continuing need for stability, security and feeding of their sense of devotion. These conditions become increasingly at risk in periods of uncertainty, change and emergence. Part of sizing up leadership challenges and opportunities, then, is being able to keep the organizational unit focused on those challenges that are time-sensitive and complicated, while working selectively with others to see the sources of calm in a sea of turbulence. Leaders need to authentically model a sense of calm and security for followers even while navigating through the whitewater. Modeling this sense of calm becomes easier as you expand your tolerance for ambiguity. As one becomes more tolerant of white water turbulence, one becomes more calm and confident that a safe way forward will be possible. So, in sizing up change opportunities in conditions of uncertainty, leaders need to be on the lookout for simple or tame landscapes (patterns and routines) in the midst of dynamic complexity.

Conclusion

Leadership in organizations today remains as problematic as it was for those who founded modern organizational theory, including Adam Smith and Max Weber. We depend on organizations for the success of modern society and our systems of governance. Yet, we also fear them for their misdirection, self-serving focus and oppressive potential. Adam Smith and Max Weber not only described modern industrial organizations and a free-market approach to industrial development, they also expressed grave concern about the kinds of effects these organizations have on employees. Smith and Weber were astute philosophers who understood that organizations must develop in a rich political culture that restrains them and tempers their corrosive effects with countervailing principles, traditions and ways of life that help align organizational practices with the broader values of the political community of which they were a part. They saw these new organizations as instruments that should serve the interests of the communities, not the other way around.

The irony of Smith and Weber's reservations about organizations is that addressing their concerns depends to an important extent on the governmental organizations that mitigate the abusive consequences of organizational life. This is done through modelling good practices, legislating, regulating, litigating, mediating, lobbying, cajoling and educating, but public organizations are commonly viewed as "sheep in wolves' clothing" (Karl, 1987), often less trusted by citizens than their private sector and nonprofit counterparts. This natural distrust of public organizations is part of the historical legacy that gave rise to the founding of the American republic. Leading in these organizations thus requires its leaders to have a heightened understanding of their moral role as agents of democratic governance. These are the issues to which we turn our attention in the three chapters that follow.

Notes

1 Throughout our discussion in the sections that follow we deliberately use the terms leadership and management interchangeably. We explain our reasons for doing so at the conclusion of our discussion of the various images of organizations.

2 We draw from Gareth Morgan's classic work (1986) to frame our discussion of organizations, using his "image" metaphor framework. Morgan identifies the following eight metaphors to organize the literature on organization theory and practice: 1) machines, 2) organisms, 3) brains, 4) cultures, 5) political systems, 6) psychic prisons, 7) flux and domination, 8) instrument of domination. To simplify the metaphors in terms of their leadership implications, we have consolidated the machine, brain and psychic prison metaphors into the machine image. We have consolidated the organisms and flux and change metaphors into the organism metaphor. We have incorporated the culture image into our institutions metaphor. We have retained the political systems metaphor, but renamed it as the "polity" image.

3 Weber (1864–1920) identified bureaucratic organizations as the defining characteristic of the modern political economy emerging in the late 1800s. His broad, comparative studies of ancient and contemporary society influenced scholars well before his works were translated into English and made available in America. His analysis of bureaucracy is scattered among a number of his works. The most influential collection of his work was published in a translation by Hans H. Gerth and C. Wright Mills in 1946/1924.

4 Key characteristics enumerated here follow Gross and Etzioni (1985), Perrow (1986) and W. Richard Scott (1992).

5 Taylor's work influenced a long lineage of organization theorists that include Chester Barnard (1938), who emphasized the importance of systematic coordination in making the internal operations of organizations effective, and Luther Gulick and Lyndall Urwick (1937), who

identified core functions of executive management that became famous as POSDCORB (planning, organizing, staffing, directing, coordinating, reporting and budgeting), Henri Fayol (1949), whose core principles. In *Chester I. Barnard and the Guardians of the Managerial State* (1992), William G. Scott analyzes the history of this influential circle of scholars in Boston who were funded by newly formed philanthropies that served to reinforce behaviors most appropriate to large organizations—behaviors that were antithetical to liberal democracy. According to Scott, the emerging social sciences served the same organizational masters.

6 For a more complete discussion of the "human relations" school see the following primary works: Mary Parker Follett (1926) and Chester Barnard (1938). Follett drew insight from work in socially oriented "helping" professions such as social work, nursing and education, where concepts of mutual adjustment, collaborative leadership and client-centered analysis prevailed. Chester Barnard stressed the importance of understanding the informal organization as an essential aspect of effective management and organizational development. This informal system, once understood, can be used to induce employees to follow organizational goals defined and articulated by management.

For secondary treatments of the "human relations" school, see Rainey (2014, 34–37) and Morgan, Robinson, Strachota, and Hough (2014, 233–39).

7 For classic studies on the sociology of professions, see Vollmer and Mills (1966), Becker et al. (1961) and Van Maanen (1976). On organizational socialization, see Kaufman (1960) and Whyte (1956). On political symbolism and interpretivism, see Edelman (1964), Bolman and Deal (1997), Daft (1984) and Berger and Luckmann (1967).

8 These early theorists developed a branch of administrative science that focuses on decisions as a unit of analysis in organizational life. Decisions are not simply isolated, discrete entities: they are typically arranged in routinized patterns called programs (Simon, 1960). This is a term now used formally as well as informally to designate many public entities. Programs are designated organizational subunits that must be linked and coordinated to achieve broader organizational goals. However, the process is not simply a matter of conscious, rational design, but of programmed competition and advocacy among coalitions of organization interests (Cyert and March, 1963). Simon noted that few decisions are ever optimal in nature. Rather, they are "bounded" by limitations of knowledge, experience, habit and capacity, and therefore require managers to make decisions that are just satisfactory and sufficient for the moment. He coined the term "satisficing" to characterize such decisions (Simon, 1947, 38–41; also see Cyert and March 1963).

From these ideas, Cohen et al. (1972) derived a model that describes complex organizations as "garbage cans" of programmed solutions which compete to solve problems. Such organizations are made up of coalitions that offer outputs from well-established routines and outcomes from political battles and compromises with competitors. Graham Allison (1971) used this schema in his classic study of the Cuban Missile Crisis to illustrate how decision models based in programmed routines and political advocacy reveal a vastly different reality than is typically portrayed in "unified rational" accounts of such affairs. He showed, for example, that the U.S. Air Force predictably lobbied for surgical air strikes as a solution to the presence of nuclear missiles in Cuba, while the Navy predictably advocated a blockade. One can easily guess what kind of solution the U.S. State Department pursued. Applying the same kind of analysis to the Russians revealed that decisions to move missiles to Cuba resulted more from bureaucratic routines and outcomes of political battles than from a rational master plan.

9 JSTOR means journal storage, which is an online service created in 1995 to provide electronic access to an extensive array of academic journals.

10 We have drawn from the following works to abstract the core principles for creating an environment of change and innovation in organizations: Eoyang and Holladay (2013), Porter-O'Grady and Malloch (2009), Scharmer (2009), Wheatley (2000) and Lichtenstein and Plowman (2009).

4 Polity Leadership

Spurred by calls to "reinvent government" and "run it like a business," many agencies over the last decades embraced the notion of a "Business Plan" as a vehicle to articulate their specific and unique values, mission and strategies. Instead of navigating the wide end of the funnel where the risk of mission creep and inefficiency is considerable, agencies migrated to the narrow end where they could winnow down the field of play, and focus on select community priorities and service areas. As a result, agency efforts were typically directed towards those services required by statute, available funding and ability to be effective. This meant that various pressing community needs were often left unmet by local agencies. These service voids, left unchecked, ultimately affect a community's quality of life.

> Don Bohn (2014, 140)

Our MISSION is to identify critical issues and support collaborative community-based solutions. We work across sectors—government, non-profit, education, business and faith— to accomplish our mission … We believe strongly that we can be more successful working together than we can working alone.

> (Vision Action Network of Washington County, Oregon, 2013)

The opening epigraphs present us with two contrasting models for achieving the public good, both of which are necessary for leadership success. One is a business-centered and hierarchical model that operates with a narrowly defined set of priorities and relies largely on rules and formal legal authority to carry out its mission. The other is a broad-based community-centered model that relies on co-production strategies to meet service needs and build trust among the business, government, nonprofit and civil society partners to achieve the common good. We introduced this co-production model in Chapter 1 and re-introduce it here in Exhibit 4.1 as part of our more extended discussion of polity leadership. This discussion consists of two parts. We start with an elaboration of what we mean by the phrase "polity leadership". The second and largest portion

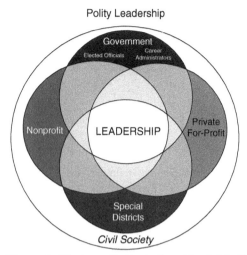

Polity Leadership

Alignment of Partners; Co-Production of the Public Good

Exhibit 4.1 Polity Leadership

of the chapter discusses the role and function of the various participants in our polity leadership model. Our assumption is that a better understanding of these polity actors will enhance the capacity of leaders to reach out and engage individuals and organizations in civic society, other governing jurisdictions and the business community to join in undertaking leadership initiatives.

What Is Polity Leadership?

The term "polity" comes from the Greek word polis, which describes the larger organic community of which the political system is a part and for which it has stewardship responsibility.[1] "Polity leadership" calls attention to the organic, fluid and interdependent relationship among the parts of our political economy in producing the collective good of the community. Since the size and degree of overlap among the sectors is constantly changing through time and is contextually different from one community to another, each generation of public servants has to rethink its leadership role, opportunities and possibilities when engaging in polity leadership. But there are some characteristics of polity leadership that endure through time, a recognition of which shapes your ability to see leadership opportunities and successfully take action.

There Are Critical Differences in Perspective, Role and Function of Polity Actors

Polity leadership is successful only when it is informed by a strong understanding of the role and function of the various sectors of the American political economy. The differences among the sectors are illustrated in Exhibit 4.2 and is based on how each sector arbitrates value differences and the breadth of interests they serve. The private sector negotiates value differences through the market, and its interests are parochial. The interests of the nonprofit sector, by contrast, are usually regarded as part of the larger common good. Special districts and general-purpose public bodies arbitrate value differences through the political process, but differ in the scope of interests they embrace. Special districts are established to pursue parochial interests in contrast to the broader common interests of general purpose governmental units. Schools, water boards and fire districts are examples of single-purpose entities created to serve a part of the larger common good, in contrast to cities or counties, which have much broader governing responsibilities.

The public sector plays a pivotal catalytic role in shaping the motivation and well-being of for-profit, nonprofit, civic and special district organizations. Markets cannot sustain themselves without a stable infrastructure consisting of communication networks, public transportation systems, financial institutions that provide stability and security, defense systems that protect and maintain international lanes of commerce, a legal system that enforces contracts, a trustworthy public safety system that protects life and property, and a regulatory system that stabilizes the rate and complexity of change in markets as well as their relations with consumers and communities. The nonprofit sector also relies on this infrastructure, depending heavily upon the grants, contracts and other forms of sponsorship by governments at all levels, not to mention its privileged tax-exempt status. This complex governmental infrastructure helps ensure the vitality of the other sectors, but it can over-reach and undermine the unique abilities of the other sectors to contribute to the common good. Knowing the "sweet

		Scope of interests	
		Parochial	Common
How values are arbitrated	Political	Special Districts	Public Agencies
	Market	For-profit private agencies and firms	Nonprofit and civil society organizations

Exhibit 4.2 Political Economy Institutional Forms that Co-Produce the Public Good

spot" between too much and too little government is an on-going exercise in prudential leadership judgment.

The private sector's concern for innovation, creativity and customer satisfaction is assumed to be the best mechanism for efficiently maximizing the allocation of society's resources. This can be the case, as long as the goals of society are compatible with those of individuals, and the demands of customers can be arranged to induce a market response. But there are numerous instances when these private market-place conditions do not exist. The following are the most common examples of market failures or exceptions that have provided justifica-tion for public-sector intervention: 1) the provision of public goods, such as national defense; 2) the amelioration of some of the diseco-nomies or externalities of collective action, such as pollution of the environment and drug abuse; 3) the avoidance of "tragedy of the commons" problems, such as natural resource depletion; 4) reaping the collective benefits of public economies, such as education and early childhood development programs; and 5) taking advantage of natural monopolies, such as water, sewer and other public utilities. In these and other instances, the public sector is encouraged to intervene in the private marketplace in the interest of promoting greater equity (Okun, 1975; Wanat, 1978, Chap. 2).

Neither the public nor private sector are as capable as the nonprofit sector in meeting individual clientele needs with the least amount of rules and costs to the client. Soup kitchens and shelters for the home-less, runaway youth and domestic violence victims rarely require clients to meet some extensive eligibility requirements. Those who provide these kinds of services to target populations are passionate about what they do, and this passion—combined with flexible, adap-tive approaches to care—is clearly reflected in the quality of treatment that is extended to each person in need. Because of these factors, more service can usually be provided for fewer dollars than is the case with either the public sector or the private marketplace. Nonprofits are also created in response to a variety of impulses, including government failure to provide sufficient public goods (for example, United Way), the American tradition of self-help (for example, Alcoholics Anon-ymous), or out of a commitment to help others (for example, Catholic Charities).

Special district governments offer still another alternative to provid-ing public services. Unlike general purpose governments that administer a broad range of services, special districts are established to administer one specialized activity on a "cost of service" basis. Fire, hospital, police, water, sewer, library and other services can be provided by creating a unit of government whose sole purpose is to administer that service at a specified cost to each member of the district. The advantage of this approach is twofold: it allows citizens to purchase additional levels of service that a city, county or school district may not be able to provide, and it controls the price they are willing to pay. One of the disadvantages of special districts is that they further balkanize public service delivery and allow those with financial resources to obtain more and better service than the poor. Under such circumstances, it becomes more difficult to build a shared sense of the larger community interest (Burns, 1994).

To summarize, the public, private, nonprofit and special district sectors are suited to perform quite distinctive tasks. It is important for public service leaders to know what each sector can do particularly well and why, as they are occasionally called upon to use their leadership role to help restructure the relationship among the four sets of community partners. The distinct characteristics of each sector are summarized in Exhibit 4.3. The summary is not meant to be exhaustive, but simply to illustrate that each of the sectors has a logic of its own. Exhibit 4.3 can serve as a check-list or reminder of what to keep in mind when you are called upon to engage in co-production activities with polity partners.

The Rise of Networked Governance

Most of the 75 different types of services that government provides are delivered by front-line employees who rely on the traditional hierarchically and legally centered bureaucratic leadership model (Morgan, Robinson, Strachota, and Hough, 2013, Chap. 20). But the complexity and trans-boundary nature of issues has generated alternative models to our traditional government hierarchies (Koliba, Meek, and Zia, 2011; Thurmaier and Wood, 2002). Today, services at all levels of government are increasingly delivered through a full array of partnered mechanisms, including: strategic and operational intergovernmental agreements (IGAs) (Thurmaier and Wood, 2002; LeRoux and Carr, 2007; LeRoux, Brandenburger, and Pandey, 2010); direct-service contracts and grants (Cooper, 2003; LeRoux, 2007; Smith and Smyth, 2010); and multi-member networked partnerships (Isett, Mergel, LeRoux, Mischen, and Rethemeyer, 2011; Provan and Kenis, 2007; Goldsmith and Eggers, 2004). In fact, the transformation of delivery mechanisms for the provision of public services has progressed to such an extent that networks of partners provide the major service delivery mechanism for many governments in the United States (Goldsmith and Eggers, 2004; Milward and Provan, 2000). A whole new set of policy tools has been developed to assist participants working in this networked environment (Salamon, 2002; see especially Cooper, 2018). Polity leadership now requires a much broader array of leadership practices than has been the case in the past.

Exhibit 4.3 Comparative Characteristics of Sectors

Private Sector	Nonprofit Sector	Public Sector	Special Districts
Mission driven	Clientele driven	Legal/rule driven	Purpose driven
Results oriented	Needs oriented	Process oriented	Service oriented
Entrepreneurial	Meeting needs with few rules and questions asked	Bureaucratic	Technical expertise
Motivating others for high performance	"Doing the right thing"	Constitutional agent of a sovereign power	Bounded legal authority
Customers	Target populations	Citizens	Target population
Flexibility	Service	Control	Service
Innovation	Flexibility for target population	Following rules	Service within narrow legal authority
Customer satisfaction	Clientele needs	Citizen rights and responsibilities	Client satisfaction
Incentives	"Doing good"	Regulations	Service
Employee empowerment	Voluntary commitment	Hierarchy	Functional competence
Delegation of authority	Informal coordination	Centralization of authority	Parochially governed
Self-interest	Responsibility	Accountability	Efficiency
Interests	Values	Rights	Service
Preferences	Needs	Equity	Effectiveness
Profit	Moral duty	Duty to the law	Duty to clients

Examples of Polity Leadership

We illustrate our notion of polity leadership with two practical examples in Exhibits 4.4 and 4.5. The Master Cases for Parts II to IV provide additional examples. In Exhibit 4.4 the government sits alongside other organizational entities in the community with no superior legal authority over other potential partners in the co-production of the common good. At the center of Exhibit 4.4 is a challenge that needs attention. It could be housing for a given target population; it could be social services for the mentally ill; it could be crime. You can pick your favorite community problem or challenge to put at the center of Exhibit 4.4.

The challenge in Exhibit 4.4 is identifying an entity that is going to take the leadership initiative to mobilize collective action among the potential co-producers. We believe that future government officials at every level will be called on to play this initiatory leadership role.

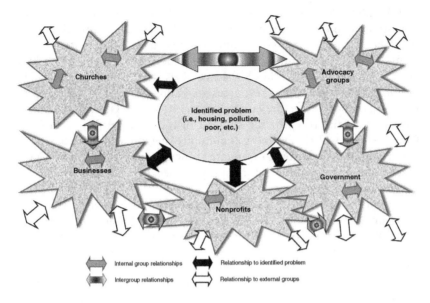

Exhibit 4.4 A Network Organized Around a Shared Challenge

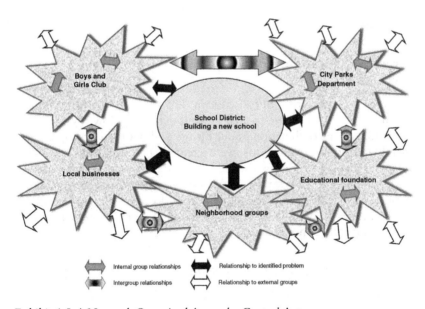

Exhibit 4.5 A Network Organized Around a Central Actor

In Exhibit 4.5 a governmental entity sits at the center of a network of potential community partners, but needs the cooperative participation of other partners in the community to maximally achieve its governmental goal. The example in Exhibit 4.5 depicts the need to build a new school, but the school district does not have the financial, political and institutional resources to build the kind of school that would maximally serve the larger community good. The school district has the potential to enlist the support of the city, the Boys and Girls Club, members of the business community, neighborhood associations and a school foundation to generate sufficient support to build a new shared multi-use facility that is jointly funded by a variety of community partners.

Exhibits 4.4 and 4.5 reflect patterns of relationships that are common throughout the United States but are found rarely or not at all in many other parts of the world. This is because each political system deliberately constructs a set of legal relationships among the private, public and nonprofit actors and civil society, which evolve through time to create patterns that norm expectations, create boundaries for discretionary action by participants and establish mutual accountability. This crazy-quilt pattern of relationships among actors in the American market economy is the product our deliberately designed system of governance that differentiates the role responsibilities of for-profit, governmental, nonprofit and civic organizations.

Government Institutions: Variety, Legal Authority and Governance

As can be surmised from our discussion thus far, the American political system is more of a bottom-up arrangement than a top-down system. This is an artifact of a combination of our history and our legal principles. The federal and state governments were created *after* local systems were already in place. In addition, the creation of these governing jurisdictions was based on a rule of law principle that prevents government from taking action unless it has been given the authority do so by the people. Taken together, these two principles create a need for a co-production approach to promoting the common good.

The Variety and Kinds of Governments

Alexis de Tocqueville, in his travels across the United States in the mid 1830s, was struck by the high levels of decentralization of governmental authority and the advantages this provided in building the trust of citizens in their public officials:

What I admire most in America are not the administrative effects of decentralization, but the political effects ... Often the European sees in the public official only force; the American sees in him right ... As administrative authority is placed at the side of those whom it administers, and in some way represents them, it excites neither jealously nor hatred ... Administrative power ... does not find itself abandoned to itself as in Europe. One does not believe that the duties of particular persons have ceased because the representative of the public comes to act.

Alexis de Tocqueville (2000/1935, 90)

If de Tocqueville were to travel across the United States today, he would likely be even more impressed by the extraordinary expansion of administrative decentralization over the past 185 years. By 2012 there are 90,108 separate governmental entities in the United States, each of which levies taxes or charges fees to deliver services to the citizens it serves. Exhibit 4.6 provides a summary overview of the types of these governing bodies and their growth over the past 50 years. As Exhibit 4.6 illustrates, these special districts have increased by more than 143 percent, growing from 12,340 in 1952 to 30,052 in 2007 (U.S. Census Bureau, 2002, 2007, 2012a). However, school districts have undergone a dramatic reduction in the number, largely as a result of the consolidation of districts that now cover a larger geographic area.

Most Americans are surprised to learn that so many governing jurisdictions have the authority to levy taxes, charge fees and borrow money to pay for the services they provide. A typical citizen may be a taxpayer of a half dozen governing jurisdictions: federal government; state; city; county; borough; township; and multiple special districts, including schools, fire, water, soil conservation, library, hospital, parks and recreation district, just to mention a few of the more common possibilities. One of the authors resides in a county with 33 separate governing jurisdictions and pays taxes to eight governing entities. This balkanized arrangement places a premium on the leadership virtue of reaching out across organizational boundaries to address issues that fall between the cracks.

The Subordination of Governments and Public Servants to the Rule of Law

Americans take for granted the principle of "limited government" even though they may not know precisely what it means from a legal point of view. At it its simplest, limited government means that public officials cannot take leadership initiative without finding the legal authority upon which to justify their actions. This authority can be found in one or more of the following sources: U.S. and state

Exhibit 4.6 Number of Government Units by Type, 1952–2007

Type of Government	1952[1]	1962	1967	1972	1977	1982	1987	1992	1997	2007	Change 1962–2007
Total units	116,807	91,237	81,299	78,269	79,913	81,831	83,237	85,006	87,504	89,527	−23%
U.S. Government	1	1	1	1	1	1	1	1	1	1	0%
Native American tribes[2]	NA	NA	NA	NA	NA	NA	NA	NA	NA	564	NA
State governments	50	50	50	50	50	50	50	50	50	50	0%
Local governments	116,756	91,186	81,248	78,218	79,862	81,780	83,186	84,955	87,453	89,476	−23%
Counties	3,052	3,043	3,049	3,044	3,042	3,041	3,042	3,043	3,043	3,033	−.6%
Municipal	16,807	18,000	18,048	18,517	18,862	19,076	19,200	19,279	19,372	19,492	16%
Townships and towns	17,202	17,142	17,105	16,991	16,822	16,734	16,691	16,656	16,629	16,519	−4%
School districts[3]	67,355	34,678	21,782	15,781	15,174	14,851	14,721	14,422	13,726	14,561	−78%
Special districts	12,340	18,323	21,264	23,885	25,962	28,078	29,532	31,555	34,683	35,052	84%

Source: U.S. Census Bureau (2002, Census of Governments, vol. 1, no. 1, Government Operations, Series GC02 (1)-1; 2007, Census of Governments).
Notes
1 1952 adjusted to include units in Alaska and Hawaii, which adopted statehood in 1959;
2 The U.S. Census Bureau does not track the number of tribes. As of October 2010 the Bureau of Indian Affairs (BIA) listed 564 tribal entities as eligible for funding and services from the BIA by virtue of their status as Indian tribes. The basic legal framework for tribal sovereignty was established by Chief Justice John Marshal in a trilogy of cases adjudicated in the 1830s and affirmed by more recent courts. See: (*Johnson v. McIntosh*, 21 U.S. (8 Wheat.) 543, 5 L. Ed. 681 (1823); *Cherokee Nation v. Georgia*, 30 U.S. (5 Pet.) 1, 8 L. Ed. 25 (1831); *Worcester v. Georgia*, 31 U.S. (6 Pet.) 515, 8 L. Ed. 483 (1832) and *United States v. Wheeler*, 435 U.S. 313, 98 S. Ct. 1079, 55 L. Ed. 2d 303 (1978). See our discussion of drivers of change in Chapter 7, where we review the history of tribal governance challenges and their leadership implications. For a list of federally recognized tribes go to www.bia.gov/cs/groups/xopa/documents/text/idc013398.pdf;
3 Includes dependent school districts, which are under the control of the state, county or other governing body.

constitutions, statutory law, administrative law, court opinions and common law. Our federal, state and local constitutions are the foundational law of the country, but they are by no means sufficient or determinative. When in doubt about whether one has legal authority to take action, most public servants ask for the advice of legal counsel. While this is both a prudent and necessary thing to do, we add a cautionary note. Legal counselors to public organizations are risk averse and see their success as preventing a jurisdiction or an employee from being sued. This backward-looking strategy often does not square well with our forward-leaning leadership model. For this reason we urge those seeking legal advice to first decide what they think is in the public interest and then ask their legal counsel how they can accomplish their goal in a legal manner.

Local Governing Bodies Are Subordinate to their Parent State[2]

Each state defines by statute the types and kinds of local jurisdictions that can exist and what authority they have. This enabling authority is codified in each state's statutes, and there is a dizzying array of models across the United States. For example, the Commonwealth of Pennsylvania organizes its local government code authority by county, subdividing each county into cities, class 1 townships, class 2 townships and boroughs. By contrast, the State of South Carolina organizes its code authority by counties (Title 4), municipal corporations (Title 5) and local government—provisions applicable to special purpose districts and other political subdivisions (Title 6). The State of Washington represents the extreme in specification of local government authority. It provides separate code authority for cities and towns (Title 35, which provides for the creation of class 1 cities, class 2 cities, and towns), home rule (Title 35A), counties (Title 36), library districts (Title 27), fire protection districts (Title 52), port districts (Title 53), public utility districts (Title 54), sanitary districts (Title 55) and water-sewer districts (Title 57).

Along the eastern seaboard of the U.S., many local governments predate their state as well as the U.S Constitution. A United States Advisory Commission on Intergovernmental Relations (1993, hereafter referred to as ACIR report) observed that during the colonial and revolutionary periods, "the custom and practice of local self-government was strong and pervasive" and they exhibited varied forms and functions (28–29). Most commonly known are the New England town governments which operated under colonial "town laws" and which practiced direct democratic governance, but local governments in other colonies also exercised considerable "local privilege," manifested in many instances through independent democratic decision processes, and in some cases were even empowered to send delegates with instructions to their colonial legislatures (27–30).

However, after ratification of the U.S. Constitution, a dominant legal doctrine emerged which treated local government generally as mere creatures of the states—as products of the reserve powers ceded to the states under the Tenth Amendment. Technically, local governments in the U.S. are not even "guaranteed a republican form" of government as the Constitution requires of the state governments in Article IV. Strictly speaking from a legal point of view states provide for the establishment of local governments, and delegate authority to local governing bodies that otherwise hold no independent authority. This legal view was fully developed into a set of principles, called the "Dillon Rule" and named after an Iowa judge who in 1868 set forth the doctrine in two important court cases (*Clinton v. Cedar Rapids* and the *Missouri River Railroad v. Lewis*).

Though the Dillon Rule is still considered authoritative, it is not the only legal doctrine recognized in statutes and case law. Thomas Cooley, a highly regarded state Supreme Court jurist from Michigan, immediately attacked the Dillon Rule, arguing in his then influential *Treatise on Constitutional Limitations* (1878, see also his concurring opinion in a Michigan case, *People v. Hurlbut, 24 Mich 44*, 1871) that "it is axiomatic that the management of purely local affairs belongs to the people concerned, not only because of being their own affairs, but because they will best understand, and be most competent to manage them" (Cooley, 1878, 378). Cooley believed that:

> local political institutions provided the fora through which people could engage in the practice of constitutionalism for themselves. The practice of local self-government would directly inculcate constitutional values in the public sphere by affording the local citizenry an opportunity to practice democracy with constitutional limitations. Through the practice of public politics at the local level, citizens would be forced in a direct and immediate way to determine for themselves which decisions would serve the "public" interests of their own communities and which would not. That experience would provide citizens with a greater understanding of what it meant to govern themselves in accord with constitutional limitations that would be possible under a regime of either centralized state legislative control or judicial supremacy.
>
> Barron (1999, 518)

While the Dillon Rule has been the dominant legal doctrine governing local government, the organic or "from-the-ground-up" aspects of local self-determination expressed by Cooley are what set local government in the United States apart from its counterparts around the world.

Neither the central government nor a controlling political party dictates how the majority of money raised from local citizens shall be spent by local government officials. This is not the case in many single-party systems or in most European countries, whose local governing bodies are the administrative agencies of the central government. While local officials are elected in counties such as France, Japan, South Korea and Italy, their discretionary authority is severely limited in comparison to local government officials in the United States. For example, in Japan, Korea, Vietnam, China and most Asian countries local government officials have very limited taxing authority. This is also the case for European democratic states such as France and Italy where local governing bodies have limited powers to collect taxes for some services like public safety, transportation, waste collection and street lighting. In these centralized governments, most of the revenue flows downward through the central ministries to local offices. This contrasts to the United States where local governments exercise significant discretionary authority over the collection and expenditure of over 30 percent of the total taxes imposed on citizens (U.S. Government Revenue, 2010. This decentralized system of governance has important implications for the exercise of entrepreneurial initiative and bottom-up leadership innovation.

Governing Structures: What Difference Do the Forms of Government Make to Polity Leadership?

Poet Alexander Pope once quipped, "For the forms of government, let fools contest, That which is best administered is best" (Alexander Pope, 1732–34). When it comes to local government, Pope's quotation might end with the line: "And over time the council-manager form has come to be judged best." Of the following four models currently in use, the city-manager form is the most popular.

Strong Mayor

This form of local government consists of a mayor and a city council, where both are independently elected through predominantly nonpartisan elections. In large cities on the East Coast and in the Midwest, mayors and council members are often elected on the basis of party affiliation. Regardless of the role of parties in local elections, under the strong mayor system both the council and mayor share in making-policy, although the mayor has near complete authority over the executive branch of government and commonly takes the initiative in making policy recommendations. The mayor appoints officers of the executive branch—the city attorney, assessor, treasurer-comptroller and heads of departments—who serve at his/her pleasure, although these appointees generally must be confirmed by the council. The city council, in its role as the legislative branch, approves key mayoral appointments and ordinances prior to their becoming effective.

Council Manager

The council-manager form of government consists of a city council (the members of which are elected predominantly in non-partisan elections), a mayor (in most cases selected from the membership of the council but elected at-large in others) and a city manager (appointed by the city council). In this system, the council determines city policy and the mayor merely presides over city council meetings. The executive branch of government is administered by the city manager, who is a professionally trained administrator. The city manager appoints executive officers, supervises their performance, develops the organization's budget and administers programs.

The council-manager form of government is the most widely used system in the United States. According to the International City/County Management Association (ICMA, 2006), the council manager form is used in 63 percent of cities with populations of 25,000 or more; in 57 percent of cities with populations of 10,000 or more; and in 53 percent of cities with populations of 5,000 or more. According to a 1996 survey of municipal forms of government by the National Civic League, 61 percent of council-manager cities have popularly elected mayors (National Civic League, 1996). More than 80 percent of all cities (mayor and manager) in the 1996 survey reported having appointed a chief official, like a city manager. This means that many mayor-council cities also have a city-manager-like chief administrative officer who answers to the mayor or the council. In the other cities, the mayor administers the day-to-day operations of the government.

Weak Mayor

Most smaller cities, and a few larger ones (i.e., Minneapolis Minnesota), have a weak mayor who performs mainly ceremonial functions. Unlike the strong-mayor system, a weak mayor does not have the power to veto council decisions, to oversee city government operations or to draw up and implement the annual budget. Most weak-mayor cities are very small, where the mayor does not have separate executive authority, but the staff performs primarily clerical and direct service functions. The weak-mayor system is the product of the Jacksonian democratic belief that too many government officials with too much power endanger the ability of the majority of working class Americans to control their government and keep it accountable (for further discussion of this issue, see Chapter 6).

Under the weak-mayor system, the budgeting and policy process is controlled by the council as a whole. The mayor facilitates the public participation activities that are part of the council's budgeting and policy role as well as serving as the ceremonial leader of the council's deliberations. The mayor is the "first among equals," which means that leadership success depends on the exercise of the soft powers of negotiation and collaboration.

Commission System

The commission system of government fuses executive and legislative functions almost completely in the hands of elected commissioners. They hold the legislative power to make policy, participate directly as administrators in overseeing the executive implementation of policy, and adjudicate appeals, usually dealing with personnel and land-use issues. Members of the commission are normally elected in non-partisan elections, and one member is designated the chair of the board to preside over meetings. In some cases, like Portland, Oregon, the mayor is elected separately but still serves as a commissioner with the lead responsibility of assigning administrative duties to each of the fellow commissioners. Again, as in the council-manager plan, the mayor has little formal power. The commission makes policy for the jurisdiction and appoints some of the executive officers, such as the city attorney, assessor, treasurer and chief of police.

Despite the differences in these formal structures of authority, in practice most local governments end up with very similar practical leadership challenges in taking initiative and building trust and legitimacy in local governing structures of authority. This is because most local governments depart from the separation of powers model that is characteristic of our national and state governments and use a "fused power" model that resembles a parliamentary system of government used in Canada, England and many European nations. We illustrate the classic separation of powers model in Exhibit 4.7. Under this model, the citizens elect legislators who make policy and then hand off this policy to an elected or appointed head of the executive branch, who implements the policy based on the technical competence of trained professionals.

This model is in place at the state and federal levels of government. At the local level it is in place with the strong-mayor form of government, where the executive function of government is controlled by an elected head that has the responsibility of implementing the policy priorities within the parameters established by the legislative body. But the strong-mayor form is the exception, rather than the rule. The most common model is the fused power system in Exhibit 4.8, where the elected officials are working closely with the chief administrators to make policy and oversee its implementation with the primary leadership

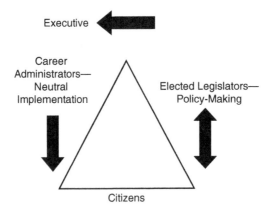

Exhibit 4.7 Separation of Powers Model of Democratic Governance

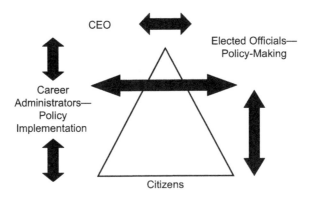

Exhibit 4.8 Fused Power Model of Government

role being taken by the city manager or chief administrative office. In practice there is no bright-line distinction between the executive and legislative functions. In this second model policy development, implementation and budgeting are a fluid and collaborative processes of exchange: it is difficult to determine where to draw the line between the instrumental role of administrative leaders and the constitutive policy role of elected officials. This is because most local government bodies, which are part-time and without significant staff support, hire a chief administrative officer or manager to serve at the pleasure of the elected body and oversee the daily operations of the government. In addition, most local jurisdictions are governed by non-partisan elections, where party affiliation is not permitted as part of the formal electoral process. Under such conditions, there has to be a close collaborative partnership between the legislative and executive functions of the organization in order for the fused power leadership model to work (see especially Svara, 1985, 1990, 1991, 1999, 2006; and Montjoy and Watson, 1995). The full-time career leadership team has to spend considerable formal and informal time understanding the priorities of individual board members. While this kind of political work is important at the federal and state levels of government, it is essential at the local level and pervades much further down into the organizational hierarchy (Morgan and Kass, 1993).

In the process of doing this facilitative work, leaders run the risk of confirming the popular prejudice that politics is an "inside game," controlled by those who hold the formal instruments of power. This is illustrated by Exhibit 4.9. It is a perceived theory that assumes "deals are cooked" long before there are opportunities for public input. This is a recipe for cynicism, burnout of administrative leaders, and avoidance of hard public-policy choices by elected officials (Morgan and Kass, 1993). It is also a condition that adds to the leadership burden of local leaders whose proximity to citizens exacerbates the challenges of building trust in democratic processes and outcomes.

The Role of Business Organizations and their Polity Leadership Implications

The role of business in the American political system is a product of the changing values and beliefs regarding individual liberty and its role in promoting the common good (see Chapter 6 for a detailed discussion of this history). America was founded on the belief that keeping government

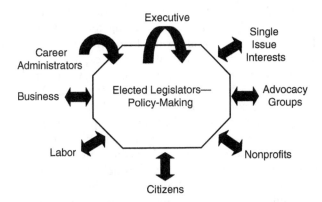

Exhibit 4.9 Perceived Theory of Public Administration

small and limited in its reach empowers individuals to be self-initiating, thus fostering the moral virtues of creativity, entrepreneurialism and innovation while at the same time guarding against excessive government control over individual liberty. These libertarian assumptions help explain why the relationship between government and the business community is a "history of sheep in wolves clothing."[3] This tension is also reflected in the role that business plays in economic development, creating civic vitality and providing moral leadership in mobilizing otherwise self-serving behavior of individuals and redirecting it to serve the larger common good (see discussions of social entrepreneurship, especially Keohane, 2013; Bornstein, 2007). In the sections that follow we provide a brief summary of the historical tension between government and the private market economy and then discus how this tension affects the various roles that the business community plays in our many democratic polities.

The Historical Tension between Business and Government[4]

From a business point of view, government has often been viewed as the taxing and regulatory bad wolf that increases the transaction costs of doing business, thus undercutting the private sector's capacity to provide goods and services as cheaply and effectively as possible. From the government perspective, businesses create jobs, generate large amounts of individual and corporate taxes and more generally are responsible for the "wealth of the nation." At the local level these jobs and taxes play a vital role in determining the well-being and quality of life in communities. But this sheep-like pro-business mindset is tempered by the fear that the incentive of business organizations to make profits and cut corners requires eternal vigilance in the collection of taxes, protecting consumers and enforcing regulatory requirements.

Taking a longer historical view of the relationship between government and business helps us put the on-going tension between government and the business community in better perspective. Those who created the intellectual foundation of modern capitalism defended private enterprise because it would, in the words of Adam Smith, enhance "the wealth of nations" (Smith, 2003/1776). It would also help foster the political system's commitment to liberty (Hirschmann, 1981, 1977). In short, the private sector existed to serve the political ends of society rather than the other way around. And this is reflected in the need for businesses to be licensed or chartered by the state, a practice that has been continuously in place since it was brought to America during the mercantilist days of the British Empire. Whenever the public interest comes into conflict with private property rights, it provides an occasion to revisit the on-going question of whether private property should enjoy the higher-level protections that are bestowed on the First Amendment freedoms of speech, press and the right to assemble. While American courts may shift the burden of proof, sometimes making it lower (*Home Bldg. & Loan Ass'n v. Blaisdell* 290 U.S. 398 [1934]) and sometimes making it higher (*Dolan v. City of Tigard*, 512 U.S. 374 [1994]), they have generally treated property rights as more contingent than is the case for First Amendment rights. You may need a permit to exercise your right of free speech or assembly, but this is intended to protect the safety of the demonstrators, unlike a license to engage in business activity.

The tension between government and business interests has been present since the very beginning of the American republic. The relationship between large commercial wealth and "modest living" by ordinary people was part of the Federalist-Antifederalists debates. The tension surfaced again during Andrew Jackson's presidency in the 1830s as he sought to right the balance between large East Coast commercial interests and the growing economic needs of the frontier. The reaction to commercial abuses surfaced again in the Progressive Era and Teddy Roosevelt's efforts to protect public lands from private exploitation and to control the monopoly interests in the oil, railroad and banking industries. As manufacturers organized to control prices, production, and shipping (Linseed Oil Trust, Cotton Seed Oil Trust, Lead Trust, Sugar Refiners' Company, Standard Oil Trust and trusts in mining, railroads, meat packing, gas, hemp and so on), it sparked government initiative to correct the abuses. The same pattern reoccurred in the New Deal and the New Frontier and Great Society eras of the 1960s and 1970s. This history is illustrated in Exhibit 4.10 and can be reviewed in greater detail in Chapter 6.

Exhibit 4.10 Illustrative Examples of Episodic Government Initiatives to Regulate Business

Populist and Progressive Period (1890–1918)

Interstate Commerce Act (1887)
Sherman Antitrust Act (1890)
Pure Food and Drug Administration (1906)
Federal Reserve System (1913)
Clayton Act (1914)
Interstate Commerce Commission (1914)
Federal Trade Commission (1914)

New Deal Period (1930–1940)

Food and Drug Administration (expanded in 1938)
Federal Trade Commission (expanded in 1938)
Soil Conservation Service (1938)
Federal Communications Commission (1936)
Social Security Administration (1935)
Federal Power Commission (1935)
Securities and Exchange Commission (1934)
National Labor Relations Board (1934)
Federal Housing Administration (1934)
Public Works Administration (1933)
Tennessee Valley Authority (1933)
Civil Works Administration (1933)
Rural Electrification Administration (1933)
Civilian Conservation Corps (1933)
Federal Deposit Insurance Corporation (1933)
Federal Home Loan Bank Board (1932)

Great Society Period (1960s and 1970s)

Department of Energy (1977)
Office of Surface Mining (1977)
Nuclear Regulatory Commission (1975)
Materials Transportation Board (1975)
Mine Safety and Health Administration (1973)
Occupational Safety and Health Administration (1973)
Consumer Product Safety Commission (1972)
National Highway Traffic Safety Administration (1970)
Environmental Protection Agency (1970)
Equal Employment Opportunity Commission (1964)
United States Commission on Civil Rights (originally created in
    1957; expanded in 1960)

A long period of deregulation and limiting the role of government began in the 1980s with the election of President Ronald Regan. But the collapse of the housing mortgage market in 2008 and the subsequent prosecution of a multitude of Wall Street traders for a variety of unlawful activities caused the three-decade-old deregulation pendulum to temporarily stop its swing, only to continue with the election of Donald Trump in 2016. For some, the election of Donald Trump in

2016 was viewed as a victory for those who wished to disassemble the administrative state that had been built over the previous hundred years of gradual government expansion (Carney, 2017).

The historical developments summarized above have important implications for public sector leaders today as they are confronted with contemporary versions of the early 20th century arguments that private businesses, like individuals, have rights protected by the Constitution (see Chapter 6 discussion of the Progressive Movement and the New Deal). In recent years this argument has been used to limit the government's ability to regulate campaign contributions by corporations (*Citizens United v. the FEC*) and to prevent the Security and Exchange Commission from imposing various kinds of financial reporting and disclosure requirements on corporations (Harvard Law School Forum, 2016). In this on-going debate over where and how to draw the line between prudent and imprudent government regulation of the private sector, there are some important assumptions that both sides of the political spectrum agree upon:

1   The government has the leading responsibility for putting in place the financial infrastructure to ensure commercial vitality. This includes exercising control of taxes, expenditures and the flow of money to ensure a vibrant and growing economy.
2   The government has the leading responsibility for ensuring that a healthy transportation infrastructure is in place to expedite the flow of people and commerce.
3   There is a presumption that government leaders should enlist the cooperative support of private businesses in achieving public purposes before invoking the hammer of regulation.

In short, government and business continue to believe that a healthy private economy creates the jobs and profits that provide the foundational base for government taxation. There is also mutual recognition that the economy cannot function without having a stable banking system, robust capital infrastructure, predictable access to international markets and all of the other conditions of social, political and economic stability that businesses need to thrive. This system of mutual co-dependence, created gradually over two centuries of history, fuels the partnership approaches that public leaders use in managing the public sector's relationship with private entities.

The Multiple Roles of Local Business as Partners in the Common Good

The private sector performs at least three roles in co-producing the public good with its government and nonprofit community partners. It contributes to local economic well-being, promotes civic vitality and provides moral leadership in mobilizing action for the common good.

Contributions to Economic Well-Being

Local communities invest considerable resources in spurring economic development by granting investment and tax reduction incentives to private businesses. How successful has this strategy been in contributing to local economic well-being? The answer depends on how you define "well-being." For example, in 2014 businesses of all types provided only 5.9 percent of the total revenue collected by all levels of government to fund government services, compared to the 37 percent of the total collected from individuals through the income tax. But for the nearly 86,000 local governments, the percentage of revenue collected from business to fund government operations was 21 percent (U.S. Census, 2011). Additional amounts are regularly collected from businesses through personal property and income taxes, which together represented the largest source of general revenue for both state and local governments. In 2011 these taxes provided 46.0 percent of the general revenue at the state government level and 39.6 percent of general revenue for local governments. Among local governments, property taxes were the most prominent source of revenue, accounting for $429.1 billion (74.2 percent) of the $578.2 billion in tax revenue received (U.S. Census, 2007).

The statistical summary provided above suggests that businesses are not the most significant sources of governmental revenue, especially at the local level. But tax revenue from local business cannot be easily separated from other sources of revenue generated from income, property and sales taxes. Businesses provide 82.4 percent of the total non-farm employment in the United States (Bureau of Labor Statistics, 2017), thus generating the bulk of wealth that serves as the basis for all of these taxes. Not only is it difficult to separate business wealth from community wealth, it is also difficult to separate business well-being from civic well-being.

The Role of Local Businesses in Promoting Civic Vitality

The civic and philanthropic role of local businesses is hard to calculate with precision because its contributions come less in the form of hard dollars and more in the form of soft service. About three-quarters of all U.S. business firms have no payroll. Most are self-employed persons operating unincorporated businesses, and may or may not be the owner's principal source of income. Of the nearly 27.7 million small businesses in the United States, 21.7 million had no payroll and another 3.7 million businesses reported having four or less employees. In short, at least 90 percent of the businesses in the United

States are clearly small, local operations, most of which are deeply rooted in the social fabric of the local community. These data provide part of the argument that fuels the growing "social corporate responsibility" (SCR) movement that has swept across the business landscape over the last decade (Conley and Williams, 2005; Carroll, 1999).

The local and small size of most businesses has significance for the quality and extent of polity leadership in the local community. For example, consider who is doing the heavy lifting in sustaining local community service organizations like the Chamber of Commerce, the Lions Club, the League of Women Voters, the Elks Club, Rotary Club and other similar humanitarian and community-centered organizations. In almost all of these cases the burden of leadership is disproportionately carried by small business owners and those they employ. This reality provides an answer to the question, what makes things local in a globalized world? What makes things local is the nature and degree of interaction among community partners. That is why the role of local business is so important. It is not so much about the economic wealth these entities produce, but their role in seeding interaction in civil society.

The Moral Role of the Business Sector

A final factor that makes business organizations an important participant in local polity-building is the value of the moral virtues that are cultivated by the world of commerce. A noted scholar of the American founding (Diamond, 1979) has observed that the principle of commercial entrepreneurship or acquisitiveness that is at the heart of the American economic system is in practice a moderating virtue that counters greed and avarice. Acquisitiveness is focused on *the getting*, while avarice is fixed on the possession or *having*. It:

> teaches a form of moderation to the desiring passion from which it derives, because to acquire is not primarily to have and to hold but to get and to earn, and moreover, to earn justly, at least to the extent that acquisition must be the result of one's own exertions or qualities. This requires the acquisitive man to cultivate certain excellences ... ventursomeness, and hard work, and the ability to still his immediate passions so as to allow time for the ripening of his acquisitive plans and measures. In short acquisitive man, unlike avaricious man, is likely to have we call the bourgeois virtues.
>
> Diamond (1979, 84)

The challenge for political leaders is to harness this acquisitive talent, energy and capacity that is spawned and cultivated by and through the spirit of commerce so that it serves the larger common good. French essayist, Alexis DeTocqville, concluded after traveling across the United

States in the 1830s that the secret for turning the natural desire of Americans to improve their well-being into a community-serving force is to get them to understand how their personal well-being is attached to the civic well-being of the larger community. De Tocqueville described this strategy as "enlightening the self-interest" of individuals through participation in civic associations. He gives the example of a new road project proposed to go through a local neighborhood, which initially may be viewed as a threat to strongly held personal values. But as the project gets discussed with friends and neighbors, the disaffected neighbor:

> will see at first glance that he has come across a relation between this small public affair and his greatest private affairs, and he will discover without anyone showing it to him, the tight bond that here unites a particular interest to the general interest.
>
> de Tocqueville (2000/1835, 487)

This strategy of intentionally arousing the self-interest of citizens and then turning that self-interest outward to embrace the interests of the larger community is at the heart of polity leadership. It is a strategy we aspire to hone in subsequent chapters.

The Special Role of Nonprofits and their Polity Leadership Implications[5]

Nonprofit organizations have always been viewed as public serving organizations that play a central role in promoting the common good (Hall, 1992). That is why they enjoy tax exempt status at the national and state levels of government (26 U.S. Code § 501 C (3)). In exchange for this tax-exempt status nonprofit organizations can not engage in activities that generate profit or engage in political advocacy. But some developments over the last several decades have altered this simple notion, complicating the leadership challenges of public servants working with nonprofit organizations to address common community issues. In the section that follows we elaborate on three of these challenges: the rise of nonprofits as public service providers, the rise of for-profit public service providers and concerted efforts by large philanthropic organizations to control or at least steer the political agenda.

Major Changes in the Nonprofit Sector

An important development over the last several decades has been the rapid rise of nonprofit, and increasingly for-profit, organizations in providing services to the community. This is a result of an important shift that has occurred in the role of government in funding services (i.e., social, health, education, culture and recreation services). Federal government spending on social services increased by 259 percent in inflation-adjusted dollars between 1965 and 1980 (Salamon, 1999, 61). However, beginning in the 1980s, government spending began a sharp reversal and experienced a 15 percent decline in inflation-adjusted dollars between 1977 and 1994 (116). Despite the decline in government funding, the total spending on community services has continued to grow as a result of the increased role played by nonprofit and for-profit organizations. For example, nonprofit revenues increased by an average of 4.3 percent between 1997 and 2007, well above the 3.5 percent average in the 1977–1996 period and well above the gross domestic product (GDP) average of 3 percent.

The growth in nonprofit revenues has been fueled mainly by increased fee for service income. In Exhibit 4.11 we show the growth in revenue sources for nonprofit organizations between 1997 and 2007. Fee revenue has grown by 58 percent compared to a growth of 12 percent in revenue from philanthropy and 30 percent from government funding. While the increased reliance on fees varies by fields within the nonprofit sector, all fields have shown significant growth, for example, 64 percent for health services, 40 percent for social services and 45 percent for culture and recreation services (Salamon, 2012, 101–106).

Lester Salamon, whose research we rely on for the information provided in Exhibit 4.11, points out that competition from for-profit service providers may be the biggest change that is occurring in the third sector over the past 30 years. In Exhibit 4.12 we draw from Salamon's work to show the growth of competition since 1977 in the fields of daycare, individual and family services, and home health care. According to Salamon, for-profits captured close to 90 percent of the growth that has occurred in home health care since 1977, accounting for 72 percent of the total employment in the field by 2007 (Salamon, 2012, 107).

A third development of note in the nonprofit community is the growing influence of large philanthropic organizations and consortiums

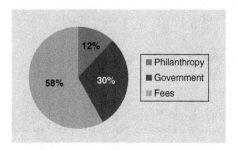

Exhibit 4.11 Sources of Nonprofit Growth, 1997–2007
Source: Salamon (2012, 105).

Exhibit 4.12 Growth of For-Profit Competition in the Fields of
Nonprofit Activity

For-Profit % of Private Employment

Field	1977	1997	2007
Day care	46.1	61.8	62.5
Individual & family services	8.5	9.2	30.5
Home health care	29.0	71.8	77.1

that shape national funding agendas, with downstream rippling effects on the priorities of state and local political communities and the mission of smaller nonprofit organizations. Take the case of education reform as an example. The Bill and Melinda Gates Foundation, the Eli and Edythe Broad Foundation and the Walton Family Foundation have taken the lead, but other mega-foundations have joined in to underwrite the "education reform movement." Some of them are the Laura and John Arnold, Anschutz, Annie E. Casey, Michael and Susan Dell, William and Flora Hewlett and Joyce Foundations. Each year big philanthropy channels about $1 billion to education reform.

> By taking over the roles of project originator and designer, by exercising top-down control over implementation, today's mega-foundations increasingly stifle the creativity, initiative, and independence of nonprofit groups. This weakens civil society. Some mega-foundations even mobilize to defeat grassroots opposition to their projects; their vast resources can easily overwhelm local groups. This, too, weakens civil society
>
> Marken (2013, 639–40)

The rise of the internet and crowd funding have added another dimension to the role of nonprofits. We are particularly interested in the impact this phenomenon is having on civic engagement, an issue we discuss in greater detail in the next section and in Chapter 7.

Some Polity Leadership Implications of Relying on Nonprofit Organizations to Set the Policy Agenda and Become Major Service Providers

What are the polity leadership implications of this enlarged role for nonprofit organizations in setting political agendas and becoming major providers of public goods and services? Our answer in the first instance is for public service leaders at all levels to become more aware of who is setting the policy agenda and to what end and, second, to become more aware of the downstream consequences of contracting out public services to nonprofit providers.

Take, for example, the consequences of educational leaders' reliance on philanthropic organizations as partners in the education reform agenda. The model being used is business-minded. The assumption of the philanthropic funders is that results will be produced by getting clear board policies that make student achievement the priority, hiring the most qualified teachers whom you pay on the basis of performance and testing students on outcomes. While these assumptions may be correct, educational leaders should not allow public programs to be launched without a vigorous policy debate about the assumptions, goals and strategies of these major educational initiatives. However, instead of this debate, philanthropic generosity has often been received and programs implemented or scaled up without much opportunity for the larger community to become part of the discourse on educational success.

The increased reliance on nonprofit organizations to deliver public services similarly has had some unintended consequences. In some cases it has caused nonprofits to alter their mission to align with contract dollars. To comply with performance-based contract requirements, it has required nonprofits to replace volunteers with accountants, contracts officers, budget managers and other trained professionals who can provide the kind of quality assurance government expects (for a more extended discussion of these issues, see Chapter 5). Smith and Lipsky ask:

> If the state no longer directly delivers services, but authorizes private parties to conduct its business, where shall we locate the boundaries of the state? Massive contracting for services should also have significant implications for the limits of government and the autonomy of nongovernmental community affairs ... More dependence on nonprofit organizations means not less but more government involvement in the affairs of voluntary and community agencies.
>
> Smith and Lipsky (1993, 5)

A clear leadership implication of the transformation of the nonprofit sector is the need for local government leaders to know their nonprofit partners. Not all are equally good polity partners in co-producing the common good. Knowing the mission and membership expectations of these organizations is an important starting point.[6]

The Special Role of Voluntary Associations and Civil Society

Standing between individuals and more formal business and nonprofit organizations that have a distinct legal status, there are millions of voluntary associations, informal networks and spontaneous acts of volunteerism across the United States in which individuals and groups engage in activities of public consequence. All sorts of organizations may fall under this umbrella, including: churches, neighborhood organizations, cooperatives, fraternal organizations, charities, unions, parties, soccer clubs, social movements, interest groups, book clubs, self-help groups, home-owner associations and families. These activities are part of what we call civil society, and enjoy varying degrees of legal recognition. Outside these voluntary associations, individuals engage in a multitude of community-building activities that never appear on any civic association index. These activities include arranging parent transportation pools to get children to and from schools, neighborhood cleaning projects, barn-raising types of activities with neighbors, assisting the infirm and elderly, and hundreds of other spontaneous acts of civic engagement.

The associational activities that occur in civil society are distinguished from the public activities of government because they are voluntary. They are also distinguished from the private activities of markets because they rely on cooperative and collaborative strategies that seek common ground and result in the delivery of public rather than private goods. While nonprofit organizations are clearly a part of what is known as the "third sector," for the purposes of our discussion here we focus only on third sector organizations and activities that do not have nonprofit status. We do so because conflating civil society with nonprofit organizations is both misleading and dangerous.

It is misleading in part because significant contributions to the good of the polity occur outside the formal legal boundaries of nonprofit organizations. These activities often provide the seedbed for the next generation of public policy issues that eventually get formalized and incorporated into law. For example, Robert Putnam in *Bowling Alone* (2000) declared that civic engagement was on the decline. But in a detailed study of Portland, Oregon, over a 40-year period, Steve Johnson (2002) discovered that the categories Putnam was using to measure civic engagement missed voluntary actions of individuals and informal groups that didn't appear on the formal radar screen. This shadow activity in civil society over a 40-year period transformed public policy in Portland on a variety of fronts (a strong bicycle culture, strong neighborhood groups, a green building ethic, a local grown food movement and environmental-centered planning). More contemporaneously, think of how attitudes, practices and laws governing gender identity and civil unions have changed over the past two decades. These changes start with individual acts of choice in civil society and gain momentum through voluntary associations and more formal advocacy organizations that eventually, through constant and unrelenting political pressure, result in changes through the formal legal system.

Second, it is dangerous to conflate the nonprofit sector with civil society because in the American rule of law system it is important to provide ample space for citizen initiatives that are not under the formal legal control of government. As we have pointed out in our previous section on nonprofit organizations, the government's control over nongovermental organizations (NGOs) both legally and through the budget contracting process, has been used in ways that have altered much of their character and purpose. We need space for private associations and individuals to build agendas that constantly ask the tough questions, thus spurring officialdom to re-examine its basic assumptions regarding the delivery of public service and the political decision-making processes that produce and provide over-sight of these services. Who is being served and who is not? Why? What are some alternatives that are more inclusive, more responsive, more effective and more capable of generating trust and legitimacy? These are the kinds of questions that have been the hallmark of churches and civic associations that have fueled major political transformations over the course of American history (the abolition movement, women's rights movement, the civil rights movement, transformations in the delivery of social service programs, the Black Lives Matter movement, etc.) and are now spawning the resurgence of interest in the role of civic society in contributing to a vibrant democracy.

Over the last three decades there has been a resurgence of interest in revitalizing civil society (see Evans and Boyte, 1992; Walzer, 1992; Cohen and Arato, 1992; Sirianni and Friedland, 1995; Boyte, Barber, and Marshall, 1994; Eberly, 1994; Rebuilding Civil Society, 1995; Schambra, 1995; Sirianni, 2009; Skocpol and Fiorina, 1999; Civic Practices Network, 2013). The resurgence is supported by the right, left and middle of the political spectrums. Where one stands in this spectrum is the result of one's very basic beliefs about the conditions that need to be in place for empowering individuals to participate within the larger community of which they are a part. How do individuals acquire a commitment to the larger good of the community? What conditions motivate individuals to express this commitment? Recall in Chapter 2 our discussion of whether a larger sense of moral purposes arises through a maturation process that starts with the needs of the individual and extends outward over time to include a commit-ment to others (i.e. Kohlberg's stages of development). Or is it the case that individuals are pre-wired at birth with a social conscience (Brooks, 2012; Haidt, 2013) and need the facilitative assistance of naturally occurring civic associations to give it expression? Often, what happens in this debate is that partisans forget about what they agree upon and focus their attention on protecting their core values from both compromise and threat (Haidt, 2013).

The left end of the political spectrum fears most the adverse consequences of state-centered political systems that provide privileged access to power and government largess at the expense of disadvantaged minority voices and causes (i.e., women's movement, LGBT movement, environmental movement, immigration movement and democracy movements around the world). The left sees civil society organizations as essential agents in the service of political justice, fairness, respect for individual dignity and economic equality. The political right also fears state-centered political systems, not so much because of the privileged access it gives to the rich and powerful, but because it displaces the role that the family, neighborhoods and local voluntary associations play in giving expression to our natural desire to attach our knowledge, skills and passions to something larger than ourselves.

The political center is concerned about restoring the mediating influence of associations where citizens learn to resolve problems, build civic skills and create social capital (Putnam, 2000; Levine, 1984; McGregor, 1984). By facilitating an environment that is relational and dialogic, associations perform a mediating function between citizens and government by collecting the interests of their members and transforming these interests into values that are expressed to governing institutions (Berger and Neuhaus, 1996; Couto, 1999; Reid, 1999). As Putnam observes:

> [w]hen people lack connections to others, they are unable to test the veracity of their own views, whether in the give-and-take of casual conversion or in more formal deliberation. Without such an opportunity people are more likely to be swayed by their worst impulses. It is no coincidence that random acts of violence...tend to be committed by people identified, after the fact, as "loners."
>
> Putnam (2000, 288–89)

And it may be no coincidence that our politics have become more extreme and deadlocked over the past several decades. Participation in associations provides an opportunity to hear and express different points of view, to test opinions, to become more informed and to gain a broader more encompassing perspective. Even if the association is narrow, partisan, exclusive and ideological in its make-up, members learn some civic engagement skills that have salutary consequences for dialogical processes of engagement outside the boundaries of the association (Talisse, 2009; Picone and Tesson, 2006).

The evidence is not so clear when it comes to participation in online social networks, which has become an extensive and growing phenomena. According to a Pew Research study of 1,233 participants, 68 percent of all U.S. adults are Facebook users, while 28 percent use

Instagram, 26 percent use Pinterest, 25 percent use LinkedIn and 21 percent use Twitter (Pew Research Center, 2016). Studies suggest that rather than create polarization, existing technology enables individuals to spend more time in their self-selected echo chambers, where communicating with other like-minded individuals has replaced loyalties based on group, policy or party identities (Bennett, 2012). These social networks do not necessarily provide experiences that serve as a corrective to disengagement from civic duty and declining participation in the formal political process (Venezuela, Park, and Kee, 2009)

What members of the civic society movement from all sides of the political spectrum have in common is agreement that our public service leaders need to be more cognizant of their moral agency in creating the conditions for a healthy civil society. This agreement reflects an appreciation for the free, unregulated space that stands between government and the business community, between nonprofit organizations and the more formally organized groups upon which they draw to fulfill their missions. Unlike engaging in business activity, citizens in civil society do not need permission from government to engage in all kinds of voluntary group activities. The civil society space provides opportunities for individuals and groups spontaneously to organize around common interests and values, expanding and contracting their size and scope to fit the needs of both the community and its members. It is a highly dynamic space that serves as a catalytic force that can spawn innovation and cross-cutting experiences for citizens in ways that link generations, races, religions, social classes and other similar "identity" markers. But it is also space that can allow fears, hatreds and sources of discontent to kindle into forces that undermine the capacity of communities to be self-governing. Our public service leaders have an influence on how this space is filled. They can use this space to expand our understanding of citizenship beyond participation in the formal processes of government decision-making, and they can also use this space to show us that freedom is not simply the product of the market actions of individual consumers and corporate producers.

The civil society movement reminds those leading from where they sit that that they exercise moral agency on behalf of both ends of the political spectrum, the left and the right. But in doing so neither the left (too wedded to government action in the pursuit of distributive justice) nor the right (too unconcerned about the destructive impact of competitive markets on the fabric of associational life) are fully adequate (Haidt, 2013). If we have been "deskilled" as citizens, it is not simply the result of the bureaucratic welfare state, but of the erosion of some of the essential citizenship-enhancing functions of our civic institutions themselves (Civic Practices Network, 2013). Polity leadership requires that we keep this citizenship-building role at the center of our moral agency (Cooper, 2004; Box, 1998; Fox and Miller, 1996).

Conclusion

This chapter builds on the understanding of your moral agency as a leader that you have already acquired by focusing on the individual, group or team, and organizational dimensions of leadership discussed in Chapters 1–3. Polity leadership adds another dimension to your leadership mindset as well as the need to acquire new leadership practices that will enable you to think and act successfully in your role as a polity leader. In this chapter we have focused on what a polity leadership mindset looks like. Revisit our polity leadership model in Exhibit 4.1: the model predisposes you to go beyond the questions that are at the forefront of attention when you take an individual, group/team or organizational perspective and ask:

1   What is the structure of the local polity landscape with respect to the relative weight of the actors across the sectors?
2   Who are the major participants in each of the sectors?
3   What kind of public service motivation provides the animus for an organization's mission and goals?
4   What kind of institutional trust and legitimacy do organizations have within the local polity setting?
5   Who are the most important civic leaders in the community?
6   What is the source of their civic motivation?
7   What are the most important types and degrees of voluntary service in your local community? How are they connected through time and by relationship to other individuals and organizations in the community? How can these activities be leveraged to serve larger public purposes? How can you help in your leadership role?

This list of questions is not intended to be exhaustive. It is an important first step in assembling an asset map of civic-serving resources. This asset map constitutes part of the "sizing up" phase of our public service leadership model when viewed from a polity perspective.

An important dimension of "sizing up" goes beyond knowing what the polity landscape looks like to discovering new leadership opportunities in the community. Like the opportunities at the individual, group or team and organizational levels, polity leadership opportunities require the knowledge and skills to tap into the full spectrum of motivations, from highly individualist and self-serving at one end to highly public serving and altruistic at the other. Leaders need to be able to tap into both ends of the spectrum. In Exhibit 4.13 we provide a conceptual map of this spectrum.

Some organizations and citizens are much more predisposed than others to thinking and acting for the public good. These are the

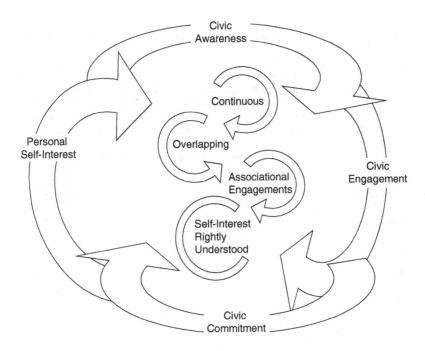

Exhibit 4.13 Polity Leadership Engagement Model

ones that may be the most important as the starting point for polity leadership. But altruism is usually not sufficient. Most citizens and organizations are at the top end of Exhibit 4.13, where they are mostly preoccupied with what de Tocqueville described as "improving their own lot in life," whether it be personal or organizational. They may need to be moved out of their mental "gated communities" and "organizational silos" to a state of awareness that over time gets transformed into "community concern." Once citizens and organizations express a community-centered concern, they are ready to be mobilized into engagement and, ultimately, collective action. De Tocqueville argued that the preeminent leadership competency needed for democratic countries was bringing associations of disparate community groups and individuals together to take common action for the community good (de Tocqueville, 2000/1935, 492). Without doing so, individuals, groups and organizations tend to fall back into their windowless silos. In the ensuing chapters (especially Chapters 9–11) we will introduce various leadership tools you can use to navigate the actors that make up the polity landscape successfully in order to take advantage of new polity leadership opportunities.

Notes

1 Polity draws our attention to the organic wholeness of the community and emphasizes the synergistic influence of history, geo-political conditions, institutions and culture in creating a shared system of values, and shared agreement on governance processes and structures, both formal and informal. This notion of polity has important implications for the "public interest" responsibilities of leaders. We view polity leaders as responsible for enhancing the moral purposes of their communities by using a value-based approach (see Chapter 9) that leverages the network of private, public nonprofit and civic relationships and resources to advance the larger common good. Polity leaders sit at the boundary nexus in Exhibit 4.1 with other government jurisdictions, nonprofit entities, organizations in civil society and for-profit enterprises. Increasingly the common good depends on the catalytic leadership initiative that public sector leaders at all levels of public organizations are willing to undertake. The dotted line through the middle of the government sector portion of the Venn diagram in Exhibit 4.1 calls attention to the need for cooperative action on the part of both elected officials and career public administrators.

Over the past decade, there has been a resurgence of scholarship that uses "regime" as the unit of analysis for understanding political change, governance and leadership development (Rohr, 1989; Morgan, Green, Shinn, and Robinson, 2008/2013; Ozawa, 2005; Elkin and Soltan, 1993; Johnson, 2002; Stone, 1989; Leo, 1997, 1998; Lauria, 1997). Our use of the term polity throughout the book is consistent with this scholarship.

2 This section draws from Green and Morgan (2014). See especially pp. 7–14. The research for this section of the paper was undertaken by co-author Richard Green.

3 We borrow the phrase "History of Sheep in Wolves Clothing" from Barry Karl, who used the phrase to describe the historical role of the American bureaucracy (Karl, 1987). We believe the phrase is also an apt historical description of the relationship between government and business over the course of American history.

4 This section draws heavily form previous work published in Morgan et al. (2013/2008), Chapter 5.

5 This section draws heavily form previous work published in Morgan, Green, Shinn, and Robinson, *Foundations of Public Service*, 2013/2008, Chapter 5.

6 See especially, Banyan (2004, 2014), Nishishiba, Banyan, and Morgan (2012, pp. 36–45). They document the factors that predispose some organizations to be better community serving partners than other.

5   The Moral Basis of Public Service Leadership

> While public morality thus in part reflects, incorporates, and is influenced by private moralities, in another respect it is sharply distinguished from, and in slight or greater conflict with, private values ... The morality of democratic government in its administrative aspects turns first of all, then, on orientation to the uniquely public interest.
>
> Paul Appleby (1952, 39, 45)

> Every political order contains, as a necessary principle of its own integrity and significance, a systematic ethical view ... which consists of the system of public authority that defines right and wrong in the realm of politics.
>
> William J. Meyer (1975, 61)

> It is quite possible for a surgeon with impeccable ethical standards in his professional life to be an absolutely irresponsible parent, a compulsive gambler, an incorrigible lecher, and so forth. Unless we are willing to acquiesce in the same possibility for government managers, we shall not make much progress in developing meaningful ethical standards for managers in the career civil service.
>
> John Rohr (1989, 16)

This chapter continues our polity argument from Chapter 4 with a more finely grained discussion of the sources of public morality that inform and guide public service leaders. Public organizations both reflect and shape the moral character of the larger organic polity of which they are a part. This organic whole is different from one country to the next and changes through time. The values that inform and guide the political systems of China or England are the product of a uniquely different history, culture, set of institutions and legal structure of authority than is the case for the values that inform and guide the leaders of public organizations in the United States. The organic whole of a New England townhall community will be different to a suburban bedroom community in Los Angeles.

It is incumbent upon leaders of these different types of communities in different geographic locations at different times in history to understand the uniqueness of the polity that they are leading and the moral values that inform and guide this whole. This is the promise and challenge of this chapter.

In Exhibit 5.1 we provide a graphic representation of the relationships between different and sometimes conflicting ethical frameworks that norm our expectations as public servants. The graphic starts with our personal ethics, which provide the backdrop for our public service leadership work. These ethics are informed and shaped by our upbringing, education, world view, race, ethnicity, geographic setting, genetic wiring as human beings and numerous other factors. There is a large body of literature that assumes these values are sufficient, if you can just "get them right" through continuous practice and hard work. Covey's highly popular "habits of the heart" series (Covey, 2004, 2005, 2006) is an example of this kind of approach. While our personal values can sometimes facilitate our ethical responsibilities as public leaders, they also can impede our responsibilities, as is illustrated by the Master Case for Part I. That is why we agree with John Rohr in the opening epigram that personal ethics is neither a necessary nor a sufficient condition for being an ethically competent public servant. We side with those who believe that leadership in the public sector is

Exhibit 5.1 Types of Public Service Ethics

especially problematic and has no easy answers (Heifetz, 1994; Heifetz, Grashow, and Linsky, 2009). Moral leadership in the public sector is more akin to what Max DePree (2008) describes as "leadership jazz," where you have to make music without any clear scripts. But that doesn't mean there aren't clear sideboards to one's moral music-making in the public sector. Our goal in this chapter is to describe these sideboards.

There are two dimensions to our ethical responsibilities as public service leaders, one that is governed by a list of proscriptions of what we can't do, and the other by a much more amorphous framework of what we should do. We call the first dimension "hygiene ethics" and the other, "doing good" ethics. Hygiene ethics keep us out of trouble, but it is never sufficient or helpful in performing the "doing good" side of public service ethics.

Doing good requires that we know what we should do, rather than simply what we can't do. What you can do and should do is almost always a matter of some discretionary judgment, thus requiring an affirmative justification. Often this justification cannot be explicitly found in the letter of the law, thus requiring us to rely on a much more amorphous body of regime values that are embedded in our political institutions and practices.

The doing good side of ethics opens up a Pandora's box of concerns, similar to the kinds of issues that surround the appointment of U.S. Supreme Court justices. Everyone wants to know how government agents are going to use their discretion to resolve ambiguity in the law and in their role descriptions. While the spotlight may be brighter and the stakes higher for Supreme Court justices, the moral obligations of local, state and federal public servants are the same: they have a duty to inform themselves on the foundational issues of democratic governance. What are the purposes of the democratic system? How do they stand on these purposes? How do they see their governance role in promoting these purposes? What is the role of government at the local, state and federal levels? How do they see their fiduciary role in relationship to other participants in the governance process (i.e., legislative bodies, the executive, citizens, states, other state and local jurisdictions)? What kind and how much discretion do I have in the specific role that I have been hired to perform? How will I use this discretion? For many participants in the Supreme Court nominating process, it is answers to these types of foundational governance questions they are seeking. We believe these questions also serve as the appropriate benchmark for measuring the moral worthiness of public service leaders to assume their fiduciary roles as keepers of the public interest. If leaders can't give answers to these questions, they can't be morally trusted to rule. Our goal in this chapter and the next is to prepare you for cultivating and deserving this trust.

In the first part of the chapter we review the major sources of public morality. This section elaborates on our overarching argument that ethical competence as a public servant is determined by the legal principles, values, structures and processes of governing institutions that both hold and give meaning to the public life through time. We progress in our discussion from the more easily identifiable sources of moral guidance for public leaders to sources that are more open-ended and fluid, but which nevertheless provide secure moral anchors to justify leadership initiative. In the last two sections of the chapter we return to a discussion of how to put this knowledge to work as a public leader from where you sit.

Public Morality Source #1: Know the Architectonic Structure of Legal Authority and its Moral Implications

Public organizations in the United States, unlike many other countries in the world, have been deliberately created to serve fairly explicit and limited purposes. In contrast to countries like England whose constitution is not found in one written document, American constitutions at all levels of government are written documents that become the focal point for public policy debates. For example, the on-going debate over whether the United States should adopt some kind of universal health care becomes a debate over whether such action is constitutionally permissible. At local levels of government the debate over restrictions on land use quickly become a debate over property rights that are protected by the Bill of Rights. The Constitution is so central to governance in the U.S. that:

> citizens in America usually ask two questions about public policy, while those of many other countries ask only one: Others simply ask '*should* their national government do this or that'; we must also ask '*may* ours do it under the constitution.'
>
> Diamond, Fisk, and Garfinkel (1966, 101)

This propensity to constitutionalize policy differences gets carried over into debates regarding the roles and responsibilities of career administrators. Americans want to know if their political and administrative leaders are exercising their discretion in a constitutionally correct fashion. Thus, the first question leaders must answer is: What is the legal basis for the authority I am exercising? To answer this question leaders need to have a clear and robust understanding of the various sources of their legal authority. This knowledge needs to be personalized, not based only on the advice of lawyers. This is because lawyers give advice to public organizations and their legal representatives based on the risk of being sued and the risk of losing a lawsuit. While such advice is important to know, it should *not* be determinative in deciding what should be done to advance the public interest. Even when agencies get sued and lose, the larger public interest is often well served. Such has been the case with civil rights (i.e., *Brown v. the Board of Education*), property rights (i.e., *Dolan v. Tigard*), religious expression (i.e., *Pierce v. Society of Sisters*), free speech (*Tinker v. Des Moines*), the rights of privacy (*Roe v. Wade*) and hundreds of other precedent-setting cases. The acquisition of legal literacy requires leaders to develop competence with the various types of law summarized in Exhibit 5.2.

America's multi-level constitutional system consisting of separation of powers, checks and balances, and divided authority, leaves career administrators in a particularly difficult quandary. To whom do they owe their primary allegiance? In England, career administrators operate under a doctrine of "ministerial responsibility," which attaches their stewardship responsibility to the government ministers of the day. This executive-centered model differs from France, where the principle of the "general will" is embodied in the doctrine of parliamentary supremacy. This means that career administrators hold stewardship allegiance to Parliament rather than to the individual government ministers. At a practical level, this creates the possibility for French career administrators to invoke their stewardship responsibility to Parliament as a whole in opposition to the policies or practices of a given minister (Rohr, 1995).

In the United States, it is not so clear where the primary allegiance of administrators should reside: Is it to the legislative body, which makes the laws and authorizes the appropriation of public funds? Is it to the chief executive, who executes the laws and to whom they report as part of the bureaucratic hierarchy? Is it to the courts, which interpret the laws? Or is the allegiance, as some argue, to the U.S. Constitution as a whole and its encompassing web of offices, processes and institutions (Burke, 1988; Rohr, 1989, Chap. 1–2)? The reason these questions can't be answered simply is because in the United States sovereignty resides in the people. In their sovereign role the people have created a complex set of constitutional structures and processes to protect liberty from a variety of dangers. When public servants take an oath to defend this legal structure, they are placing this loyalty above loyalty to individuals, offices, parties, ideology and programs whenever the two come into conflict.

The moral obligation to preserve the integrity of America's architectonic legal structures of authority is frequently at the center of debates over leadership scandals. When has a leader merely made an error in personal judgment (committed an ethical impropriety)? When has a public official engaged in practices that are illegal (corruption)? Or when has a leader undermined the very foundations of public authority by abusing and misusing the structures of public authority (tyranny)? For example, an administrator may not respond to a legislative request for information, either ignoring the request altogether, or, worse, falsely claiming it is not

Exhibit 5.2 Forms of Legal Authority

Types of Law	Key Features	Leadership Implications
Constitutional	• **Powers of Government:** Specifies the limited powers of government. • **Structures and Processes of Government:** Establishes who can exercise what authority and how. This includes separation of powers, checks & balances and federalism. • **Judicial Review and the Supremacy Clause:** The U.S. and State Supreme Courts have final authority to determine what their respective Constitutions means. An important adjunct to the supremacy of the Supreme Court is the *supremacy clause* of Article VI of the U.S. Constitution, which establishes federal law as the supreme law of the land. • **Bill of Rights and Fourteenth Amendment:** The first 10 (of 26) amendments to the U.S. Constitution constitute the Bill of Rights; they were passed by the first Congress shortly after ratification of the Constitution. The Fourteenth Amendment contains *due process* and *equal protection* clauses that apply to state and local governments as well as to the federal government, and it gives Congress the power to pass laws enforcing its provisions. The Fourteenth Amendment was passed shortly after the Civil War to ensure the protection of the civil rights of newly freed slaves from abuses by southern states.	• Public administration serves three maters: it receives its budget and statutory authority to implement legislation from the powers enumerated for the legislative branch, and operates mainly, but not exclusively, under the supervening authority of the executive branch as specified in the constitution and/or the authorizing state charter under which local governments operate. Courts are the final arbiter. • The supremacy clause provides the basis for a preemptive claim by federal administrators over state- and local-level interpretations of federal law when the two may be in conflict or when a state/local law conflicts with a federal law (i.e., criminalizing medical marijuana, or in state efforts to control illegal immigration). The equal protection and due process clauses of the Fourteenth Amendment have been interpreted by courts to apply most of the Bill of Rights restrictions to states and local governments as well as the U.S. government, thus broadening local leadership responsibilities.

Statutes	Laws passed by legislative bodies (called ordinances at the local level) provide government with the authority to act.	Laws provide administrators with the authority to execute programs and spend money.
Administrative Law	A prescribed legal process whereby administrators can "fill in gaps" in legislation.	Rule-making is the major tool used by administrators to clarify the law when statutes are unclear, ambiguous, contradictory or specifically delegate authority to administrators.
Judicial Law: Constitutional, Statutes & Common Law	In addition to interpreting what the constitution and statutes mean, courts create *common law*, which is case law established through litigation (see, for example the standards governing liability for "faulty or dangerous" products, Levi 1949, 8–27).	Public officials are subject to the legal interpretations of statutes and ordinances by courts.
Executive Orders, Proclamations, Memorandum, Directives and Signing Orders	Presidents, governors and mayors can issue proclamations, orders, executive determinations, executive memorandums, executive notices, executive guidelines and signing statements. Executive orders were used to place Japanese Americans in internment camps in World War II. Use of these executive tools have expanded, raising questions about the abuse of executive power (Cooper, 2014/2002, 2005).	Local executive orders and memorandum are usually more ceremonial than substantive. At the federal level they can be substantively significant, such as stopping oil drilling (https://www.whitehouse.gov/the-press-office/2016/12/20/presidential-memorandum-withdrawal-certain-areas-atlantic-coast)

available or can't be provided. Such actions, absent special claims to protect privacy rights, confidential information, the national secrurity, etc., undermine the integrity of the democratic deliberative process and the need to maintain legislative oversight. They are not merely legal infractions; more importantly, they constitute small acts of tyranny. This kind of offense is recognized at the national level in the provisions for impeaching a president and in the provision in many jurisdictions for the removal of public officials from office, even when they have not engaged in corruption or have committed ethical improprieties. In cases like President Clinton's infamous sex scandal involving Monica Lewinsky, the Watergate break-in scandal during President Nixon's administration, and Russian influence in the Trump administration, the question was whether those who had fiduciary responsibility misused the powers of their office to undermine the integrity of the collective decision-making structures and processes of the governance system as a whole. It is one thing to be a personal lout or to engage in acts of lying, stealing and cheating for personal gain. It is quite another matter to engage in tyranny. As noted by William J. Meyer in the opening epigraphs to this chapter:

> [s]imple corruption in government ... represents the stuff of popu-
> lar scandals in the modern state, but it is presumptuous to think
> that this represents the full range of ethical disorders to which the
> state is susceptible ... Every political order contains, as a necessary
> principle of its own integrity and significance, a systematic ethical
> view ... which consists of the system of public authority that
> defines right and wrong in the realm of politics.
>
> Meyer (1975, 61)

One of the ethical challenges of being true to one's moral obligations as a public servant is the problem of "dirty hands." This is a condition that involves the use of morally dubious means to protect the moral well-being of the community (Walzer, 1973; Nye, 2008). Those respon-sible for public safety and national security commonly face a dirty hands problem. For example, when is it appropriate to lie to a terrorist who has just killed a dozen people and is holding another ten hostages? When do you compromise due process requirements or endanger the lives of innocent civilians in the name of apprehending public enemies? Such questions reflect the need for public leaders sometimes to respond to matters of urgency or to take advantage of windows of opportunity that may arguably violate the principles of public morality. President Lincoln faced this issue in using his executive powers as commander in chief to free the slaves in military zones and subsequently in using morally dubious means to muster enough votes in Congress to pass the 13th Amendment prior to meeting with Jefferson Davis to accept the surrender of the Confederacy and bring an end to the Civil War. Less famous examples occur commonly throughout every level of public service, where individuals have to decide when it is justifiable to violate a rule, a legal principle or the rights of individuals in the service of the larger pubic good. Fortunately, the passage of whistle-blowing laws have reduced the dirty hands problem. While protecting individuals from prosecution or dismissal for bringing attention to wrongdoing, these laws do not remove the moral angst that comes from reconciling the use of morally dubious means to protect the larger public good.

The problem of dirty hands can be an especially problematic for professionals like doctors, lawyers, social workers, psychologists, etc. who operate simultaneously under their own professional code of ethics as well as their public service ethical obligations. Professionals not only are essential to high-quality public service, but they bolster the legitimacy to government initiatives. This can sometimes put professionals in morally difficult positions. A good example is the role of professional psychologists during the famed waterboarding torture of terrorists held in custody under the American Patriot Act of 2001 (115 Stat. 272). The torture techniques were developed with the secret complicity of the American Psychological Association (APA).[1] When this information came to light, the APA commissioned an investigation and subsequently amended its ethics code in 2010 to prohibit APA members from participating, facilitating or otherwise engaging "in torture, defined as any act by which severe pain or suffering, whether physical or mental, is intentionally inflicted on a person, or in any other cruel, inhuman, or degrading behavior" (APA, 2018, section 3.04). But what is a professional to do when asked by government to undertake actions that are believed to violate their professional code of ethics? They are faced with the dilemma of serving their government, but potentially at the expense of losing their license to practice. Such examples reinforce our larger point that public morality rests on standards that are not reducible to personal, professional or some other form of universalist ethics.

Public Morality Source #2: Know What Is Prohibited

Most of public service ethics focus on prohibiting various forms of self-dealing. Look up your state or local ethics commissions to see what kind of activities they engage in. You will find that they focus on the kinds of issues summarized in Exhibit 5.3, all of which deal with enforcement of explicit legal requirements to prevent various kinds of personal and organizational wrong-doing. The focus of these laws and practices is on hygiene ethics, or the negative merit of preventing the use of public resources and power from serving the personal interests of individuals, and the corruption of the legally defined mission of our public institutions. Getting hygiene ethics right is necessary, but never sufficient for guiding the exercise of your affirmative discretion to serve the public interest.

Exhibit 5.3 Types of Ethical Abuse and Controls

Types of Abuse	Accountability Solutions
1 Rewarding partisan loyalty	Hatch Act Civil service reform Anti-nepotism rules Codes of ethics
2 Self-dealing	Conflict of interest legislation Financial disclosure laws Professional audit and financial standards Post-employment prohibitions Contracting requirements Restrictions on acceptance of gifts, favors, etc. Codes of ethics
3 Incompetence/inefficiency	Civil service reform Personnel training and development Management approaches (Theories X, Y, Z) Codes of ethics
4 Insensitivity to rights/ interests of citizens and clients	Citizen oversight bodies Right to privacy acts Restrictions on use of private information Freedom of information processes Codes of ethics Rule-making Copyright and patent laws
5 Agency self-aggrandizement	Right to privacy acts Freedom of information acts Open government provisions Legislative oversight Executive control Codes of ethics Rule-making
6 Lack of representation	Notice and comment rule-making Public hearings Open meeting laws and quorum requirements Citizen advisory and oversight boards Negotiated and hybrid rule-making Mandatory representation requirements Collaborative governance and networks Neighborhood associations

Public Morality Source #3: Know the Kind and Source of Your Leadership Discretion

No amount of legal clarity and certainty can eliminate the need for the exercise of discretionary authority. There are obvious reasons for this. First, legislative bodies sometimes cannot agree on the purposes of a law or may build conflicting purposes into law or statute, leaving administrators with the responsibility of figuring out what a specific provision of the law means. For example, when legislators believe that some citizen involvement may be required in the administration of federal programs but can't agree on how much is enough, they may use widely interpretable language like "maximum feasible participation."[2] At other times, legislative bodies do not know what the cause of a given problem may be or what solutions might be appropriate. Under such circumstances they often deliberately leave it to administrative bodies to decide on the meaning of goals like "fair competition," "safe drugs," "responsible risk" etc. Finally, in the rush to judgment to get a bill passed, all of the homework may not have been done to be clear about the meaning and consequences of a given policy solution. Administrators are left to do the best they can with what the legislative body has served up.

While opportunities for leadership discretion are ubiquitous throughout public organizations, discretion is viewed quite differently depending on where you sit and what role you are performing. This produces quite contradictory reactions to the existence of such discretion. What may be an appropriate exercise of discretion by engineers working in a local transportation office may not be appropriate for public servants working in a state department of environmental quality, or for those working in the mayor's neighborhood community action program. Engineers tend to see discretion as relatively safe, because decisions are governed by commonly accepted technical criteria and professional best practices. Those working for the mayor will see discretion as safe only when it is in the hands of those who can accommodate the changing needs and preferences of citizens and stakeholders in the community.

Consider the Master Library Case for this section. The director of the Library and the board for whom she works have additional measures of success in dealing with the values and preferences of citizens in the community than the technical expertise of a member of the professional library staff. For those working in the field where conditions vary from one geographic setting to another, flexibility and discretion is needed to make the technical adjustments necessary to accomplish the goals of a given project. Discretion at the field level typically requires more flexibility, while central office officials seek policy consistency. Middle managers generally have to balance these competing objectives. The various kinds of programs they are required to implement derive from differing moral and legal foundations for administrative authority. This complex variation in types of responsibility means that administrators cannot easily respond to citizen demands with formulaic reform. They must take into account the types of policy issues they are responsible for implementing and the implications these types have for the amount and kind of discretion they need to exercise in order to be successful.

In addition to political and organizational factors that affect the amount and kind of leadership discretion you have, discretion also varies by the kind of public policy you are charged with implementing. For example, Exhibit 5.4 demonstrates the importance of distinguishing between those who have responsibility for administering services and those who bear regulatory and policing responsibilities. Most of us respond more favorably to our mail carrier than to an Internal Revenue Service (IRS) agent. In fact, this difference creates terribly difficult management problems for public organizations that are simultaneously charged with both customer service and enforcement responsibilities. Consider a state liquor control agency that is simultaneously responsible for promoting sales and collecting taxes, while also responsible for enforcing the drinking age and preventing other abuses by licensees. Being responsible for both sales and enforcement requires creating complex structures of authority and personnel processes that do justice to inherently conflicting organizational missions.

One way to understand the significance of different types of policy on the exercise of administrative discretion is to review the mix of motivations that create public policy in the first place.[3] Although legislative intent is not always clear and unambiguous, there exists a basic logic in the legislative process that is fairly obvious and holds important implications for the exercise of administrative discretion. The logic starts with the very limited amount of time and interest that elected officials have in the wide range of issues that cross their desk. They can't pay equal attention to everything, especially if they are citizen legislators with part-time staff. They pay more attention to issues that require a low investment of their time and energy and they pay more attention to issues where there is strong and well-integrated pressure from interest groups. These two motivators are captured respectively at the left and bottom of Exhibit 5.4. Together these

Exhibit 5.4 Policy Types and Corresponding Types of Administrative Discretion

Degree of Integration by Stakeholders	Integrated	Redistributive Policy Produces Administrative Political Discretion	Self-Regulatory Policy Produces Administrative Professional Discretion
	Fragmented	Distributive Policy Produces Administrative Technical Discretion	Regulatory Policy Produces Administrative Planning Discretion
		Low	High
		Administrative and Political Costs of Reaching a Decision	

Source: Morgan et al. (2013/2008, 62).

legislative motivators produce the four different types of administrative discretion in each of the four cells in Exhibit 5.4.

Distributive Public Policy and Technical Discretion

Distributive or pork-barrel policies tend to put administrators in the position of using their technical discretion and professional competence to build a dam, construct an aircraft bomber or improve a waterway. Since the ends of the policy are usually uncontested, and the means are assumed to require the application of commonly accepted technical knowledge, discretion tends to be narrower and less controversial than is the case with the other three policy arenas. At least at the political level, elected officials do not assume they need to worry much about what administrators do to carry out their will. Once a decision has been made to authorize a project and to appropriate the funds, administrators are generally trusted to use their technical competence to get the job done. Technical requirements and competence act to limit and constrain administrative discretion.

Regulatory Policy and Social Planning Discretion

Regulatory policy does not generally carry the same trust and confidence of elected officials. The definition of the ends that regulatory agencies are supposed to achieve is often a matter of some disagreement among legislators. While there may be a common desire to create safe working environments, clean air and water, and safe foods, our uncertain state of knowledge means there is always some disagreement over exactly what is harmful and how the harm should be addressed. Even when there is agreement that a certain substance is toxic, the level of risk we are willing to assume varies from one person to the next, especially when there is a trade-off between the risk and the additional cost of the regulation on businesses. Legislatures generally saddle administrators with handling the resulting problems of risk assessment and balancing trade-offs. These inherent difficulties place regulatory administrators in the position of answering two questions: Will it work? Will it be acceptable? These questions often put administrators in the political catbird seat.

The question of whether a given policy will work requires the administrator to perform the relatively technical and rational task of finding solutions to a particular problem. But rational problem solving is only one of the tasks regulatory policy demands of administrators. In addition, they must consider whether a particular course of action will be acceptable. They generally rely on a combination of hearing processes and advisory committees to assist with this task. But these processes often become volatile, difficult to predict and uncertain with respect to the outcomes they produce.

Redistributive Policy and Political Discretion

The kind of discretion inherent in social planning needs to be distinguished from the kind of political discretion exercised by administrators in implementing redistributive policy. When deciding redistributive policy questions regarding such matters as taxation, poverty, gender and race, politicians create conditions of discretionary administrative authority not because they are uncertain of what the problem is, but because a proposed solution may well create enemies politicians cannot afford to make. Administrators under these conditions are presented with ambiguous rather than vague laws (Jowell, 1975; Leys, 1943). An ambiguous law is one in which the legislature refuses to resolve competing political criteria and, instead, enacts a law that passes the decision-making difficulties on to administrators. One of the best examples is the Community Action Program passed by Congress in the 1960s. The law required the establishment of local citizen advisory committees for each community action program. These oversight committees were required to provide "maximum feasible participation"—a phrase deliberately left ambiguous by the authors of the legislation, since making it specific would necessitate deciding between those who believed the solution to poverty required a dominant leadership role for professionals in the field, and those who believed that the poor themselves were the best judges of how poverty could be solved. This ambiguity was passed on to administrators who could not sidestep the quarrel as they set up and administered these programs in the major cities in the U.S. (Blumenthal, 1969). As a result, administrators were caught up in a maelstrom of controversy as they tried to work their way through the debate, frequently resulting in lawsuits in which courts ultimately decided the issue (Horowitz, 1977).

Vague laws, in contrast to ambiguous laws, are most often the result of inadvertent and unintended consequences of legislative actions rather than a deliberate attempt to obfuscate. Examples of vague laws abound. For example, you can be subject to prosecution for "excessive speed," "reckless endangerment," "unfair competition," "contributing to the delinquency of a minor." These kinds of vague legal provisions are the result of legislative bodies not knowing enough of the detail to be specific. So they craft language that permits lots of discretionary interpretation for the professional experts responsible for implementation.

Self-Regulatory Policy and Professional Discretion

The final category of discretion is associated with the independent judgement exercised by doctors, nurses, dentists, lawyers and other similar certified professions. Professionals are assumed to possess the judgment necessary to determine what competence is required to perform their job, and all are assumed to be in agreement on what the job is—for example, preserving life in the case of doctors. When these conditions occur, legislative bodies delegate large amounts of unfettered discretion to professionals to self-regulate who is entitled to practice in a given field.

There are numerous instances of administrators invoking this kind of functional autonomy to justify their interpretation of what is legally appropriate, which has occasionally resulted in spectacular public controversies. For example, in 1969 Richard Nixon ordered the U.S. Justice Department to petition the courts on behalf of southern school districts to delay court-ordered busing. President Nixon invoked his policy of New Federalism to argue for control of desegregation policy, instead of citizen committees at the local level. This precipitated a civil disobedience letter from more than 15 U.S. Justice Department lawyers who asserted they had a professional duty to press forward on the court desegregation order (Greenberg, 1984, 80). Implementation of environmental laws involving spotted owls and other endangered species have put natural resource administrators similarly at odds with elected officials in both branches of government (Yaffee, 1994).

What happens when our best efforts to find moral guidance in the laws and structures of authority leave us in the dark as to the moral purposes that should guide our leadership action? Where do we turn for guidance? Our answer is that we should be guided by a robust understanding of the moral purposes of the American political system as those values are reflected in our political institutions over the course of its history. While this understanding will seldom tell us precisely what to do, it will, much like membership in any moral order, keep our moral agency at the forefront of our attention and sharpen our thinking regarding the multiple moral purposes that ultimately will provide a justification for the exercise of our leadership action. In the remainder of this chapter we will focus on moral lessons from the American founding. In the next chapter we focus on the moral lessons from the development and transformation of this founding institutional legacy through time.

Public Morality Source #4: Know the Moral Legacy of the American Founding[4]

The founding of the American political system was a fortuitous achievement. Nowhere in the history of the world had a democratic republic been established and maintained over such a large and diverse territory as the United States. The framers of the republic were acutely aware of the unique moment in history when they gathered in Philadelphia in 1787 to reconsider ways of correcting defects in the Articles of Confederation. The Articles had proven too weak to guarantee the successful conduct of the Revolutionary War. The authority to raise taxes, the capacity to organize and supply armies, and the ability to respond quickly to external threats proved frighteningly difficult. As with the

United Nations, the North Atlantic Treaty Organization (NATO) and other loosely coupled confederations, it had become difficult to act decisively when consent from nearly all, or at least the major members, was required on nearly everything. Without solving these problems, democratic liberty was at risk. That was the end, the ultimate prize of the Revolutionary War. It was not simply a war to gain independence from a foreign power, it was a Revolution to establish and secure individual liberty for all citizens. While there was fundamental agreement on this prize, there were profound differences in what was thought to most endanger liberty and the correctives that needed to be put in place to address these dangers.

There were four dangers to democratic liberty identified by the founders that played a decisive role in shaping the outcome of the Constitutional Convention: 1) too much government, 2) too little government, 3) government that fails to protect the minority from the tyranny of the majority, and 4) government that provides too little opportunity for local autonomy. These problems reflect quite distinct and on-going challenges for public service leaders. Together they provide the framework for measuring the moral success of all public service leaders who function as democratic agents of the American political system. In the sections that follow, we will summarize these differences and the moral implications they have for public service leadership.

Too Much Government: King George and the Problem of Concentrated Wealth

The excesses of King George and an overbearing monarchy sparked the American Revolution. Famous events such as the Boston Tea Party and the ride of Paul Revere represented a call to check the abusive exercise of tyrannical governing power, especially executive reliance on general warrants (as opposed to specific warrants) to send troops into private homes to search for whiskey that had not been properly taxed. This was an early version of the current debate over the indiscriminate collection and storage of private information of citizens by government without a specific search warrant. In response, each newly adopted state constitution (except New York's) concentrated governmental power in the popularly elected legislative branch, providing for only a very weak executive branch (Thach, 1969, Chap. 2). And under the Articles of Confederation, the national government remained totally dependent upon the good will of the states for its resources and exercise of its meager powers.

An important undercurrent that fueled hostility toward a powerful executive branch (and more generally the concentration of political power wherever it occurred) was the fear of the consolidation of wealth and power that would be used to the advantage of the rich and the disadvantage of the poor. This had been the history of the mercantilist system that had used its colonial outposts to fuel the treasury of the mother country and enhance the benefactors of this wealth. When added to the physical abuses of executive authority in the colonies, there was a prevailing attitude that "We do not want too much government!" The excitement resulting from giving all power to the people soon foundered, however, on the dual shoals of incompetent government and majority tyranny.

Incompetent Government: The George Washington Problem

The inability of General Washington to acquire the necessary troops, arms and supplies during the Revolutionary War demonstrated the need for unity of command operating within a stable and more robust system of funding. It was nearly impossible to conduct coordinated and sustained military campaigns under the authority of the Articles of Confederation, which gave this responsibility to a committee. Severe war losses and economic depredations taught painful lessons about the need for unity of command, coordinated planning, adequate powers to implement legislative will and the ability to respond quickly to emergencies. The lesson learned, at least by some of the founding generation, was that too little government was as bad as too much. Expertise, specialization and strong executive capacity were essential parts of the recipe for securing the blessings of liberty for posterity. This lesson has grown in importance over the last two centuries, and is reflected in the adoption of a professional civil service system, the rapid growth of the council-manager form of government, steady expansion of the executive branch of government, and growing reliance on expertise judgment (see Chapter 6 for a fuller discussion of these issues).

Majority Tyranny: The Shays' Rebellion Problem

In 1786 and 1787, the fear of tyrannical majorities was always a background concern, but it surfaced in practice when debt-ridden farmers in western Massachusetts took up arms to prevent the courts from foreclosing on their mortgages. Since debtors always outnumber creditors in a large commercial republic, many of the framers realized that the success of Shays' Rebellion would undermine fundamental rights and threaten the kind of long-term stability necessary for the new nation's economic growth and development. By the time of the call for a Constitutional Convention to revise the Articles of Confederation, unchecked legislative majorities seemed as threatening to the protection of liberty as a tyrannical executive.

Local Autonomy: The Engaged Citizen Problem

The Jeffersonian spirit hovered over the Constitutional debates, even though Jefferson was not present to participate. This spirit was carried by the Antifederalists who strongly believed that small relatively homogeneous communities of engaged citizens were important to the survival of democratic institutions for three reasons.[5] First, it would provide the best oversight of those in power. Second, it would result in policies and practices that were informed by local knowledge. Third, direct democracy provided the enabling conditions for cultivating good citizenship and strong commitment to the large public good.

The overarching fear of the Antifederalists was that the newly proposed constitution would create a mutually co-dependent relationship between private wealth and public power. In doing so, it would gradually erode civic engagement as citizens spent more and more of their time trying to improve their economic lot in life. Over time, this large commercial republic would undermine vigilance over each other's liberties and civic-mindedness more generally.

The current version of the Antifederalist argument has been captured in Robert Putnam's book, *Bowling Alone* (2000). Putnam documents the decline in civic engagement in the United States over a period of four decades and argues that such a development has adverse consequences for the long-term health of American democratic governance. Civic engagement cultivates the habits and skills of give and take, prudence and the ability to appreciate multiple perspectives. When the intensity and number of social relationships are in decline, it places a heavier burden on political institutions to resolve conflicts among citizens who have little experience in engaging differences in social settings with strangers. Thus, political differences become sharper and more difficult to resolve (Putnam, 2000, 23–24, 341–44, 357–63; Field, 2003,1–2; Haidt, 2012). There is now a range of evidence that communities with a high amount of such social capital are more likely to benefit from lower crime rates, better health, higher educational achievement and better economic growth (Halpern, 2009).

To summarize, for the founding generation, securing the public interest was a problematic balancing act. It required government to be 1) energetic, efficient and effective, 2) responsive to popular will, 3) protective of minority rights, and 4) supportive of local autonomy and civic engagement. Attempts to address any one of these four major dangers to liberty seemed only to exacerbate the other three. For example, creating a more energetic government, with greater executive power to protect against various external threats and tyranny of the majority, potentially endangers the liberty of citizens from internal abuses of power by governing officials. The corresponding lack of civic engagement dulls the development of a vigilant citizenry to check the abuse of governmental power. For the Federalists, too little governmental power at the center and majority tyranny were far more deleterious to the public interest than the Antifederalists' fear of too much power at the center and the desire for a civic republic. Thus, from each of the four threats to liberty there emerged corresponding and rival institutional correctives that are summarized in the following beatitudes:

The Founding Beatitudes
Too much power begets usurpation, to which majority rule is a
   corrective;
Too much majority rule begets majority tyranny, to which separation
   of powers and checks and balances is a corrective;
Too much separation of powers and checks and balances begets
   incompetent government, to which unity at the center is a
   corrective;
Too much unity at the center begets usurpation, to which civic
   engagement is a corrective.

Adapted from Morgan (2011, 85)

The tensions captured in these beatitudes provide a moral framework for public service leaders at all levels and in all types of public organization in the United States. Regardless of position. title, organizational type and jurisdictional form, public servants are morally obligated by virtue of their constitutional agency to be keepers of the following four core regime values: protecting rights, being responsive to citizens, managing public organizations and resources efficiently and effectively, and fostering civic engagement to create ownership by citizens in their governing institutions. These values constitute the Doing Good circle of the venn diagrams in Exhibit 5.1.

In Exhibit 5.5 we summarize these core values, which operate within an extended republic of federal states, local governing bodies and a multiplicity of interest groups. Over the course of American history

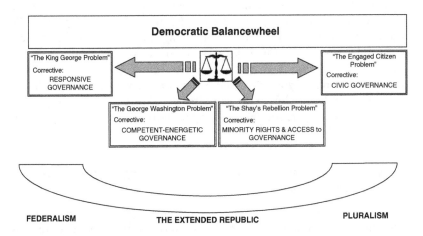

Exhibit 5.5 The Founding Leadership Legacy

these four core values and the extended republic within which they operate have been broadened and deepened by various reform movements that have added meaning to each of the values sets. In Chapter 6 we review the historical legacy of these reforms and the moral implications for guiding the discretionary exercise of leadership authority by public servants.

Together the U.S. Constitution and the founding debates provide us with a necessary starting point for understanding the moral values that should guide public service leadership. But this is far from sufficient. The values of the past get altered by the accidents of history, by surprises, by intentional reforms, by changes in technology, by demographic changes and by political movements to right past wrongs. For example, those who created the 4th Amendment protection against "unreasonable searches and seizures" were concerned about warrantless searches by the visible agents of government trespassing on private property. But what should "unreasonable searches and seizures" mean in a rapidly changing global community with technology that is used by both public and private entities to acquire access to very personal and detailed private information? As we debate and temporarily settle this moral question, it will change the moral value we attach to the phrase "unreasonable searches and seizures." As these changes occur, the values of the past get imbedded slowly over time in institutions that give them further depth and meaning. In Chapter 6 we continue our discussion of the sources of moral authority of public servants by examining the leadership implications of the institutional legacy of changing public service values and reforms since the American founding.

Principles and Practices for Tempering Public Service Ethical Conflicts

In this final section of the chapter we provide some principles, strategies and practices for reducing ethical conflicts in your leadership role. We would like to provide you with a single magical tool that makes ethical conflicts disappear, but this is impossible in the kind of setting you are in charge of leading. The best we can do is to arm you with some strategies that make you more self-aware of the various moral dimensions of your leadership work and to provide you with some core principles that temper, soften and mitigate unproductive and sometimes destructive ethical conflicts.

Becoming Comfortable with Moral Conflict: Being Self-Reflective About Our Moral Agency

One of the challenges leaders face is learning how to become comfortable with moral ambiguity, uncertainty and conflict. These conditions may not be good for your soul, but they are the common stuff of democratic leadership. In the face of conflict your role is to facilitate community dialogue to get working solutions, not to resolve the conflict on behalf of the community you serve. Take solace in the fact that the American founders created political institutions that ensured the perpetuity of moral conflict with respect to the best means of securing a regime of ordered liberty. Your job is to keep this debate alive and to make it as productive as possible.

As a starting point for growing more comfortable with moral conflict in the political arena, we have provided a series of self-reflective questions in Exhibit 5.6. The goal of these questions is to jump-start a process of self-reflection where you have a clear understanding of your moral agency and the confidence to undertake leadership action.

Exhibit 5.6 Key Questions for Sorting and Ordering Public Service Ethical Dimensions

1. What kind of ethical issue am I facing?

   - Personal ethics
   - The ethics of avoiding wrong-doing
   - The ethics of doing public good

2. What is the source of my legal authority?

   - Constitution (U.S. or state)
   - Laws, statutes, ordinances
   - Administrative rules
   - Court cases
   - Institutional norms and practices
   - Other

3. What kind of discretion do I have?

   - Planning
   - Regulatory
   - Distributive
   - Professional
   - Other

4. What unique public good values are at risk?

   - Abuse of government power
   - Inadequate representation
   - Violation of individual and minority rights

- Abridgement of protected process values
- Failure to honor community values

5. What substantive rights are at risk?

   - Liberty
   - Property
   - Equality
   - Other

6. What public values are in conflict/need to be balanced?

   - Abusive government power
   - Inadequate representation
   - Protection of individual and minority rights
   - Violation of process values
   - Community values

7. What kind of ethical conflict am I facing?

   - Conflict of interest
   - Principle-based conflict
   - Integrity-based conflict
   - Other

8. What is the impact of history in shaping how I define the ethical conflict I am facing?

   - See Chapter 6 for a discussion of these historical institutional values.

9. How has reflective practice influenced my understanding of the ends I am serving and the choice of means to effectuate these ends?

   - See Chapters 9 and 12 for a more detailed discussion of the process and purpose of reflective practice

The Role of Self-Interest in Promoting the Public Good: What Do We Mean by the Public Interest?

One of the barriers to good leadership action is the often held assumption that leaders and followers need to be self-less and motivated by high-minded moral aspirations. When these conditions do not exist, leaders sometimes feel reluctant to undertake action or feel morally unworthy for taking credit of good results that are not the product of virtuous motivations. But we need to disabuse ourselves of this notion and remember the key assumption of the American founders in creating a completely new set of political institutions in 1787: the public interest can be achieved mainly by preserving and promoting the private interests of individuals. In fact, the public interest is the product of such promotion.

The American founders relied on the principle of self-interest to generate confidence in securing liberty over such a large geographic area as the United States. For example, in Federalist No. 10 (Hamilton, Madison, and Jay, 1961/1787–1789), Madison explained how the pursuit of self-interest by various social, economic, religious and political groups would mitigate the danger of the formation of a tyrannous majority. Madison used the principle of self-interest again in explaining the logic of the systems of separation of powers and checks and balances. The system was based on the principle that "the interest of the man" be "connected with the constitutional rights of the place." Hamilton illustrated this kind of thinking in Federalist No. 72, when he defended giving the president unlimited terms of office because it would appeal to a person's love of fame, thus holding in check his petty ambition, vanity, avarice and other less desirable forms of self-interest. As Hamilton argued in the New York Ratifying Convention in a debate with his colleague Melancton Smith, concentrating on the kinds of vices that are most favorable to the prosperity of the state is much more productive than concentrating on virtues (*Elliot's Debates*, II, 257).

Ways of Viewing and Resolving Moral Conflict

How we think about ethical conflicts matters. Some approaches increase our odds of resolving conflicts, at least temporarily, while other approaches escalate conflict. A common method of distinguishing ways of thinking about moral conflicts is summarized in Exhibit 5.7. The interest-based model is the most commonly used approach for resolving conflicts. There is a large body of literature that has developed around what has come to be called "interest-based negotiation" (O'Dowd and Barrett, 2005). In their best-selling book *Getting to Yes*, Fisher, Ury, and Patton (1992) argue that when people define their dispute only in terms of *position*, they often appear to be intractable since one side wants something that the other completely opposes. Conflict resolution facilitators use this simple insight to encourage stakeholders to redefine the situation in terms of the *interests* that underlie their positions. This technique is widely used in labor-management negotiations. It is also widely used to facilitate agreement across sectoral and organizational boundaries, an issue we discuss in much greater detail in Chapters 9 and 11. By focusing on one's *interests* rather than overt positions, resolution-resistant conflicts can become solvable. This is because, in many cases, interests are compatible even when stated positions are not. Clarifying interests helps to identify what part of the issue is important to each party (Whitall, Thomas, Brink, and Bartlett, 2014).

A values- or principle-based conflict is frequently the most difficult to resolve. This is because values are relatively enduring conceptions about the most important principles of life such as what is good or bad and desirable or undesirable (Allen, Wickwar, Clark, Potts, and Snyder, 2009, 23-30). These principles do not change much over time. As a result, they are so closely identified with one's sense of moral identity that it is hard to compromise without feeling that you have given away part of who you are. Much of the history of human civilization is a history of warring ways of life where armed conflict becomes the only way of settling moral differences. That was why the American founders argued so hard for keeping government out of the business of regulating religion and private

Exhibit 5.7 Types of Ethical Conflict

	Interest-Based	*Principle-Based*	*Integrity-Based*
Source of Conflict	Conflicting interests	Conflicting values	Personal sense of identity
Strategy for resolution	Bargaining and negotiation	Agreement with opposing values	Ability to live with the process and outcome
Degree of change over time	Medium–high, depending on how interests get defined.	Low, since values tend to remain consistent over time	Medium–high, depending on the extent to which experience adds new information that is incorporated into one's personal sense of identity
Advantages	Facilitates compromise	Makes values difference and goals very clear	Facilitates agreements while preserving personal moral values
Disadvantages	Pragmatic process and outcomes that obscure value differences	Makes compromise and negotiation difficult	Doesn't provide an external standard by which those outside the process can judge the ethical outcome

moral beliefs. The primary business of government, they argued, is to regulate conflicting interests. Of course the distinction between interests and values is not always a self-evident or bright-line distinction, thus requiring leaders to be knowledgeable agents of conflict management. Citizens, religious groups and morally centered advocacy groups will always lobby for government assistance in protecting and expanding the reach of their moral view of the world. One of the important lessons of the American governing tradition is the need for government leaders to be cautious about how they use their discretion as an instrument of moral agency. They need always to ask where and how they are using their discretion to maintain the appropriate boundaries between private beliefs and public purposes. This is illustrated by the librarian in the Master Case for this section. She wonders whether her personal moral beliefs are an appropriate reason to test the adequacy of existing library policies regarding internet filtering. This kind of self-awareness of boundary issues is the starting point for ethical competence in public service.

The third way of viewing the resolution of ethical conflict in Exhibit 5.7 is called the integrity-based approach. As the word integrity suggests, emphasis is placed on preserving one's sense of moral wholeness rather than a set of principles that stand independently and outside of ourselves (Benjamin, 1990; Dobel, 2002; Fairholm, 2013, especially his discussion of "whole soul" leadership). An example of the integrity-based approach is frequently seen during a collective family decision to end life support for a loved one. There is often some factual uncertainty; there is moral ambiguity; members of the family may be in conflict over what can and should be done; and the decision can't be put off forever. In such situations, it is common for the differences among the parties to be dealt with through a dialogical process, the outcome of which is that everyone can live with the final result even though it is not something they would have done if left on their own. The moral test for the final decision is whether each of the participants can live with it, that is, the decision does not leave anyone feeling they have compromised their integrity, the overall moral sense of who they are as an ethical agent.

The integrity-based view of ethical compromise is a developmental- and experience-centered approach which assumes that humans are moral works of progress and participate in a larger moral community (Brooks, 2012). We discover what exactly our values and principles mean when we have to make practical decisions. The complexity and ambiguity of particular decision settings adds nuance to our moral competence and capacity. It is a view that encourages moderation and temperance, which are particularly important qualities for leaders working within the American rule-of-law context. But the integrity-based approach has some obvious shortcomings. Since the standards for knowing what is morally acceptable are held internally, individuals and groups can become morally siloed. This is what happened to Albert Speer as Minister of

Armaments and War Production in the Third Reich. By all accounts, Speer was the model of a good "Theory Y" manager. He created a high-performing organization culture by relying on team work, continuous quality improvement and valuing the opinion of employees. He developed a strong sense of ownership by everyone in the organization (Singer and Wooton, 1976). When the war ended, Speer expressed no remorse for what he did. He possessed a high level of integrity, as probably did most every one of his employees. What was missing was moral self-reflection and discourse on the moral ends of their actions.

The Importance of Space for Moral Reflection and Dialogue Among a Diversity of Views

There is an important lesson to be drawn from the story of Albert Speer. The conditions for creating a high-performing organization may not be the same as the conditions for creating an ethically aware and ethically competent organization (Adams and Balfour, 2004; O'Leary, 2006). There are plenty of examples of the adverse consequences of "group think" and the doppelganger effect in organizations where everyone marches over the moral cliff together like lemmings jumping into the deep (see the Tuskegee syphilis experiments, Jones, 1993; the Cuban Missile Crisis, Allison, 1971; the Challenger space shuttle accident, U.S. NASA, 2003; and the torture of prisoners at Abu Graib, Hersh, 2004). Most of the participants in these events believed they were acting with integrity. But feeling a sense of integrity about what you do is not enough. One needs external standards and critical perspectives to foster a constant process of moral self-reflection. These conditions become difficult if one operates in a homogeneous and morally tepid or sterile environment where there is no moral discourse. Albert Speer came to realize the moral evil of what he did only at the end of his 20-year imprisonment in Spandau as he was prompted by his reading and self-reflection to confront the moral standing of his actions as a brilliant administrator. He observed, that,

> in the isolation of imprisonment, I learned to look inside myself to study my own weaknesses and strengths and for the first time in my life, I had the leisure and opportunity to read and absorb works of philosophy and theology.
>
> Norden (1971, 202)

Conclusion: Putting Our Ethical Thinking into Practice

We end this chapter with an example of integrating the materials we have covered in the previous sections into a personal ethical framework to guide leadership action. Exhibit 5.8 presents an administrator's personal journey from just seeing ethics as being a good person to seeing public service ethics as entirely something else and even at times in conflict with her personal ethics. The journey is also a story about the development of prudential judgment, which is at the very heart of being an ethically competent public servant. Prudence, as we will argue in Chapter 12, is a moral virtue, and, like the acquisition of all other virtues, it requires practice. Both space and moral conflict are necessary preconditions for becoming an increasingly competent moral agent of the public good.

Exhibit 5.8 Public Service Ethics and Personal Ethics: How I Came to Know the Difference, by Debbie Ellis

At the time of writing this reflection, I was serving as a program manager for Parent Information Resource Centers (PIRCs). The U.S. Department of Education created the first PIRCs in 1995 to provide parents, schools and organizations with the training, information and technical support needed to understand how children develop and what they need to succeed in school. The program was founded on the belief that family engagement is critical to increased student success, reduced drop-outs rates, increased college attendance, decreased achievement gap and increased positives outcomes for children. While federal funding for the PIRC program ended in 2012, I am working to keep the program intact through a combination of state, local, nonprofit and fee-for-service funding alternatives.

This is a story of my personal journey as a public servant from viewing ethics as just "being a good person" to now viewing my ethical responsibilities as a matter of personal and public morality in which I must balance democracy with authority (Meyer, 1975), and civic engagement with our strong spirit of individualism (Lane, 1988). This journey has come half-way through my public service career and is the result of lots of self-reflection promoted by discussions with my Executive MPA colleagues and the readings in the previous sections of this book.

When I first began thinking about administrative ethics and values, I relied on my own internal definition and understanding of morals. Like many in America, my viewpoint was based on my home and religious upbringing, which in my case was an extremely rigid Pentecostal heritage founded on a narrow set of moral principles. I believed I was using my own personal standards of ethics to help me determine what was appropriate and acceptable in my public role. Because these moral standards were so deeply engrained (and so "black and white"), I thought my considerations of ethical principles as applied to my work were almost automatic and unintentional. Upon further reflection, I began to realize that the standards and criteria which I used for guiding my judgment as a public servant were much more complex and maybe not even the same at times. For example, I noticed that my frustration with the performance of some of my co-workers was not always the result of a violation of my personal ethical views of "hard work, honesty, integrity, civility, etc.," but because they did not show proper respect for basic demo- cratic values and legal principles, such as protection of client rights, transparency, citizen engagement and a commitment to equitable processes for resolving client grievances. It was not simply a matter of getting my fellow colleagues to become "nicer human beings." I gradually came to appreciate that my ethical framework encom- passed more than just the personal ethics that were the result of my upbringing. They encompassed my stewardship responsibility for basic constitutional and democratic values. This discovery posed two challenges to my new-found locus of administrative responsi- bility. First, how do I square the conflict between the values taught as part of my upbringing and the values I now hold as a public servant? Second, how do I become better as an ethical public servant?

Administrative Ethics: Personal Integrity and Public Responsibility

My ethical framework is founded on both my personal morals and the commitment I have to the common good. Fortunately for me these two sets of values are not frequent in conflict. But what happens when that is not the case? How do I resolve the conflict? For example, from a young age, I was told how to act, what to say and what to think and believe—creating for me a much narrower meaning of morals and ethics which took the form of negative "thou shall nots," and Puritanical or Victorian "no-nos" (Diamond, 1977). From the point of view of my family who hold to the strict religious values of their upbringing, I am probably viewed as a moral chameleon—anxious to accommodate others, "temperamentally indisposed to moral controversy and disagree- ment ... [and] quick to modify or abandon previously avowed principles in order to placate others" (Benjamin, 1990, 47). The work of Martin Benjamin (1990) has played a significant role in helping me make sense out of the person I have become and to reduce the conflict between my personal ethical values and my moral values as a public servant.

Benjamin argues that there are three approaches to resolving ethical conflicts: an interest-based approach, a principle-based approach and an integrity-based approach. With the interest- based approach, negotiation and compromise are viewed as an ethically good thing. This is because negotiation and compromise are seen as part of the process of producing a shared common good, which stands on higher ground than the separate interests of the parties. This view contrasts with the principle-based approach, which organizes life around "a single most important goal to which all others are subordinate" (Rawls quoted in Benjamin, 1990, 21). The principle-based approach is common among those who use their religious beliefs to determine which values, principles, feelings and intuitions are given serious consideration, while paying little or no attention to competing goals. This is the view that was part of my upbringing. To my family, compromising on any concepts within their single dominant end constitutes a betrayal to themselves and their God.

I have found Benjamin's integrity-based approach helpful in understanding how it is possible to alter one's ethical views while at the same time holding true to a core of ethical, personal and religious beliefs and values that remain with you throughout life. The integrity approach to ethics assumes that our moral beliefs and values are altered by our experience. With each new experience comes a more nuanced understanding of the ethical complexity of a given situation that requires action. Benjamin gives an example of family members and health care specialists standing around a patient who is on life support with no medical data that supports recovery. When someone who is on principle opposed to the withdrawal of life support decides to join in a group decision to withdraw life support, has the individual sold their soul? A principle-based approach would argue yes, while the integrity-based approach would simply ask whether one's integrity remains intact. Integrity is about the moral wholeness of a person at any given point in time, even when this wholeness may be composed of conflicting values that take on urgency at different points in time and where the wholeness itself is composed of different parts in a different order over the course ones life. It is similar to someone believing in the commandment that "thou shall not kill," but taking another person's life to save a loved one or participating in the medically assisted suicide of a love one. These experiences, while life changing, do not automatically alter ones moral integrity, although they may not square with ones first principles.

Over time, I have learned that, because of my sense of civic responsibility, my strong commitment to equity, and my passion for the work I do and the people I serve, I have reframed the meaning of my previous values to include my values as a public servant. I still have most of the same basic moral values and character traits that my family espouses (integrity, honesty, trust-worthiness, respect, responsibility, fairness, caring, etc.), but reframing has enabled me incorporate a more diverse array of values that are essential to the achievement of the common good. In doing so, I would argue that my integrity has remained relatively unchanged over my life course. What is critical to an integrity-based view of ethics is the commitment to a constant process of introspection in which we re-examine our personal moral code and the way in which it can be more closely aligned with the larger stewardship values that are integral to our public service roles.

Standards of Public Morality: How Do I Become a More Ethical Public Servant?

Given my integrity-based view of ethics and my commitment to introspection, I believe that we become better in our ethical role as public servants in the same way we become better as moral human beings: it requires practice, not simply thinking morally virtuous thoughts. For me, having a catechism of public values of the kind provided in the previous section of this text (i.e., efficiency, effectiveness, responsiveness, protecting rights, honoring civic engagement) serves as a good daily test of whether we are doing all that we can to become morally better public servants. That is why I find it useful to benchmark my work against what I have come to call "The Ten Public Service Commandments.. This exercise has been especially important to me in my transitional role of trying to secure the future of my PIRC program by finding alternative sources to the federal funding that has now come to an end.

1 **Constitutional Sovereignty.** Throughout the process of negotiations regarding the future of the PIRCs, the program directors had to be fully aware of their role as institutional stewards. As a large group, we informed citizens and state officials of the impact of our work and of the proposed changes in legislation—being ever mindful of not crossing the bounds of lobbying for our own efforts. We had to put in place checks and balances to ensure that no government funds were used in any of the efforts to inform the public. Because of our informational efforts, current legislation is still in place that authorizes PIRCs.
2 **Subordination and Autonomy.** The grant program under which I operated my program was created by a deliberately ambiguous law, which kept us subordinate but also allowed us considerable autonomy. The law was deliberately created this way, in part, as a response to too much government (a.k.

a. the "King George Problem") with the goal of giving more flexibility and control at the state level. My grant had four main goals; two of which were fairly specific as to the actions required to carry them out and two were quite vague. This discretionary authority allowed us to use a constitutive approach (see Chapters 1 and 5) when developing our activities. Based on feedback from clientele during our training workshops, feedback from partner organizations during meetings, and evaluation reports and studies across the state we could adjust our activities to gain trust and legitimacy with our community partners.

3 **Representation.** Due to the exponentially growing population of Latinos, when we first wrote the grant we focused on increased services for Spanish-speaking families. In addition to providing them with services, we hired a staff member who was a Spanish-speaking parent of children who had previously been educated in Mexico. As part of our efforts to retain funding for the PIRCS, citizen groups were informed of the proposed changes to elementary and secondary education policy. They then took their opinions to their state representatives to voice their desire for continued services. In addition, we continue to work with parents (as outlined below) in additional empowerment efforts to assist them in having a voice on the micro level (their own child's classroom) to the macro level (state and federal government).

4 **Civic Engagement and Participation.** At our micro level of service provision, we are actively engaged in citizen participation. In fact, our main mission is getting families more engaged in their child's education in ways that lead to school and lifelong success. To achieve this mission we must sometimes bypass the "experts" and empower family members to be the driving force behind parental education and advocacy efforts. In order to nurture this type of civic engagement, we have collaborated with parent groups to design and develop their own packages of training materials that they will use with other families in order to understand the school system and to become active participants in the educational processes. For one group, we told them we were just the "administrative conduits" who were taking their words and ideas and putting them into a form that could be used across their district and the state.

At the macro level, we are assisting families and parent-serving organizations to be more engaged in educational policy. Since there is no longer any federal funding or federal/state mandates regarding family engagement, we are working with partner organizations to develop policy guidelines for family engagement that we will propose first to state officials and then to our federal legislators. We have also drafted language regarding family engagement that has been delivered to the state's Education Investment Board in hopes of enhancing their vision of family engagement for the state's public schools. In addition to policy formation, we are using this collaborative effort to map the services currently being provided to the families within the state, determine the gaps in services or service areas, and assess the most effective way to meet the needs of students and their families.

5 **Effective Governance.** The goals of the PIRC are ones of facilitation, service provision and education. For facilitation, we coordinate school–family partnerships activities among agencies and organizations to ensure that families and schools are served statewide. This facilitation takes place in many of the civic engagement activities outlined above. Our educational services include personal, one-on-one technical assistance activities carried out with families or educators to large-scale statewide conferences. We generally tailor our educational ventures to the specific needs of the audience and try to engage in long-term educational processes versus the single workshop in order to build sustainable change. Education is one of our services, as well as guidance regarding compliance issues, product development and technical assistance.

6 **Responsiveness.** In order to meet the needs of the entire state, we structured our services to provide easy access and efficient response to request for services. For individuals outside the Metro area, we provided services online so that they could access our products or access technical assistance through email/text communications. In addition, we added a toll-free telephone number that was monitored by individuals who spoke English and Spanish. We also created a response system that required us to return a phone call or email within 24 hours of its receipt (during business hours). So that more parents could attend our training sessions and our annual conference, we kept our costs low, provided translation, educational stipends and a range of other services at no charge. In order to maintain this level of responsiveness in the future, we have incorporated these provisions as a basic part of our proposed service model.

7 **Due Process and the Rule of Law.** Within our grant obligations there was a stipulation that we be governed by a Board
of Directors made up of a diverse representation of parents
and parent-serving organizations across the state. The Board
provides oversight of our activities to ensure compliance with
our legal and due process requirements.

8 **Equity.** Equity was a major consideration within all our
activities. As stated earlier, we proposed the grant to meet
the needs of the Latino families (and families with limited
incomes) in the state. We knew that educational equity issues
were a major focus of education reform. The No Child Left
Behind act specifically called for the accountability of schools
and districts in their services to, and outcomes for, low-
income and minority children. In order to achieve both fairness in procedures and in results, the families of these children
were targeted (by the federal grant-makers) in order to assist
them in gaining the information and knowledge that the
parents of higher achieving students already possessed. But,
in addition to these targeted services, universal services were
made available to all families in the state.

9 **Accountability and Open Government.** As a grant-funded
organization, we were subject to multiple performance
reviews and legislative oversight. In addition, we were
accountable to the citizens of the state and responsible for
achieving the funds and grant goals supported by our funding. Also, considering our options for future funding, I am
very mindful of the impact of the service fees that partner
organizations are considering for their administrative services. I take seriously my responsibility to be a good steward of the money we receive so that our clientele can enjoy
best services at the most reasonable costs.

10 **Protection of Rights.** As I mentioned in point 8, protection of
rights is a major consideration in all our activities. We proposed the grant to meet the needs of the Latino families and
families with limited incomes, especially to build their capacity to fully benefit from federal programs. Education, in and
of itself, is a major component in the attainment of our other
constitutional rights of freedom, equity and property. Without
education (and the knowledge it provides), one is not fully
able to participate in and secure these rights.

As I continue my efforts to transition the PIRC program to some
kind of alternative funding, all kinds of ethical issues are at the
forefront of my concern. From a personal point of view, I have a

great passion and great sense of civic responsibility in advocating for the type of family engagement that increases the likelihood that children will be successful in life and school. I started with the narrow view that was primarily focused on maximizing service to a target population in the most efficient and effective manner possible. But now I see my role as a steward of democratic governance. With this shift in focus I now am more concerned about how I can leverage all of the assets from the private, nonprofit and for-profit sectors to achieve the larger common good of the polity. The notion of polity leadership developed in Chapter 4 has transformed the ethical meaning and purpose of my public service role as an administrator. I have come to appreciate the importance of constant reflection on the moral purposes of my work. Without such reflection one can quickly succumb to the plight of Albert Speer, a remarkably gifted administrator who ran the Ministry of Armaments and War for Hitler with great efficiency and productivity, who was sentenced to a life in prison for war crimes.

> [I]n the isolation of imprisonment, I learned to look inside myself to study my own weaknesses and strengths and for the first time in my life, I had the leisure and opportunity to read and absorb works of philosophy and theology.
>
> Norden (1971, 202)

The lesson for me from the story of Albert Speer is that as administrators we need to constantly subject the ends we serve to the same kind of rigorous questioning that we apply to the means we use to carry out our work.

Notes

1 For a good account of the sequence of events that resulted in a change in the American Psychological Assoication standards see Risen (2015).
2 For an excellent example of the use of this legislative strategy and the consequences, see Blumenthal (1969). Blumenthal's discussion of the maximum feasible participation requirements built into many of the antipoverty programs put in place during the Johnson administration shows how deliberately fuzzy language ends up in legislation, which results in extensive law suits throughout the United States.
3 It is important to remember in our discussion of discretion in this and the following section that we are viewing it from an inside perspective, i.e., from the view of the person who has been delegated discretion by the legislative process. Our goal is to assist administrative leaders in understanding the political dynamics that explain the amount and types of discretion they hold.

This contrasts with Nye's discussion of discretion, which is viewed from the outside perspective of citizens and followers. Nye reminds us that in viewing the exercise of discretion from the outside as leaders and followers, we are looking at the performance of public leaders in terms of: 1) how well intentioned they are; 2) how well they adhere to appropriate public processes and 3) how well they achieve good results (Nye, 2008, 112).

4 The material for this section has been adopted from previous work published in Morgan et al. (2013/2008), Chapter 4, 75–80.

5 The Antifederalists were a loosely coupled group of opponents of the newly proposed constitution of 1787. They favored small and weak government with lots of oversight by yeoman farmers who were thought to be more vigilant, frugal and trustworthy than members of the commercial class. For the best account of their beliefs and contributions to the America founding, see Herbert Storing (1981a, 1981b).

6 Thinking in Time

Using Our Institutional Legacies to Improve the Public Good[1]

Thinking institutionally is nothing dramatic, new or flashy. It is more like revisiting a forgotten old home place and experiencing a recognition—a bringing to mind again—of valuable things that only appear to have been forgotten ... [I]t pushes a person to go beyond being instrumentally rational—that is simply making intelligent choices regarding means to some arbitrary and self-validating goals we happen to have chosen simply to please ourselves. It calls on substantive rationality regarding intelligent choices about the ends of action worth choosing.

Hugh Heclo (2008, 186–87)

[C]hanges of the moment commonly enfold the history of the past like an oyster enfolding the speck of sand that becomes the pearl, or the tree growing over the broken limb or fire scar. In each case, history is etched into what becomes the future. If government and public administrators are expected to take a leadership role in reconsidering the role responsibilities of the various actors in our political economy in coproducing the public good, it is important that the agents of change have a deep and active understanding of the institutional traditions and history of values that can provide a stable grounding to guide changes in the delivery of public services at our local levels of government.

Morgan, Shinn, and Cook (2014, 321)

Public service leadership opportunities are significantly shaped by our ability to think and act institutionally. By "institutionally," we do not simply mean the kinds of polity knowledge discussed in Chapters 4 and 5: knowledge of the changing boundaries across sectors of our political economy, knowledge of our political structures and processes, knowledge of the role and function of the various actors in the political economy, and knowledge of the moral purposes of our system of limited government. Surely, this knowledge requires an understanding of institutions, but it is not necessarily knowledge that is informed by the stream of history, or what we call "thinking in time." Our various social, economic and political institutions get transformed by the processes of history, much like the treasured axe that belonged to our great-grandfather, but whose handle and head have been replaced three times through intergenerational use. We still regard the axe with institutional reverence even though it is not the same axe used by our forbearers. Thinking institutionally enables us to discover the values that are the foundation of taken-for-granted leadership practices that provide leaders with the ability to connect the past to the future and that give these practices legitimacy through time.

While institutions are often leaders' best friends, they are also at times their worst enemy. Institutions are responsible for embedded practices of racism, sexism and other forms of exclusion, marginalization and oppression that undermine the public good. Institutions constrain leadership possibilities and initiatives. Knowing the downside of institutions is an important first step in the process of transforming our institutions into morally enduring objects of respect. But to make these transformations as agents of change from the inside requires that we know this history, we have an understanding of the "bright side" of this history, and that we have some practice in using the "bright side" to change the "dark side." This can be done only if our institutional traditions are sufficiently rich, diverse and flexible enough to provide us with moral correctives. We believe the American public service tradition meets this test.[2] Our purpose in this chapter is to arm you with this rich treasure-trove of knowledge so that you can make our governing institutions better.

For purposes of our review, we rely on the conventional categories that are frequently used in describing historical periods relevant to the development of American public service: Jacksonian, Populist, Progressive and New Deal (see Van Riper, 1958; White, 1958, 1951; Morgan, Green, Shinn, and Robinson, 2013, 97–118).[3] Our review builds from our discussion in Chapter 5 and uses the following core value conflicts as the framework for our discussion:

- The role of government in relationship to the market economy and civil society;
- The role of the central government and Native American tribes in relationship to state and local governments;
- The trade-off of efficiency, effectiveness, protecting rights, being responsive and promoting and strengthening civic engagement;
- The type and kind of public service leadership needed to promote the common good.

Each of the above categories provide us with various polity leadership opportunities. In these roles, however seemingly small and invisible, we carry responsibility for managing the relationship of government to the market economy and civil society. We carry responsibility for the role relationship between the central government and state and local governments. We use our discretion to balance competing public values, giving priority to some over others. In carrying out these roles we draw from a variety of public service leadership models to undertake this work. In the closing section of this chapter we summarize these leadership models that have become a part of our institutional legacy of public service.

Jacksonian Democracy (1829–1869): Servant Leadership, Ordinary Virtue and Representative Bureaucracy, Limited Government and the Voluntary State

Andrew Jackson's presidency was the product of growing resentment by an expanding western frontier opposed to financial and governmental control by a perceived class of eastern wealthy oligarchs. President Jackson used his power to elevate the status and control of ordinary citizens. He abolished the National Bank that Alexander Hamilton had fought so hard to create. He introduced rotation in office, later known as the "spoils system;" and he exercised popular leadership over a mass political party movement. Perhaps Jackson's most unique contribution in strengthening the executive branch was the belief that energetic use of executive authority should be exercised in the name of the people themselves. He believed the people were best served by a president who vigilantly used the power of the office to limit government. This fore-shadows the modern-day presidencies of Ronald Reagan, George W. Bush and Donald Trump who claimed to be the servants of the "silent majority." Carried to its extreme, it is an argument that justifies making the bureaucracy "representative."

Limited Government and the Voluntary State

Jackson used the vigorous exercise of his executive leadership to check "bigness" in all its forms, both within government as well as in the private sector. During his second term in office, Jackson took on "bigness" at the national level by vetoing the renewal of the charter of the National Bank, first established in 1816 to bring safer, uniform standards and predictability to banking throughout the nation. Jackson viewed these arguments as a subterfuge that undermined state and local banks. He extended his attack on "bigness" to the private sector by issuing the Specie Circular in July 1836, requiring payment in gold or silver for the purchase of all public lands. This measure contributed to a run on banks by depositors who wished to convert their paper bank notes into gold or silver. Bank failures began in the West and spread quickly to the East. By the spring of 1837, the entire country was gripped by a financial panic (Temin, 1969). Jackson, nevertheless, remained steadfast in his belief that unshackled business competition was "the best guaranty of the prosperity of the country ... If the door is thrown open to every competent man, the public wants will be attended to" (quoted in White, 1958, 448).

Jacksonian democracy provides public service leaders with a vision and a strategy for securing the economic well-being of their community and the larger nation state. Jacksonian democracy established a new and clearer standard regarding the separation between the public sector, the private market economy and the voluntary sector. For Jackson, the private market economy constituted the engine of progress, with government playing the limited role of removing barriers to competition. This meant using the power of government to remove the monopolistic advantages of inherited wealth and corporate concentrations of power. In addition to this constraining role, Jackson believed government should encourage the disposal and settlement of public lands, much of which were taken from Native Americans and mixed-blood Hispanics. Securing the frontier for expansion and development formed part of Jackson's vision of making America a land of opportunity for the hard-working, ordinary citizens who could be trusted to do the right thing. The rapid growth of voluntary associations between 1820 and 1840 added fuel to the entrepreneurial spirit of the ordinary man and gave real meaning to the voluntary sector as a vital political force.

The Jacksonian legacy left us with two countervailing leadership propensities. One emphasized the subordination of public servants to a popularly elected chief executive who embodied the will of the people. The other emphasized a representative bureaucracy that directly reflected the will and energy of the people throughout all levels of the governing process. The representative bureaucracy message to public servants was an empowering one: "You shouldn't wait to be given executive direction from above. Interpretations of the public will at higher levels of government may be different, but no better, than the interpretation from where you sit." But this message stood in sharp tension with the first message: "As President, I am in charge of the entire executive branch of government. Don't act until I tell you what, when and how."

Servant Leadership: Who Is Accountable to Whom?

Jackson was the first president to articulate the novel theory that the president was a direct representative of the people, rather than an agent of a larger constitutional order. He was the first president to recommend the abolition of the electoral college, arguing in his first annual message to Congress that "as few impediments as possible should exist to the free operation of the public will" (Richardson, 1899, II, 448). He returned to this view in his famous protest message to the Senate, justifying his right to dismiss William Duane, secretary of the Treasury, for his refusal to remove deposits from the U.S. Bank.[4] Jackson claimed that by electing him president, the people had conferred upon him "the entire executive power" of government (Richardson, 1899, II, 85). Carried to its logical conclusion, this view would turn executive subordinates into mere ministerial agents of the president without independent accountability to either the Constitution, or to the legislative and judicial branches of government. This principle resurfaced in the presidency of George W. Bush, who developed a unitary theory of the chief executive that entitles the president to exclusive authority over administrative agencies, even when it is contrary to the expressed will of the legislative branch (Cooper, 2005). This view significantly expands the purpose of an energetic executive beyond the original goal of ensuring more competent governance; it also creates potential tensions between administrative agencies and the legislative branch, which has oversight and funding responsibilities. The lesson for leading from where you sit is the need to be clear about your agential role. When you initiate leadership are you doing so because you are representing the public will, fulfilling your constitutional obligations, serving as the spokesperson for efficiency and effectiveness, meeting the policy goals established by the legislature, carrying out your instrumental role within a chain of command, or some combination of the above?

Ordinary Virtue through Rotation in Office: Representative Bureaucracy or the "Spoils System?"

President Jackson converted Antifederalist and Jeffersonian suspicions about long-term government service into an operating principle called rotation in office. The rule of frequent rotation of government officials was premised on a two-pronged belief that, over time, power tends to corrupt, and that everyone possesses the necessary qualities to rule (Richardson, 1899, II, 448). Jackson argued that public employees needed a constant reminder that office is not a species of property, but an instrument created solely for the service of the people. He believed that too much time in office allows individuals to divert government from its legitimate ends and make it an engine for the support of the few at the expense of the many. We need not worry about frequent personnel changes, since "the duties of all public offices are, or at least admit to being made, so plain and simple that men of intelligence may readily qualify themselves for their performance" (Richardson, 1899, II: 448–49). Jackson wished to apply the principle of rotation in office throughout all levels of public service, from the very top to the very bottom. The downside of Jackson's philosophy is that it resulted in the creation of a system that rewarded individuals for their loyalty to party platform and officials, not their competence for public service. It also reduced predictability and continuity in administrative practice. Over time the abuses of this system and the rise of party boss systems in the large cities resulted in a major reform movement that became part of the populist agenda.

Populist Reform (1869–1910): Neutral Competence and the Rise of the Regulatory State

The Civil War ended the debate over slavery and cast dark shadows over the claimed right of states to independent sovereign authority. Another important outcome was that out of the war emerged a unifying transformation of Hamilton's vision of a large and feverish commercial republic. Rather than being organized around the centralized power of a national government, this unifying transformation was organized around private wealth and power. The success of the Civil War resulted less from newfound administrative competence at the center, and more from the military, logistical and financial support offered by private organizations like the United States Sanitary Commission, which took responsibility for providing medical care to the Union Army. This private organization in the 1860s was explicitly created to provide a public good, which today would likely be undertaken by nonprofit organizations.

> Institutionally, evangelical enterprises of the antebellum period provided the bureaucratic organizational models for the mobiliza-tion as well as the expertise and personality types necessary for the effective operation of these administrative hierarchies. The victory of the Union was seen both by its organizers and by the significant elements of the general public as a legitimation of the claims of the organized private sector ... The Jacksonian persuasion, with its prejudices against private power and the institutions and elites associated with it, was on the defensive in the face of a triumphant assertion of political nationality that identified itself with private wealth and power.
>
> Hall (1992, 36)

The unifying national vision created in the aftermath of the Civil War grew rapidly in the following decades as a result of economic develop-ment, which created an increasingly integrated and interdependent national economy. Manufacturing investment ballooned from $2.7 bil-lion in 1879 to $8.2 billion in 1899. During this period the value of manufactured products rose from $3.8 billion to $11 billion in constant dollars. The nation had just 23 miles of railroad track in 1830; by 1890, it had 208,152 miles. The age of high-volume production drew workers to the cities. In 1870, less than 8 percent of America's workers were engaged in manufacturing, while only one out of five Americans lived in cities larger than 8,000. By 1910, almost a third of the population worked in manufacturing, and half the population lived in cities. Immigration skyrocketed during this period. Almost half the population of Ireland left for the United States. By the 1870s, 280,000 immigrants arrived annually, and this number rose to more than a million by the turn of the century.[5] The migration to major cities resulted in the development of large political machines and rampant corruption. It is often said that New York's Tammany Hall, under its notorious boss, William Marcy Tweed, provided more services to the poor than any city government before it, although a large share of the money went into Tweed's own pockets. One of Tammany Hall's loyal lieutenants, George Washington Plunkitt, made famous the distinction between honest and dishonest graft. The distinction rested on serving one's parochial interests versus serving the good of the larger community.

> Everybody is talkin' these days about Tammany men growin' rich on graft, but nobody thinks of drawin' the distinction between honest graft and dishonest graft ... I'm getting' richer every day, but I've not gone in for dishonest graft—blackmailin' gamblers, saloon keepers, disorderly people, etc.—and neither has any of the men who have made big fortunes in politics ... I might sum up the whole thing up by sayin': "I seen my opportunities and I took 'em."
>
> Just let me explain by examples. My party's in power in the city, and it's goin' to undertake a lot of public improvements. Well, I'm tipped off, say, that they're going to lay out a new park at a certain place ... I go to that place and I buy up all the land I can in the neighborhood. Then the board of this or that makes its plan public and there is a rush to get my land, which nobody cared particular for before. Ain't it perfectly honest to charge a good price and make a profit on my investment and foresight? Of course it is. Well that's honest graft ... I made my pile in politics, but, I served the organization and got more big improvements for New York City than any other livin' man. And I never monkeyed with the penal code.
>
> Quoted in Riordon (1963, 3, 29)

Plunkitt's distinction between honest and dishonest graft raised basic questions about the nature of enlightened self-interest and about what kinds of correctives one should apply to the public service to remove the abuses and excesses of the system. Is the best corrective to remove all temptations to the passions and interests of public service officials? Or is it better to turn temptation and self-serving interests to more public-serving ends? Or do we recruit individuals to public service who have the "fitness of character" to resist whatever temptations may come their way? As corruption began to infiltrate the highest levels of government, reformers needed a way to stem the tide. During Ulysses S. Grant's administration (1869–1877), the president and his cabinet were implicated in a half-dozen major scandals that included Crédit Mobilier, the Gold Conspiracy, the Whiskey Ring, the Indian Ring and the Salary Grab.[6] This animated public ire and focused attention on the problem. When a disaffected office-seeker assassinated President James Garfield in 1881, it provided the spark for reformers to mobilize action against the spoils system.

The Role of Public Servants and the Principle of Neutral Competence

After winning the moral battle over slavery, reformers turned their attention to the abuses of the Jacksonian spoils system and the industrial excesses of the Gilded Age. They sought, in the words of James Stever, to throw the rascals out "by muckraking and otherwise arousing the public to vote." Then they would fill offices with honest, diligent, and educated "moral" men. They assumed that these "good candidates would implement good policies" (Stever, 1988, 30).

The passage of the Pendleton Act of 1883 and the creation of a civil service merit system institutionalized the best thinking of the day about how to correct the abuses of the spoils system. The goal was to temper greed and to restore moral integrity to public service by isolating it from undue political influence. Career administrators would be appointed and promoted on the basis of written qualifications to perform the job, not on the basis of friendship or partisan political loyalty. The Pendleton Act established the modern civil service system for the federal government and served as the template for replicating the system in all 50 states and most local jurisdictions.

The standard of neutral competence became a lasting legacy of Populist reform for public administration and the most important legacy carried forward into modern public service. The commitment to protect the neutral competence of public servants takes a variety of modern forms, including conflict of interest legislation, financial disclosure laws, open government requirements and various Hatch Act regulations (prohibiting public employees from engaging in partisan political activity) at the state and local levels of government (Morgan and Rohr, 1986; Rohr, 1981).

The Beginnings of the Regulatory State: Rethinking the Balance between the Public, Nonprofit, Special District and Private Sectors

The post-Civil War period is commonly known as the Gilded Age, a period of wealth accumulation by some of America's great families, many of whom became famous for their philanthropy and public service. Examples include Andrew Carnegie, who made his money in steel production; Edward H. Harriman, who accumulated a fortune building railroads; John D. Rockefeller, who became rich drilling for oil; Cornelius Vanderbilt, who earned his wealth in transportation systems; and J.P. Morgan, who became famous for banking. The discovery of gold, silver and oil, the rapid expansion of transportation, the large influx of immigrants for cheap labor, and the increased demand for goods and services created large concentrations of wealth. This accumulation of money, power and influence was justified by the doctrine of "survival of the fittest." Similar to Charles Darwin's argument in *The Origin of the Species* (1859), Herbert Spencer believed that freedom of individuals in the social sphere to pursue their own interests, like the natural selection of the species in the physical world, resulted in the development of superior talents. Competition, not cooperation, produced these superior talents, and they became the engines for innovation, creativity and social progress. Government intervention should be kept to a minimum in social and political life in order to reap the full advantages of "social Darwinism" or survival of the fittest (Spencer, 1994).

There were two countervailing influences on the raw application of the survival of the fittest doctrine, both of which tempered its potential for excess. First, people of wealth were assumed to have a moral obligation to the poor and less fortunate. Second, Spencer's argument assumed that government had an important role to play in ensuring that the rules of market competition were fair and did not unduly corrupt the operations of government.

In *The Gospel of Wealth and Other Timely Essays* (1962/1889), Andrew Carnegie argued that all personal wealth beyond that required to supply the needs of one's family should be regarded as a trust fund to be administered for the benefit of the community. It must be administered wisely to deal with the causes of misfortune, rather than simply the effects. Carnegie argued that:

> one of the serious obstacles to the improvement of our race is indiscriminate charity. It were better for mankind that the millions of rich were thrown into the sea than so spent as to encourage the slothful, the drunken, the unworthy. Of every thousand dollars spent in so-called charity today, it is probable that nine hundred and fifty dollars is unwisely spent—so spent, indeed, as to produce the very evils which it hopes to mitigate or cure ... The best means of benefiting the community is to place within its reach the ladders upon which the aspiring can rise—libraries, parks, and means of recreation, by which men are helped in body and mind; works of art, certain to give pleasure and improve the public taste; and public institutions of various kinds, which will improve the general condition of the people; in this manner returning their surplus wealth to the mass of their fellows in the forms best calculated to do them lasting good.
>
> Carnegie (1962, 26–27)

Carnegie followed his own advice and became both the wealthiest and most generous philanthropist of his day. His doctrine was radical, primarily because he called for the use of private wealth to attack the conditions of misfortune and dependency, rather than to provide charity for individuals. The use of private wealth for public purposes was based on Carnegie's view that individuals were part of a larger community—a joint venture, much like a private corporation. While the doctrine of survival of the fittest meant hierarchy and unequal distribution of talents, it was a hierarchy of mutual interdependence, whether in a private corporation or in a community of fellow citizens. This principle of mutual interdependence was reflected in the growing role that the nonprofit sector played in promoting the public good. Its importance to government was officially codified in the Tariff Act of 1894, when Congress granted tax exemption status to nonprofit charitable, religious, educational and fraternal associations.

The close symbiotic relationship between private wealth and public power was reflected through all dimensions of the American political economy during the latter half of the 19th century. For example, railroads became vital to the nation's economy. In many regions of the United States, a single company enjoyed a monopoly of rail transportation, which enabled the railroads to adopt policies that large numbers of customers believed unfair and discriminatory. The states adopted measures to cope with these abuses, such as laws to prevent the railroads from engaging in freight pricing and rebate abuses.[7] When these were declared unconstitutional in a series of decisions by the U.S. Supreme Court, pressure groups turned to the federal government for relief. Influential eastern businessmen, who believed that they, too, were the victims of discrimination by the railroads, joined western farm organizations. This populist political alliance persuaded both major political parties to include regulation of the railroads in their national platforms in 1884; it also induced Congress to establish the Interstate Commerce Commission (ICC) in 1887 and then enact the Sherman Antitrust Act in 1890.

The ICC Act prevented unjust discrimination by the railroads, prohibited the pooling of traffic and profits, and made it illegal for a railroad to charge more for a short haul than for a longer one. It also required that the railroads publicize their rates, and established the ICC to supervise the enforcement of the law. The ICC was empowered to eliminate many of the monopolistic practices that spawned a farmers' revolt in the west and the Populist movement as a whole.

The 1890 Sherman Antitrust Act declared illegal all business combinations that restrained trade between states or with foreign nations. Although it was aimed at eliminating the monopolistic practices of the railroads, more than ten years passed before the Sherman Act was used to break up any industrial monopoly. Contrary to the hopes of those who pushed for its passage, it was initially used to obtain an injunction against a striking railroad union accused of restraining interstate commerce. Such results outraged reformers. The growing extremes between the power of wealth and the powerlessness of poverty became politically violent with the Homestead Strike in 1892 and the Pullman Strike in 1894. There were growing fears of a new civil war that would be fought on the economic front. These fears were reflected in the Populists' Progressive successors who placed a much higher emphasis on the role of administrators in promoting social justice than had been the case with their reform-oriented predecessors.

The Sherman Antitrust Act and the ICC constituted the beginnings of what is now called the *modern administrative state*. It marks a recognition that government administrative oversight is essential in coping with the complex industrial and economic problems created by an increasingly complex economic system. This was a point argued by Alexander Hamilton one hundred years earlier. But the move in this direction was hard fought and very gradual, largely due to U.S. Supreme Court decisions that to this day treat private corporations as "persons" under the due process clause of the Fourteenth Amendment (*Slaughter-House Cases* 1873, *Citizens United v. FCC* 2010). By treating corporations as persons, the courts opened the door to arguments by private businesses that government regulations constitute a deprivation of property "without due process of law." Such arguments were invoked to prevent government regulation of wages, hours and working conditions until the U.S. Supreme Court begin to soften its stance in 1935 during the presidency of Franklin D. Roosevelt (Swindler, 1969).

Re-Striking the Federal Balance by Returning to Direct Democracy

The relationship between the states and the federal government during the latter decades of the 19th century began to change in response to political pressures to control the abuses of the Gilded Age. But the increased leadership role for career public servants at the federal level did not come at the expense of the continuing role that states played in controlling the affairs that mattered most in the lives of average citizens. The restructuring of the relationship between citizens and their governments had more to do with the invention of new forms of direct democracy during the Populist period. The Populists pushed the principle of "popular control" to a whole new level.

Frustrated by the unwillingness of legislative bodies to control the growing abuses by private business, and by the unresponsiveness of elected officials to the electorate, Populist reformers introduced a variety of new accountability mechanisms that included recall, the initiative, referendum and direct election of numerous officials that had previously been appointed (i.e., county clerks, attorneys, auditors, sheriff, coroners, treasurers, etc.). While some scholars include these reforms as part of the Progressive movement in the early decades of the 20th century, they were Populist in origin and were included in the national Populist Party platforms of 1892 and 1896 (Johnson and Porter, 1973, 110). In fact, most of the electoral reforms advocated by the Populist movement became reality decades later under the banner of the Progressive movement.

While these reforms expanded the accountability of public service leaders, they also further balkanized the political landscape, making it more difficult to coordinate public services across separately elected offices within the executive branch of government. The values of responsiveness and accountability gained prominence while the values of efficiency and effectiveness lost priority. This is not surprising, since the primary purpose of the Populist reform agenda was to protect against moral corruption rather than to promote greater government efficiency.

Summary of Institutional Legacies Carried Forward into the 20th Century

Several institutional legacies have been created since the later decades of the 18th century and over the course of the 19th century which have important leadership implications for leading from where you sit:

1 The Federalist idea that administrative leaders have to be master designers of organizations.
2 The Federalist and Antifederalist notion that a sense of public duty and commitment to the common good is a less reliable motivator than appealing to the enlightened self-interest of individuals.
3 The Jacksonian and Antifederalist notion that leadership is less about getting ambitions projects done efficiently and effectively and more about building a base of trust with the grassroots followers.
4 The Jacksonian notion that administrative leaders play a representative role in addition to their roles as experts.
5 The Populist idea of a career public service based on competence.
6 The Populist institutions of direct democracy, including the long ballot, referendum, initiative and citizen oversight commissions.
7 The social responsibility role of private wealth and nonprofit organizations in contributing to the common good.
8 The Antifederalist, Jacksonian and Populist legacies that view concentrations of wealth and power as requiring the vigilant exercise of state oversight and regulatory power.

Progressive Reform (1910–1921): Scientific Management and Moral Leadership

The Populist Era reaffirmed the long-standing rule-of-law principle that public service leaders are never to use their office to promote or acquire personal gain. But if discretionary choices by career administrators are not to be governed by personal loyalties, political favoritism and personal visions of the public good, what ought to fill the discretionary vacuum for administrative leaders? If politics is taken out of administration, what should replace it? In short, what precisely is meant by neutral competence? What values should guide, inform and check this competence? The Progressives gave two kinds of answers to this question, one drawing on the scientific impulse within Progressivism and the other drawing on the pragmatic and moral side of the movement (Stever, 1990), which we will discuss more fully in the sections to follow.

The Growing Dominance and Abuses of the Market Economy

The turn of the 20th century was marked by an accelerating pace of economic development that benefited evermore-concentrated centers of power and wealth. Manufacturers organized to control prices, production and shipping (Linseed Oil Trust, Cotton Seed Oil Trust, Lead Trust, Sugar Refiners' Company, Standard Oil Trust and trusts in mining, railroads, meat packing, gas and hemp are all examples). What started as informal associations grew into tightly integrated systems of control and domination of the marketplace by private organizational entities. These concentrations of wealth and power came at the expense of the growing ranks of poor people concentrated in urban areas.

> Approximately one third of the nation's manufacturing assets were consolidated into 318 giant companies with capitalization of $7.3 billion. The high tariffs that America imposed on raw materials and supplies from abroad encouraged further consolidation: the new giants preferred to buy up domestic suppliers rather than pay them high, protected prices. Thus, when tariffs prevented U.S. Steel from obtaining cheap pig iron and coking coal from Canada, the firm simply purchased Pennsylvania iron and coal producers outright rather than let them enjoy the extra profits of the protected market.
>
> Thus arose the modern corporation in America. Some of the mammoths that emerged bore names that would become synonymous with American industry—names that reflect the unambiguously national identities to which they aspired: U.S. Steel, American Sugar Refining, American Telephone and Telegraph, American Rubber, United States Rubber, American Woolen, National Biscuit,

American Can, American Tobacco, Aluminum Company of America, General Electric, General Motors, Standard Oil, and, even more grandiosely, International Harvester.

Reich (1992, 36)

The abuses of the industry magnates were exposed through a variety of writings, starting in the 1890s and continuing through the first decade of the 1900s. Jacob Rijs exposed the poor living conditions of the tenement slums in *How the Other Half Lives* (1890). In *The Shame of Cities* (1904), Lincoln Steffens exposed the rampant political corruption in the party machines of Chicago and New York, arguing that they served the interests of businessmen who sought government contracts, franchises, charters, and special privileges. *The Jungle*, published by Upton Sinclair in 1906, traced an immigrant family's exploitation and the dangerously unsanitary practices prevalent in Chicago's meat-packing industry. These efforts collectively resulted in increased federal and state oversight of the private business sector.

The Expanding Role of Both the Federal Government and the Nonprofit Sectors

In the early decades of the 20th century, the federal government expanded its responsibility on a variety of fronts. It continued to increase its oversight of big business with the passage of the Clayton Act (1914), the Federal Trade Commission (1914) and the Federal Tariff Commission (1916). During Teddy Roosevelt's administration (1901–1909), nearly 40 companies were sued for price fixing and other antitrust violations. The exposure of abuses in meat packing, tenements and public health by muckraking journalists produced results. Significant new legislation was passed, including the Pure Food and Drug Act and the Meat Inspection Act (both in 1906), and laws establishing minimum safety and housing standards in tenements. A third area of expansion of federal oversight and regulation occurred on the natural resource front with the formation of the National Forest Service in the Department of Agriculture (1905), the Bureau of Reclamation (1902), the National Park Service (1916) and a much-expanded role for the Army Corps of Engineers in managing harbors and rivers.

Ironically, the excesses of the private marketplace spurred the expansion of nonprofit organizations far more than it increased the role of the federal and state governments. The increasing gap between the rich and poor spawned the expansion of private philanthropic organizations in the growing cities (Hall, 1992, 47–51). Women organized to push for reform legislation, seeking to secure their own right to vote while also advocating for a wide range of progressive social issues. This included the establishment of settlement houses that provided immigrant families with various services (Stivers, 2000b). The Women's Christian Temperance Union attacked alcohol abuse and succeeded in lobbying for passage of the Eighteenth Amendment (1919), better known as Prohibition. Women won the right to vote with the Nineteenth Amendment in 1920. Women activists were prominent in many associations, including the Women's Trade Union League and the National Consumers' League (NCL), which worked to educate the public on issues of wages, hours and working conditions. The NCL developed a "white label" program, an award for employers whose labor practices met with the NCL's approval for fairness and safety. It made the issue of fair wages and working conditions a front-page concern.

Reform of corporate practices came slowly, not simply because of the power and wealth of industry giants, but because of Americans' ambivalence about the role of large corporations in their lives. On the one hand, large corporations were defended in the name of efficiency, effectiveness and economies of scale achieved through mass production. On the other hand, they were guilty of greed and the accumulation of massive wealth that came at the expense of a rapidly growing class of urban, working poor. Progressive reformers reflected this ambivalence by promoting efficiency as the polestar of the public interest, while also advocating for the moral and physical improvement of all citizens. They believed that corporations, like governments, should embody a moral commitment to efficiency while providing for the material welfare of workers and customers.

For those entering public service, the big question for Progressive reformers centered on what kind of professional expertise was most needed to efficiently promote the public interest. How should we prepare this new generation of public servants? Two schools of thought emerged, one emphasizing the importance of scientific analysis and the other emphasizing the importance of the values and traditions at the contextual center of administrative practice.

Public Service as Scientific Management and Administrative Efficiency

Woodrow Wilson has become famous in public administration for articulating the claim that science should be at the center of preparing the next generation of career administrators.[8] In his now-famous 1887 essay "The Study of Public Administration," Wilson called for making public administration a separate field of study in order to deal successfully with the growing complexity of managing the business of government.

> The object of administrative study is to rescue executive methods from the confusion and costliness of empirical experiment and set them upon foundations laid deep in stable principles ... There

should be a science of administration which shall seek to straighten the paths of government to make its business less unbusiness-like, to strengthen and purify its organization and to crown its dutifulness.

Wilson (1887, 18)

While Wilson's essay went unnoticed in his day, it captured the effusive confidence that Progressives shared about the ability of science to improve the efficiency and effectiveness of any organization, be it public or private. Reformers such as Frederick Taylor called for a more systematic approach to administrative practice. Taylor introduced principles of scientific management that emphasized empirically grounded research on work processes in order to identify the "one best way" of doing business (Taylor, 1911). This was the beginning of a very long tradition of borrowing practices from the private sector to "make government run more like a business."

The scientific methods of the era spawned a variety of new innovations that are now taken for granted as an integral part of public service (Stever, 1988). For example, the movement spawned research bureaus that for the first time emphasized data-based policy recommendations and evaluation of results. These bureaus laid the groundwork for performance measurement of managerial operations, which could then be fed into the budget allocation process. Institutionally, the Progressives established the council-manager form of government, which remains common today and is responsible for the professionalization of local administration. The council-manager model embodies the Progressives' reliance on professionals to meet the needs of citizens, whether through social work, public health, public works, law enforcement, or the management of the general affairs of the community (Stever, 1988; Stivers, 2000b).

Public Service as Moral Leadership

Alongside the vision of public administration as scientific management stood a vision that saw professional career administrators as exemplars, as tutors, as goads to moral and intellectual excellence (Stever, 1988, Chap. 3). This vision rested on the belief that:

[the] common citizen can become something of a saint and something of a hero, not by growing to heroic proportions in his own person, but by the sincere and enthusiastic imitation of heroes and saints, and whether or not he will ever come to such imitation will depend upon the ability of his exceptional fellow-countrymen to offer him acceptable examples of heroism and saintliness.

Croly (1964, 454)

This larger moral vision of the Progressive movement transforms the practice of public administration from a merely scientific and technical enterprise into what Stever calls a "polity profession." Stever use of the term polity is similar to our own.[9] By combining the words polity and profession, Stever calls attention to the increasingly important role that trained professional career administrator play in exercising their policy development and implantation role in the service of the larger public good (Stever, 1988, 31). In short, the task of "speaking truth to power" was more than a matter of making things work, or making them work efficiently (Dror, 2005, especially Part 4; Wildavsky, 1979). It was a matter of keeping the democratic system on a moral course by at least modeling the appearance of civic virtue, if not cultivating its actual practice. This is strikingly similar to the founders' conception of a natural aristocracy wherein those who seek fame before the eyes of posterity will at least mimic civic virtue.

Summary of Institutional Legacies Carried Forward from the Progressive Era

In retrospect, the Progressive Era left administrators with two seemingly different leadership roles to play in the American system of democratic governance. One emphasizes the purely instrumental role of scientifically managing public organizations, using state-of-the-art techniques in policy development and implementation. The other emphasizes the moral leadership role of public leaders in elevating public discourse and fostering human development. The moral and instrumental strands of the Progressive movement left the legacies of the 18th and 19th centuries intact, though playing down some and elevating others:

1   The Progressive Era reinforced the Populist era notion that leadership requires reliance on specialized competence and expertise. Institutional legacies include the council-manager form of government, systematic budgeting and accounting practices, research bureaus and in general the transformation of public service into a modern-day profession.

2   The Progressive Era reinforced the earlier Antifederalist and Jacksonian notion that administrative leaders use their expertise to facilitate the implementation of the community's will.

3   The Progressive movement builds on the Federalist vision of an administrative elite that protects democracy from unenlightened impulses of the masses. But the moral goal of both the Federalists and Progressives was primarily instrumental and utilitarian, falling far short of the Antifederalist concern for the cultivation of civic virtue and community.

The New Deal (1933–1976) and the Rise of the Administrative State

The Progressive movement's reliance on professional expertise, combined with the moral urgency of meeting the needs of the less fortunate, set the stage for the emergence of a new era of positive government, staffed by an elite corps of technically trained career administrators committed to using government to solve problems and deliver services. This legacy came to fruition during the New Deal period. Between the start of the Great Depression, precipitated by the stock market crash in 1929, and President Lyndon B. Johnson's Great Society initiatives through the 1960s, this elite corps of "good government" professionals created and implemented entirely new programs and organizational structures that further strengthened the American administrative state.

The Expansion of Government through Regulation and Entitlement Programs

At the programmatic level, the administrative state consists of a variety of social services and subsidies known as entitlement programs. These include such benefits as social security, unemployment payments, health care, public housing assistance, aid to dependent children, and other types of social welfare assistance. Like President Jackson, Franklin D. Roosevelt succeeded in winning the affection of the poor and the working class, and thereby made the presidency an instrument of popular will and individual rights.

> FDR and his supporters sought and achieved a transformation in the conception of rights and integrated it into a social services or welfare conception of the positive state. In other words, insuring the delivery of basic social services, now often referred to as the social "safety net," was the same as protecting and advancing individual rights. "With the advent of the New Deal political order, an understanding of rights dedicated to limited government gradually gave way to a more expansive understanding of rights, requiring relentless government identification of problems and the search for methods by which these problems might be solved" (Milkis, 1993, 131). This identification of problems began with FDR's articulation of a "Second Bill of Rights," addressing economic security; but by the 1960s and 1970s it had expanded much farther, to encompass broad health, welfare, and "quality-of-life" problems that reformers argued required delineation of additional basic rights as part of their resolution.
>
> Cook (2014, 144)

The expansion of new social service programs reached its zenith during President Johnson's Great Society initiatives in the mid-1960s. His administration tried to tackle the intractable problems of poverty, racism, unemployment and inadequate education. During the Johnson presidency, Congress enacted two major civil rights acts (1964 and 1965), the Economic Opportunity Act (1964) and two education acts in 1965. In addition, legislation was passed that created the Job Corps, Operation Head Start, Volunteers in Service to America (VISTA), Medicaid and Medicare. During the 15-year period beginning in 1965, government spending on social welfare grew by more than 660 percent in current 2007 dollars (230 percent in inflation-adjusted dollars), more than 15 percent a year in real dollars. As a percentage of gross national product, social welfare spending expanded from 11.5 percent to 19.5 percent in 1976 and then leveled off at 18 percent (Salamon, 1999, 61). By 1999, the United States was spending 21 percent of its gross domestic product on government-funded social welfare services, compared to 30 percent or more for Western European countries (Salamon, 1999, 53).

Although the Great Society made significant contributions to the protection of civil rights and the expansion of social programs, critics increasingly complained that the antipoverty programs were ineffective and wasteful. Their costs, combined with the staggering expense of the Vietnam War, soon overtook Johnson's domestic initiatives.

The Triumph of Executive-Centered Administration

The New Deal also institutionalized a vision of good executive leadership that is perhaps even more significant than all the agencies it established. The vision was clearly articulated in a famous report by one of the intellectual leaders of the New Deal, Louis Brownlow. The *Brownlow Report* (officially called the U.S. President's Committee on Administrative Management *Report with Special Studies*, 1937) provides the underlying rationale for more than 100 executive-level reorganization plans submitted to Congress since 1939.[10] It places priority on the dual principles of centralized political accountability and administrative efficiency.

Political Accountability to the Chief Executive

The Brownlow Report's chief premise is that the president is the all-encompassing political leader of the community—"leader of the party, leader of the Congress, leader of a people" (Shafritz and Hyde, 1992, 90). This view, a direct descendent of Andrew Jackson's view of the chief executive, collapses what had previously constituted multiple, independent streams of accountability into a single person and office. Three developments during the New Deal contributed to this unitary view, making administrative officials much more subordinate to the elected chief executive than had been the case at any time in American history. First, the presidency became the symbolic embodiment of the nation and the destiny of its people. Second, the nondelegation doctrine in the courts came to an end. Third, a successful executive initiative was launched to deal with the growth in the number and size of federal agencies during the early decades of the 20th century. Each of these developments, and their present-day implications, are described in the sections that follow.

THE PRESIDENT AS NATIONAL SYMBOL AND VOICE OF THE PEOPLE.

The stock market crash of 1929 plunged the nation into a chaotic economic state. By declaring in his first inaugural address that there was "nothing to fear but fear itself," and by submitting a flurry of bills in his famous first hundred days, President Roosevelt instilled hope and courage in the people of the United States. He galvanized the nation's focus on the chief executive as the source of energy, power and solutions to reverse the nation's misfortunes. This view of the executive function as the focal point of leadership and accountability persists to this day.

NONDELEGATION DOCTRINE.

At a legal level, administrative agencies had been governed for more than a century by the doctrine of separation of powers. According to this doctrine, it is a violation of the U.S. Constitution for Congress to delegate its legislative authority to the executive branch of government unless there are clear standards to guide the exercise of administrative discretion. Justice George Sutherland succinctly summarized a version of this doctrine in the early years of the New Deal: "Congress cannot delegate any part of its legislative power except under the limitation of a prescribed standard."[11] In the mid-1930s, the U.S. Supreme Court applied this doctrine to strike down significant pieces of New Deal legislation. President Roosevelt responded in frustration by rolling out a plan that would nominate six new justices to the Court—one new justice for every justice over the age of 70. He argued that the Court was composed of nine old men who needed help to carry out their increasing workload in a responsible manner. While the plan was rejected, the Supreme Court softened its view of the nondelegation doctrine.[12] By 1940 the Court declared that "delegation by Congress has long been recognized as necessary in order that the exertion of legislative power does not become a futility."[13] No longer was non-delegation necessary to preserve the power of the legislative body. Indeed, the opposite was true—delegation was the only way of preventing the legislative power from becoming futile.

GREATER POLITICAL ACCOUNTABILITY TO THE EXECUTIVE.

The doctrine of greater political accountability to the chief executive formed the cornerstone of the Brownlow Report. Members of the Brownlow Committee called attention to the fragmentation of political responsibility as the federal government had grown willy-nilly since the latter decades of the 19th century. The solution required greater unity of political command by the chief executive. The report argued that proliferation of administrative agencies by Congress, combined with overlapping bureaucratic responsibilities, necessitated more centralized coordination and control by the president. Without this centralization, political accountability and control of the federal bureaucracy would continue to be compromised. Though Congress statutorily creates the mission of federal agencies and provides these agencies with their budget authority, the report recommended more administrative centralization. Nearly all of the 100 reorganization plans proposed since the mid-1930s have accepted this Jacksonian principle, which has resulted in the creation of a separate and ever-larger chief executive White House staff) and more executive control over agencies (i.e., Office of Management and Budget). This executive-centered approach has been replicated in most of the 50 states, as well as in most local government jurisdictions. As we pointed out in Chapter 4, over 80 percent of local governments have a council manager or CEO form of government, which delegates to administrative leaders the major responsibility for daily operations of government as well as doing the homework for developing new policy initiatives for the elected body.

Administrative Efficiency

The second core principle of the Brownlow Report was greater efficiency through the elimination of overlap and duplication of administrative functions. In addition to the political agenda served by consolidation, there has always been a consistent administrative agenda driven largely by private-sector managerial principles that emphasize control, coordination and efficiency. These private sector models are claimed to be necessary to overcome the defects of public-sector structures that divided sources of accountability within a constitutional system of checks and balances.

The New Deal represents the triumph of an instrumental view of administrative agencies, subordinate to the popular will embodied in the president. It was a view first advanced by the Antifederalists and was strengthened institutionally by the Jacksonian and Progressive movements, which collectively created governance institutions that reinforced popular control operating under the supervening authority of a chief executive. The New Deal represents the triumph of the view that career administrators are the ward of the chief executive.

The Rise and Transformation of the Nonprofit Sector

One of the less noticed consequences of the growth of the administrative state since the New Deal has been its impact on nonprofit organizations and private-sector service organizations. Government spending on social services increased by 259 percent in inflation-adjusted dollars between 1965 and 1980 (Salamon, 1999, 61). But, beginning in the 1980s, government spending began a sharp reversal and experienced a 15 percent decline in inflation-adjusted dollars between 1977 and 1994. Despite this decline in government, overall support for the social service sector continued to grow as a result of the increased role played by the nonprofit and for-profit sectors (Salamon, 1999, 116. For example, between 1977 and 1992 private social service agencies grew by 130 percent, numbers of employees working for these agencies grew by 140 percent, and the reveneues of these agencies grew by 240 percent above what they had been in 1977.

Much of this growth was triggered by a deliberate strategy to shrink the government sector by contracting out an increasing number of public social service programs to nonprofit community organizations (see Smith and Lipsky, 1993, Chap. 3). From one point of view the increased reliance on nonprofits represents the triumph of the Antifederalist and Jacksonian view that associations and organizations in the voluntary sector are the anchors for achieving the common good of the community. As President George H.W. Bush observed in his 1989 Inaugural speech "all the individuals and community organizations spread like stars through the nation, doing good." But excessive reliance on these nonprofit stars as contractees for delivering public services has had some unintended adverse consequences, including:

- Professionalizing nonprofit organizations with less money available for direct services and less reliance on volunteers (Smith and Lipsky, 1993; 83–87, 100–108);
- Centralizing of headquarters in Washington D.C. where professional staff can work directly with government policy makers. In doing so, many nonprofits have become part of America's system of interest group liberalism where power is brokered by professionals representing interest group lobbyists, congressional staff and administrative leaders within the bureaucracy (Smith and Lipsky, 1993; 175–76);
- Transforming the mission of nonprofit organizations away from providing maximum service to a target population to meeting government accountability requirements to deliver specified levels of service to given numbers of clientele with the dollars available (Smith and Lipsky, 1993, 229, 122–32);
- Meeting demand for greater economies and efficiencies by consolidating and merging their operations, leaving fewer providers in the community than in the past (Smith and Lipsky, 1993, 177–82).

Smith and Lipsky conclude that the nonprofit sector now reflects "a shift ... from the informal to the formal care systems, greater homogeneity of service within particular service categories, a diminished role of the board of directors in agency governance, and destabilization among nonprofit agencies" (1993, 215). In short, many service providing nonprofits have become more instrumental than constitutive in their mission and culture, and are thereby weakened in their ability to promote citizen engagement in governance.

The next generation of public service leaders face the challenge of rethinking the role of nonprofit organizations in building and sustaining a healthy system of democratic governance. Part of this re-rethinking requires a better understanding of which nonprofits make the best government partners. Studies have shown that by virtue of their mission and membership some nonprofits are significantly better government partners than others (Banyan, 2003, 2004). A second part of this re-thinking involves a better understanding of which civic associations are best suited to cultivate the knowledge and skills for good citizenship. Narrowly focused organizations that exist primarily to serve the needs of their members aren't always the best organizations for fostering the dialogical and collaborative skills needed for building agreement in public forums.

The Rising Importance of Local Government

The New Deal began a process that has resulted in significant expansion in both the sizes and types of local government. President Franklin Roosevelt began the process by encouraging the creation of public corporations to float revenue bonds as a way of avoiding municipal defaults. He urged the creation of water, sewer and electric power districts, arguing "that these governments should be used to circumvent debt limits and referendum requirements for issue of bonds" (Burns, 1994, 53). Roosevelt provided model legislation for enabling citizens to form housing authorities and soil conservation districts, and tied federal funding exclusively to the creation of these jurisdictions. Their numbers exploded as a result.

The impetus for expansion continued in the post-World War II period as a result of pressure for economic development. For example, the expansion of industry and housing caused the real estate industry to reorganize and apply political pressure to establish new cities and special districts. Race played heavily as another factor in the expansion. It was common practice prior to the 1950s for neighborhood improvement associations to create restrictive covenants that excluded individuals on the basis of race. The U.S. Supreme Court declared in 1948 that race-based restrictive covenants were unconstitutional. This decision encouraged cities to use their zoning authority in new and creative ways (Burns, 1994, 60, 54–55).

A fourth pressure to expand cities and special districts occurred during the 1960s with the New Frontier administration of President John F. Kennedy and the Great Society administration of President Lyndon B. Johnson. Federal aid to cities almost doubled. It came in the form of programs for housing, urban renewal, mass transit, education, job training, poverty, model cities and grants-in-aid (Burns, 1994, 62). These initiatives yielded two consequences. First, they changed the expectations of the role that cities could play in meeting the redistributive social needs of the community. In addition to planning for growth and providing infrastructure, Great Society and New Frontier programs laid the groundwork for a larger community-building role to be played by public administrators. Second, these new programs increased the complexity of local government and placed new challenges of interorganizational and interjurisdictional coordination on local government leaders. For example, transportation planning had to be coordinated with a growing number of local jurisdictions as well as with newly created administrative bodies. The elected and career officials responsible for these new arrangements were placed in the catbird seat.

The fifth factor that spurred the growth of cities and special districts was the significant increase in state and local taxation during the 1960s. Starting in 1961, taxpayers at the local level experienced the largest increase in taxes since the 1930s. This increased burden induced businesses and residents to create new cities and special service districts in the attempt to escape these tax burdens. New special service districts also gave them options in deciding whether they wished to purchase additional services (Burns, 1994, 62). As we discussed in Chapter 4, if suburban dwellers wish to live in the pastoral setting of the countryside but still have access to city-level police and fire services, they can create special districts to purchase additional levels of police, fire, health, education or other services. During the decades following the local taxation crisis of the 1960s, special districts grew in number from 21,264 in 1967 to 35,052 in 2002, an increase of more than 60 percent (see Exhibit 4.6 in Chapter 4).

The expansion in the number, complexity and role of local government jurisdictions since the New Deal has greatly increased the challenges of leading from where you sit. Local administrative leaders have to coordinate more of their work with other jurisdictions. For example, when a city shuts down a group home for its inability to comply with code restrictions, the service burden is pushed to the county and surrounding local jurisdictions. Whether it is policing, education, parks, library service, transportation planning or most other local services, it is hard to imagine these activities being carried out in silos.

Institutional Legacies Carried Forward from the New Deal

The New Deal is one the major watersheds in American history. The period transformed the socio-economic, political, legal, intergenerational and administrative landscape and established new institutions that have become a normal part of the moral legacy of administrative leaders wherever they sit. But as with most all institutional legacies, they sit alongside previous legacies that often place administrators in the position of integrating the past into the present, while seeking to make these legacies relevant to the future. The following three major administrative leadership challenges will continue as legacies of the New Deal:

• *Executive-Centered Leadership: The Problematic of the Administrative State.* The New Deal built on Hamilton's 1975/1787–1789 executive-centered vision and produced a significantly strengthened presidency to advance the values of a more effective and efficient government and expanded social programs to assist those in economic and social need. While the New Deal left administrators with a strong sense of efficacy in executive-centered leadership, at the same time it tempered this efficacy with a much-expanded vision of equality and social justice, with local governments and nonprofit organizations serving as important partners in this vision. The size and role of the federal government in this partnership will continue to remain an important leadership challenge.
• *The Growing Importance of Local Government and the Rise of the Regulatory State: The Problem of Unfunded Mandates.* One of the downstream consequences of the New Deal was a large array of new regulatory and entitlement programs that are administered by state and local jurisdictions without the funding to do so. The National Conference of State Legislatures (NCSL) monitors the number and costs of these mandates (NCSL, 2017). The NCSL estimated that the U.S. Congress had shifted over $131 billion in costs between the financial years 2004 and 2008 to states and local governments (NCSL, 2010). These developments resulted in the passage of the Unfunded Mandates Reform Act of 1995 (109 STAT. 48), which placed limitations on the practice of unfunded mandates. Even with these limitations in place, figuring out how to pay for expanded services and increased regulatory costs is a leadership challenge that will continue for the foreseeable future. This challenge has become even more daunting in the face of rapidly rising pension obligations by state and local jurisdictions and the growing importance to most all Americans of the role of government in the provision of some kind of health care.
• *The Creation of the Administrative State: The Rise and Transformation of the Nonprofit Sector.* The New Deal created a legacy of

reliance on nonprofit and voluntary organizations in civic society to carry major responsibilities in contributing to the common good. But taken to its extreme, excessive reliance on these providers can result in treating them as subcontractors who should be held to the same accountability and performance standards as any other business. This "contracting out" mindset can quickly become part of "running government like a business." While that is certainly part of our measure of leadership success, it often is not the most important when seeking to build trust and legitimacy in governing institutions. One of the on-going leadership challenges of the New Deal legacy is how to structure contracts with nonprofit service providers that enables both government and service providers to perform their quite distinct and separate roles without compromising the integrity of each of the partners (see previous discussion in this chapter).

Some Leadership Conclusions Regarding the Moral Legacy of American History and Political Institutions

We have devoted considerable attention in this chapter to reviewing the historical development of American political institutions and the social conditions that have transformed these institutions over time. We have done so because of our simple belief that these institutions provide public service leaders with a rich tapestry of moral values that can be used to build trust and legitimacy in democratic governance. This historical legacy is summarized in the lower half of Exhibit 6.1. It builds on the upper half of leadership legacy created by the American founding (see Exhibit 5.3 in Chapter 5) and shows how the origins of the leadership models that emerged during the founding period have been broadened and deepened by several periods of reform. Each of these periods has added institutional values, structures and process that have become part of the moral tradition of public service in the United States. Like the legacy of the U.S. Constitution and the debates surrounding the American founding summarized in Exhibit 6.1, core democratic values are in conflict with one another. In fact, one could view the historical legacy of American governing institutions as an ongoing process of re-debating the American founding. When the leadership pendulum swings too far toward being responsive to the popular will, the pendulum swings back to be less responsiveness and more reliant on the judgment of experts to protect minority rights and deliver public services effectively and efficiently. The Antifederalists, Jacksonian Democrats, Populists and modern-day members of the Tea Party recognize that liberty cannot be secured by relying solely on the good intentions and voluntary support of ordinary citizens. The leaders of all of these movements wanted strong government support and

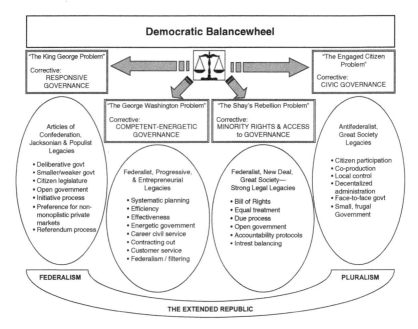

Exhibit 6.1 Public Service Leadership as Democratic Balancewheel

intervention to realize their libertarian reliance on private and voluntary sector solutions to public challenges. Likewise, the Federalists, Progressives and New Dealers recognized that government alone cannot provide the conditions for securing the blessings of liberty to the most vulnerable members of our population. However limited or expansive government may become in its reach at a given point in history, expertise and organizational capacity are essential both in government as well as in the institutions of civil society and the private market place. These obvious truths draw us to the conclusion that successful public service leaders need to develop competence in multiple leadership models that are part of the American institutional legacy. In Exhibit 6.2 we organize this institutional legacy into six public service leadership traditions, which we elaborate more fully in the sections to follow.

Leaders as Guardians of Individual Rights and Abuses of Government Power

The moral lesson that has most endured over the course of American history is the popular belief that government "power tends to corrupt, and absolute power corrupts absolutely" (Lord Acton, 1887). The American Revolution and the subsequent constitution it produced have become global symbols of the rule of law, limited government, the

Exhibit 6.2 Public Service Leadership Models and Traditions

Competent Governance and Executive-Centered Tradition	Interest-Balancing Tradition
• Strong government needed to protect rights • Unity in the executive, but embraces diverse organization principles • Career, professional service • Initiative and entrepreneurialism/competitiveness • Efficiency/effectiveness • Systematic planning • Federalism/filtering	• Open, transparent government • Deliberative decisions • Diffusion of power • Citizen legislatures • Lobbying, interest groups • Initiative/referendum: direct democracy • Small, frugal governments • Preference for markets and market mechanisms (i.e., contracts, competition, etc.)

Entrepreneurial Tradition	Civic Governance Tradition
• Using data, analysis and reflection to generate new understandings of challenges and solutions • Synthesizing and applying known principles in new ways • Reconsidering how the interface of governance structures and human motivations can be maximally structured to increase government performance • Continuous re-examination of how government performance can be structured to strengthen the market sector and civil society to better co-produce the public good	• Volunteerism (low pay for public servants, emphasizes dedication to community/service) • Citizen participation/engagement • Close collaboration and co-production • Resource sharing • Nonprofit activism • Local control • Private property protections • Decentralized administration • Proliferate jurisdictions • Face-to-face government • Under-resourced, weak governments: fiscal conservatism/balanced budget

Minority Rights & Access to Governance Tradition	Equality and Equity Tradition
• Rule of law • Divided government • Bill of rights: an open field! (free exercise, association, speech, privacy, property, etc.) • Equal treatment (through process especially) • Due process • Interest advocacy and balancing • Accountability protocols • Court advocacy • Open government: emphasis on access	• Strong government to protect against economic abuses (Jacksonian, Populist, Progressive, New Deal, New Frontier and Great Society movements) • Social safety net programs • Special needs programs for those with physical, emotional, mental and social impairments • Expansion and professionalization of social service specializations

Source: Derived and modified from Morgan et al. (2013/2008, 147).

guarantee of individual rights (i.e., free exercise, association, speech, privacy, property, etc.), open access to government, transparency in political and judicial decision-making, equal protection of the law and due process. These values have been the touchstone of many reforms movements that have sought to renew the importance of protecting citizens from the over-reaching and self-serving arms of rulers whose purposes do not always align with the common good of the citizens they serve. The Jacksonian, Populist and their contemporary counterparts are visible reminders of the enduring need to tame government from excessive and abusive use of its power to govern.

Leaders as Interest-Balancers

Leadership as interest-group balancing derives from James Madison's view that a multiplicity of interests in the economic and social spheres is the best check against the tyranny of an overpowering majority. As the founders observed in *The Federalist Papers*: "The regulation of these various and interfering interests forms the principal task of modern legislation and *involves the spirit of party and faction in the necessary and ordinary operations of government*" (Madison, 1787, Federalist No. 10, emphasis added; also see Hamilton, 1788, Federalist No. 79). The public manager shares responsibility for balancing these interests in the daily operations of the administration.

In addition to relying on the informal checks from a contending multiplicity of interest groups, Madison's leadership model relied on an "auxiliary system" of formal checks and balances between and within each of the branches of government. This formal system has been incorporated into administrative practice in the form of independent audits, evaluations, elaborate rules of procedure and multiple avenues of redress when agency actions threaten basic rights or vested interests.

The pluralist leadership legacy is alive and well in the modern administrative state. Everywhere we turn, organized interests are at the administrative doorstep, sometimes seeming to co-opt or even paralyze decision-making processes. We use the term "pluralism" to describe theories of governance that affirm the dominant role that interest groups play in the operation of the American systems of government, as well as the legitimacy of these interests in making the systems work effectively. Pluralism assumes that political interests affect all aspects of policy-making and implementation. Good leadership under the legacy of pluralism creates an atmosphere of openness on an issue and then supports discourse until common agreement and action is possible. Compromise and trade-offs are assumed to be central and morally necessary.

The pluralist model works best when interests are well developed and securely attached to stable groups in the larger society, and when the issues under discussion are well understood by all of the participants. This model is particularly effective in reconciling pragmatic differences; however, it is not especially useful when dealing with strong ideological differences, attempting to optimize the use of limited resources, working to achieve a planned set of objectives, or trying to resolve problems that are fundamentally technical. Moreover, since the model starts with the status quo, it neglects interests that are not well organized and funded. The model is not always appropriate when planning for long-term needs; and it frequently results in inefficiencies through prioritizing private interests over the public good.

Leaders as Champion of Efficient, Effective and Competent Government

The story of George Washington at Valley Forge is the story of the failure of government to carry out its assigned work efficiently, effectively and energetically. In short, it is a story of incompetent government—one not up to the task of achieving the goals it was assigned. Over time, the continued failure of government to deliver the goods and services that citizens expect is a recipe for the erosion of popular confidence and support. This is a message that has been repeated throughout history, including the more recent call (in the 1990s) to "reinvent government" in order to improve its performance.

Both as army general and as president, George Washington joined with Alexander Hamilton to bring greater energy to the executive branch of government. This energy entailed putting more emphasis on systematic planning, coordinated implementation with adequate resources, and the ability to act quickly and decisively. The conditions to create and sustain this energy required unity of command, duration in office, competent powers, sufficient resources and a core group of experienced, knowledgeable officials, all of which characterized President Washington's administration. Washington's presiding leadership and sound judgment enabled subordinate colleagues such as Hamilton to develop sophisticated plans and proposals, and to help establish new institutions and practices that would help stabilize the new nation and set it on course for commercial and agricultural prosperity (Green, 1919). The Washington administration either bolstered or put in place the basic elements of a stable commercial economy, a sound defense, a basic communications system, a transportation infrastructure and a revenue system, all of which instilled broad public confidence in the viability of the new nation.

This executive-centered leadership model works best when problems require systematic solutions, where there is general disenchantment with the current state of affairs, and when experienced and knowledgeable people are needed to address problems that are widely viewed as legitimate. Such conditions tend to be in place during times of war and economic crisis. The executive-centered model doesn't work as well when dealing with challenges where there is lack of agreement on the ends of action, where there is no shared vision, or when the nature of the expertise needed to solve the problems is in dispute. For example, it works much better when applied to fighting wars or dampening economic cycles than it does in combatting racism, poverty and economic inequality. But even in fighting wars, we have learned that if the end goals are not clear, the executive-centered model will not serve us well.

Leaders as Champions of Entrepreneurism and Innovation

Much of the leadership literature over the past decade has focused on the role of leaders in fostering innovative cultures and championing creativity (see especially Sahni, Wessel, and Christensen, 2013; Shalley and Gilson, 2004; Baer, Oldham, and Cummings, 2003; Thornton, 2010). This literature assumes that the motivation and ability to be innovative is much greater in the private sector than in public and nonprofit sector organizations (Sahni et al., 2013). The public sector is constrained by rule of law principles and accountability requirements that place a much greater priority on operating within organizational missions and budgets than being innovative and creative in designing and implementing better ways of doing what has been done in the past or in inventing new solutions to old problems. As a consequence, it is common practice to give the private sector credit for being the stewards of core values like innovation, creativity and entrepreneurialism.

But consider for a moment the audacious creativity and entrepreneurialism represented by the framers of the American constitution. Alexander Hamilton spoke for most of his fellow countryman when he observed in Federalist No. 9 that "wholly new discoveries" had made it possible for new principles to be creatively applied to construct a totally novel form of republican government. Hamilton continued to be the champion of government innovation as secretary of the Treasury. He borrowed and improved upon best practices from Europe in fashioning the American financial system. His system of public credit and debt management helped stabilize the young American economy, set the stage for its prosperous commercial and agricultural development and provided the underlying conditions for citizen trust and confidence in the long-term stability of the socio-political system (Green, 1919). The regulation of the economy through the Federal Reserve Board's use of refined monetary policies to manipulate interest rates exemplifies this model at work today.

The story to carry forward from Hamilton's legacy is that entrepreneurial leadership is needed most when conditions are uncertain and unstable and when collective trust needs to be built. That is the whole purpose of entrepreneurial activity in the private sector. The goal of the private sector is to create products and services that clients and customers will have confidence in over the long run. You don't need to be very entrepreneurial when things are going well, customers are happy and you can count on your past products serving you well into the future. But because of competition in the private sector, leaders can't sit for very long on their past successes; they have to be thinking about "the next best answer." For this reason, the entrepreneurial leadership model is often associated with a free-market philosophy that emphasizes a strictly hands-off approach to administrative oversight of the economy. But that was not what entrepreneurial meant to the early leaders of the American republic who viewed innovation as a necessary condition for building, maintaining and renewing trust and legitimacy in the institutions of democratic governance. For example, Hamilton argued that a robust economy required robust governments with firm regulatory powers as well as economic stimulants to provide stable infrastructure and moderated business cycles. Under this model, the government must aggressively regulate those markets deemed essential to our national interests, and it must counteract the self-destructive aspects of market behavior (Green, 2002, 1993, 1919). We are reminded of these problems when contemplating abuses such as those that occurred in the savings and loan industry in the 1980s; the industry-breaking actions of Enron, MCI WorldCom Inc. and other Wall Street insider trading scandals of the 1990s; and the rampant speculation, fraud, and abuse in the financial industry that led to the financial crash of 2008 and subsequent Great Recession. All of these severely damaging events were due in large part to extensive deregulation and refusal by key public officials to use the regulatory powers still assigned to them by law (cf. Green, 2014, 2012). Hamilton would have been appalled, less perhaps because of the particular misdeeds of individuals and companies in the private sector, but because of the slow response of public institutions to deal with the loss of trust and confidence in governing both public and private institutions.

Our argument throughout this book is that public innovation becomes imperative as complexity increases. Whether it is the complexity of the brain, the solar system or interdependent social systems, new ways of "sizing up" challenges and opportunities are required when seeking to understand and successfully act within systems characterized by high levels of complex interdependencies. We develop this argument more fully in the next chapter and provide leadership tools for deliberately spawning innovation in public contexts in Chapters 9 and 11.

Leaders as Champions of Equality and Equity

America was founded on the promise that differences in economic status were a consequence of one's personal efforts and not a consequence of one's birth or condition. This is why the American Revolution was fought in the name of liberty, not equality. Americans shared the common belief that giving individuals their liberty to take advantage of America's natural abundance would result in a high level of equality of social condition. De Tocqueville was struck by this social equality in comparison to the European continent when he first visited the United States in 1831. But President Andrew Jackson was struck otherwise when he succeeded in winning the presidency in 1828 on a campaign against the economic elites whom, he argued, had acquired their power and money on the backs of the "common man." This notion that American democracy requires a minimum condition of economic and social equality has been a consistent theme throughout American history. Artifacts of this agenda are found in the legal and public policy legacies of the Populist, Progressive, New Deal, New Frontier and Great Society agendas over the last 150 years.

Three developments have pushed this equality agenda to the forefront. One is the growing income disparity between the rich and the poor. Between 1967 and 2012, U.S. household income inequality grew by 18 percent, with nearly half of that growth occurring during the 1980s (U.S. Census, 2012b; see further discussion of this issue in Chapter 7, "Growth in Income Inequality"). This income inequality will continue to play an ever-larger role in the American public policy debates at all levels of government.

A second factor that has made equality an issue of growing concern is the on-going and unresolved issues surrounding race, gender identity and the treatment of immigrants. Regardless of one's personal views on these issues, public service leaders are unavoidably made participants in these debates as a result of public policy obligations they have under the law. Sometimes these obligations may be in conflict. For example, social workers employed in "safe harbor" jurisdictions may find themselves at odds with their obligations to adhere strictly to federal program eligibility and reporting requirements.

Finally, our commitment to equality has been increasingly institutionalized as a result of the professionalization of many areas of public service leadership. Consider the role of counselors, psychologists, therapists, social workers and other specialists we rely upon to carry out our public service roles. These professions have been called into service as advocates for the best interests of their patients and clients.

The commitment to equality has now become an integral part of the American public service leadership legacy. This commitment is officially recognized in the American Society of Public Administration's Code of Ethics, Provision 4: "Strengthen social equity. Treat all persons with fairness, justice, and equality and respect individual differences, rights, and freedoms. Promote affirmative action and other initiatives to reduce unfairness, injustice, and inequality in society."

Leaders as Community Capacity-Builders

Jefferson and his Antifederalist colleagues reminded participants in the founding debates that civic engagement and active participation in providing for the well-being of our local communities is a peculiar kind of democratic virtue that cannot be taken for granted. It requires living shared lives in a common place—usually "within the fabric of a relatively small and homogenous community" (Brinkley, Polsby, and Sullivan, 1997, 93). It requires direct face-to-face communication and assumes that differences among individuals and groups can be bridged through a web of long-standing relationships and mutual obligations. This assumption places considerable weight on the leadership practices of facilitation, conflict resolution and civic dialogue. It produces a system that tends to produce a frugal governance arrangement that relies extensively on volunteerism and an engaged citizenry. Tenure in office is short, part time and generally low paid. The role of administration under this model is to gather people together to transform sharp differences of opinion into a common agenda, to give voice to this agenda and to develop the necessary support over time to realize it. This vision of democracy is carried forward in many of our local institutions, whether it be the New England town councils, special districts, neighborhood associations or ethnic communities.

The communitarian model works best when the groups and individuals involved have a history of working together over time on tough issues. This stream of engagement builds two kinds of trust, together called social capital (Putnam, 2000). One kind of trust arises from a sense of solidarity and group identity exemplified by fraternal organizations, church-groups and ethnic communities. This kind of trust is called "bonding capital," "a kind of sociological superglue" (Putnam, 2000, 23) that generates a lot of in-group psychological support. What prevents this in-group trust from turning into out-group antagonism is "bridging capital," which arises from working together with others who have different views, backgrounds and beliefs. Both kinds of trust rely on face-to-face relationships that hold everyone accountable for what they say and do (McCullough, 1991; Skocpol and Fiorina, 1999). Accordingly, this model is poorly suited to settings where the participants are transitory, where there is no sense of shared past or future, and where an issue is easily shifted to another venue or external authority. Thus, the conditions for the success of the communitarian model, with its emphasis on dialogue, stand in opposition to those found in the pluralist, interest-group balancing model and the energetic and entrepreneurial models. The communitarian model's inherent dangers lie in oppressive community majorities and weak institutions that can do little to resist them.

The rise of modern technology raises the question of how it might be used to facilitate the communitarian model, and to serve the ends of good government more generally. For example, can virtual political communities be created that disassociates people living in a common place and substitutes a virtual community organized around common challenges, issues, interests or questions? We leave this question for further consideration in our discussion of the future role of technology and government in the next chapter.

Conclusion

The six administrative leadership traditions we have summarized above and in Exhibit 6.2 are deeply embedded in the practices of American democratic governance. It is our hope that a deep understanding of these traditions and the institutional legacies that support them will embolden you to lead from where you sit. Sometimes this leadership may require recovering the moral purposes of current activities, programs and practices that have gotten lost over time. At other times it may require standing up to alter the course of action and to justify doing so by drawing on portions of America's long and diverse administrative leadership legacy to elevate values that have been given short shrift or are in need of re-balancing. Taken together, these traditions provide public service leaders with a robust set of public service principles, practices and values to build legitimacy and trust in the institutions of democratic governance.

Notes

1 For this chapter we have drawn from Morgan, Green, Shinn, and Robinson (2013), Chapter 4, 97–118.
2 We urge our readers to immerse themselves in the growing body of scholarship that re-examines American history from the vantage point of the oppressed, the underprivileged and the forgotten. This history adds immeasurable depth and breadth to our argument in this chapter that an institutional perspective requires a heightened understanding and vigilance on the part of our leaders who have stewardship responsibility for the moral well-being our institutions. For works especially relevant to public service leadership we have found the following particularly useful as supplemental reading in our courses: Vance (2016), Kendi (2016), Stivers (2000a, 2000b, 2002), Wilkerson (2006) and Zinn (2015/2005).
3 We have relied largely upon Paul Van Riper's excellent summary of the history of the United States Civil Service to organize the major eras of development. However, we have distinguished the Populist and Progressive eras here because of the significant differences in goals and objectives (Van Riper, 1958).
4 President Jackson opposed the existence of a national bank, which had been established by Congress in 1816. His opposition was based on the belief that a national bank created an exclusive monopoly, which benefited privileged stockholders at the expense of the hard-working American people. He ordered the secretary of the Treasury, William Duane, to transfer

deposits out of the U.S. Bank to 12 designated private banks. When Secretary Duane refused, Jackson dismissed him from office. The protracted battle over the role of the National Bank was symbolic of a much larger and more fundamental set of issues that President Jackson set forth in his famous veto message of the renewal of the Bank Charter in 1832. "Many of our rich men have not been content with equal protection and equal benefits, but have besought us to make them richer by act of Congress. By attempting to gratify their desires we have in the results of our legislation arrayed section against section, interest against interest, and man against man, in a fearful commotion which threatens to shake the foundations of our Union" (Richardson, 1899, II, 1139–54).

5 For a more detailed account of these changes see Robert Reich (1992), especially 26, 27, 31–32; and William Swindler (1969).

6 These scandals involved typical abuses of the public trust that have their contemporary counterparts. All were variations on the same theme—using your position of public trust for personal gain:

Crédit Mobilier (1872). The vice president of the Union Pacific Railroad, George Francis Train, created a private construction company called Crédit Mobilier of America, which was the sole bidder for certain construction contracts from Union Pacific. The company was paid hefty fees through federal subsidies approved by members of Congress who were provided with cheap shares of stock in Crédit Mobilier.

Gold Conspiracy (1869). Two private speculators, Jay Gould and James Fisk, persuaded the assistant treasurer of the United States to tip them off when the government intended to start selling large amounts of gold that was intended to buy back paper currency, called "greenbacks," issued during the Civil War. The speculators created a financial panic called Black Friday when their hording caused prices to rise and stocks to plummet. The crises ended when the government began selling gold.

Whiskey Ring (1875). A conspiracy of government agents, politicians, whiskey distillers and distributors diverted millions of dollars in federal taxes on liquor for personal gain through the creation of a network of bribes involving tax collectors, storekeepers and others.

Indian Ring (1876). President Ulysses Grant's secretary of war, William W. Belknap, accepted bribes from companies with licenses to trade on the reservations of many Native American tribes. He was impeached by the House of Representatives, but acquitted by the Senate in August 1876.

Salary Grab (1873). Congress gave itself a 50 percent salary increase on the last day of the session in 1873 and made the increase retroactive for the previous two years.

7 These state laws were called Granger Laws because they were designed to protect the interest of farmers who had organized into local associations, called granges, to advance their interests against the monopolistic practices of price fixing by railroads. The laws were overturned in a series of Supreme Court decisions: *Munn v. Illinois,* 94 U.S. 113 (1877); *Budd v. New York,* 143 U.S. 517 (1894); and *Brass v. North Dakota ex rel. Stoesser,* 153 U.S. 391 (1894)

8 While Wilson is often regarded as the father of viewing public administration as a science, Brian Cook's excellent review of Wilson's scholarship correctly points out that this narrow interpretation is incorrect. In fact, Wilson emphasized that "popular sovereignty is never fully expressed and national purposes never full realized," making it necessary for administrators to complete the vital tasks of carrying out public laws and continually refining the law's shape and substance (Cook, 2007, especially 261).

9 Stever's use of the term "polity" is similar to our own (see especially Chapter 4). In both cases polity calls attention to the moral integrity of the community viewed from the perspective of an organic whole. It calls attention to the functional interdependence of the political economy, including the voluntary, public, for profit and nonprofit sectors.

10 See U.S. *Report on the President's Commission on Administrative Management*, 1937; *President's Message to the Congress*, March 25, 1971; Mansfield (1969), Nathan (1976), Rohr (1989, Chap. 9), National Academy of Public Administration (1983), and National Performance Review (1996).

11 *U.S. v. Chicago., St. P. & P.R. Co.*, 282 U.S. 311, 324 (1931). The view expressed by Justice Sutherland in 1931 was much less strict than the version of the non-delegation doctrine articulated by Justice Stephen J. Field toward the end of the 19th century: "That Congress cannot delegate legislative power to the President is a principle universally recognized as vital to the integrity and maintenance of the system of government ordained by the Constitution" (*Field v. Clark*, 143 U.S. 649, 692 (1892)).

12 *Panama R. Co. v. Ryan*, 293 U.S. 388 (1935); *Schechter P. Corp. v. U.S.*, 295 U.S. 495 (1935). In addition to changing its view on the non-delegation doctrine, the court shifted its interpretation of the due process clause. It had interpreted the due process clauses of the Fifth and Fourteenth Amendments to prohibit legislative bodies from passing various kinds of economic and public health regulations on the grounds that they restrict property or liberty without "due process of law." Businesses used this interpretation to challenge government market regulation, including efforts to establish standards for wages, hours, working conditions and competition (Pritchett, 1968, Chap. 31). The Supreme Court's sudden shift (in 1937) in interpretation of the due process clause and the non-delegation doctrine became known as the "stitch in time that saved nine."

13 *Sunshine A. Co. v. Adkins*, 310 U.S. 381, 397 (1940). Judicial deference to administrative discretion has developed over the past 50 years into some reasonably clear standards of review (Cooper, 2007, Chap. 7). With the appointment of new Supreme Court justices during the Bush II and Trump administrations, there is evidence that deference to administrative discretion may be less in the future than it has been in the past. Justice Gorsuch is well known for his desire to breath new life into the non-delegation doctrine.

Part II
Identifying Leadership Opportunities
"Sizing Up" Possible Leadership Action

Master Case: The Mt. Hood National Forest Strategic Stewardship Plan

This case explores the creation of an environmental stewardship plan, the goal of which is to protect multiple and highly valued community resources in the face of declining resources. The plan illustrates the value of leading from where you sit, not asking for permission and being careful in "sizing up" the vertical and horizontal authority structures that are needed for success. The case illustrates the complexity of contextual settings, which provide challenges to navigate, even for seasoned administrators.

This case study is drawn from administration of Mt. Hood National Forest in Oregon, one of the 155 national forests in the National Forest System. The forest covers 1.1 million acres, including 1,000 miles of hiking trails, 8 wilderness areas, 76 campgrounds, and 11 developed skiing/snowboarding areas. Recreation in the forest system brings in more than $33 million in annual revenue to local communities, and the forest generates an estimated 2,700 local jobs. The particular case study is of the Mt. Hood National Forest Strategic Stewardship Plan, completed in 2006 (U.S. Forest Service, 2006). The plan was developed in response to external divers of change to reduce the size and cost of government. The plan used two core political strategies to respond to these pressures: 1) enlisting citizens, groups and corporations in co-production, and 2) broadening the basis of citizen engagement.

Drivers of Change

The leadership initiative in this case was prompted by three drivers of change: reduction in resources, increasing demand for goods and services and environmental protection and a highly articulated policy environment.

Pressure to Reduce the Size and Scope of the Federal Government

The U.S. Forest Service is a large federal agency of 30,000 employees within the U.S. Department of Agriculture. As such, it is in the mainstream of successive administrations' efforts through the Office of Management and Budget (OMB) to make government smaller and more effective. The President's Management Agenda (U.S. OMB, 2002) began in earnest to make government agencies smaller and more efficient when, during the administration of George W. Bush, it undertook five government-wide initiatives: 1) strategic management of human capital, 2) competitive sourcing, 3) improved financial performance, 4) expanded electronic government and 5) budget and performance integration. The Forest Service was strongly affected by these initiatives. The breadth of scope was matched by the fervor of the rhetoric:

> The need for reform is urgent. The General Accounting Office ... identifies areas throughout the federal government that are most vulnerable to fraud, waste, and abuse ... New programs are frequently created with little review or assessment ... wasting money and baffling citizens ... The work of reform is continually overwhelmed by the constant multiplication of hopeful new government programs ... The President's vision for government reform is guided by three principles. Government should be:—citizen-centered, not bureaucracy-centered;—results-oriented;—market-based, promoting rather than stifling innovation through competition.
>
> U.S. OMB (2002, 3–4)

Mt. Hood National Forest budgets were decreasing significantly, in large part as a result of OMB's desire to make government smaller and more effective. Budgets declined from $45 million in 1991 to $23 million in 2002, and full-time equivalent employees (FTEs) declined from over 800 to a low of 300 in the same time period. As of 2013, the forest employed fewer than 200 FTEs. The reduction of employees and resources resulted from centralization, competitive sourcing and downsizing due to reduction in funds.

Increasing Pressure for Goods, Services and Environmental Protection

Despite the downsizing, the pressure for goods, services and environmental protection continues to increase. The Mt. Hood National Forest, along with the entire Pacific Northwest Region, has been at the center of considerable environmental litigation over public forest protection issues for the last four decades. A national analysis of litigation and appeals showed hundreds of agency decisions in litigation and thousands of decisions under appeal (Larsen, Lynn,

Kapaldo, and Fedkiw, 1990). The number of species that are rare, threatened or endangered in Oregon is large and growing. In 2010, the list included 746 vascular plant species, 430 nonvascular species, 239 vertebrates and 235 invertebrates (Oregon Biodiversity Information Center, 2012). Many of them occur on the Mt. Hood National Forest, which necessitates extensive surveys and consultation with regulatory agencies be conducted in advance of any contemplated ground-disturbing activity.

Pressure from a Complex Policy Environment

Two hundred principal federal laws were identified in 1993 that relate to Forest Service activities, starting with the U.S. Mining Laws Act of 1872 and ending with the Tourism Policy and Export Promotion Act of 1992 (U.S. Forest Service, 1993). Many new laws affecting administration of the forest have been passed since 1993. One example is Congress's passage of legislation in 2009 that expanded five existing wilderness areas on the forest, established three new areas and expanded the Wild and Scenic Rivers System. In addition, the act specified three land exchanges, created a national recreation area, added protections for three particular watersheds, and made provisions for tribal planning and studies (Omnibus Public Land Management Act, 2009). While the administrative and financial burden of implementing the act was immediate and large, no new funds were appropriated for its implementation, which caused already scarce funding for the forest to be redirected.

Administration of the Mt. Hood National Forest is guided by overlapping agency, regional and local policy, including the agency mission, national laws, national and regional strategic plans, goals and forest working principles. The Forest Service Strategic Plan is guided by the Forest Service mission "to sustain the health, diversity, and productivity of the Nation's forests and grasslands to meet the needs of present and future generations" (U.S. Forest Service, 2008). The plan defines six strategic goals to accomplish the mission of the agency. The goals include:

1 Reduce the risk from catastrophic wildland fire. Restore the health of the nation's forests and grasslands to increase resilience to the effects of wildland fire.
2 Reduce the impacts from invasive species. Restore the health of the nation's forests and grasslands to be resilient to the effects of invasive insects, pathogens, plants and pests.
3 Provide outdoor recreation opportunities, while sustaining natural resources, to meet the nation's recreational demands.
4 Help meet energy resources needs. Contribute to help meet the nation's need for energy.

5   Improve watershed condition. Increase the number of forest and grassland watersheds that are in fully functional hydrologic condition.

6   Conduct mission-related work in addition to that which supports the agency goals and fulfills statutory stewardship and assistance requirements.

While each of the aforementioned six goals is laudable and important, each also reflects conflicts in values, policy and appropriations. For example, in the case of fire prevention and suppression, citizens care urgently about having their communities protected from wildfire. Fire, however, is part of the natural functioning of ecosystems. On many of the nation's 193 million acres of national forest lands, fire has been actively suppressed for most of the last 100 years to protect communities. The result is that when fires burn on wildlands now, they are often dangerous and very expensive to fight. While it takes a multi-pronged approach to reduce the intensity and severity of wildfires, restoring the health of ecosystems is a central part of any solution. Restoration means investment of public funds to restoration activities. Because of the immediate importance of putting out fires, the agency reports that the fire portion of the Forest Service budget has increased from 13 percent to 42 percent over the past 15 years (U.S. Forest Service, 2007). As a result, funds available for management of lands continue to decrease dramatically. This example illustrates a broader phenomenon: while laws, regulations and executive policy provide a rich, often conflicting, and finely articulated policy environment, the funds appropriated to agencies and allocated to field units on a yearly basis are targeted in a highly instrumental fashion. Funding is tied directly to accomplishment of specific enumerated targets. The other goals similarly embed deep conflicts.

Taken together, the reduction in resources, a highly articulated policy environment, and increasing demand for goods and services and environmental protection have had a large impact on citizens, permittees, partners and natural resources. When permittees or partners propose any action for use or occupancy of Forest Service lands, the law requires significant analysis, which does not move forward unless the permittee or partner agrees to pay for the process. Recreation in the forest is increasing, with 4.5 million visitors per year as of 2013. The number of cars being broken into at trailheads and the disturbing rise in violent crimes and homicides has exceeded the capacity of the organization to deal with them. The ability of the Forest Service to administer and manage recreation has decreased significantly, resulting in an increased potential threat to capital improvements and natural resources. The Forest Service's ability to maintain roads has also been diminished, resulting in rough road surfaces, potholes, brush encroachment or roads being washed out completely, all leading to more accidents. Interestingly, environmentalists filed a lawsuit aimed at stopping fees being charged to use the forest. These are the pressures that led to the Strategic Stewardship Plan.

The Genesis of the Stewardship Plan

For a decade, Mt. Hood National Forest relied on partnerships to meet the increasing demand in goods and services in the face of significantly diminished resources. These methods of operation conflicted with the traditionally held view of employees and the public—that it was the job of Forest Service employees to provide goods and services directly. In fact, it was reaching the point where the only Forest Service employees who dealt face-to-face with citizens were law enforcement officers and receptionists. With rare exception, every other person who came in contact with the public was a permittee, vendor, contractor, volunteer or someone from a different agency. Cognitive dissonance was high. One of the forest supervisor's biggest motivations in creating the Strategic Stewardship Plan was to normalize and institutionalize the new way of doing the agency's business through partnerships.

Because the plan was attempting to capture and standardize a new business model, the forest supervisor commissioned the leadership team of the district rangers and staff officers to actually work with the public and write the plan. It took three years to complete, but the time and attention to detail made it *their plan—the people's plan—*and demonstrated how the forest was doing business at its best. The plan was developed using two core principles that are an inherent part of new public governance (NPG): 1) enlisting citizens, groups and corporations in coproduction; and 2) broadening the basis of citizen engagement.

The Mt. Hood National Forest Strategic Stewardship Plan was signed by the forest supervisor, on April 22, 2006, Earth Day (U.S. Forest Service, 2006). The plan was successful in memorializing and institutionalizing the commitment to partnerships that the forest had cultivated and refined for a decade preceding the plan. It represents careful deliberative thinking on the part of the forest leadership team and many interested citizens about how best to create a future envisioned by agency leaders and the citizens they serve.

Guiding Principles and Propositions

The plan's guiding principles include ecosystem restoration, citizen stewardship and economic sustainability. The first is an important part of the agency mission; the second seeks to institutionalize citizen stewardship by naming it; and the third captures the essence of the economic throes in which the agency and forest found itself. The plan is based on five propositions about the forest and people who care about it (U.S. Forest Service, 2006, 1):

1   People care deeply about public lands in the Pacific Northwest.
2   People across the Pacific Northwest regard Mt. Hood and its environs as their own.
3   Citizens increasingly recognize that stewardship of the Forest is not the sole responsibility of government officials, but is instead a shared civic responsibility. And increasingly, citizens recognize that stewardship is more than a duty; it is a privilege and an honor.
4   In addition, through business relationships (permits, contracts, partnership agreements, and memoranda of understanding) many more people help us deliver services to and for the public.
5   Employees of Mt. Hood National Forest are similarly dedicated to protecting and conserving the Forest and its natural resources, and to serving people. We are especially interested in ... partnership for the best stewardship of the Forest we love. That's the purpose of this strategic stewardship plan—to foster citizen stewardship.

Setting forth these principles in an official plan provided participants with a transparent foundation upon which to anchor the new approaches in organizational and community culture. These values resonated with citizens and employees and were useful in guiding how the forest would better position itself to face the challenges of increased dependence on horizontal collaboration rather than direct vertical production of goods and services to meet the agency mission. The plan helps illustrate the power created when leaders articulate, memorialize and thus name and create the social norms necessary to guide intended change.

Overview of the Strategic Stewardship Plan

The plan outlines and organizes a framework for expanding partnerships for citizen stewardship of the Mt. Hood National Forest. The term *citizen stewardship* is used in the plan in its broadest sense to include individual citizens; special interest groups; communities of interest; local communities; nonprofit organizations; other federal, state and local agencies; individual outfitter guides; permittees; small companies; and large corporations. The goals of the plan were to better understand and meet the needs of citizens, foster citizen stewardship and provide a starting point for dialogue and a catalyst for learning and change on the part of the Forest Service through citizen stewardship. The leadership of Mt. Hood National Forest took a critical step early on in the process, being abundantly clear about the role of the agency in the past and the present, and what it should look like going into the future. This clarity was important for building understanding, enlisting support of employees and the public, and creating a common table of shared knowledge and expectations.

The Logic of the Plan

Management of the Mt. Hood National Forest is guided by U.S. Forest Service national and regional policy, strategic goals, priorities and budget considerations. In addition, the forest is subject to many regulations enforced by other agencies. These goals, guidelines and regulations frequently conflict, providing an inexhaustible supply of fuel for the long-held acrimony surrounding the management of public forests. Although this framework fits largely within the discretionary function of government, when action is taken it needs to align with agency direction and comply with regulations. It was essential for participants reach some initial agreement on what values the forest should protect. This agreement is reflected in the following five strategic stewardship challenges:

1   protecting communities from wildfire;
2   restoring critical public and private lands stream habitat for the recovery of aquatic species;
3   managing for a healthy forest that sustainably provides goods and services for people;
4   working with public, private and civic interests for sustainable regional recreation;
5   assuring relevance of public lands, goods and services in an increasingly diverse society.

These five values provided the underlying logic of the plan. Citizen stewardship opportunities are created when the strengths of the forest organization and its financial and human resources are matched to an array of potential collaborative projects arising from the stewardship challenges. When citizens who care roll up their sleeves to take on one of the projects, citizen stewardship is enacted.

Results of the Plan

The Mt. Hood Strategic Stewardship Plan is listed first under stewardship contracting success stories on the Forest Service's national website (U.S. Forest Service, 2013). There are many reasons why the Stewardship Plan became a national exemplary model for creative governance solutions to "wicked problems." One of the most important of these has been a reduction in acrimonious conflict among multiple users of the forest and new initiatives by stakeholder groups to address the five challenges around which the stewardship plan was organized. The plan was successful in mobilizing citizen coproduction and engagement. The

Forest Supervisor's goal was to meet the forest agency's mission regardless of significant fluctuations in yearly congressional appropriations—a goal that was met. A major result of the plan was seeing more than 1,000 citizens engaged in stewardship and perhaps another 1,000 people involved in business and collaborative partnerships in citizen stewardship related to the forest. Illustrating this point, nearly 400 forest partners are recognized in the preface of a book (Marbach and Cook, 2005) commissioned by the Forest Service to commemorate its Centennial—itself a project born of collaboration. The forest supervisor dedicated the book: "To the many partners in stewardship, in the name of the American public and the 4.5 million people each year who enjoy recreating on the Mt. Hood National Forest."

Another positive and quite unexpected outcome has been support for a new fee—the Northwest Forest Pass. Various organizations have come together to support this fee and to take on the task of administering recreation programs supported by the fee. For example, the Back Country Horsemen and several other groups have become wilderness stewards whose role is to protect the environment and people. Off-road dirt bike enthusiast organizations help keep motorbikes on designated trails, close dangerous trails and repair damage caused by careless users.

Even though conservation education funding has remained close to zero, by working with partners the forest has created popular conservation education programs that deliver high-quality conservation education experiences to over 100,000 people, primarily students, every year. By working with the proprietor of Timberline Lodge, the forest meets the needs of 1.9 million visitors per year to the lodge, only 500,000 of whom pay fees for the service through ski lift tickets or lodging. The remaining 1.4 million guests are not charged a fee because the proprietor is committed to public service.

Over 1,000 people volunteer nearly 50,000 hours per year helping to maintain trails, plant trees, clean up trash and do whatever else is needed to make the forest a better place. Citizens have also been willing to work with us when invited to participate in collaborative community stewardship planning.

From an organizational management standpoint, staff leaders, officers and citizens alike understand and support the forest's mission. Each leader also has a clear vision of the way forward in the areas of his or her own responsibility.

From a budget standpoint, individual forests compete on a yearly basis for their portion of the regional budget. The region sets priorities each year that guide the allocations. Because citizens were so strongly engaged in formulating the Strategic Stewardship Plan and because so many are partners in coproduction of goods and services provided by the forests, they became a strong, politically significant voice in helping shape the region's priorities. As a result, the forest enjoyed increased budgets in the areas where citizens were most engaged—in watershed restoration through road decommissioning, in fisheries habitat restoration, in historic structure renovation, in habitat-improvement projects, in transportation system planning, and in several other equally important areas.

From a policy standpoint, the forest was successful in changing its level of public support from long-standing and acrimonious protests over timber harvest on public lands to present-day public support of controversial policy decisions, among them the forest's Off-Highway Vehicle Travel Management Plan. The forest has active citizen groups and communities who participate in planning timber sales and stewardship contracts.

The Sandy River Basin Partners have worked together to form a comprehensive basinwide restoration strategy for habitats of all salmon and steelhead populations on both public and private lands (Sandy River Basin Partners, 2007). The highest priority restoration projects already have been completed. From a programmatic standpoint, the forest was recognized, in large measure as the result of this partnership, as having the highest quality aquatic restoration program in the nation.

Case Analysis

The creation of the Mt. Hood Forest Strategic Stewardship Plan touches on a variety of themes central to Part II of this book, in addition to reinforcing themes we have already discussed in Part I. First, the case illustrates the possibility of finding leadership opportunities even when the sky seems to be falling. The forest supervisor rose above the common "Chicken Little" attitude in the face of continuous declining resources, intractable political conflicts among stakeholders and a seriously constrained policy environment. Instead of saying "this is impossible," he looked around to see what assets were already in place as a result of decades of efforts to save money and to reduce the size of government. He found community assets that could be leveraged to create community ownership of the challenges faced by the agency. Once these challenges were owned, he created a process that turned this ownership into new resources that the agency could use to fulfill its mission.

This case study also illustrates the need for public leaders to have a functional road map—a working theory—of governance that lays out and links the vertical and horizontal dimensions of leadership in a way that it can be navigated successfully. As noted by the forest supervisor in this case:

The clarification that came with the planning process helped me to see how best to (1) align the organization of my staff, (2) legitimize my actions to those above me, (3) harness organizational resources to support the plan, (4) memorialize and institutionalize organizational commitment internally and externally, and (5) galvanize external support, engagement, and coproduction. More simply, theory helped me to better recognize drivers of change, better name the challenges, and better deploy my own and organizational resources (time, money, people, procedures, and values) toward a larger people-centered conception of what natural resource management in a public national forest is all about. The grand prize, if I had to name it, is threefold: (1) having my own organization really understand that the forest mission is not just a natural resource–centered mission but also a people-centered mission, (2) being able to legitimately deploy official resources toward the people side of the mission, and (3) being able to involve citizens in the larger enterprise of natural resources stewardship.

Larsen (2014, 137)

A third lesson from this case is the need for public administrators to embrace working with multiple public, nonprofit, private and civic actors whose cooperation must be earned, not commanded. The forest supervisor earns each partner's cooperation through interest-based relationship building: being clear about his own organization's interests, striving to understand the interests of potential partners, and developing collaborations in areas of mutual interests.

Fourth, this case illustrates that leaders need to be very clear about your own and your agency's authority and the framework of political, executive and judicial working parameters. It is important to articulate contemplated collaborative endeavors in language that comfortably resides in and can be easily supported by your agency. While administrators are sometimes annoyed by the frequency of policies du jour, reference to them can serve as an important legitimizing influence to contemplated collaborative endeavors that might otherwise seem questionable.

Fifth, because of organizational stasis, it is the duty of leaders to make the case for change. The more consequential a contemplated change, the more robust the argument for change must be (see Kotter, 1996 for a full discussion of creating organizational change).

Sixth, it is important for leaders to pick partners carefully and purposefully. As we observed in our discussion of polity leadership in Chapter 4, collaborations need to be based on dependable organizational strengths that create synergy and forge connections to important people, public opinion, a pool of able volunteers, an ability to organize large-scale multiparty field projects, etc.

A final leadership lesson that can be drawn from this case concerns the core interests of the participatory organizations. It is important to measure and report results of collaborations in metrics that are responsive to those interests. Doing so ensures continued relevancy of the partnership to its respective organizations and memorializes results in a way that counts.

7 Sizing up the Leadership Context
Drivers of Change in the 21st Century

> the present is the opening in the door through which the light [of the past] is able to shine. The essential executive action, then, is opening that door. Opportunity knocks often, but never waits long. If we keep shut our various doors of opportunity, the light can never shine on us.
>
> Kouzes and Posner (1995, 107)

> we're all puppets, and our best hope for even partial liberation is to try to decipher the logic of the puppeteer.
>
> Robert Wright (1995, 37)

Leadership requires seeing the opportunities that lie hidden beneath the seeming bewildering array of external forces that impinge on human action often making us feel like puppets on a string. Our goal in this chapter is help you feel less like a puppet and more like the puppeteer. We summarize the major drivers of change in the 21st century that affect our ability to take leadership initiative in our respective public organizations. Our goal is to encourage leaders to view these external forces as doors that can be opened to let the light of change shine in, rather than as constraints. We undertake this summary in two parts. In the first part of the chapter we identify the major drivers of change in the 21st century. In the second part we discuss how the profession of public administration has chosen to respond to these drivers of change, first in the form of the New Public Management (NPM) movement and then with the New Public Governance (NPG) movement.

There are two reasons why we believe aspiring public service leaders need to have a good understanding of the forces of change summarized in this chapter. First, the various external forces of change that surround us create a logic that, when understood, opens the doors of opportunity for undertaking meaningful leadership initiatives. Our argument draws upon path dependency theory, which contends that options for change are to be found in the historical conditions that sow the seeds of change. Knowing these historical conditions and their current manifestation arms us with the knowledge of what kinds of change is possible and how the change can best be undertaken (Peters, Pierre, and King, 2005). For example, we show in our discussion of the NPM movement that one could anticipate the NPG movement that followed the first wave of reform by examining the values and institutional actors that were being advantaged by NPM compared to the values and actors that were being marginalized.

But there is a second and perhaps more important reason for reviewing the forces of change in this chapter. We believe that a review of these drivers makes a good case for the insufficiency of both our current public service leadership mindset and the tools needed successfully to address an increasing array of what we call "wicked problems." This conclusion sets the stage for our argument in Chapter 8 where we present a leadership framework for assessing "wicked challenges" and summarize the kind of leadership mindset that needs to be cultivated to successfully address emergent leadership challenges that have no clear definition or set of solutions.

Drivers of Change in the 21st Century[1]

There are known and knowable forces of change on the horizon that leaders must take into account if they are to successfully "size up" the opportunities to make a difference. In the sections that follow we review the most important of these drivers of change that shape as well as limit opportunities for leadership initiatives. None of these drivers should surprise anyone who has been paying attention to current trends that affect public policy, programs and the administration of the public's business. Ignoring these trends imperils our chances for leadership success. Some of these drivers affect organizational missions, leadership and administrative operations directly. Other drivers are more indirect and less subject to organizational control and influence. For example, organizations can design strategies to deal with succession planning and demographic changes in society more quickly than they can design strategies to deal with global warming or the decline in citizen trust in governing institutions. The latter may require a more concerted and centralized policy approach that goes far beyond what a single organization or jurisdiction can accomplish. Accordingly, we organize our discussion of drivers of change to start with those that are more accessible to local organizational action and move toward a discussion of those drivers that may require more concerted collective action at higher scales of governance.

Workforce Changes: Generational Differences and the Demise of Professional Expertise

Public-sector organizations currently face major issues due to retirements, workforce transition and succession planning. The Government Accountability Office (GAO) reported that 31 percent of the federal workforce will be qualified for retirement by 2017 (U.S. GAO, 2014). Likewise, retirements and staffing turnovers place critical burdens on state, county and city governments, whose employees constitute 60 percent of public employment (Ehrenhalt, 1999, 19–22). Much of the expected waves of retirement in public sector organizations have been delayed by the collapse of the economy in 2008. However, as the retirement wave regains momentum, it will pose obvious problems of preserving institutional memory, sustaining best practices, supporting long-standing relationships among cooperating institutions, and transferring to successors the subtleties of prudential practice that account for much of current success. This is especially true in local communities where much of public sector work is carried out through partnerships and other collaborative arrangements among public, nonprofit and for-profit institutions. Implied promises made to stakeholder groups, expectations of the sequencing of public service projects when funding becomes available, and similar kinds of agreements make it possible for social capital to be built and sustained over time. Without continuity in the workforce and proper leadership, this capital is in danger of being eroded.

Workforce demographics pose additional challenges for identifying, acquiring and retaining the kinds of abilities that will be most needed in the future. The impact of technology, globalization and the resulting changes in culture have created growing generational differences within the workforce that have important implications for motivating employees (Taylor, 2014). Exhibit 7.1 summarizes the major generational differences and the impact these differences have on work environment expectations and performance. Millennials enjoy work settings that are flexible, provide opportunities to make a difference, ensure good work-life balance, take advantage of making the highest best uses of technology and have opportunities for career growth. The Baby Boomer and Generation X employees value career advancement more than feeling listened to by the organization; they value tangible and more instrumental benefits than the intrinsic benefits of public service. While Baby Boomers are workaholics, they do not have high tolerance for organizational rules, procedures and protocols that get in the way of good results. Finally, the traditionalists are fast becoming organizational relics. Taken together, these generational differences require leaders at all levels of public services to be armed with a rich portfolio of motivational tools and strategies.

Exhibit 7.1 Generational Differences Chart

	Traditionalist: 1928–1945	Baby Boomers: 1946–1964	Generation X: 1965–1980	Millennials: 1981–1996
Current Age	63-86	44-62	28-43	8-27
Other Names	Veterans, Silent, Moral Authority, Radio Babies, The Forgotten Generation	"Me" Generation, Moral Authority	Gen X, Xers, The Doer, Post Boomers, 13th Generation	Generation Y, Gen Y, Generation Next, Echo Boomers, Chief Friend-ship Officers, 24/7s
Influencers	WWII, Korean War, Great Depression, New Deal, rise of corporations, space age Raised by parents that just survived the Great Depression Experienced hard times while growing up which were followed by times of prosperity	Civil rights, Vietnam War, sexual revolution, Cold War/Russia, space travel Highest rate of divorce and 2nd marriages in history Post-War babies who grew up to be radicals of the 70s and yuppies of the 80s Strong belief in "The American Dream" As a result they are seen as being materialistic and ambitious	Watergate, Energy Crisis, dual income families and single parents, first generation of latchkey kids Y2K, Energy Crisis, activism, corporate downsizing, end of Cold War, moms work, increased divorce rate Perceptions shaped by growing up having to take care of themselves Came of age when U.S. was losing its status as the most	Digital media, child-focused world, school shootings, terrorist attacks, AIDS, 9/11 Typically grew up as children of divorce Grew up more sheltered than any other generation as parents strived to protect them from stress, harm and the evils of the world Came of age in a period of economic expansion Kept busy as kids; first generation of children with schedules

Core Values	Adhere to rules, law and order, respect for authority Commitment to the collective good; giving back; duty before pleasure Dedication/sacrifice Delayed reward Discipline; loyalty Family focus Hard work; responsibility Patience Trust in government	Anti-war Low attraction to government Anything is possible Equal rights; equal opportunities Extremely loyal to their children Optimistic Personal gratification and growth Question everything Spend now, worry later Team oriented Commitment to work Want to "make a difference"	powerful and prosperous nation in the world The first generation that will NOT do as well financially as their parents did Highly educated High job expectations Independent Informality Lack of organizational loyalty Pragmatic Seek work-life balance Self-reliance Skeptical/cynical Think globally High techno literacy	Achievement oriented Most educated generation Avid consumers Strong sense of civic Duty Self-Confident Embrace diversity; highly tolerant Enjoy fun High morals Competitive Like personal attention Members of global community Highly techno savvy High spirituality
Work Ethic and Values	Dedicated Pay your dues Work hard Respect rules and authority Age = seniority	Driven Workaholic-60 hr. work weeks; Work long hours to establish self-worth and identity and fulfillment Work ethic = worth ethic	Commitment to work-life balance Work smarter and with greater output, not work longer hours.	Believe that because of technology, they can work flexibly anytime, anyplace and that they should be evaluated on work product, not how, when or where they got it done

(*Continued*)

Exhibit 7.1 (Cont.)

Traditionalist: 1928–1945	Baby Boomers: 1946–1964	Generation X: 1965–1980	Millennials: 1981–1996
Company first	Challenge authority; dislike conformity to rules that compromise quality Loyal to team Process oriented	Output/outcome oriented; eliminate unnecessary tasks, rules and procedures Self-reliant Move easily between jobs and employers; criticized for having no attachment to a particular job/employer	Expect to influence the terms and conditions of the job Less career ambition in favor of more family time, less travel, less personal pressure High expectations of bosses and managers to assist and mentor them in attainment of professional goals Goal and career oriented; training and education important Want long-term relationships with employers, but need meaningful, challenging and innovative opportunities Prefer diverse, collaborative and fun work environment

While high levels of technical competence will continue to be important in the future, they will no longer be sufficient, even within public service activities dominated by technical specialists. The flattening of public organizations, increased emphasis on customer service and the need to build collaborative partnerships at the lower ranks of public organizations place much greater emphasis on recruiting individuals who have the capacity to make sense out of muddles, to deal with ambiguity and to stay calm in tense, conflict-ridden settings. This has been the case for those occupying leadership positions in the upper ranks of the public service for quite some time, but these qualities are now increasingly required at lower ranks of public service. Robert Reich finds these qualities in new kinds of workers, whom he calls "symbolic analysts:"

> Symbolic analysts solve, identify, and broker problems by manipulating symbols. They simplify reality into abstract images that can be rearranged, juggled, experimented with, communicated to other specialists, and then, eventually, transformed back into reality. The manipulations are done with analytic tools, sharpened by experience. The tools may be mathematical algorithms, legal arguments, financial instruments, scientific principles, psychological insights about how to persuade or amuse, systems of induction or deduction, or any other set of techniques for doing conceptual puzzles.
>
> Reich (1992, 178)

It would be a mistake to assume that these symbolic analysts are trained exclusively in some new kind of specialty. As Reich argues, they most often are the product of a robust liberal arts education which cultivates the capacity to see the "big picture" and to integrate the broad view with the details and specific needs at hand. The acquisition of this kind of generalist and integrative capacity becomes especially urgent for technically trained career officials who are now next in line for promotion. Leadership training programs that cultivate the qualities of the symbolic analysist will become much more important than they have been in the past.

Not only is professional expertise changing and becoming thinner through retirements, it is also under attack. The information age has made all of us experts, which is turning the professional world upside down. The history of the 19th century could be called the "Rise of the Professions." It was a period in which we experienced the formalization of public professions like law, social work, education, health care, planning and public management. We came to depend on these cadres of trained professional to diagnose and design solutions for public problems using their stocks of knowledge and conventions of practice. Society ordained this class of people with the authority to address a set of problems on our behalf—acting in our interests individually and collectively (Stever, 1990, 1988). However, the high esteem enjoyed by professionals is crumbling as a result of a variety of cross-cutting drivers of change. These include the democratization of knowledge resulting from rapid changes in technology; the emergence of overlapping and emergent problems that no one set of professionals can address; social and political hyper-pluralism that makes value advocacy often more important than "professional facts;" and the balkanization of the professions into ever-more numerous subsets of specialists who are more attached to their specialty than they are to the larger profession of which they are a part. All of these changes mean that professionals in the future will need to expend much greater effort in legitimating the value of their expertise, as it can no longer be presumed.

Growing Demographic and Ethnic Diversity

In the years ahead, most local communities will grow in size and be composed of an older and more diverse group of citizens. Between 1990 and 2000, nearly 33 million people were added to the national population, the largest ten-year increase in U.S. history. The fastest growing regions were the Sunbelt areas of the West and the South. Projecting to the year 2015, the U.S. Census Bureau (2018) suggests that America will remain predominantly "white," but that other racial groups will continue to increase disproportionately. Perhaps the most dramatic result of these changing population trends during the last few years has been that African Americans have been replaced by Hispanics as the nation's largest minority group. This is the result of large numbers of immigrants entering the country from Latin America and high birthrates among first-generation Hispanics. More recent census research conducted by the Pew Research Center indicates that:

> Hispanics will account for the vast majority—74 percent—of the 10.5 million workers added to the labor force from 2010 to 2020. That share is higher than in the previous two decades. Hispanics accounted for 36 percent of the total increase in the labor force from 1990 to 2000 and for 54 percent from 2000 to 2010.
>
> Kochhar (2012)

Hispanic workforce numbers are increasing at the same time that white labor force numbers are beginning to decline. The percentage of women in the workforce appears to have peaked at around 59 percent.

The patterns of diversity are not uniform throughout America. Most ethnic and racial minorities are concentrated in major urban centers and specific states. For instance, Hispanics of Mexican ancestry have their highest populations in California, Arizona, New Mexico and Texas. While these individuals make up only 12.5 percent of the U.S. population,

Hispanics now constitute 32.4 percent of California's population, with 77.3 percent being of Mexican heritage. Greater Los Angeles is, in effect, the second largest Mexican city in the world—only Mexico City has a larger Mexican population. Half of all U.S. Hispanics live in California and Texas, however, the presence of people with Hispanic ancestry is now growing rapidly outside of the Southwest as well. This is particularly true in the urban centers of New York City, Chicago and Florida, and in major farming regions such as the upper Midwest, the Willamette Valley in Oregon and the Yakima Valley in Washington State.

The 2010 U.S. Census report indicates that the Hispanic population grew from 35.3 million in 2000 to 50.5 million in 2010, accounting for over half of the overall growth in the U.S. population (Ennis, Ríos-Vargas, and Albert, 2011). The impact of this diversity on local communities will vary, but issues of race and ethnicity are becoming a growing priority for public leaders generally. There are two visions that have governed the debate over the relevance of minority group identity in the United States. One vision begins with a normative *assimilation* framework, which assumes that the melting pot model experience of European immigrants is the preferable public policy objective. However, this model is challenged by a *multicultural* alternative, which argues that assimilation is neither possible nor desirable for the kind and character of diversity present in many American communities. First, most European immigrants have been able to assimilate within the first or second generations due to their similarity in physical appearance to the majority population. People with darker skin have not been able to assimilate as readily or at all in some cases. This has been particularly true of African Americans and some Hispanics. As a result, assimilation is now often rejected as a goal by "minorities of color" in favor of gaining respect and acceptance as economically, politically and culturally equal but separate ethnic groups. Second, many point out that the assimilation model works best when the size and concentration of ethnic groups is small. However, when the ethnic group is large enough that it can effectively insulate its members from the dominant cultural patterns of the national society, the assimilation model does not work so easily. This is borne out by the history of large concentrations of ethnic groups in the larger U.S. cities. For example, many African American communities, Mexican Americans and Central Americans in eastern and southern Los Angeles, and some of the Vietnamese immigrants who arrived in the United States in the 1970s and settled in urban areas rather than in small towns have not followed the assimilation model. In situations like these, pressures to assimilate are often ignored (Rodriguez, 2003).

Those Americans who favor a society that acknowledges the permanent existence of unassimilated or only partially assimilated ethnic/racial minorities generally advocate for multiculturalism (or pluralism). This is essentially a celebration and encouragement of continued diversity, similar to the policy introduced by Canadian Prime Minister Pierre Elliot Trudeau in 1972 in order to hasten the acceptance of a permanently unassimilated French-speaking society in Quebec Province. Today, multiculturalism in Canada is a deep-rooted policy at every level of government and has been expanded to cover all ethnic groups. For many, this serves as the model to be emulated in the United States.

There are those like Richard Rodriguez (2003), a leading American essayist and social commentator, who argue that the debate between the multiculturalism and melting pot models is largely irrelevant. Constant close contact among people of different ethnic and racial groups in the United States is progressively resulting in a blurring of the differences between them. Rodriguez suggests that Americans are melting into each other genetically and culturally. More and more children are being born with two or more different ethnic or racial backgrounds.

The 2010 Census provides dramatic evidence in support of Rodriguez's argument. Between 2000 and 2010, the number of mixed-race children in America rose by 50 percent, to a total of 4.2 million. Overall, the total number of adult Americans who self-identify as mixed race rose by 134 percent, to 1.8 million (Humes, Jones, and Ramirez, 2011). Since the mixed-race population is "overwhelmingly young," these numbers translate into more mixed-race peers for all children, especially in southern and Midwestern states, where increases in numbers of mixed-race Americans have been "far greater than the national average" (Saulny, 2011). Rodriguez refers to this phenomena as the "browning of America" and asserts that a distinct national culture is developing—one formed largely by various ethnicities borrowing from each other and thereby creating a new cultural synthesis. Rodriguez (2003) points to the recent experience of Hawaii and the southwestern states as examples of this homogenizing of people and their cultures into something distinctively new.

In addition to browning, local communities are also graying. By 2025, the Baby Boomers born in 1955 will be 70. Just under 20 percent of the U.S. population will be younger than 15, slightly less than today, according to the U.S. Census Bureau. The middle of the age spectrum will hollow out, and the number of those 65 and older will swell from 12.4 percent of the population to 18.2 percent. The nation in 2025 is projected to have 43 social security beneficiaries for every 100 workers. The graying of America will result in important changes in the configuration of local communities, as resources in all sectors are shifted toward health care clinics, home health services, hearing aid providers, hospitals and hospital equipment stores, physical therapists and residential care facilities (for additional changes see Hobbs and Stoops, 2002; U.S. Census Bureau, 2002; Pew Research Center, 2017).

Future public servants will be challenged by the "graying" and "browning" of America to craft and implement policies that take into account the unique age, cultural and language needs of various subpopulations. This will be especially true in the delivery of social services and public education, where scarcity of resources is already straining the capacity of public service systems to meet existing needs. For the foreseeable future, the greying and browning of America wiil provide a fiery cauldron for political debate over "who belongs," how much and what kind of diversity is enough, and the more enduring issues of institutional racisim (Haidt, 2012; Dionne, 2016; Dionne, Ornstein, and Mann, 2017). In the short run, these political debates will not change the tradjectory of demographic realities, but they will make the work of our career public servants harder. Throughout the length and breadth of the land, our local public servants will have rich opportuntities to hone their conciliatory leadership knowledge and skillls (see especially discussion of Exhibit 7.3 in this chapter and a discussion of conciliatory practices in Chapter 10).

The Urbanization of Rural Communities

Urbanization commonly assumes we are referring to the creation of "global cities" (Global Cities Initiative, 2018) and the concentration of populations in urban areas. But this is a misperception of how urbanization is affecting the larger landscape. Urbanization is occurring in rural areas, particularly in the more open spaces of the western US and the Midwest. Families are moving from farms and ranches to live more proximately to town centers and then commuting out to farms and ranches. These "new west" urban centers are attracting migrants who are not placed based in terms of household income. Some are retirees. Others are people who can telecommute to their work from any place with sufficient IT connectivity. Web designers in Choteau, Montana, for example, or World Bank employees in Joseph, Oregon, illustrate what we mean by rural urbanization. There are now 24/7 project management teams where a team dispersed by location track the work day in every time zone with team members in Oregon, India and Germany—all working from the same electronic base of information. There is a paradox of urbanization in these areas as the life style choices are clearly drawn by the natural landscapes of rural areas even while technology both shrinks the world and makes global products and ideas readily available in rural areas, a process that has come to be known as "glocalization."

Permanent Fiscal Crisis with Increased Emphasis on Managing for Results

It is likely that public service leaders of our public organizations will face continued fiscal stress for the foreseeable future (Osborne and

Hutchinson, 2004; Green, 2012). Many officials have been sounding the alarm for decades over rising debt, growing costs of entitlements and ownership of the U.S. debt by China and Japan. David Walker, a former comptroller general of the United States, has estimated that if the present U.S. rates of spending and taxation continue, the U.S. government will be bankrupt by the year 2040 (Walker, 2007). The major tax bill passed in December 2017 has made the debt even higher and driven an ideological political wedge between those who believe the cuts will significantly stimulate the economy and increase tax revenue and those who believe that some combination of cuts in entitlements, Medicare and the military will be essential. The continuing taxpayer revolt, along with the protracted recession, makes significant tax increases an unlikely solution, and the heated politics surrounding public debt has led more to stalemate than progress.

A complicating factor at the local level is the proliferation of government jurisdictions and special districts (see extended discussion in Chapter 3 on polity leadership), which tend to fracture the political will and the economic resources that could be pooled to help cope with the fiscal crisis. All of these jurisdictions depend heavily on property tax revenue, which has been severely restricted by a combination of property tax limitations and a depressed housing market. At the same time, local jurisdictions, like the national government, are facing a growing pension and retirement obligations as the Baby Boomer generation retires. These conditions will result in increased pressure on local career administrators to coordinate with other jurisdictions for tax levies, service consolidation and educating citizens about what they are getting for the taxes they pay. Pressures will increase to do more with less or to provide the same levels of service while cutting expenditures. At some point, it will no longer be possible to continue operating programs at meaningful levels of service. The financial collapse of cities across the United States over the last decade, including Detroit, Michigan, and Stockton, California, provide telling reminders that service cuts have become part of the new normal. Elected officials risk their careers when trying to remedy these situations with tax increases. Career administrators will need to take a leadership role in convincing both the public and the elected officials of what to do when public institutions reach the breaking point; clearly, only certain programs will be salvageable with the funds available. But there also will be leadership opportunities to explore new kinds of partnerships that blend the resources of the public, private and nonprofit sectors.

The Rising Importance of Native American Indian Tribes and Tribal Governments

Since the early 1960s, there has been a fundamental transformation in the relationship between Native American tribes and U.S. state and local governments. Charles Wilkerson (2006) argues that the rise of modern Indian Nations, particularly since World War II, is one of the great civil rights struggles in American history. This struggle has resulted in a new area of self-determination that makes Native American tribes a full and equal partner in the co-production of the common good.

More than 60 million acres nationwide are under the control of 565 tribes and count some 3 million Native Americans as enrolled members. Each tribe, and each portion of each tribe, has its own institutional history with the federal government, other tribes and other proximate state and local governments. The booming years following World War II gave rise to new pressure on tribes by the federal government to gain access to tribal lands and resources. Termination and relocation became the official policy of the federal government toward Indians in 1953, with the passage of House Concurrent Resolution 108. Subsequent laws gave certain states authority to extend jurisdiction over tribal people on tribal lands in specific areas of law. Though not in statute, federal policy in the late 1950s included a massive effort to relocate Indian people from reservations to urban areas. Chicago, Oakland and Minneapolis, among other cities, were established as targets for relocation efforts with transition offices and programs. Other urban centers—for example, Los Angeles and Portland, Oregon—saw rapid increases in the population of Native Americans through "voluntary" migration pushed by termination of tribes, sale of homelands and the crushing poverty in Indian country. The concentration of Indian peoples in urban areas had the unintended consequence of spawning a new identity among Native Americans based on the commonalities of their histories. It allowed a small but critical number of Native people to complete higher education, become lawyers and activate interest in a generation of leaders willing to lead the struggle to regain self-determination. This "rights-taking period" reversed the termination act, Public Law 280, and re-established rights to fish, determine tribal membership and self-govern.

Federal policy for the last 40 years officially supports the principle of self-determination and the recovery and enforcement of rights for Native American Indian tribes. However, this struggle is an unfinished work. Tribes continue to seek restoration of tribal recognition; the restoration of homelands; remedies for losses such as the mismanagement of mineral extraction based on trust funds administered by the Bureau of Indian Affairs (BIA); and the achievement of tangible outcomes on the land for rights that have already been secured, including water in the stream and fish in the river.

If an earlier generation of tribal leaders emerged to champion the struggle for basic rights, a new generation is emerging to lead governance within tribes, bridge interjurisdictional management among tribes and other governments, and implement the increased responsibilities that have come with these newly secured rights. A generation ago, it was common to find non-tribal professionals working for tribes to implement tribal policy. Today, it is more common that the these professionals are Native Americans and increasingly enrolled members of the tribes they serve. These professionals work across policy domains with expertise in fisheries, social work, business management and health care. Tomorrow will be different, as tribe after tribe builds governance capacity to administer a broadening range of fundamental services such as housing, health, energy, natural resource, economic development and social programs. Public service leaders at all levels of federal, state and local government will need to attend to the dynamic changes in the 565 currently recognized tribal governments, where the balancing of rights and responsibilities, trustee responsibility and self-determination, and independence and co-production are added to everyone's leadership portfolios.

Proliferation of Governmental Jurisdictions and Overlapping Structures of Authority: Mergers, Consolidations and Shared Service Agreements

As we noted in Chapter 3, the number of local jurisdictions has grown dramatically since the 1960s. The willingness to accommodate the desire of citizens to live in enclaves that protect them from the perceived adverse consequences of growth, increased taxes and undesirable diversity, whether socio-economic, ethnic or racial, has resulted in the creation of a complex array of local governing institutions. The pressures that have created these governing entities are not going to dissipate in the foreseeable future; in fact, they will likely continue to increase. As a result, local jurisdictions are preoccupied with issues of taxes and tax bases, annexation, infrastructure provision, land improvement, zoning and provision of services. These issues place a premium on managing interjurisdictional relationships, and they will grow in importance as jurisdictions are forced to cooperate in managing shrinking resources and accommodating increased concerns from citizens for "getting their money's worth." Such pressures will likely lead to mergers, consolidations and shared administrative functions in order to reduce overhead costs and increase efficiencies in maintenance, information technology and purchasing. The current push for decentralization will cycle into recentralization. Evidence for this already exists in the consolidation of police and fire services into unified districts, and in nonprofit-sector delivery of social services, where small nonprofits are banding together or being swallowed by larger entities in order to sustain or improve capacity.

Decline of Civic Engagement and Public Participation: How to Build Trust in Governing Institutions

In this section we build on our discussion in Chapter 3 of the role of civic associations in carrying out our polity leadership responsibilities. A variety of factors have come together to reduce the motivation and interest of citizens in participating in civic life and public decision making processes. In *Bowling Alone*, Robert Putnam traces this decline to a variety of factors, including technology and mass media, mobility and sprawl, increased work pressures and generational demographic differences (Putnam, 2000, 277–284). By far the biggest factor is the generational differences that show up in how individuals feel about big issues like patriotism, money and self-fulfillment. Each generation born after 1930 places more and more emphasis on money and self-fulfillment than patriotism and service to the common good (273).

As ordinary citizens have withdrawn from direct participation in civic and political institutions, the vacuum has been filled by the rise of large associational networks. Many of these networks have moved their headquarters to New York City and Washington D.C., where their professional staff can work directly with government policy makers (Skocpol, 1997, see especially 472). Professionalization of civic associations is part of a much larger phenomena called "interest group liberalism."

Interest group liberalism is a system of independent but powerful interest groups that are run by professional experts who have close working relationships with government officials at the legislative and executive levels of government. Sometimes called the "iron triangle," the three sides of the triangle consist of: key members of Congress who are responsible for funding and providing oversight of a particular program, a federal agency that administers the program, and the trade associations and lobbying groups who are the chief beneficiaries of a particular program. There is a common interest among these three sets of participants to craft solutions to problems that result in a weak government oversight (Lowi, 1979).

One of the most important implications of interest group liberalism is that ordinary citizens are not a part of this system of governance. Over time citizens may become cynical and feel disenfranchised. Despite elections, the same groups of insiders end up being the "real decision makers" and citizens start to feel that they no longer can "band together to get things done either through or in relationship to government" (Skocpol, 1997, 472). The Occupy Wall Street movement of 2011 and the presidential election of 2016 are poignant examples of the rising of the disengaged to "take government back" from vested interests.

The general decline of civic engagement and public participation places a burden on local governing bodies, both professional staff and elected officials. They have to spend more time anticipating what citizens feel and want. They have to deliberately design strategies that will build engagement and produce outcomes that the majority of the citizens can own. Local governing bodies can no longer simply assume that citizens have more trust in their local governing institutions and officials than state and federal levels of government. Citizen trust is a kind of social capital that needs to be replenished. Like any other capital, once it is gone, it takes heroic efforts to restore.

The Changing Boundaries of the Political Economy

As we documented in Chapter 6, the boundaries between the public, nonprofit and private sectors have been in a continuous process of change. But since the 1980s with the election of Ronald Reagan, the boundary shifts have been quite significant and will continue for the foreseeable future. Consider some of the more significant markers of these changes:

- President Reagan's deregulation of business initiative in 1980 remains fully intact (especially with the election of President Donald Trump in 2016), despite the Wall Street hedge fund scandals of the 1980s and 1990s and the collapse of the stock market in 2008.
- Businesses and unions have been given the same right as individuals under the first amendment to spend unlimited sums of money for the election or defeat of individual candidates (see *Citizens United v. Federal Election Commission*, 558 U.S. 50, 2010).
- The faith-based initiatives of the George W. Bush administration (Executive Order 13,199 [2001]) that provide avenues of federal government support to churches and other faith-based groups for the provision of social services are very much an active part of the public policy agenda.
- Contracting out social services to nonprofit and even for-profit organizations has become the norm (see further discussion of this in our review of New Public Management in the last section of this chapter).
- One of the less well-known developments in recent years is the deliberate creation of hybrid organizations, what are sometimes called *quasi-governmental organizations* ("quagos") and *quasi autonomous nongovernmental organizations* ("quangos"). The federal government has created 300 of these in the last few decades (Moe and Kosar, 2005). While these agencies carry out government-sponsored activities and provide money or mechanisms for funding government activities, they operate outside the legal authority of Title 5 of the U.S. Code. This means that they cannot

be held accountable through the traditional tools of executive oversight (the budget and general management laws, for instance).

The reshaping of government boundaries, with more reliance on third parties to provide governmental services, has sparked renewed interest in key questions that were at the center of the constitutional debate in 1787: What role should government play in a democratic society? How can that role be assured under a rule-of-law system? What kind of accountability mechanisms should be in place to ensure that third parties conform to public values? For the foreseeable future, public administrators will play a leadership role in answering these questions at every level of American democratic government, particularly as they are called upon at the local level to use the nonprofit and private sectors for the delivery of public services.

The Increasing Reliance on Technology and the Promise of E-Government

The increasing prominence of modern technology raises the prospect of using it to facilitate citizen engagement and to serve the ends of good government more generally. For example, can virtual political communities be created that disassociate people living in a common place and substitute a virtual community organized around common challenges, issues or interests that are constitutive of a larger common good? The evidence so far suggests that absent intentional, structured and sustained intervention, individuals will continue to use technology to reproduce a world they find most consistent with their own beliefs, attitudes, values and common interests (Iyengar and Kinder, 2012; Prior, 2005). Technology allows individuals to avoid differences rather than confront them, which is the opposite of what happens when individuals are living together in a common space and have nowhere else to go or to hide. Now that modern technology allows us to go anywhere to be with anyone at any time, what are the implications of this for our political work as leaders?

The evidence suggests that we have a large opportunity to use technology to improve access to government information, to influence and improve government decision-making, to educate citizens, to hold government accountable and to improve government services (see Marche and McNiven, 2003; Saxena, 2005). But the confidence that our citizens have in this happening is not very high, as the Pew summary in Exhibit 7.2 suggests. According to this study, citizens are fairly evenly split on the use of technology to improve governance participation, decision-making and outcomes. These results may be less a statement about the technology and the good intentions of those using it, and more a statement about the impact of technology on changing the formal institutions of governance and the self-referential habits and behaviors that information technology creates among users.

There are at least four major leadership challenges that are posed by modern technology for those who want to use it for collective action. The first is information overload. While technology provides easy access to more information, more information does not produce greater knowledge and better-informed decision-making. In fact, excess information can create information overload and pose increased challenges for sorting and ordering the array of data in ways that create relevance and meaning for the common work of the community (Levitin, 2014, 3–33). It can complicate choices, steer citizens in the wrong directions and confuse citizens as to which choices to make (cf. Thaler and Sunstein, 2009). In short, data overload can produce confusion, conflict and indecisiveness, what has come to be called "the paradox of choice" (Schwartz, 2005).

A second leadership challenge is using technology in ways that enhance the possibility for creating a shared sense of community, rather than having it used to further divide the community into ever-narrower factions. The balkanizing effect of technology certainly provides a safeguard against tyranny of the majority. But this argument in favor of technology misses Madison's larger point about the value of competing interests in enlarging the range of interests that individuals take into consideration as a result of deliberation with others who hold

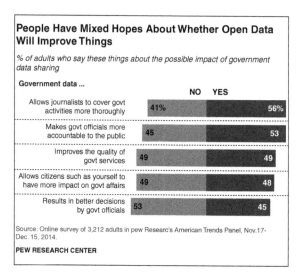

Exhibit 7.2 Perceptions of Possible Government Data Sharing Impacts

Source: Online survey of 3,212 adults in Pew Research American Trends Panel, November 17 to December 15, 2017.

differing views. The challenge is figuring out how we can use technology to conduct public discourse in a manner that facilitates rather than exacerbates compromise.

A third challenge in using technology for collective action is finding ways to put elected officials at the center of the information dialogue. As Madison argued in Federalist #10, American democracy depends on refining and enlarging:

> public views by passing them through the medium of a chosen body of citizens whose wisdom may best discern the true interest of the country and whose patriotism and love of justice will be least likely to sacrifice it to temporary or partial considerations.
>
> Madison (1787, Federalist No. 10, quoted in Rossiter, 1961)

Tweeting will not suffice, especially when the goal is to create an information exchange and dialogue that facilitates group decision-making by the elected officials and a shared sense of community on the part of the participants. It is hard to imagine this problem being solved without altering the ways in which elected officials currently collect and use information for decision-making purposes.

A final, and perhaps the most problematic, challenge of using technology is the protection of privacy. This concern has been exaccerbated by the influence of Russsia in the 2016 presidential election and by the revelations of information sharing by Facebook and Google. These major breaches of security are likely to make citizens even more wary of using technology to expedite goverance decisions and service delivery.

The Growth of Income Inequality

The gap between the rich and the poor in the United States has grown over the past several decades. Since 1967, U.S. household income inequality grew by 18 percent. Nearly half of that growth occurred during the 1980s (U.S. Census, 2012b). Between 1979 and 2000:

> the real income of households in the lowest fifth (the bottom 20 percent of earners) grew 6.4 percent, while that of households in the top fifth (the top 20 percent of earners) grew 70 percent, with the top 1 percent achieving real income gains of 184 percent. In contrast, during the 1950s and 1960s real income almost doubled for all groups.
>
> Mishel, Bernstein, and Allegretto (2005, 2)

In a report titled, *The State of Working America: 2004/2005*, the Economic Policy Institute estimated that the bottom 80 percent of

American households control only about 16 percent of the nation's wealth. Meanwhile, wages, benefits and working conditions for workers at the bottom continue to decrease (Mishel, Bernstein, and Allegretto, 2005, 12). The United States ranks third to last among the Organization for Economic Co-operation and Development (OECD) nations in terms of income equality.

Since 2000, the number of poor Americans has grown considerably. The official poverty rate hovered at about 15 percent in the four years between 2008 and 2012, up from 12.1 percent in 2002. The 2012 Census indicates that 49.1 million Americans have fallen below official poverty thresholds, up from 42.9 million Americans in 2009 and 34.6 million in 2002 and slightly over 22 million in 1973 (U.S. Census Bureau, 2012b). The official poverty rate in 2000 (11.3 percent) was about the same as 1973 (11.1 percent) despite the fact that real capital income grew 66 percent over the same period (Mishel, Bernstein, and Allegretto, 2005, 12). Any changes in the poverty rate since 1981 are almost entirely the result of market forces, not the result of any changes in the tax system or transfer payments to the poor (Mishel, Bernstein, and Allegretto, 2005, 339–40).

While the Census Bureau figures reveal a significant number of Americans living in poverty, many experts argue that the measures used by the federal government drastically underestimate the real scale of poverty in America—primarily because the official poverty thresholds are considered "too low." The Economic Policy Institute believes a more realistic poverty threshold for a family of four would be in the area of $30,000 a year—and that a more accurate estimate of the poverty rate in America would be at least 30 percent of the total population (Mishel, Bernstein, and Allegretto, 2005, 12). The 2010 Census provides new supplemental measures of poverty and lower-income levels that rise as high as 146 million, almost half of the population. There are clear public service leadership implications for the growing income gap between the bottom and top of the economic spectrum. Politically, it means heightened tension between the haves and the have-nots, and this can easily spawn grassroots movements such as Occupy Wall Street in 2011 or the Bernie Sanders campaign for president in 2016. These grassroots initiatives reflect a heightened concern over the vast disparities in wealth; the multiple problems of the poor, including jobs, housing, health care and wages; and the shrinking of the middle class in the United States.

Managing the issue of income inequality is especially problematic for public service leaders at the local level. They do not make national and state policy; instead they are legally responsible for funding local services like police, fire, parks, education, transportation, water, sewer, zoning and land use planning. In the face of state limitations that have been placed on local property taxes (which is the major revenue source for funding most local government activities; see Chapter 4), these jurisdictions have increasingly turned to a fee-for-service approach to funding many activities. But there are examples of using the current state of affairs as a stimulus to think "outside the box" in terms of developing new approaches to addressing the problems of affordable housing, employment and homelessness at the local level (Government Innovations Network, 2018).

The fee-for-service approach has expanded beyond sewers and water to include parks, libraries, street improvement, lighting districts, health clinics, etc. The customers and clients paying these fees do not clearly separate their tax bill from their water, sewer or other charges for a designated service. This leaves citizens experiencing an undifferentiated increase in the costs of government. Alternatively, the proliferation of fees for services and special tax rates for enumerated services leave citizens wondering what the "general government taxes" actually pay for. All of this leaves our public leaders in the unenviable position of reminding and educating a polarized public of the enduring needs of communities, the importance of investing in infrastructure, the need to build in equity provisions in fee-for-service programs that take into account income inequality and the obligation to take care of the growing number of dispossessed people in our society who require a social service safety net.

Climate and Environmental Changes

Climate change is almost universally listed among the top ten drivers of change (Friedman, 2005). It directly and indirectly impacts all aspects of our life—ecological, economic and social. While some ecological impacts are obvious—more precipitation as rain and less as snow—other impacts are less apparent. For example, we are seeing changing patterns in "home range" of plant and animal species both in the wild and in cultivated settings. Perhaps less visible but more dramatic are changes in ocean conditions serving as a predicate for all manner of physical and biological changes. Economic impacts of climate change are becoming more apparent as well, as whole communities in coastal and riverine settings begin planning for rising water levels by physically moving community centers uphill from the rising tide of the oceans and the increased flooding of our rivers. Changing climate patterns create more turbulent events with consequences for built infrastructure and the communities affected. Flooding, fire and wind events are all becoming more common and harder to predict. We are experiencing a social response to these changes as recreation patterns adjust to reflect snow and water levels. And what homeowners expect to be growing in their yards changes almost yearly—lawns, the icon of home ownership, are a dwindling relic of past ambitions.

Every year for the last decade most jurisdictions in the Western United States have set a new record for "drought." For most world watch organizations focused on human health, agriculture, forestry and economic development, water scarcity is a top driver. Water shortages are predicted not only to impact lives directly but give rise to greater conflict as scarcity requires historic social bargains among water rights holders to be revisited. In 2016, the State of California captured the headlines globally for its aggressive efforts to cut back water use and to create programs that would incentivize those who own water rights to forego the use of those rights. These restrictions are driven by growing water needs for agriculture (which accounts for 80 percent of human consumption) and population and industrial growth (which accounts for the other 20 percent). The growth in consumption is coming at the expense of water to protect wild and scenic rivers, which has decreased by half since 2006 (USGS, 2016).

Part of the water shortage story is the changing patterns and locations of water for natural resources and agriculture. Nut farmers are migrating from California to Oregon, for example, and winegrowers are already thinking of shifting varieties in vineyards established just decades ago. There is evidence that water scarcity is driving population migration as well (Nagourney, Healy, and Schwartz, 2015). These changes have a disproportionately adverse impact on those at the lower end of the socio-economic scale. Creating equitable allocation of scarce resources and providing appropriate compensation for property losses will generate heated public debate regarding equity and social justice.

Global Energy System Dynamics

For the last 50 years, energy access and use has been a global issue, comprised of several parts. One is a dramatic geopolitical shift in where fossil fuels are coming from and the markets to which they are going. This is not a simple issue, but an evolving one where technology and market prices change types, sources and markets for fossil fuels. While coal is on the downturn in the US, until recently it has been on the rise in China (although China, too, is making serious efforts to reduce its coal reliance). New sources of oil and gas have emerged in North America, shifting the geopolitical balance of oil and gas imports. Fossil fuels as a resource for electrical energy production are also changing as a result of environmental regulatory policies (i.e., clean energy standards and policy goals for more sustainable fuels, including state renewable energy portfolio standards), and because of changes in energy production and incentives to economize consumption. With more renewable energy sources entering the generation side of the energy system, there is a need for load balancing of energy resources like hydro and natural gas turbines, which can be turned on and off to balance wind and solar.

And energy systems are linking with information technology to develop systems that are literally smart. The emergence of "smart energy systems" is replacing our century-old reliance on technology improvements by regulated monopolies to provide us with continuous energy efficiency. Smart energy systems take advantage of technology to disperse energy production and incentivize the reduction of consumption. Net-zero consumption homes, while not standard, are a reality today. Rooftop solar systems that allow households to produce and consume electricity are a growing expectation. These systems rely on conservation, timing of use and energy-independent devices to reduce demand. Developing countries can now skip the long-linked centralized energy monopoly systems and go directly to dispersed systems. These changes will radically impact institutional arrangements, infrastructure design and policy. Second- and third-order impacts of the "smart energy" systems will be far-reaching. They include the reallocation of resources, changes in local communities dependent on extraction economies, improved environmental impacts, a new energy economy and, ironically, increased value of big hydro and reliance on regional anchor institutions that have responsibility for stabilizing regional transmission systems, load balancing and storage of potential energy.

Responses to the Normal: The Rise of New Public Management (NPM) and New Public Governance (NPG)[2]

The drivers of change discussed in the previous section are both a reflection as well as the cause of changes in the traditional role of government, a role that has been taken for granted since the New Deal and the World War II. Two sets of factors began to coalesce in the 1980s, calling into question the traditional assumption that a large centralized government was the preferred approach to addressing socio-economic problems. First, there was a resurgence of support for a smaller and less intrusive government that would reduce the regulatory and financial burden on individuals and property holders (Green, 2012; see Chapter 6 of this volume). This call for smaller and less government was reflected on a variety of fronts, including taxpayer revolts in several states that succeeded in putting into place limitations on tax increases and spending. It was reflected on the regulatory front in the call for reduced restrictions on the rights of property owners to develop their land, and on businesses burdened by environmental, occupational safety, healt, and employment regulations (Cooper, 2009). The call for less government was also fueled by the belief that the private and nonprofit sectors could provide many government services more cheaply and efficiently

(Cooper, 2003). Underlying much of this call for smaller and less government was a philosophical belief that democracy is safer when government is smaller.

A second major factor challenging the viability of the World War II and New Deal administrative state was concern over a growing national debt and the escalating costs by state and local governments for health and retirement plans for employees (Walker, 2007; Morgan, Green, Shinn, and Robinson, 2013/2008, Chapter 1). Taken together, these forces for change have resulted in two movements over the last three decades that call into question the capacity and appropriateness of government to be the primary agent in addressing society's problems. The first movement, called *new public management*, took the business or market model as the standard for measuring government success. The second movement, called *new public governance*, emphasizes the importance of taking a collaborative approach to providing public services with partners within and across the public, nonprofit and private sectors. This model is more emergent and bridges communitarian aspects of the nonprofit sector with aspects of the market model. Neither model claims to be exclusive; each one emphasizes different kinds of strategies designed to reduce the size, scope, costs and inefficiencies of government.

In the sections that follow we review the NPM and NPG movements and assess their implications for administrative leadership and practice. We will undertake our review in four steps. In the first part we provide an overview of the reform periods in the field of public administration. This will help show the reader where and how New Public Management and New Public Governance fit into the development of the field. In the third part we focus on rise of New Public Management, its assumptions and accomplishments. In the third part we discuss the distinguishing characteristics of New Public Governance, its assumptions and accomplishments. We then summarize some of the leadership assumptions and implications of NPG. This sets the stage for the next chapter where we argue that neither the vertical rule-centered leadership model of NPM nor the horizontal collaborative-centered model of NPG is sufficient. We introduce the EMERGE leadership framework that emphasizes the knowledge, skills and competencies to lead in a state where conditions faced by leaders are more emergent than known and knowable.

An Overview of the Reform Periods in Public Administration

In Exhibit 7.3 we locate the place of NPM and NPG within the larger evolution of the study and practice of public administration through five stages of development. We call the first stage "preclassic" because it precedes the conscious creation of public administration as a formal field of study and captures what leaders are expected to do when undertaking nation-building and state-building. Studies of the role of public administration during these successful founding periods (in the United States and elsewhere around the world) document the importance of administrative leaders who used their discretion to assist founding political leaders in building the trust and legitimacy of the political order. This was the genius of both Genghis and Kublai Khan, who together united China and laid the foundations for the modern world (Weatherford, 2004); of the founders of the Greek and Roman city states; of Ataturk, who founded the Turkish Republic (Bay, 2011; Mango, 2000); of Mao Tse-tung, who founded modern China; of Ho Chi Minh who reunited Vietnam; and of the American founders as well (cf. White, 1958; Green, 2002). All of these founders viewed the work of administrators as essential to government performance. They consciously recruited members of their administrative cadre based on their: 1) competence in building systems, 2) sensitivity to the needs and values of local citizens, 3) ability to increase the reputation and trust in the larger political system, and 4) ability to create and maintain a shared sense of common values and purpose. In short, the work of administrators was not seen as simply being instrumental and loyal but as being an integral part of shaping the meaning, value and legitimacy of the political order itself. This makes the work of public administration—from its inception—political, constitutive and value-centered.

The third column of Exhibit 7.3, labeled "classic public administration," represents the emergence of public administration as a distinct field of study. It has its origins in the United States in the Populist and Progressive eras of the late 1800s and early to mid-1900s. Salamon observes that classic public administration theory "posited a new type of institution, the democratic public agency, that would overcome the three major problems long associated with government bureaucracy—that is, excessive administrative discretion, special-interest capture, and inefficiency" (2002, 9). From the beginning, public administration has concerned itself with the business of restricting government agencies to the administration of policy rather than the making of it, the staffing of agencies based on competence rather than influence, and management principles aimed at efficient dispatch of duties.

Represented by the fourth column in Exhibit 7.3, new public management became the dominant paradigm in the 1980s. There is widespread agreement that the NPM agenda has succeeded in accomplishing multiple goals, among them increasing government efficiency, improving service access and delivery to citizens, and downsizing government while expanding the private and nonprofit sectors (Brookes, 2008, 3). NPM has strengths that are important for building citizen trust in government, including: 1) an emphasis on customer service; 2) the need to foster professionalism, managerial skills and accountability in

Exhibit 7.3 Distinguishing Characteristics of Public Administration Leadership Philosophies

	Pre-classic Nation Building	Classic Public Administration	New Public Management (NPM)	New Public Governance (NPG)	Value-Based Performance Governance
Theoretical basis	Regime theory	Political science, public policy, organizational theory	Rational/public choice theory, management science	Institutional, network, theory of agency	Political economy, regime theory, complex interdependence
Concept of state	Unitary	Unitary	Regulatory and privatized	Plural and pluralist	Regime-dependent
Management focus	Nation	Organizational hierarchy	Organizational performance	Values that are coproduced by networks and partners	Value-based performance
Leadership actions	Nation-building and statecraft	Output management	Coordination	Interest-based conflict resolution	Diplomacy
Leadership scope	A people and their destiny	Management within an organization	Coordination among organizations	Forging collective horizontal leadership	Collective vertical and horizontal leadership
Leadership results	Institutions and processes of state	Hierarchical and professional control: efficiency and effectiveness	Customer satisfaction, efficiency, effectiveness	Agreement on actions	Agreement on the nature of the problem and solution
Value orientation	Variable	Agnostic values Hierarchy	Explicit values	Limited explicit value conflicts	Unlimited explicit value conflicts

Value arbitration	Institutions and processes of state	The market and classical or neoclassical contracts	Networks and relational contracts	Renewed institutions and processes of the state
System orientation	Monocentric; internal focus	Polycentric; internal focus	Mini-centric; external focus	Polycentric; external focus
Performance unit of analysis	Outputs; transactions	Outcomes	Conflict resolution	Consensus-building, trust and legitimacy
Leadership archetype	Tactical and operational management	Strategic management	Strategic leadership	Transformational leadership

Source: Adapted and expanded from Osborne (2010, 10).

public administration; 3) and the important role of leaders in creating and maintaining high-performing organizations.

The critical responses to the deficiencies of classic public administration and new public management have spawned new public governance, represented by the fifth column in Exhibit 7.3. NPG represents a shift in focus from what it takes to make things work in vertical structures of authority to what it takes to make things work in horizontal structures, or what has come to be called "leading in a power-shared world" (Morgan et al., 2013/2008, Chapter 13; Crosby, 2010; Crosby and Bryson, 2005). These horizontal structures are represented by cooperative agreements between and among public agencies, nonprofit organizations and participating entities from the market sector. Joint actions like these require a focus on identifying and reconciling conflicting values with a reliance on different policy instruments and tools than those used in traditional hierarchical structures (see the Master Cases for Parts II, III and IV of this volume for excellent examples of this type of leadership). Salamon (2002) outlines five key areas of change that result in this transition from classic public administration and new public management to new public governance:

- a shift in focus from agencies and programs to the kinds of policy tools and instruments needed to create and sustain network agreements,
- a shift in organizational form from hierarchy to network,
- a shift in dynamics from public v. private to public and private,
- a shift in exercise of power from command and control to negotiation and persuasion,
- a shift in orientation from management skills to enablement skills.

One of the important consequences of NPG is that it taps into what Bellah and his colleagues characterize as the second language of American discourse (Bellah, Madsen, Swindler Sullivan, and Tipton, 1996/1985). This language is rooted in the civic republican tradition (Kemmis, 1990, Chapter 2) and places high emphasis on civic engagement and the role of civic and voluntary associations in sustaining healthy democratic governance through their educative and mediating role in tempering interest group and ideological conflicts (Skocpol, 1997; Skocpol and Fiorina, 1999; Sirianni, 2009; Putnam, 2000; Putnam, Feldstein, and Cohen, 2003). Fairholm's emphasis on value-centered leadership, what he calls "whole-soul" leadership, is a reflection of this new emphasis on going beyond interest-based politics to achieve moral agreement among members of a common community (2004, 588). This approach emphasizes tapping into the unique cultural and historical identity of a community and using this reservoir of shared history and values to build mutual agreement that advances the common good. In the sections that follow we explore the factors that gave rise NPM and NPG movements in greater detail and the implications they have for future public service leadership.

The last column in Exhibit 7.3, "value-based performance governance," captures our guess of where the field of public administration is headed in the decades to come. It will be a period characterized by the need to build agreements at the community levels of public service where citizens may be quite divided in the values that inform their understanding of the scope and reach of different levels of government. If successful, these value-centered leadership approaches will create stronger local communities by strengthening civic capacity and building resilience. But these successes are likely to occur despite national partisan divides. But that is a good reminder that we should not equate politics with governance. Sometimes these two sets of political activities grow quite far apart. This is one of the reasons we have deliberately organized our leadership framework around the governance roles of public officials in the nonprofit, public and for-profit spheres. The destiny of our communities will depend as much, if not more, on how these leaders in the various sectors perform their governance roles than on how well our leaders in our formal structures of authority perform their roles. We return to this theme in the concluding section of this chapter.

The Rise of New Public Management

There has been a concerted effort since the 1980s to reframe the model of public service from a rule-centered system of accountability to one that makes government run more like a business. This movement began following the election of Ronald Reagan to the U.S. presidency. Labeled the New Public Management movement, it strives to make the services provided by government more responsive and accountable to citizens by applying businesslike management techniques with a strong focus on competition, customer satisfaction and measurement of performance. There is general agreement among scholars and practitioners alike that these efforts to measure what gets done have produced a variety of worthwhile results:

- Measures of efficiency and effectiveness have inspired managers, supervisors and frontline employees to improve their capacity to diagnose and correct operational problems (Ammons and Rivenbark, 2008).
- An emphasis on performance measurement has heightened interest in creating systems that improve the overall management and governance of political entities (Hatry, 2010, 2002; Moynihan and Pandey, 2005; Wholey and Hatry, 1992).
- Performance measurement systems have expanded to embrace an increasingly larger array of values, including cost and efficiency

measures; various effectiveness measures such as outputs, outcomes and impacts; and qualitative measures such as satisfaction, responsiveness and quality of life (O'Flynn, 2007; Stoker, 2006; Jørgensen and Bozeman, 2007).

But there are two major weaknesses of using private-sector business principles to improve the performance of government, regardless of what gets measured. First, there is no common denominator—such as profit, market share or return on investment—that can serve as the basis for comparison across the wide range of criteria that build trust and legitimacy among citizens in their political institutions. Furthermore, efficiency, effectiveness and responsiveness to citizens (government's customers) are not the only values needed to build trust and legitimacy in democratic governance. As we have argued in Chapter 5, values like fairness, equity, protection of rights and transparency play important roles in determining the legitimacy of political institutions, processes and outcomes (Cooper, 2003; Rosenbloom, 2005, 2003; Moe, 1994; Moe and Gilmour, 1995; Lynn, 1998; Kelly, 1998; Moore, 1995, 1994; Hefetz and Warner, 2004). How do you put these more elusive values on the same plane as those that can be measured more easily, and how do you create a common denominator that allows for meaningful comparisons?

The second weakness of using private-sector models for improving government performance is that the public sector is comprised of increasingly fragmented structures of authority that confound the possibility, and even desirability, of moving in a straight line from goals and objectives to instrumentally and rationally linked performance measures. The proliferation of local governments (see Chapter 4), coupled with the entrepreneurial push to outsource public service to nonprofit and private-sector organizations, shifts performance away from a single-minded focus on the efficient, effective and customer-sensitive achievement of goals and objectives to a focus on achieving and sustaining agreements between and across structures of authority. This has been described as "leading in a power-shared world" (see Chapters 4 and 10 of this volume; Robinson and Morgan, 2014, Chapter 12) and is the focus of our discussion in the next section.

Some of the weaknesses of using a business-centered approach can be illustrated by seeing what can happen over time to both nonprofit and public organizations that have aggressively taken advantage of the NPM agenda to contract out public services to third parties. We start with the impact on nonprofit organizations. In order to comply with government accountability and performance standards, many small nonprofits have had to fundamentally alter the structures, staffing and operations of their activities. Instead of relying on volunteers, they have had to spend more money on professional accountants, grant writers, contract managers, finance officers, etc. Or, to be competitive, many small nonprofits have been merged to form larger organizations, leaving fewer nonprofit providers on the community landscape. The providers that remain rely less on passionate volunteers and more on career professionals who develop a co-dependency relationship with their counterparts in government. This unintended chain of events undermines the capacity of nonprofit organizations to serve as potential sources of meaningful social and institutional change (Smith and Lipsky, 1993, 5; Berry and Arons, 2003, Chapter 5).

The impact of the NPM contracting-out agenda on public organizations is no less far-reaching but much less noticed. When government is the direct service provider, the citizens have an opportunity through the annual budget process and changes in program authority to understand and participate in the debate over the social service needs of the community. But when these services are contracted out to third parties, the oversight is transferred away from the political process to contract managers. Under this kind of system, it takes a concerted effort by leaders to keep the social service needs of the community at the center of community deliberation.

To summarize, the NPM business-centered agenda is based on a truncated view of the purpose of government, which is more than simply being accountable to citizens or providing efficient and effective programs and services. Government is also responsible for collecting the values of the community and creating integrated responses to these values across increasingly fragmented government systems (Kelly, 1998; Lawrence, 1998). When the values of the community are in conflict, or when they are contrary to the interests of significant minorities, government officials have a fiduciary responsibility to make decisions that are in the larger public interest. This kind of accountability model was pushed into the background with the emergence of NPM and replaced with a business model. The Vision Action Network Master Case for Part III provides a good illustration of what happens when the NPM model becomes the standard for measuring the success of governmental entity. It loses sight of its community governance role, which is the goal of New Public Governance.

The Rise of New Public Governance

Concerns with NPM's narrow instrumental focus generated a counter-movement among practitioners and academics to place substantive political values more firmly at the center of the governance debate. This New Public Governance movement emphasizes three trust- and legitimacy-building characteristics of public governance that are ignored and/or undervalued by NPM. First, NPG is value-centered; it believes the goal of government is to promote the larger common good. Mark Moore has called this new emphasis "the public value approach" (Moore, 1995, 1994; also see Smith and Huntsman, 1997), while Stoker and others have called it "the collective preference approach" (Stoker, 2006; Alford, 2002). NPG is interested in advancing the value created by the whole of government activities, not just improved efficiency, effectiveness or responsiveness in the implementation of a given program. This shift has broadened the objectives of performance measurement and management to include service outputs, satisfaction, outcomes, a wide array of substantive political values and, ultimately, citizen trust and the very legitimacy of government itself.

A second characteristic of NPG is its emphasis on the creation of government processes that facilitate the generation of implement agreements among wide-ranging stakeholders who may disagree on what courses of action will produce the maximum public value (Yang and Holzer, 2006; Sanger, 2008). These conciliatory processes have spawned the creation of new tools, like "multiple stakeholder processes" (Zimmermann and Maennling, 2007; Lelea, Roba, Christinck, and Kaufmann, 2015) and atelier gatherings that bring people together from different communities of practice and disciplines to engage in dialogue, identify shared interests and differences and collectively problem-solve shared challenges. We discuss some of the most important of these tools in Chapter 11.

NPG and its complementary governance and leadership tools assume that politics is mainly about creating collectively determined preferences through value-centered mediation processes (Alford, 2002; Moore, 1995; O'Flynn, 2007). This is a sharp contrast to the philosophy of NPM, which views politics as the aggregation of individual preferences. The consequences of this difference are nicely illustrated by thee major steps the United Kingdom has taken over the last decade to reform the delivery of its education, medical and justice and social services to citizens at the local government level. In recent years, public officials in the U.K. have chosen to treat government performance not as a set of rationally planned objectives that are the consequences of interest-based political outcomes at the polls but an on-going process of political mediation among contending stakeholders. These stakeholders have very legitimate differences regarding the public values that need to be preserved to ensure the integrity of the larger public good. The on-going role of government administrators and elected leaders is to be honest brokers and agents of the larger public interest. Such efforts have resulted in the creation of a wide variety of new policy instruments, negotiated agreements and performance measures that would have been difficult, if not unthinkable, under NPM (Brookes and Grint, 2010; Grint, 2000; Osborne, 2010, especially Chapters 16, 19 and 22; Salamon, 2002; Koliba, Meek, and Zia, 2011).

A final characteristic of the NPG movement is that it views the creation of the public good as a coproduction process involving the public, private market, and the nonprofit sectors (see Crosby, 2010; Crosby and Bryson, 2005; O'Toole, 1997; Osborne, 2008). Under this model, the role of government is not simply to regulate, distribute or redistribute public benefits, but to serve as a catalytic agent to invest private and nonprofit stakeholders in shared ownership of the public good. In this catalytic role, government performs two functions: it brings stakeholders to the table, and it ensures that the process of negotiating agreement is undertaken in the public space and carried out in a manner that insures shared ownership of both the process and the outcome. This is illustrated by community policing programs or much more complicated forms of networked governance such as watershed management over a very large geographic area that involves multiple stakeholders and structures of authority (see Mt. Hood Stewardship Master Case for Part II of this volume).

To summarize, NPM is interested primarily in using the private and nonprofit sectors to deliver a service cheaply, efficiently and effectively (Osborne and Gaebler, 1993; Osborn and Hutchinson, 2004), while NPG is interested in enhancing the capacity of local organizations as a means of building civic infrastructure and the overall capacity of a community to be self-authoring (Banyan, 2003, 2004; Smith and Lipsky, 1993; Smith and Smyth, 2010). The three characteristics of NPG discussed above emanate from a common belief that government plays a catalytic leadership role in bringing the public, private and nonprofit sectors together to contribute to the distinctive way of a life of a political community.

Conclusion

The ability of societies to survive through time depends to a very large degree on the capacity of their governing systems to respond to the socio-economic, demographic, technological and environmental forces of change. In his effort to discover why civilizations collapse, Jared Diamond found that more often than not it is was the failure of government leaders to see or respond quickly enough to the dangers at hand (Diamond, 2011). The United States has deliberately created a system of government that balkanizes the exercise of official power and authority in all three sectors. This has been one of the strengths of the United States over the last 250 years of its young existence, but it remains to be seen whether this will continue to be a strength in the future. Centralized national responses to looming challenges are difficult to come by and even more difficult to sustain over an extended period of time. These conditions create opportunities, and even a special responsibility, for public service leaders at all levels of government to "size up" the external drivers of change and assess the kinds of response that will best build the trust of citizens in their democratic institutions.

The legacy of New Public Management and New Public Governance, combined with the leadership models that are part of the American administrative legacy discussed in Chapter 6, provide a rich repertoire of resources upon which leaders can draw to help identify challenges and opportunities. But these are not enough. The pace of technological change and the interdependency of multiple "drivers of change" are exceeding our capacity to make sense out of what is going on in time to create durable solutions. Take for example, our response to the financial collapse of 2007. The reforms put in place are no longer thought to be needed, which is leading experts to think about responses that anticipate a constant state of adjustments to deal with dynamic unknowns. This has prompted one critic of the existing regulatory system to remember the advice of von Clausewitz: "If you entrench yourself behind strong fortifications, you compel the enemy to seek a solution elsewhere" (Caprio, 2009, 22). In the chapter that follows we introduce a new leadership framework that is intended to arm leaders with the ability to "size up" challenges and opportunities and take leadership action in conditions of emergence where there are more unknowns than knowns. In doing so, our goal is to prevent leaders from succumbing to the danger of entrenching themselves behind strong fortifications and then being surprised by the outcome.

Notes

1 For this section we have drawn from our previously published work, Morgan et al., (2013/2008, Chapter 14, 454–65).
2 For this section we have drawn from Chapter 1 by Morgan and Sinn in Morgan and Cooke (2014, 3–8).

8 The Normal v. the New Normal and the Rise of Wicked Problems

Leadership for Emergence

Leaders must have the ability to make something happen under conditions of extreme uncertainty and urgency—a condition we label *emergence*. In fact, leadership is needed more during times of uncertainty than in times of stability: when confusion over ends and means abounds, leadership is essential. Leaders master change—and they master uncertainty, seizing the imperative to act.

Kouzes and Posner (1995, 76)

The search for scientific bases for confronting problems of social policy is bound to fail because of the nature of these problems ... [I]n a pluralistic society there is nothing like the indisputable public good; there is no objective definition of equity; policies that respond to social problems cannot be meaningfully correct or false; and it makes no sense to talk about "optimal solutions" to these problems ... Even worse, there are no solutions in the sense of definitive answers ... social problems are never solved. At best they are only re-solved—over and over again.

Rittel and Webber (1973, 160, 168)

Some problems are so complex that you have to be highly intelligent and well informed just to be undecided about them.

Peter (1982, 24)

The opening epigraphs establish the central themes of this chapter. We build on the argument of Chapter 7 that our current public service leadership mindset and the tools are insufficient to deal with what we call "wicked challenges." By "wicked" we mean challenges that have no clearly identifiable solution and that are embedded in a highly fluid and interconnected set of causal influences. These conditions make it impossible to know the best path forward. We develop this argument more fully in the first part of the chapter and discuss the reasons why wicked challenges are becoming more and more common, what we call the "new normal." In the second part of the chapter we present a framework for identifying different kinds of leadership challenges, ranging from simple, complicated, complex and chaotic or wicked. In the final part of the chapter, we draw from the conceptual work of Snowden and Boone (2007) to discuss the implications of these different kinds of challenges for public service leaders.

Wicked Problems: What Are They and Why Are They Becoming More Normal?

Rittel and Webber first popularized the use of the phrase, "wicked problems," in the early 1970s in their effort to make sense out of the emerging complexity of the public policy landscape in the United States (Rittel and Webber, 1973). Recall that the early 1970s were the years following various social initiatives like the War on Poverty, The New Frontier, the Great Society Programs, the Civil Rights Movement and an awakening of the environmental movement (see Chapter 5). Rittel and Webber saw in this emerging complexity and moral diversity of views a need for the development of a new leadership mindset that is more focused on problem identification in an unstable socio-economic and political environment than focused on finding permanent solutions and fixes.

Despite their call for a new leadership mindset, we continue to rely on solution-centered approaches to most leadership challenges. This solution-focused paradigm provides the *raison d'être* for many of our regulatory policies and public programs dealing with land-use planning, managing financial markets, and public health and safety. Some issues can certainly be treated as problems with solutions, such as stopping the spread of food poisoning in a local restaurant, building and repairing our capital infrastructure, preventing point source pollution by a business or reducing unlawful game and timber harvests on public lands. But other challenges cannot be approached with the assumption that there is a solution. Protecting our local communities from various kinds of natural and man-made disasters, finding solutions to homelessness, managing our natural resources for multiple uses and reducing crime and drug addiction are examples of what systems scientists call an emergent order (Kurtz and Snowden, 2003, 464; Kauffman, 1993), or a set of conditions with too many causes that is too unstable and too disorganized to be known with certainty.

The Master Cases for each of the parts of this volume and the opening leadership vignettes in Chapter 1 illustrate the greying of boundaries between simple leadership challenges and truly wicked ones. The local librarian who wants to revisit the Board's policy on protecting children from access to inappropriate internet materials or the forest supervisor managing the development of a stewardship plan can quickly find themselves in a hornet's nest of contested and unresolvable issues. Leading in conditions that have the potential to become a hornet's nest has come to be called "the new normal," a previously unfamiliar or atypical situation that has become standard, usual or expected.

Wicked problems are becoming more common in the political, economic and social settings for two reasons. First, problems have become more complex and interdependent (Keohane and Nye, 1987). Second, our social and political institutions have become less able to achieve collective agreements that last through time, thus resulting in conditions that are highly dynamic and inherently unstable. There are three sources of evidence we have examined to understand and to illustrate the idea of complex interdependence and environments that are highly unstable. One is the growing body of literature dealing with the impact of globalization on the nation state. The second is the emerging body of research on strategies for dealing with accidents and surprises. The third is the testimony of clinical practitioners. We summarize the relevance of this literature for our argument in the sections that follow.

Globalization and Complex Interdependence: Localizing the Sources of Legitimacy and Trust

There is growing global recognition that nation states no longer enjoy the trust and legitimacy anticipated by the Peace of Westphalia in 1648. This Westphalian model assumed the principle of sovereignty based on territoriality and the absence of a role for external agents in domestic governing structures. Most importantly, it assumed that states could control their destiny through wise leadership and self-contained governance practices. That view has been undermined by the rise of increasingly complex, interdependent and dynamic multidimensional networks of multinational corporations, international regulatory and governing bodies, global associations, sectarian and religious advocacy groups, regional organizations, along with a growing number of officially recognized political entities (Held, 2004; Keohane and Nye, 2000; Rosenau, 1998; Johnson, 2001). These networks rely on information that is produced and shared through constant technological innovations. Together these conditions have created a reduced capacity of nation states to control their destiny, and caused nation states to no longer take for granted the unqualified trust of their citizens.

Pulitzer Prize winning journalist Thomas Friedman, in his book called *The World is Flat* (2005), uses the metaphor of a flat globe to emphasize the increased interdependence of human beings who share a world that is quickly becoming "hot, flat and crowded." These conditions create complex and dynamic systems that have replaced order and hierarchy. "Causal relations are numerous, interrelated, difficult to identify, and always shifting. Comprehensive understanding of most issues has become impossible, uncertainty has increased, and predictability has become a vestige of the past" (Magis, Ingle, and Duc, 2014, 446).

So what are the implications of these conditions of global complex interdependency for "leading from where we sit"? In his book on the *Five Literacies of Global Leadership* (2007), Richard Hames argues that future leadership success requires us to tap into the power of what he calls the "café," a metaphor for the network of individuals where the informal discussions within organizations take place. This is contrasted with the "cathedral" with its arrangements of centralized power. Hames (2013, 23-24, 130, 317) argues that "we are headed to a world without the traditional dominance of nation states. In this new world order, regions and cities will have more power and resources than many existing nation states." Whether or not you agree with Hames' thesis on the demise of the nation state, it is certainly true that more and more challenges will be addressed locally by those who understand what is going on and by leaders who are able to mobilize the resources from where they sit. Looking up in the hierarchy for solutions to challenges or for directions on what to do next and how to do it is increasingly less successful, especially when you are required to innovate in conditions of emergence.

One of the less observable consequences of globalization for local leadership action is its impact on local businesses and nonprofit organizations. As we observed in our discussion of polity leadership in Chapter 3, nonprofits and local businesses have historically played key roles in providing seed corn for civic engagement and building civic capacity. But globalization has weakened this linkage to local communities through consolidations, expansions and mergers that make a corporation or nonprofit organization's global network more important than the place-based networks where corporate headquarters or satellite operations are located. As globalization continues to weaken the linkages of individuals and organizations to their local communities, public service leaders will need to rely more on their polity leadership role in building organizational, citizen and stakeholder trust in local governing institutions.

Accounting for Surprises: Using Science to Contain and Control Complex Adaptive Systems

A second source of evidence in support of the need for emergence leadership is provided by the "science of surprises", more commonly known as complex adaptive systems theory (CAST). Students of CAST are interested in understanding how the interactions among the parts of complex systems can reciprocally interact to produce widely unexpected and surprising outcomes. Typical examples of complex adaptive systems include the global economic network of relationships regionally, nationally and locally; an ecosystem's relationship to the larger biosphere; the impact of brain functioning on our immune system; and the internet and cyberspace, which is composed, collaborated and managed by a complex mix of human and computer interactions. What can leaders learn from these complex adaptive systems that generate surprises? Are there understandable and foreseeable patterns that can be identified in the seeming endless flux?

We turn to the patterned flight of a flock of birds or the foraging behavior of an ant or bee colony to provide accessible examples of what CAST researchers are trying to understand. What explains the behavior of the whole? The answer is not to be found in having a leader, but in having organized followers who act in concert because each individual member of the group follows a set of basic rules. When any one of the parts behaves unpredictably, like the intricately connected strands in Charlotte's Web, it can set off catastrophic and unpredictable results in other parts of the web. For example, while the September 11 attacks were a surprise, even more surprising to the insurance industry was that the event resulted in a major flight of capital from the world insurance market to the tune of about $40 billion. To those in the insurance industry who have a vested interest in assessing risk and accidents, these events provided an opportunity to create more reliable and encompassing models for guessing better the next time around (MacKenzie and Tzar, 2002).

But there is another optional set of responses to surprises, and that is to assume that you cannot ameliorate the problem of guessing wrong by developing better predictive models. What if you assume that you can never create a model that can reduce surprises? What if you assume, instead, that you need to adjust leadership behaviors and assumptions to respond more creatively to surprises? This kind of research question looks at the bright side of surprises, rather than the dark side. In doing so, it positions leaders to develop an innovation-oriented predisposition and to possess greater confidence as they face an environment of uncertainty.

Changes in Clinical Practice

A final source for understanding the leadership implications of complex interdependence and highly dynamic systems is the testimony of practitioners. Exhibit 8.1 contains a summary of findings by a group of students who interviewed leaders in the Portland, Oregon, health care industry (Janac, Evjen, Edge, and Lasich, 2012). The central point of their inquiry, reflected in the questions posed to leaders, was, "What is the 'new normal' and its impact on your work?"

Exhibit 8.1 Summary of Leader Views on Changing Conditions in the Health Care Industry

Leader #1: Constant change has become the norm for me. In the early 1980s hospitals were decrying the advent of Diagnosis Related Groups (DRGs) reimbursement strategies, arguing that this would bring ruin to the industry. In the 1980s experts were decrying the advent of health care exceeding 13 percent of gross domestic product (GDP). In the 1990s, the industry awaited its ruin at the hands of managed care. Over the last 30 years leaders have come to assume that instability is common, uncertainty is ever-present, change continues to escalate, disruption occurs regularly, and we can neither fully predict nor govern the future. Instead of a "new normal," leaders believe we will continue to face "not normal" times. Leaders need to:

- Expect the unexpected,
- Take advantage of the "good weather" and "good luck" that we will also continue to encounter, and
- Learn how to thrive in the face of uncertainty, chaos and adversity.

The strategic context of health projects will be different in the future—more complex, more dynamic, more difficult to comprehend with lots more uncertainty than from when project management was invented in the 1940s and 1950s, so it will be more difficult to "project into the future" (we never can step into the same river twice) so project management will need to shift the balance of attention from looking inward to more looking outward. In essence we will need to pay more attention to people and relationships and implement/construct our futures "on the go," spending less time on up-front planning. Rather than "ready, aim fire," we will be doing "fire, ready, aim."

Leader #2: I have not been in health care for very long, but it is something that is constantly evolving. There is a big shift from an illness model to a wellness view; prevention is becoming increasingly emphasized. Related to this focus on prevention is cost and insurance, which are highly contentious and will be debated and on the forefront of health care most probably for a very long period of time. Also, continual advance in health IT and how to utilize technologies effectively and prove "meaningful use" is something that continues to burgeon and will do so for the foreseeable future.

Leader # 3: In the field of technology where I work, the pace is much faster. Everyone expects a quick response and expects you to be available. That is different from the past. In practice, although you are not told so explicitly, expectation and responsiveness is really high. That puts pressure on managers and leaders. For public sector managers, nothing is sacred and there is heightened scrutiny and accountability. Public service leaders face more challenges and experience greater risks than in the past.

How to Assess the Types and Characteristics of Leadership Challenges

As leaders face an increasing number of challenges for which there are no clear paths, they need to be armed with a new emergent leadership mindset and some additional leadership tools. But at the same time leaders will continue to operate in a world of normal, where drivers of change can be identified and successfully managed with good data analysis, appropriately designed and staffed public organizations, and diligent community outreach and communication with all of the vested external stakeholders. In short, we see a leadership landscape that requires some careful sorting and ordering. Building on the work of Snowden and Boone (2007), we present a typology of leadership challenges in Exhibit 8.2.

Simple challenges are characterized by both low levels of complexity and value conflicts. Sometimes called tame problems by scholars (Conklin, 2006), simple challenges have: 1) well-defined and stable problem statements; 2) a recognizable point at which a solution is reached; 3) a solution that can be objectively evaluated as right or wrong; and 4) a limited set of appropriate solutions. Simple problems can be hard, but they can always be dealt with in a straightforward manner. This is because there is a science, a set of best practices or a protocol for dealing with simple problems. For example, most infrastructure maintenance and repair issues in large urban areas may be quite difficult to undertake because of the desire to mitigate adverse impact on the expectations and convenience of the affected parties, but the projects are simple compared to large and complicated infrastructure design and construction of new projects.

Complicated challenges are characterized by lots of parts and, like a complicated jigsaw puzzle, take considerable time, resources and analytic work to get the parts properly ordered and sequenced in order for a challenge to be successfully addressed. Examples include building a local light rail system, creating an integrated 911 communication network, or building new infrastructure overlays in large urban areas ("The Big Dig" highway tunneling project in Boston, for instance).[1] Complicated problems represent the home of classic public administration, where the expertise of a specially trained cadre of professional career administrators is needed to sort, order, plan, coordinate, develop and implement solutions to challenges, both simple and complex, under the direction of elected officials.

With chaotic challenges the leadership strategy is to learn to live with and gradually improve the condition, not control it. Major earthquakes, homelessness, drug addiction, hazard waste spills and wildfire conflagrations are examples where "managing" rather than "controlling" is the order of the day.

Exhibit 8.2 Types of Challenges and Implications for Leadership

	THE CONTEXT'S CHARACTERISTICS	THE LEADER'S JOB	DANGER SIGNALS	RESPONSE TO DANGER SIGNALS
SIMPLE	Repeating patterns and consistent events Clear cause-and-effect relationships evident to everyone; right answer exists Known knowns Fact-based management Low level of conflicting moral views	Sense, categorize, respond Ensure that proper processes are in place Delegate Use best practices Communicate in clear, direct ways Understand that extensive interactive communication may not be necessary	Complacency and comfort Desire to make complex problems simple Entrained thinking No challenge of received wisdom Over-reliance on best practice if context shifts	Create communication channels to challenge orthodoxy Stay connected without micro-managing Don't assume things are simple Recognize both the value and the limitations of best practice
COMPLICATED	Expert diagnosis required Cause-and-effect relationships discoverable but not immediately apparent to everyone; more than one right answer possible Known unknowns	Sense, analyze, respond Create panels of experts Listen to conflicting advice	Experts over-confident in their own solutions or in the efficacy of past solutions Analysis paralysis Expert panels Viewpoints of nonexperts excluded	Encourage external and internal stakeholders to challenge expert opinions to combat entrained thinking Use experiments and games to force people to think outside the familiar

Fact-based management

Technically complex, but not conflicting moral purposes.

COMPLEX				
Flux and unpredictability	Probe, sense, respond	Temptation to fall back into habitual, command-and-control mode	Be patient and allow time for reflection
No right answers; emergent instructive patterns	Create environments and experiments that allow patterns to emerge	Temptation to look for facts rather than allowing patterns to emerge	Use approaches that encourage interaction so patterns can emerge
Unknown unknowns	Increase levels of interaction and communication	Desire for accelerated resolution of problems or exploitation of opportunities with a tendency to obfuscate conflicting moral values and purposes	Use dialogic approaches that enable conflicting values to surface
Many competing ideas	Use methods that can help generate ideas: open up discussion (as through large group methods); set barriers; stimulate attractors; encourage dissent and diversity; and manage starting conditions and monitor for emergence		Build in the time needed to creating sustainable agreement with respect to competing values
A need for creative and innovative approaches			
Pattern-based leadership			
Conflicting moral values among groups and individuals	Use methods that recognize and can mediate conflicting moral views of what is in the public interest		

(Continued)

Exhibit 8.2 (Cont.)

	THE CONTEXT'S CHARACTERISTICS	THE LEADER'S JOB	DANGER SIGNALS	RESPONSE TO DANGER SIGNALS
CHAOTIC	High turbulence	Act, sense, respond	Applying a command-and-control approach longer than needed	Set up mechanisms (such as parallel teams) to take advantage of opportunities afforded by a chaotic environment
	No clear cause-and-effect relationships, so no point in looking for right answers	Look for what works instead of seeking right answers	"Cult of the leader"	
	Unknowables	Take immediate action to re-establish order (command and control)	Missed opportunity for innovation	Encourage advisers to challenge your point of view once the crisis has abated
	Many decisions to make and no time to think		Chaos unabated	
	High tension	Provide clear, direct communication		Work to shift the context from chaotic to complex
	Pattern-based leadership			
	High levels of moral conflict	Focus on what is ethically most urgent, i.e., personal survival and public safety		

Source: Adapted from Snowden and Boone (2007, 73).

Complex and chaotic challenges pose the greatest difficulties for leaders because there are high degrees of uncertainty, which is why they are called "wicked" (Brown, Harris, and Russell, 2010; Batie, 2008, Rittel and Webber, 1973). It is important to distinguish two quite different sources of wickedness in Exhibit 8.2. One stems from a lack of determinacy, or cause and effect certainty. This kind of uncertainty can be reduced to a knowability issue with reliance on research or science to transform the unknown to the known. In Exhibit 8.2 this kind of uncertainty is labeled "known unknowns" in the matrix representing complicated and complex problems and is distinguished from "unknowables" in the matrix representing chaotic problems.

The other basis for wickedness stems from moral ambiguity—how it is we individually and collectively feel about whatever "it" is. Most commonly moral ambiguity arises when individuals are in disagreement with respect to the values that should guide public policy and the allocation of resources. In such cases gathering and analyzing more data often does not resolve the conflict. Less commonly, value-centered challenges arise when individuals in the community are unsure how they feel about a given issue. A good example is the debate over immigration and the legalization of marijuana. Many of those favoring decriminalization of marijuana are not so sure how they feel about making it freely available in state licensed stores. In such cases it is common to take a "wait and see" approach to issues about which we are morally uncertain. In other cases we may be of two minds on a given moral issue, as is commonly the case on immigration issues. As one Iowan was quoted by a *New York Times* interviewer on the issue of immigration, "I'm as prejudiced as the day is long ... It's a bad thing that all these illegal Mexicans are here ... But they're hard workers. They're doing jobs that lazy Americans won't do" (Bosman, 2015). Because of the important role that moral ambiguity and value differences play in creating conditions of emergence (see especially Bao, Wang, Larsen, and Morgan, 2013; Moore, 1995; Grint, 2000; Brookes, 2008), we have added this dimension to Snowden and Boone's analytic framework.

Some Leadership Implications of Emergence

In the second column of Exhibit 8.2 we summarize the role of leaders in dealing successfully with each of the four kinds of challenges. For simple challenges, leaders rely heavily on delegating responsibility to those with the right expertise to address the challenge at hand. They insure that proper processes are being followed and that there is good communication among those seeking to address the challenge. For more complicated issues, leaders focus their attention on identifying the range of expertise and processes that need to be in place and the proper sequencing of actions that need to be taken. For complex issues where answers are not clear, the leader's role is to create an active learning environment where followers and different kinds of experts are brought together and encouraged to voice their views, respectfully listen to the views of others and be open to new ideas. Challenges that are truly chaotic (i.e., a mass shooting or a natural disaster) require leaders who can "get things done" now that reduce the chaos and give participants a sense of confidence that they are making a difference.

In spite of what we are learning about different kinds of leadership challenges, our prevailing model assumes a process where leaders rally followers around a commonly shared vision, and empower them to take ownership of both the vision and action needed to address a targeted challenge. While this kind of leadership will certainly be needed in the future, it will sit alongside other models where understanding and mastering the leadership control board will become more important than expertise- or role-centered approaches. There are several control-board characteristics of leading in conditions of emergence that open up leadership opportunities to a much wider range of positions throughout every level of public and nonprofit organizations.

Knowing Leadership Strengths of Your Team and Matching with Contextual Needs

Knowing the strengths of others and putting these strengths to the highest and best use in the situation at hand will become increasingly important to leadership success. This includes building and maintaining high-performing work groups and organizations that match the unit's capacity with the nature of a given set of challenges. It also includes building community support so that leadership initiatives enjoy the trust of the citizens and clients they serve.

Sizing Up Challenges

A second control-board function of leadership is the ability to "size up" multiple challenges that are in different stages of evolution and determine what response is most appropriate for the moment. It is important to remember that Exhibit 8.2 is intended to serve a heuristic function, not to suggest that challenges faced by leaders can be discreetly and neatly put into one of the four rows in the matrix. The nature and priority of a given leadership challenge is frequently characterized by high degrees of fluidity that require trial-and-error, challenge-reduction and problem-solving techniques. One of the chief tasks of a leader in these settings is to interpret the noise surrounding a given challenge and organize its dimensions into prioritized actionable paths forward. We use the term paths to emphasize that a given challenge may necessitate undertaking a mix of initiatives over time, some of which treat the challenge narrowly with a short-term focus, and others that take a more long-term set of actions that confront both the cause-effect uncertainty and the value trade-offs. The literature refers to this kind of flexibility as agile leadership (Ryan and Ali, 2013). An example might be the installation of traffic-sensitive lights at intersections while building a new subway system. The language of pathways also captures the tentative or contingent nature of any given course of action, which will likely require reconsideration as new information and circumstances arise.

Need for Innovation

In the world of the normal, success is defined by sticking to pre-existing norms, accepted rules, scripted protocols and best practices. But in an emergent world of the new normal, leaders need to invent on the fly and use the creatively of followers and stakeholders to design processes of implementation that build trust and legitimacy in both the substance of policy outcomes and the changing processes along the journey of engagement. What we have in mind here is illustrated by the Vision Action Network, the Mt. Hood Stewardship and the Medler School System Master Cases for Parts II to IV respectively. All of these cases illustrate the inadequacy of solely relying on traditional approaches and practices and the need to think and act outside the box.

Heightened Prudential Judgment

We have painted a leadership landscape from where you sit that is filled with a combination of the routine and the unusual. But something as seemingly routine as a local road maintenance project can quickly trigger a movement to "stop urban sprawl." Or a port dredging project to enhance the commercial viability of a local community can become an international issue involving the control of invasive species. A seemingly typical economic development project to assist a local glass manufacturing business can quickly get transformed into a clean air and public health issue as a result of harmful pollutants emitted during the manufacturing process.

This ability to switch from a simple definition of a problem to something that is complex, from an analytic approach to one that is synthetic, from a linear way of viewing a situation to a more organic approach, is nicely illustrated by Major General Michael K. Nagata's challenge of designing a U.S. strategy for fighting the Islamic State of Iraq and the Levant (ISIL). As commander of American Special Operation forces in the Middle East, General Nagata openly conceded that he was operating in completely unknown and uncharted waters where defaulting to traditional approaches was totally inappropriate:

We do not understand the movement, and until we do, we are not going to defeat it ... We have not defeated the idea. We don't even understand the idea ... What we have been asked to do will take every ounce of creativity we have. This may sound like a bizarre excursion into the surreal, but for me it is about avoiding failure.

Schmitt (2014)

In the chapters that follow we provide you with a leadership that can prepare you for the surprises, improve your ability to "size up" leadership challenges and opportunities, match leadership strategies that are most appropriate to the challenge at hand, and take innovative action from where you sit that is informed by a heightened capacity for prudential judgment.

Note

1 The Big Dig was a highway tunneling project in Boston in the 1980-2007 period that re-routed the chief highway through the heart of the city into the 3.5-mile (5.6 km) Thomas P. O'Neill Jr. Tunnel. The project also included the construction of the Ted Williams Tunnel (extending Interstate 90 to Logan International Airport), the Leonard P. Zakim Bunker Hill Memorial Bridge over the Charles River, and the Rose Kennedy Greenway in the space vacated by the previous I-93 elevated roadway. Initially, the plan was also to include a rail connection between Boston's two major train terminals. The official planning phase started in 1982; the construction work was done between 1991 and 2006; and the project concluded on December 31, 2007, when the partnership between the program manager and the Massachusetts Turnpike Authority ended.

The Big Dig is the most expensive highway project in U.S. history. It was plagued by escalating costs, scheduling overruns, leaks, design flaws, charges of poor execution and use of substandard materials, criminal arrests and one death. The project was originally scheduled to be completed in 1998 at an estimated cost of $2.8 billion (in 1982 dollars, $6 billion adjusted for inflation as of 2000). However, the project was completed only in December 2007, at a cost of over $14.6 billion ($8.08 billion in 1982 dollars), resulting in a cost overrun of about 190 percent as of 2006. *The Boston Globe* estimated that the project will ultimately cost $22 billion, including interest, and that it will not be paid off until 2038. As a result of the death, leaks and other design flaws, the consortium that oversaw the project agreed to pay $407 million in restitution, and several smaller companies agreed to pay a combined sum of approximately $51 million (Haynes, 2008; Flint, 2015).

9   EMERGE Leadership[1]
"Sizing Up" Challenges and Opportunities

Public leadership ... needs a new framework with which to negotiate this world [of continuous change]. The framework must be one in which complexity is not treated as an anomaly, but rather as part of the natural order. This new framework must (1) enable leadership to work successfully with changing levels and degrees of complexity; (2) make it possible to see patterns and trends in apparent chaos, to recognize the opportunities and threats associated with the emergent order, and to respond constructively to surprises; (3) provide sensibilities to find and nurture relationships beyond artificially imposed boundaries; (4) ensure that leadership is ready to respond to unintended consequences with positive adjustments in strategy; (5) create in leadership the desire to learn continuously and prepare organizations to integrate that learning into structures and practices; and (6) coach leadership to stay grounded in the core values, institutions, and legal principles of the state's regime even as they engage in the complex worldwide network.

Magis, Ingle, and Duc (2014, 240)

The upside of today's political-technology platform is that leaders can come out of anywhere—fast ... In the long run, the only thing that will save us is if more people—no matter what age, color, gender or faith— build moral authority in their respective realms and then use it to do big, meaningful things. Use it to run for office, start a company, operate a school, lead a movement or build a community organization. And in so doing *you* can help put the "We" back in "We the people".

Friedman (2017, emphasis in original)

The 21st century calls for a new kind of leadership to inspire confidence in the ability of technology to enhance human potential rather than substitute for it.

Davis and Samans (2017)

The opening epigraphs argue that we need a new approach to leadership—one that facilitates our ability, regardless of our position, to take leadership initiative to deal with the kinds of emerging conditions we introduced in our discussion of the "new normal" in Chapter 8. There we presented a typology for sorting and ordering different kinds of leadership challenges based on a variety of characteristics (see Exhibit 8.1). We return to this typology in this chapter as the starting point for introducing our EMERGE public leadership approach. The EMERGE approach provides public leaders with the necessary mindsets, practices and tools for addressing contemporary challenges in an effective and ethical manner. The general concepts and supporting evidence for EMERGE Leadership are presented in Chapters 9 and 11.

Summary Overview: The EMERGE Performing Stage for "Sizing Up" and Taking Action

The world where we sit often appears like a tangled web of impossibilities. Much like looking down on a complicated course of whitewater rapids, we often feel like inexperienced amateurs who do not possess the knowledge, skills and discretionary conditions to navigate safely through the turbulence. The EMERGE Public Leadership Performance Platform serves to dispel this feeling of powerlessness that most public servants have when thinking about taking leadership initiative to address organizational performance issues, especially those that affect moral justice within the community.

The EMERGE approach consists of three integrated elements:

1   The EMERGE Public Leadership Performance Platform can be analogized to a virtual performing stage. But instead of re-enacting the work of an author, those engaged in a leadership activity are simultaneously the actors and the authors. This performing stage is comprised of individuals, teams, organizations and community members who are committed to making a difference for the common good (Nonaka, 2010).

2   These public actors address their shared challenge along two dimensions. One is a continuous sizing up of themselves, their fellow actors and the performance context. The other is taking action to ensure the most effective and ethical performance possible while intentionally learning about leadership practices that work well and those that do not—what in EMERGE we call "prudential judgment" (see Chapter 12).

3   To enhance the capacity of leaders to perform well in both the sizing up and taking action dimensions, we present 12 EMERGE tools that public actors can readily learn and apply. These tools are intended to be mixed and matched in a recursive and adaptive manner as the situation demands. Each of the

core EMERGE tools is aligned with a corresponding set of EMERGE practices. Like other practices, whether it be carpentry, dentistry or musicianship, mastery requires developing proficiency in the various sub-activities that constitute the practice writ large. For example, being a good carpenter requires being good at knowing what materials and techniques are best suited to the task at hand, using the right tool to complete a given stage of a project, and adapting to changes in external conditions. These sub-activities are learned through "doing," "reflection" and "continuous leadership learning" in the context of real world challenges. The product of what is learned is called prudential judgment.

A graphic depiction of the EMERGE Public Leadership Performance Platform is presented in Exhibit 9.1. EMERGE public leadership is a multifaceted and recursive process representing both the intentional movement toward, and the attraction by a shared and inspirational vision of improvement in the common good over time.

Exhibit 9.1 The Performing Stage for Prudential Judgment

The major elements of the EMERGE Public Leadership Performance Platform are further elaborated in Exhibit 9.2. The exhibit describes the two dimensions of the leadership performance stage, giving a brief description of the leadership practices contained in each and the tools that correspond to those practices.

The EMERGE sizing up tools and leadership practices are further elaborated in Chapter 9, and the taking action practices and tools are elaborated in Chapter 11. We take seriously the view that effective and ethical leadership, e.g. prudential judgement, is a "learned practice." This means that the application of the EMERGE approach in the context of real public challenges is essential to strengthening prudential judgment. The Master Cases for this volume as well as the leadership vignettes in Chapter 1 provide illustrations where the EMERGE Public Leadership Performance Platform can be applied both to serve the public good and to strengthen the prudential judgement of those involved in the leadership process. In the following sections of this chapter and Chapter 11, you are encouraged to think about applying the EMERGE tools to your own leadership challenges.

The EMERGE tools share in common the goals of creating openness to change, encouraging a predisposition to see change as an opportunity rather than a problem and fostering reflective processes to reconsider earlier conclusions. The EMERGE Public Leadership Performance Platform enables leaders to deal comfortably with changing levels and degrees of complexity, see patterns and trends in the midst of turbulence, and create an organizational environment that empowers followers to participate in the identification and ownership of leadership initiatives.

Tool 1: Assessment of Leadership Readiness: "Know Thyself and Be True to that Knowledge"

> Polonius to His Son Laertes:
> This above all: to thine own self be true,
> And it must follow, as the night the day,
> Thou canst not then be false to any man.
> Shakespeare (*Hamlet*, Act 1, Scene 3,
> verses 78–82)

While most of us can and do lead from where we sit in everyday situations, not all of us are equally aware of our pre-disposition for effective and ethical public leadership in the "new normal" era as described in Chapter 8. A commitment to leading effectively and ethically from where we sit in the public arena—in any of a variety of roles ranging from a concerned citizen, community activist, nonprofit organization official or government administrator—should begin with leaders coming to "know thyself,"[2] or

Exhibit 9.2 EMERGE Public Leadership Performance Platform: Performance Stage Dimensions by Core Practices and Tools

Performance Stage Dimension: Sizing Up Leadership Challenges and Opportunities

Leadership Practices	*EMERGE Leadership Tools and Descriptions*
	1: Assessment of Leadership Readiness
Practice One: **Develop Awareness of** **One's Readiness for Public Leadership**	This tool enables individuals to become more aware of their pre-disposition toward effective and ethical public leadership. Pre-disposition for public leadership is assessed along three interrelated dimensions: motivation to serve the common good, alignment of one's personal values with enduring polity values and readiness to embrace change.
	2: Leadership Challenge Understanding
Practice Two: **Know the Nature of a** **Wicked Leadership Challenge**	This tool assists prospective leaders along with interested others to identify and understand the characteristics of a wicked leadership challenge, including the degree of a challenge's wickedness and the salient elements of its historical evolution.
	3: Leadership Opportunity Identification
Practice Three: **Identify a Practical Leadership Opportunity** **that Addresses a Wicked Challenge**	This tool enables leaders—in collaboration with followers—to frame an initial, multi-faceted leadership opportunity that both responds to the wickedness of a defined challenge and contributes through a multifaceted action strategy to an initial vision of an improved state of the common good at some specified time in the future.
	4: Leadership System Framing
Practice Four: **Frame the Key Dimensions** **of the Multifaceted Leadership Opportunity as**	This tool enables leaders to frame an identified leadership opportunity as a multifaceted system embracing three essential perspectives: 1) at the "system level," embracing the

(Continued)

Exhibit 9.2 (Cont).

Performance Stage Dimension: Sizing Up Leadership Challenges and Opportunities

Leadership Practices	EMERGE Leadership Tools and Descriptions
a Complex and Dynamic System	concept of the "expanded now" that brings together the institutional lessons of experience with the vision/values of the future; 2) at the "sub-system level," seeing both one's-self and followers within a leadership team and organizational cultural setting, and 3) at the "supra-system level," focusing on common interests and areas of conflict among relevant stakeholders.
Practice Five: Discern Emergent Patterns in a Dynamic Situation as the Basis for Persuasion	**5: Contextual Intelligence (CI) Discernment** This tool enables leaders to graphically depict the five most salient contextual conditions embedded in a leadership opportunity, thus allowing for the enhancement of Contextual Intelligence (CI). As CI is developed, a leader can gain foresight—defined as being able to discern emergent patterns that are useful in persuading followers and others to join in a leadership journey.
Practice Six: Embrace a Mindset of Continuous Leadership Learning	**6: Continuous Leadership Learning** This tool enables leaders to approach leadership learning as an adaptive and generative process. Continuous learning, driven by collective reflective practice, is the foundation for the exercise of effective and ethical prudential judgment.

Performance Stage Dimension: Taking Action to Realize a Shared Vision

Practice Seven: Model Trusting Relationships with Leadership Team Members and Others	**7: Model with Relational Trust** This tool enables leaders, through a process of open dialogue, to model a high level of relational trust with leadership team members and relevant stakeholders with the intent of growing and nurturing transformational trust throughout the leadership initiative.

Practice Eight:
Inspire a Shared and Moral Vision/Values related to a Leadership Initiative

Practice Nine:
Use Contextual Intelligence to Develop and Act with a Smart Power Strategy

Practice Ten:
Convene and Nurture a Coalition to Realize the Vision

Practice Eleven:
Pioneer Breakthrough Innovation in the Public Arena

Practice Twelve:
Intentionally Strengthen Prudential Judgment through Reflective Practice

8: Inspire Vision with Moral Grounding

This tool embeds inspiration into the initial vision and values associated with a leadership initiative, thereby expanding ownership, providing moral grounding and enhancing the ability of the shared inspiration to become "alive" in everyday public action.

9: Persuade with Smart Power

This tool enables leaders to make use of the emergent patterns discerned from the Contextual Intelligence (CI) Tool in developing and acting with a responsive "smart power strategy"—one that represents the "smartest" balance of hard and soft power—for persuading others to engage in a leadership journey.

10: Convene Stakeholder Coalitions

This tool empowers leaders in collaboration with their leadership team to convene and institutionalize a robust network of organizational followers and external stakeholders to realize the common good embedded in the leadership initiative's shared vision.

11: Guide Organizational Innovation

When a leadership initiative involves a "pioneering effort" in an organizational context, this tool guides leaders "in blazing a breakthrough trail" with a high level of confidence that they are taking a course that improves the public good.

12: Strengthen Prudential Judgment

This tool provides leaders with a systematic approach to reflective practice—encompassing open dialogue, generative learning, and ethical decision-making—with the intent of strengthening prudential judgment.

developing a deep sense of self-awareness of one's readiness to lead. Self-awareness is extremely important in the context of the EMERGE public leadership approach since it serves as a basic building block for carrying out all types of leadership roles and relationships (see Chapter 2). Self-awareness is essential to being a successful leader at the individual, group/team, organizational and community levels and in operating at different scales of leadership complexity. Self-knowledge is also timeless, which means that what is gained in one stage of your leadership journey gets carried over and is eventually passed on to subsequent generations.

The first EMERGE sizing up tool, "Readiness for Leadership," enables leaders to become more aware of their pre-disposition for "new normal" leadership. Pre-disposition for individual public leadership is assessed along three interrelated and overlapping dimensions: pre-disposition to serve the common good, alignment of one's public service values with polity values, and readiness to embrace continuous change. These dimensions are displayed in Exhibit 9.3, and each is developed as its own assessment in the sections that follow.

How Pre-Disposed Are You to Serving the Public Interest?

EMERGE draws from a large body of literature that treats public service leadership as a passion or calling to serve others and contribute to the larger common good. We define passion as an intense emotion, an emotional excitement, a deep aspiration or an agitation. To perform well in "new normal" contextual settings, individuals need to possess some level of deeply held dedication to making a positive

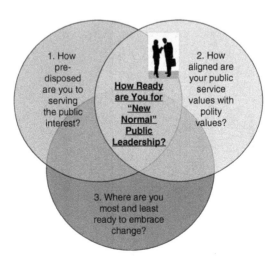

Exhibit 9.3 Tool 1: Readiness for Public Leadership Assessment

difference and leaving a legacy for the citizens and communities they serve. We view this as part and parcel of caring deeply about something or someone beyond one's own self-interest. As one of our former students was fond of saying, "For something important to happen, someone has to care."

There are a large number of studies on public service motivation (PSM), which document the generalized conclusion that those entering public service possess a higher predisposition to serve others and make a difference in the lives of others than those seeking employment in the private sector. The conceptual elements that comprise PSM include: attraction to policy making and to politics, civic duty, commitment to the public interest, compassion/self-sacrifice (Perry and Hondeghem, 2008; Perry and Wise, 1990). As defined by the pioneers of this research, PSM is an individual's orientation to delivering services to people with the desire to do good for others and contribute to the public interest, even when it requires self-sacrifice (Perry and Hondeghem, 2008; Bright, 2013).

PSM is the basis of a leadership framework that was popularized in the late 1990s called "servant-leadership," which is defined as serving the interests of others first. Robert Greenleaf, who first introduced this framework, explains the meaning of servant-leadership as follows:

> It is not the individual who decides that he is a leader or will become a leader, but the community that places him in that particular role ... The individual's choice is only whether or not he will accept the responsibility given him by the community ... Leaders are ordinary people who, through the needs of the community, emerge as "special" people. Through certain events and situations, they acquire extraordinary and compelling powers that attract followers. It is the community's responsibility to control that power while at the same time supporting that leader who is voicing the opinions of the community. These words are part of the leadership equation. The other part is the will and the personal strength to opt for leadership as a meaningful lifestyle, toward which an individual may progress by conscious preparation.
>
> Greenleaf (2003, 34)

The first step in the three-part process of assessing leadership readiness draws from this PSM research and the servant leadership framework. It asks you to assess more particularly the nature and strength of your passion to make a difference. Following is an example of a "high level of readiness" response to this assessment: "I would like to explore the idea of empowering disadvantaged communities to have access to and the ability to make healthy choices for themselves." The immediate advantage associated with this assessment is that it provides prospective leaders with heightened self-awareness about areas where they might invest their energy and passion to make a difference.

How Aligned Are Your Public Service Values with Polity Values?

We argued in Chapters 4–6 that public leaders have an obligation to understand and advance the core polity values that comprise the common good of the regime they serve (assuming the regime is pursuing values consistent with international standards of justice and respect for human rights). In the American republic, these core polity values are democratic in nature and public leaders are expected to place these values at the center of their work. These values include impartiality, justice and due process to sustain a nation of law; liberty, equity and human dignity; accountability (and hence disclosure); and promoting a responsive process that is accessible and responsive to the citizens and citizenship rights and obligations, such as informed participation and compassion (see extended discussion in Chapter 6).

But these values are not static. As we illustrated in Chapter 6, the scope and meaning of American democratic values have evolved through time. For example, the meaning of equality at the time of the American founding was quite different than in 1900, and it was different still in 2000. Equality has broadened from just having the same political rights that are guaranteed to all citizens (i.e., right to vote, hold public office, serve jury duty) to include some measure of economic and social equality (i.e., equal access to public accommodations, freedom from workplace discrimination, a minimum level of social security and the extension of protected classes to include age, national origin, ethnicity and conditions of birth). At the same time the meaning of equality has deepened. For example, gender and racial equality have been extended beyond the right to vote to include workplace and social equality. And efforts continue to broaden and deepen the application of equality while insuring that we secure performance on past gains.

Before stepping onto the public leadership performance stage and enlisting others in an initiative, actors have a personal responsibility to consider the extent to which their own public service values are aligned with their regime's core values. This is especially important for leaders who will necessarily have to mediate competing values among participants who may desagree on the priority and meaning of different polity values. For example, what does our regime commitment to equality require in terms of equity and inclusion practices? Fostering agreement out of contending polity values is a central part of a leader's meaning-making work. As illustrated by the Librarian Master Case for Part 1 and Exhibit 5.6 in Chapter 5, the inherent tensions among our personal, professional and polity values are not only healthy, but necessary. These tensions keep us on our moral toes in making leadership decisions and, more importantly, create and fuel targets of opportunity for under-taking leadership initiative. These tensions create the space where we can maintain our integrity and sense of moral identity while honoring the values of the regime that we are bound to serve.

In our leadership development work, we find that most mid-level officials, including those with a deep and enduring passion for serving the public good, are not well versed in our regime's core polity values. Fewer still are aware of how their own personal values align with the prevailing regime values. To address this lack of understanding, we have developed a polity value assessment instrument focused on the degree of alignment between one's own values and the polity's core values. We have found that developing this self-awareness heightens the self-efficacy of leaders who have to function simultaneously in multiple structures of authority by identifying the polity values that are unique to each setting. Some of these values require being successful in tradi-tional legal and bureaucratic structures that are normed by rules, roles and hierarchical accountability relationships (what we call vertical structures of authority). Others are more horizontal in nature, requiring a reliance on slowly building trust and legitimacy interpersonally over an extended period of time. These structures require the capacity to lead in what is called a power-shared world. This values alignment assess-ment can assist public leaders in identifying areas of value misalignment and point to issues that need further self-reflection.

The Polity Values Alignment Assessment includes ten core polity values abstracted from our discussion in Chapter 5. The relative impor-tance of these values depends on the institutional and organizational settings where leadership initiatives are launched and executed:

1 **Stewardship.** Committing to uphold the constitution, laws, rules, due process and democratic regime values of equality, liberty, property and the rights of individuals. Stewardship includes respecting checks and balances, separation of powers, federalism, the role of the private, nonprofit, special district and civil society sectors.
2 **Voice.** Allowing citizens and representative groups to participate in governance by ensuring that decisions account for the aspirations of current and future generations.
3 **Fairness.** Playing by the rule of law to ensure that there are just and fair procedures along with fairness in intent and in results.
4 **Integrity.** Displaying high ethical standards including an accurate, transparent and accountable representation of the truth based on evidence and facts.
5 **Respect.** Being respectful of the opinions, conditions and life-cir-cumstances of others with a commitment to treat all citizens with equal dignity.

6 **Trustworthy.** Being counted upon to do what you say you will do in faithfully executing one's duties, as determined through the political and legal processes, in support of the public interest or the collective good.

7 **Caring.** Being kind and compassionate by assisting others in need.

8 **Loyalty.** Demonstrating pride in and love for one's country and community.

9 **Humility.** Serving the public with respect, concern, courtesy and responsiveness, recognizing that service to the public often requires sacrificing one's own interests.

10 **Balance.** Using one's discretion to ensure that competing polity values are appropriately used to create governing processes and policy outcomes that advance the common good of our regime of ordered liberty.

Exhibit 9.4 provides an example from one of our executive leaders who completed the Polity Value Alignment Assessment. Exhibit 5.8 in Chapter 5 provides another example of what this regime values self-assessment looks like in practice.

Exhibit 9.4 Example of Value Alignment Exercise

My values are based on the words I've carried to each position over the last two decades: Mission, People, Leadership, Teamwork and Integrity. My personal values are based on family, public service, loyalty, patriotism, honesty and integrity and a focus on people. These values are clearly indicated in my top Clifton Strength Finder Theme of "Belief." I strongly believe that taking the time to both identify and "model" or discuss your values is critical for any leader. Living by these values, even though they aren't necessarily shared by those who work with you, will insure that you are seen as an honest and predictable leader which is absolutely critical to insuring that you are seen as trustworthy.

Where Are You Most and Least Ready to Embrace Change?

The final leg of the three-legged Readiness Assessment tool focuses on a leader's pre-disposition to embrace change. As was discussed in Chapter 8, the new normal public leadership arena is characterized by high levels of dynamic complexity and moral ambiguity. Somewhat surprisingly, this dimension of personal readiness for leading change and innovation is a missing link in most of the leadership literature. For example, Kotter's classic eight-step model for leading change does not include this personal readiness element (Kotter, 2012, 2014).

Our experience in working with successful public leaders is that they have a high degree of self-awareness about how their personal traits impact their ability to lead within high-change environments. This self-awareness allows leaders to readily step into and thrive in the context of dynamic complexity. They do this by asking this basic question: "Where am I most and least ready to embrace continuous change?"

To assess a leader's predisposition to embrace change, we adapted an assessment instrument from Dr. T.J. Jenney at Purdue University.[3] The instrument includes seven personal change readiness traits that can be assessed and compared. The Personal Change Readiness Assessment is available in the online EMERGE Tool Platform. This assessment is useful for "knowing thyself" along seven personal traits important for embracing versus resisting change. This information arms leaders with the ability to decide the types of leadership challenges and opportunities they are most likely to be successful in pursuing. The results also provide a solid basis for authentic communications with followers and stakeholders.

The seven change-readiness traits are elaborated below:

1 **Resourcefulness.** Resourceful people are effective at taking the most of any situation and utilizing whatever resources are available to develop plans and contingencies. They see more than one way to achieve a goal, and they are able to look in less obvious places to find help. They have a real talent for creating new ways to solve old problems; they lean into change. When people who are low in resourcefulness encounter obstacles, they often get stuck, dig in their heels and go back to the old way. Those with low resourcefulness scores might overlook obvious solutions and create more work than is necessary.

2 **Optimism.** Is the glass half empty or half full? Optimism is highly correlated with change-readiness since the pessimist observes only problems and obstacles while the optimist recognizes opportunities and possibilities. Optimists tend to be more enthusiastic and positive about change. Their positive outlook is founded on an abiding faith in the future and the belief that things usually work out for the best. Sometimes optimism can cloud a rational and realistic assessment of the facts.

3 **Adventurousness.** Two qualities comprise the adventurous spirit: the inclination to take risks and the desire to pursue the unknown, to walk the path less taken. Adventurous people love a challenge. They often break the rules in service of the public interest but are careful not to break the law. Since change always involves both risk and the unknown, individuals high in adventurousness usually perform well during organizational shake-ups. They are the pro-actors or positive deviants—the employees who initiate and create change.

Individuals high in this trait may demonstrate a tendency toward recklessness.

4 **Drive.** Drive is the fuel that maximizes all the other traits. If you have internal drive, nothing appears impossible. If you don't, change can be exhausting. Drive is the individual's level of personal dynamism. It shows up in a person's level of intensity and determination. To make a new procedure work, to overcome the myriad of problems that any plan for change unwittingly produces, it helps to have drive and enthusiasm. However, too much drive may indicate bullheadedness or obsession.

5 **Adaptability.** Adaptability includes two qualities: flexibility and resilience. Flexible people have visions and dreams like everyone else, but they're not overly invested in them. When something doesn't work out, they'll say, "Plan A doesn't work, let's go to Plan B." Resilience is the capacity to rebound from adversity quickly with a minimum of trauma. Failure or mistakes do not derail adaptable leaders. Scoring very high on this trait may indicate a lack of commitment or stick-to-it-ness.

6 **Confidence.** If optimism is the view that a situation will work out, confidence is the belief in your own ability to handle it. There is situational confidence—"I know I can swim across this channel, learn this program, write this report"—and self-confidence—"I can handle whatever comes down the pike." Self-confidence is the kind of confidence the Change-Readiness Scale measures. High scorers are generally individuals with a strong sense of self-esteem. They often believe that there is more than one right answer to a problem situation, and are able to call on different perspectives to find appropriate pathways forward. They believe they can make any situation work for them. Very high scorers may indicate a cocky, know-it-all attitude and lack of receptivity to feedback.

7 **Tolerance for Ambiguity.** The one certainty surrounding change is that it spawns uncertainty. No matter how carefully you plan an initiative, there is always an element of indefiniteness or ambiguity. When a high level of moral ambiguity is added to contextual change, then the uncertainty and ambiguity is much greater. Without a healthy tolerance for ambiguity, change is not only uncomfortable; it's downright scary. But too much tolerance can also get a public leader in trouble as it may indicate a difficulty in making decisions and finishing tasks.

As with the previous two readiness assessments, the personal change-readiness assessment can provide potential leaders with a general level of self-awareness at a particular point in time. When the assessment results align with one's own experience, then it is important to be mindful of those traits and to own them. Where results do not align, leaders may want to explore the results with trusted peers or retake the assessment after some period of time. Always check in with others when some aspect of the assessment does not feel right. And be open to learning some new insights about your own traits and readiness for change. Finally, treat the assessment as another perspective on your current mindset, but not one that definitively typecasts your change readiness. If you are not very ready to embrace change in one area, then you can treat that as a signal that you need to partner with others who are more predisposed for change-readiness in that area.

Concluding Thoughts on the "Readiness for Public Leadership Assessment" Tool

The EMERGE Readiness for Public Leadership Assessment tool brings together three important dimensions of a positive pre-disposition for public leadership in the "new normal" era: a passion for public service, an alignment with polity values and a readiness to embrace change. In using this tool, prospective public leaders can become proficient in the first EMERGE practice of "Develop[ing] Awareness of One's Readiness for Public Leadership." When leaders are aware that they are ready to engage in "new normal public leadership" along each of the three dimensions, there should be minimal hesitation in moving on to the second EMERGE sizing up tool for understanding a leadership challenge. For those who are not quite yet ready on one or more of the dimensions, this might be a signal to move more slowly into the new normal leadership realm. As readiness for different types of leadership typically ebbs and flows over time, stepping back for a while may be an appropriate response. While stepping back, leaders may want to consider one of several reflective actions. For one, leaders can look more deeply into the results of the readiness tool dimensions based on self-knowledge and the experience of others. For another, leaders can gain additional insight by reading more from the references that accompany this tool. We highly recommend that prospective leaders also consider additional self-assessments including the Strengths-Based Leadership Assessment (Rath and Conchie, 2008) and an emotional intelligence assessment (Bradberry and Greaves, 2012). Finally, leaders can test out their newly gained self-awareness on small initiatives, and learn more by probing, as described in Tool 6 of this chapter. In all of these actions, leaders can gain in authenticity in their relationships by aligning their actions with awareness of "knowing thyself."

Tool 2: Leadership Challenge Understanding: "Don't Eat the Mushroom Without Knowing What it Is Good For!"

> Certain societal problems become so complex that no single individual or organization can resolve or provide straightforward answers to them. Such intractable problems have been described as "wicked problems."
>
> McGrandle and Ohemeng (2017, 218)

As we discussed in Chapter 8 (Exhibit 8.1), not everything is a leadership challenge and not all challenges are the same. Leaders must have the ability to create strategies that align with the particular characteristics of a problem that they are seeking to address. For example, you can't discipline employees in the same way you provide customer service; you can't create organizational performance improvements in the same way you generate greater stakeholder involvement; you can't get support for an idea from your supervisor in the same way you get support from your fellow workers. While there are some common techniques (i.e., active listening), you can't assume that strategies which have been successful with one group of followers will work with another. Successful leaders adapt their leadership strategies to the nature of the challenges and the attentive participants they are seeking to involve.

In addition to challenges being different, the same challenge in two different settings can involve different levels of risk. For example, delaying the installation of a new roof in one school may involve much greater risk than in another school because of the age of the structure, the vulnerability of the school population, the political engagement of the community, etc. These context-specific factors generate different sources for uncertainty. Some result from not having enough information, for which research and science provide solutions. Other sources of uncertainty arise from moral ambiguity caused by value conflicts, overlapping value commitments and moral uncertainty about how one feels about a given set of issues. These different sources of uncertainty have important leadership implications. For example, if uncertainty arises because we don't know the causal dimensions of a challenge, leaders might ask for more information, assuming there is the time and budget to do so. If not, leaders might need to help groups partition technical risk and assign value to become either more certain or more comfortable with the level of technical uncertainty. Sometimes simple problem framing, system outlining or mind mapping helps with this "root causality" basis of uncertainty (Fullan, 2001). If, however, the uncertainty arises from societal complexity or moral ambiguity, then other tools are called for, such as facilitated dialogue, deep listening, value clarification, criteria enumeration, test balloons, voting, consensus processes, etc. In the remaining sections of this chapter and

Chapter 11 we introduce you to some of these leadership tools for narrowing the focus of a given leadership challenge and for selecting the right combination of approaches and tools for addressing it.

Once leaders are ready to step onto the leadership performance stage, as explored in EMERGE Tool 1, then they are ready to identify and understand the characteristics of a leadership challenge that lie within their sphere of discretionary influence. EMERGE Tool 2 assists leaders with this. The tool uses a three-step process as displayed in Exhibit 9.5.

This Tool 2 template can be used by leaders to identify and understand a real-time leadership challenge. You will be able to continue using this leadership example as you work with additional EMERGE tools that we will explain in the ensuring sections of this chapter and in Chapter 11.

The sizing up steps included in the Leadership Challenge Understanding Tool are intended to walk prospective leaders through a systematic process to cultivate a deep understanding of your leadership challenge. This is intended to develop the EMERGE Practice 2 of: Know the Nature of a Wicked Leadership Challenge. The tool's three steps are explained more fully below. The tool has been designed to steer the user toward the selection of a "wicked problem" in order to cultivate the leadership skills needed for this kind of challenge.

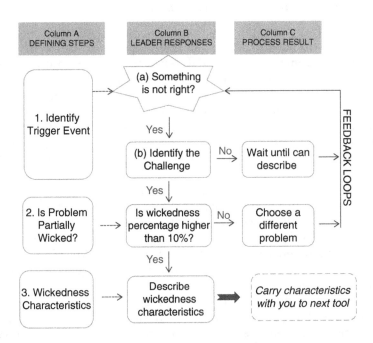

Exhibit 9.5 Tool 2: Leadership Challenge Understanding

Step 1(A). Perceiving a "Trigger Event"

A trigger event for public leadership is represented by a prospective leader's perception that something in the public arena is not right, or that there is a gap between the way things are (either now or at some point in the future) and the way they could and should be. For example, in our Mount Hood Forestry Master Case for Part II, the trigger event was a perceived gap between accomplishing the legally required mission of the organization and the budget allocated to support it.

Step 1(B). Identifying the Challenge

After a problematic has been triggered, a leader can restate the problematic as a leadership challenge and describe it in narrative form. At this stage in the identification process, the challenge description can be brief. However, it should be clearly stated and include a time dimension. Again, to illustrate with the Master Case, the challenge could be described as: "This forest is deteriorating because we are not receiving Congressional funding to support our requirement to meet our legal mandates to hikers, snowboarders, forest harvesters (i.e., firewood, mushroom, blueberries, game) and other user groups."

Step 2. Determining if the Challenge Is Wicked

This step draws on the description of the four major types of problems provided in Chapter 8. Tool 2 provides leaders with the template for completing an initial assessment of the nature of their challenge, including the mixture of challenge types. Wicked challenges are "conundrums." A wicked challenge is defined as one where the amount of "dynamic complexity" embedded in the challenge is greater than 10 percent of the total. If a leader's challenge has less than 10 percent of dynamic complexity, then leaders should not proceed with the use of the EMERGE approach for that challenge. Rather, leaders should choose another leadership approach (e.g., operations administration, complicated managerial or crisis response) that is more suited to the nature of the specific challenge at hand. To proceed with the application of the EMERGE approach, leaders should begin the process from the beginning by selecting a different, and potentially more wicked, trigger event. In our Mt. Hood Master Case example, it was determined that the challenge was about 60 percent "wicked" in nature, primarily due to recent and projected changes in the political priorities of legislators in Congress, a reversal of thinking about a regulatory-centered approach to forest management, and increased pressure on the use of the forest by growing numbers of stakeholders.

Step 3. Describe the Wicked Characteristics

The final step in this tool is to assess and describe the specific "wicked-ness characteristics" embedded in the challenge. In this text, we refer to problems that are wicked in nature as a special class of problems—they are "challenges" (beyond problems). They are embedded with multiple dimensions and cannot be successfully resolved by uni-dimensional policy solutions. "One of the most important aspects of wicked pro-blems is the lack of clear root causes and therefore no one best solution" (Head and Alford, 2015, 715).

To avoid the term wicked challenge being applied to every social challenge and becoming ubiquitous, Rittel and Webber (1973) identified ten key characteristics for identifying such challenges. In EMERGE Tool 2, we synthesize Rittel and Webber's original list into seven key wickedness questions. And to ensure full coverage of the moral ambi-guity issues that usually accompany wicked challenges, we have also added an additional question. The Problem Identification Tool therefore includes the following eight questions:

1 How is the challenge complex with many interconnecting parts and a high degree of uncertainty?
2 How is the challenge novel and different from other problems?
3 In what way is the challenge very difficult or impossible to com-pletely understand?
4 Describe why the challenge requires exploration and collaboration across various people with complementary and divergent knowledge/ skills to gain a better understanding of it and to address it effectively?
5 Describe how the challenge is dynamic in nature, i.e., continually changing?
6 Describe how the challenge is open-ended without a clear end point at which it will be clearly resolved?
7 In what way does the challenge lack a proven strategy to success-fully address it?
8 How is the challenge morally ambiguous with multiple different values and interests at play?

The EMERGE leadership approach encourages leaders to discuss the char-acteristics of the challenge with a few others, and then to capture these initial perspectives in writing. In our Master Case example, it was discovered through this discussion that the Mount Hood Forest challenge was com-prised of at least 15 interconnecting parts, many of which had high levels of uncertainty. There were no less than ten stakeholder groups, depending on how narrowly you wished to label a group. We used the following three questions to determine whether a stakeholder deserved to be labeled a recognized group for purposes of the exercise: 1) Does the group have a claim recognized in law? 2) Is the group politically well-organized at the local level? 3) Is the group's livelihood highly dependent on use of the forest (i.e., mushroom harvesting by the Muong and Vietnamese)?

In addition to the complexity caused by multiple user groups, there were multiple vertical relationships among the various functional units of the local organization (i.e., fire, timber, recreation, budget, personnel). As this vertical complexity was followed upward through the chain of bureaucratic commend, it led to a very complex array of contending political forces in Washington D.C. and in the country at large with respect to the regulatory role of government. For all of these reasons, we concluded that the case easily qualified as a wicked challenge.

Concluding Thoughts on the Leadership Challenge Understanding Tool

One goal of the EMERGE leadership approach is to cultivate the capacity for prospective leaders to initiate leadership from where they sit. This capacity requires continuous identification of challenges along with an understanding of the underlying internal and external dynamics that give meaning to the challenge within its context. The EMERGE Leadership Challenge Understanding Tool assists leaders to lean into challenges and to understand the degree and nature of challenges' wickedness. Using this tool, public leaders can become proficient in the second EMERGE Practice of "Know the Nature of a Wicked Leadership Challenge." Understanding this wickedness provides the basis for identifying a leadership opportunity in EMERGE Tool 3. Leaders also continue to elaborate the contours of wickedness, and to develop foresight, in Tool 5 on Contextual Intelligence (CI).

Tool 3: Leadership Opportunity Identification

> Every interaction is an opportunity for leadership.
> Dr. Phyusin Myint (informal communication, 2007)

Effective and ethical public leadership must be learned and nurtured through reflective practice. The best mechanism for this leadership practice is in the actual public-sector work setting. These settings contain many challenges that can be reframed as opportunities for leadership. The Master Cases for each of the parts of this book provide a multitude of examples at and across every level of the organizational hierarchy. Whether you are functioning at the first-line service level, as a program manager in the middle of a public organization, or as a member of an organization's support and logistical staff, hardly a day goes by without some challenge or frustration with the "way things are." These challenges, identifiable by using Tool 2, provide the stage for stepping into a potential leadership opportunity. By leadership opportunity, we simply mean taking personal responsibility for initiating action that leads to some improvement in the way things are.

Finding ways to initiate change from where we sit is more difficult than selecting a leadership challenge. The opportunity identification process usually requires a fundamental change in one's leadership mindset. This is because we see and experience the manifestations of challenges in our everyday work but we often don't see any way that we can make a difference. We are surrounded by rules, structures, processes, norms and expectations that remind us daily of the boxes we are in. We feel constrained for a couple of reasons. First, we often believe that we are not in a formal position of leadership. No one has told us, and it is not explicit in our job descriptions, that we have any discretionary authority to take some initiative. Second, more than likely, the culture we are working in does not place high value on risk taking for fear of failure and public ridicule. Finally, we are often overwhelmed by the complexity and enormity of figuring out very practical activities that we might initiate. In the face of this assumed lack of discretion, our risk averse culture and minimal spare time to think out of the box for a pathway forward, we default to doing nothing. We hold ourselves harmless for taking moral responsibility for acting by blaming the system and the moral failings of individuals we think do have responsibility for making the changes we want to see happen.

The EMERGE leadership approach sets out to change this "I can't be a leader" mindset by providing a structured and easy to apply Leadership Opportunity Identification process supported by an EMERGE tool. As a result of following this process, we believe public servants will learn the everyday practice of identifying practical leadership opportunities in their work settings.

The Leadership Opportunity Identification Tool consists of three steps that help you whittle down a leadership challenge into manageable action. These steps are illustrated in Exhibit 9.6 and are elaborated in the text below; the supporting tool for the opportunity identification process is also included in the online EMERGE Public Leadership Performance Platform. This tool enables leaders—in collaboration with followers and key stakeholders—to frame an initial multifaceted leadership opportunity that responds to the wickedness of a defined challenge. It also supports defining an early vision of an improved state of the common good at some specified time in the future through a multiphased action strategy.

Step 1. Transform the Challenge into a Multifaceted and Responsive Leadership Opportunity

Being successful in leading from where we sit requires finding the ray of light shining through the clouds that provides a potential opportunity to

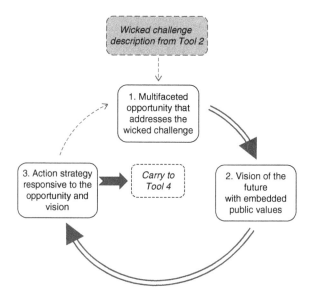

Exhibit 9.6 Tool 3: Leadership Opportunity Identification

take leadership action. But like most clouds, the ray of light you see now is soon transformed by the moving stratosphere to create slightly different possibilities in a different places and times. This is the spirit with which we want you to approach the identification of a leadership opportunity. It is not a clear fixed point in time but rather a discursive process that requires you to go through several steps before you have identified a robust leadership opportunity with the confidence you need to begin thinking about taking leadership action.

One of the best ways to undertake the process of "whittling down" down wicked challenges so they become manageable leadership opportunities is through dialogue with others on the leadership performance stage. Having multiple perspectives, degrees of organizational experience, levels of authority and diversity of perspectives increases the richness, variety and innovative leadership opportunity possibilities (Senge, Hamilton, and Kania, 2015; Williams and O'Reilly, 1998; Milliken and Martins, 1996).

Step 2. Co-Create a Future Vision of the Common Good with Embedded Public Values

A vision represents our polestar for our public leadership journey; it provides direction for our leadership opportunity and is a source of inspirational attraction for our leadership team and coalition members.

An inspirational vision—embedded within selective polity values as discussed in Tool 1—needs to be articulated early in the leadership journey by the initial champions, and then revisited and nurtured though intentional sharing with others throughout the process. Creating and revisiting a shared and inspirational vision is a reminder that leaders take responsibility for giving meaning to collective action. Public leaders play a key role in generating agreement on shared ends and the priorities that should be given to what are often multiple, and competing, courses of action. The visible manifestation of the completion of this task is the co-production of a statement of shared vision and values—in both graphical and narrative formats—by core members of the leadership team. It is important that the process be continued until there is one shared future vision (Kouzes and Posner, 2017). The vision presents a desired image of some point of time in the future when our leadership challenge is successfully addressed and our desired improvements to the common good have been created. In this sense, the vision is aspirational, and not necessarily something that is expected to be fully achieved. It represents a desirable future state of improvement in the public good from the perspective of where we are now and what we think we can do to make improvements.

We prefer to think of a vision as something more than a statement that is emotionally inspirational to individual members of the team; we think of it as a force that simultaneously pushes and attracts the leadership team. The vision is the visible manifestation that we are succeeding in "getting to yes."

Step 3. Draft an Action Strategy Responsive to the Leadership Opportunity and Vision

The Leadership Opportunity Identification Tool recognizes that opportunities are not neat clean bundles that come in packages that you can tie up with a bow. They are often, like the wicked challenges they address, fuzz balls consisting of some elements that might be time sensitive, others that might be technically complex, and still others that will surely be morally contested in their intent, their modes of delivery and their outcomes (Nye, 2008). Sorting and ordering these strategic parts and sequencing the various action steps is a hard process requiring dual mindsets of disciplined deconstruction and dialogical innovation. By that we mean listening to others with an eye to generating new possibilities that you may not have originally entertained as possible. At the conclusion of this exercise you will have untangled the various characteristics of your leadership opportunity in ways that are responsive to your wicked challenge and that give you confidence in tackling the opportunity in manageable steps (Brown, Harris, and Russel, 2010). This process of deconstruction and innovation will yield a strategy of multifaceted and doable leadership actions that you can take from where you sit.

Recent research on tackling wickedness suggests that a leader's action strategy requires three things: a means whereby the leadership team can increase its knowledge for dealing with the opportunity through time; a mechanism for following stakeholder negotiations to adapt and stay robust through time; and an explicit pathway to increase the number and diversity of collaborating third parties into the coalition-building process over time (McGrandle and Ohemeng, 2017, 233). Flexibility needs to be designed into the strategy (Brinkerhoff and Ingle, 1989) so that it retains its "requisite variety" (Ashby, 1957; Jantsch, 1975). The response must fit the challenge (Head and Alford, 2015).

Concluding Thoughts on the "Leadership Opportunity Identification" Tool

In practice, the EMERGE Public Leadership Performance Platform intends to reduce value divergence through the successful engagement of multiple stakeholders who are active on the public-sector performing stage. As they perform together, these stakeholders will gradually develop more positive beliefs about each other where "cooperation transaction costs go down" due to increases in trust (Fullan, 2001). Success depends on a highly adaptive leadership team whose members: 1) expand their knowledge over time through curiosity and continuous learning; 2) create partnerships to bring multiple perspectives and pathways to the table—to mitigate differences and foster value congruence—so the best alternatives can be selected and requisite variety can be maximized through working together; and 3) innovate by going outside the box to create new strategies that are more aligned with citizen and stakeholder needs.

The Leadership Opportunity Identification Tool helps leaders transform wicked challenges into manageable actions that can be taken from where they sit. In using this tool, public leaders can become proficient in the third EMERGE practice: "Identify a Practical Leadership Opportunity that Addresses a Wicked Challenge." Having an initial conception of our leadership opportunity, along with the vision it addresses and the strategy for moving it forward, is an essential sizing-up performance element. This information is essential for framing our "leadership system," which is the focus of Tool 4.

Tool 4: Leadership System Framing

If we are to survive and prosper, and if our children and grandchildren—and their children and grandchildren—are to enjoy the benefits of our ability to make the world better, we must find ways to think and act more effectively in a power-shared-world.

Crosby and Bryson (2005, xi)

Leadership increasingly requires sizing up opportunities that require the participation of actors in all sectors and in multiple jurisdictions. Leadership roles encompass interconnected relationships within and across this complex vertical and horizontal system. This interconnected system of vertical and horizontal structures of formal and informal authority needs to be understood so that the support of participants throughout the system can be enlisted in the service of your leadership opportunity. Since these potential resources are dispersed, leadership is less about having a good idea and more about recruiting partners, champions, fellow travelers and potentially sympathetic patrons who can use their resources and moral authority to be part of your leadership opportunity.

The EMERGE Leadership Framework views public leadership from an open systems and relational perspective. Systems are defined as purposive sets of elements together with relationships between the elements and their attributes. A systems perspective focuses on the internal and external interactions that occur in complex situations at and across different levels of abstraction and scale. This perspective therefore shines a light on the complete set of leadership systems and subsystems that can be enlisted to support your leadership opportunity.

Taking full advantage of leadership opportunities is possible only if you have an accurate understanding of the leadership systems of which you are a part. There are three system levels that need to be taken into account: your leadership system (LS) level, the sub-system level and the supra-system level. The basic building block for public leadership is your LS level, which we have previously referred to as the leadership performance stage. The LS is defined by an action strategy aligned with a vision and informed by its historical setting. The LS is comprised of three sub-systems, e.g., the leader, the followers and the organizational setting within which you wish to initiate your action strategy. As these sub-systems are dynamic and evolve over time, public leaders need to continuously update their knowledge of the prevailing system frame, including their leadership roles, and adapt their action strategy in order to remain responsive.

Knowing how the public leadership performance stage is wired is an important part of successfully sizing up your leadership opportunity and accompanying action strategy. The EMERGE Leadership Framework uses a systems framing tool for unearthing additional sizing up information on your leadership opportunity. The Leadership System Framing process consists of several steps that help you "size up" and understand how the different parts of the leadership opportunity are linked. It also elucidates four key dimensions of your public leadership role. The Leadership System Framing Tool is visually presented in Exhibit 9.7, and is further elaborated in the text below. The supporting tool for the Leadership System Framing process is also included in the online EMERGE Public Leadership Performance Platform. The intent of this system's identification tool is to switch the units of analysis discussed in Chapter 2 from individuals, teams and the organization, to the interconnected system as a whole (Lichtenstein, Uhl-Bien, Marion, Seers, and Orton, 2006). This requires taking a systems perspective that includes all of what we have discussed in Chapters 2–4.

The tool enables leaders to frame an identified leadership opportunity as a multifaceted system embracing three essential perspectives: 1) the system level, which is the caretaker and repository of the "expanded now" (Hames, 2007; see Chapter 6 of this volume) and is responsible for integrating the vision and polity values of the aspirational future with key institutional perspectives and lessons from the past; 2) the sub-system level, which is composed of yourself as a leader and your followers within a leadership team and organizational cultural setting; and 3) the supra-system level, which is comprised of stakeholders whose policy preferences on issues related to your potential leadership imitative create complexity and moral ambiguity.

The Leadership System Framing Tool illustrated in Exhibit 9.7 high-lights four key leader roles that are explained more fully in the sections that follow.

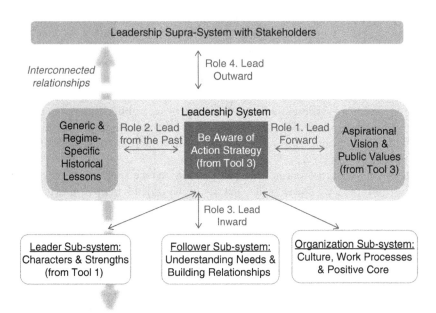

Exhibit 9.7 Tool 4: Leadership System Framing

Role 1: Leading Forward

As already mentioned, public leaders have an important role of always "leading forward" with an eye on the aspirational vision and polity values to which their leadership opportunity is directed. As we have argued throughout various chapters (see especially Chapters 3, 9 and 11), leaders take responsibility for inspiring and giving meaning to collective action. They play a key role in generating agreement on shared ends and the priorities that should be given to what are sometimes multiple and competing courses of action. The visible manifestation that leaders have accomplished this task is the co-production of a statement of shared vision and values by members of the leadership team that is aligned with the leadership challenge and opportunity.

Role 2: Leading from the Past

An effective and ethical leadership system needs to be tethered to the past. This requires leaders to understand the relevant institutional history and key lessons, and to bring that experience into the action strategy. Leadership opportunities are part of what Hames (2007) calls "the extended now." They reside within a time-warp that extends from the past through the present into the future. Understanding the particular history of an issue is of paramount importance to leaders, especially those who are faced with complex and dynamic challenges. This history is likely to reveal a treasure-trove of important information regarding individuals, groups and institutions that are essential for the success of any leadership initiative. Prior relationships, norms and expectations may be buried deeply within this history. Leaders need to develop the capacity to "think in time."

Richard Neustadt and Ernest May have provided us with some very practical "sizing up" ideas that enable us to think historically. Their insights are based on two decades of experience (1950–1970) serving as political advisors across three presidential administrations. In their famous book, *Thinking in Time* (1986), the authors provide a variety of useful methods that help leaders not only stand above the dance floor, but to do so with an eye to asking what is different about what they are seeing from what they may have seen before. Looking down from above is not the only direction for sizing up what is going on. It is also important to look backward to see what is relevant for carrying forward into today and tomorrow. Many may find Neustadt and May's multipronged approach too complex for identifying the historically relevant antecedents for simpler organizational or personal leadership challenges. If so, you can use the following simplified list of questions we have developed for use in our leadership training programs:

1   What are the precursors to the issue you have identified, both the challenge and the opportunity?
2   What key individuals have been involved in different ways with the issue? Who were they and what did they do?
3   What previous interventions were undertaken to address the issue?
4   What positive and negative results did the interventions generate? Were there unanticipated consequences?
5   What implications does your historical analysis have for the leadership opportunity you have identified? Do you still believe the leadership opportunity you are pursuing is appropriate?
6   If it is appropriate, but requires revisions, please re-frame your opportunity, taking into account the historical information you have surfaced.

Role 3: Leading Inward

Successful public leaders are keenly aware of the need to continuously lead inward by knowing yourself in relation to your followership team and your organizational setting. The EMERGE Leadership Framework sub-divides your leader role into three interrelated sub-systems, one for you as a leader, another for your followers and a third for the organizational setting where your leadership opportunity is anchored.

Your role related to the Leader Sub-system is to "know thyself" (as discussed in EMERGE Tool 1) and to continuously strive to enhance your prudential judgement as an effective and ethical public leader (as will be discussed in Tool 12 in Chapter 11). In a team setting, public leaders need to know how their strengths, and those of followers, align with the four functions of a high-performing team: strategy, execution, relationship development and influence. We recommend using the Rath and Conchie (2008/2017) assessment instrument for identifying the strengths of individuals.

In the EMERGE Leadership Framework, followership is viewed as intricately linked to leadership. Thus, your role related to the Follower Sub-system is to understand how to relate to followers and how to energize them to join you on your leadership journey. In EMERGE, a follower is NOT synonymous with a subordinate (Chaleff, 2003). A subordinate is one who occupies a lower rank than another, who is bound to perform duties dictated by others regardless of personal preference, and is held accountable to standards set by others. A follower can occupy any rank in relation to a leader, co-creates a vision with the leader, makes decisions about personal contributions, and is mutually accountable for achieving the vision along with the leader. The EMERGE Leadership Framework places the follower role on parity with the leader role, because both perform critical roles required successfully to tackle a wicked challenge. In this sense, we view public leadership as having a focus on the purposive and dynamic relationships between leaders and followers who share responsibility within the context of a "leadership (opportunity) team." Within the context of this team, leader and follower roles are often in flux. Everyone in the team thrives on the provision of four basic relational needs: trust, compassion, stability and hope (Rath and Conchie, 2017/2008; Kouzes and Posner, 2017).

The Organization Sub-system is comprised of the organization's culture, its work processes and its operating core (Mintzberg, 1983). The leader's role in relation to this sub-system is to be aware of the forces that will serve to support and inhibit the leadership opportunity as it is implemented (Bridges and Bridges, 2016). The Organization Sub-system is explored more deeply in EMERGE Tool 11 on Leading Organizational Innovation in Chapter 11.

Role 4: Leading Outward

Public leaders must also pay keen attention to leading outward by considering the larger supra-system to which their leadership opportunity is linked. The supra-system consists of key stakeholders, interest groups, organizations and other political forces at work in the leadership environment. Since relationships need to be forged with many of these external groups, a public leader needs to know who will make a good strategic partner and how to develop these partnerships. The EMERGE Leadership Framework gives high priority to a deeper understanding of the supra-system in the Contextual Intelligence (CI) Tool 5 and the Convening Coalitions Tool 10 in Chapter 11.

Concluding Thoughts on the Leadership System Framing Tool

Our argument throughout the book has been that vertical and horizontal structures of formal and informal authority need to be understood so that you can enlist the support of others in the service of your leadership opportunity. Since these potential resources are dispersed, leadership is less about having a good idea and more about recruiting partners, champions, fellow travelers and potentially sympathetic patrons who can enlist their resources and moral authority to be part of your leadership opportunity. The purpose of Exhibit 9.7 is to provide a template reminder so that you can create a leadership system profile for your leadership opportunity.

The EMERGE Leadership System Framing Tool assists leaders to concurrently see the whole and the parts of their leadership opportunity from where they sit (Heifetz and Linsky, 2017)—to simultaneously stand on the balcony watching while performing on the stage below. In using this tool, public leaders can become proficient in the third EMERGE practice of "Frame the Key Dimensions of the Multifaceted Leadership Opportunity as An Complex and Dynamic System." Having an initial conception of our leadership system is another essential sizing up performance element. This information is essential for deepening our Contextual Intelligence (CI) and Foresight, which is the focus of Tool 5.

Tool 5: Contextual Intelligence (CI) Discernment

No problem can be solved from the same level of consciousness that created it.

Albert Einstein

In the previous chapter we discussed the importance of standing above the dance floor to see the patterns that may not be visible to the dancers down below (Heifetz and Linsky, 2017). As argued by Nye (2008), an important part of the sizing up process is to get a good reading of the context. The Contextual Intelligence (CI) Discernment Tool, including mind-mapping and foresight development, provides a metaphorical balcony upon which to stand to view the critical contextual elements of your leadership opportunity. This tool is readily accessible to those occupying seats at various levels of organizational authority and in all types of public settings.

A mind map is a visual portrayal of the known factors shaping the outcome of a given course of action and the inter-relationships among all of these known factors. It visually organizes information. When applied to a challenge, an image of the challenge is placed at the center of a blank space, and related issues and associated ideas connected to the challenge at the center of the map are added. This process of trying to connect related issues branches out into many related and ever-smaller sub-branches. These maps are drawn by hand, either individually or in teams. The process is iterative so that each round of mapping results in a closer approximation of what the group believes captures the best representation of the challenge, and resembles the way a composite drawing of a criminal suspect is constructed from multiple pieces of information from various witnesses. The process is designed for team dialogue and group learning.

Mind maps help us better understand the nature of the complexity of a leadership opportunity by deconstructing the whole into identifiable and interconnected parts, including multiple sectoral actors, organizations, associations, and individuals acting both in their personal and organizational capacities. Some of a challenge's complexity lies in the nature of the problems addressed. For example, public safety, education, public health and transportation planning are inherently complicated. But the legal and political ways in which we deal with these issues are made more difficult by our governing principles, structures and processes. This is illustrated in Exhibit 9.8 with a Green Necklace trail proposal in a local metropolitan area. The leadership challenge is how to take advantage of the existing unconnected trails and link them together using the green space dots running through multiple pieces of private property as well and dozens of government jurisdictions. This is illustrated in Exhibit 9.9, which summarizes the kinds of agreements that have to be negotiated with different kinds of landowners. There are more than 100 landowners, that include the private sector, the federal government, the state, 25 cities, 27 school districts, 3 counties, 6 park districts and 28 other special districts.

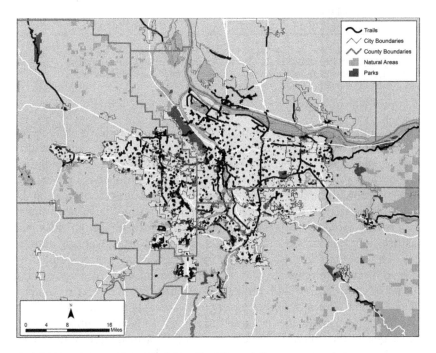

Exhibit 9.8 Metro Green Necklace Trail Proposal

Source: Prepared by Paul Manson, Senior Research Assistant, Center for Public Service, Hatfield School of Government, Portland State University from Metro Regional Government Regional Land Information System (RLIS), Portland, OR.

Exhibit 9.9 Greenspace by Type and Size of Ownership

Types & Number of Jurisdictions	Sum of ACREAGE
Cities - 25	14345
Regional - 1	7493
School Districts - 27	5837
Other Special Districts - 28	3899
Park Districts - 6	1840
US Forest Service	1676
State Parks and Recreation	941
Non-profit Other	854
US Fish and Wildlife	846
Private - Other	807
Unknown	730
Counties - 3	310
Other State	303
Non-profit Conservation	239
Other Federal	59
Private - HOA	59
Grand Total	40239

Source: Prepared by Paul Manson, Senior Research Assistant, Center for Public Service, Hatfield School of Government, Portland State University from Metro Regional Government Regional Land Information System (RLIS), Portland, OR.

Making such a plan actually work, therefore, requires leaders to coordinate actions across many organizational boundaries and jurisdictions, with each facing different legal, organizational and political imperatives (see Chapter 4). The Green Necklace trail may appear as a typical program management problem that requires coordination of multiple participants. The difference is that program management, as it is typically understood and applied in the private sector, does not assume that participants have equal and independent governing authority. This means that "what counts for success" may not be defined by the project requirements, but may be defined by larger governing principles, structures and processes of authority that are in conflict. This is what makes the project complex, rather than complicated.

One of the complexities is a result of the way in which multiple jurisdictions deliver their services. Development and implementation of the Green Necklace plan will require a series of land-use ordinance changes, alterations to public landowners' management plans, and some land exchanges with willing sellers to balance private with public interests. The constellation of jurisdictions affected by the new plan may require the services of a local land trust or a special-purpose intermediary such as the Wetlands Joint Venture or the Nature Conservancy to focus collaborative efforts on achieving a workable land exchange. Furthermore, private landowners may not be interested in selling their lands, but might be willing to condition them with easements or other legal mechanisms. If this happens, questions arise about who can or should hold the easement, with options ranging from the local governments to a nonprofit trust or a homeowners' association. Creating the desired policy outcomes thus requires familiarity with a wide variety of coordinative mechanisms to accommodate a multitude of jurisdictions, the business and nonprofit sectors, and dozens of interested individuals and groups.

The conditions described above explain why and how mind maps can be especially helpful to leaders in enabling them to understand the many sources of complexity and how the parts are all inter-related to each other. Once this sizing up is done, leaders have a better idea of where to start figuring out what leadership initiatives are needed where and in what order.

The EMERGE Leadership Framework uses a CI Discernment mind-mapping tool for unearthing additional sizing up information on your leadership opportunity and allowing you to envision emergent patterns in a dynamic situation as a basis for persuading followers and stakeholders to join in your leadership journey. The CI Discernment tool is presented graphically in Exhibit 9.10, and is further elaborated in the text below; the full tool is also included in the EMERGE Public Leadership Performance Platform. The tool consists of two sequential assessments. First, you carry out a CI mind-map assessment of your leadership opportunity by probing five key CI areas. Based on the CI assessment insights, you then discern emergent patterns in the evolving terrain of your leadership opportunity. The intent of this tool is to seek out emergent patterns in the context that can be used in persuading followers and others to join in your leadership journey. The tool enables leaders to visually depict the five most salient contextual conditions embedded in a leadership opportunity. This allows for the enhancement of CI, and for leaders to gain foresight related to the realization of the leadership opportunity as this development occurs.

Contextual Intelligence Mind-Map Assessment

In completing the CI mind-map assessment, information is gathered on the following five key dimensions of the context in which the leadership opportunity operates.

Cultural Tolerance for Risk Taking

The cultural setting is a broad category of factors that include demographic, historical, geographic, linguistic, ethnic, racial, religious and other similar factors that give a people, a place or an organization its particular sense of identity. This identity can be organized around a place (i.e., Napa

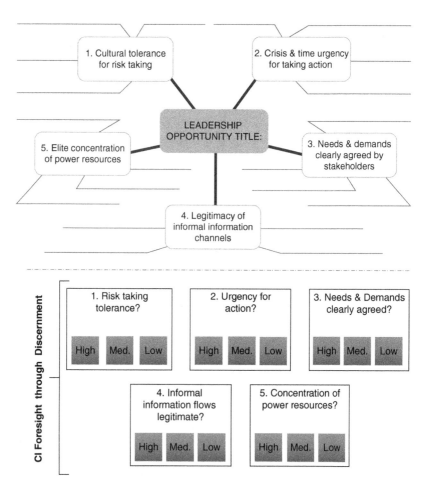

Exhibit 9.10 Tool 5: Contextual Intelligence (CI) Discernment—Mind Map with Foresight

Valley, Harlem, New Orleans), an organization (i.e., The Green Bay Packers, the United Way, the National Rifle Association), a set of values (i.e., the Amish, the American Civil Liberties Union, the Tea Party), history (i.e., The Declaration of Declaration of Independence, the Constitution, the Civil War), race (i.e., African American, Native American, Hispanic) or any one of several other sources. For each of the above listed sources of cultural identity, it is hard to separate one factor from all of the others that weave together over time to generate a cultural identity. The one thing these sources all have in common is that cultural identity and values become embedded in institutions, which carry the culture forward through time and perpetuate cultural practices, both for better and for worse. This CI dimension is assessed by looking at how much risk-taking is tolerated by the cultural setting and who is assuming or supporting that risk-taking. The focus of attention in this area is on cultural tolerance for risk-taking.

Crisis and Time Urgency for Taking Action

A perception of crisis and time urgency for taking action is the second critical factor for leaders who need to "size up" the most propitious moment for galvanizing the support needed to tackle a leadership challenge. Calculating the urgency and time sensitivity for taking leadership initiative is not simply a matter of counting votes from superiors and followers, but it requires that you put yourself in the shoes of everyone else you need to be part of your initiative. What are their personal, organizational and program-related priorities? How much control do your potential partners have over the time they can devote to a leadership initiative? How does this square with the time-sensitive issues within the organization like getting budget agreement, closing the books on the fiscal year, contract deadlines, union negotiations, election or appointment of governing policy boards, etc.? The focus of attention within this factor is on "the crisis and time urgency for taking action."

Needs and Demands Clearly Agreed on by Stakeholders

A third kind of contextual intelligence is the needs and demands of collaborators and opponents. Our CI assessment separates out the needs and demands of collaborators from the needs and demands of opponents. A conventional political approach would simply require that you prepare a list of friends and foes. But leadership in a shared-power world requires that you not only "count noses," but that you look beyond the votes to obtaining and building trust and legitimacy with potential partners.

Leaders must know what followers and collaborators need. For decades, there was widespread belief that followers need what President George H.W. Bush famously called "the vision thing," a quality that his critics claimed he lacked (Ajemian, 1987). President Bush may have been right to downplay the importance of this quality. In a study by Gallup of a random sample of 10,000 followers over a four-year period (2005–2009), Gallup discovered that "vision" did not rank at the top of the followers' list of leadership qualities they seek. Trust, compassion and stability ranked above hope, which is certainly a part of the "vision thing." But hope is a more encompassing quality than vision (Rath and Conchie, 2017/2008, 92–91, 251–256).

The Gallup study did not differentiate the needs of followers in public service organizations from the needs of followers in the private sector. But as we noted above, we do know from research that public service followers generally possess a higher level of public service motivation than their private sector counterparts (Bright, 2003; Perry, 1996, Perry and Wise, 1990). This may give public service leaders a marginal advantage when calling upon followers to enlist their support in the service of a noble public service goal. But this marginal advantage does not detract from the four essential qualities of trust, compassion, stability and hope identified in the Gallup study. The focus of attention within this factor is on "the clear and agreed needs and demands of collaborators and opponents."

Legitimacy of Informal Information Channels

The fourth contextual dimension is the legitimacy of informal information channels. The flow of information, both formally and informally, plays a decisive role in influencing people, budgets, programs and clients, both inside and outside the organizations. In fact, it was this argument that helped spawn the movement in the 1990s to flatten organizations through the elimination of middle management layers that were seen as "superfluous," "hour glass bottlenecks" and "make work" featherbedders (Morgan, Bacon, Bunch, Cameron, and Deis, 1996, 360). The movement accused middle managers of "stopping ideas coming down and stopping ideas going up" in the organization (former United Airlines President Ed Carlson, quoted in Peters and Waterman, 1982, 313). This accusation is a powerful reminder to those wishing to take leadership initiative of the importance of sizing up the communication and information flows as part of their CI assessment. This assessment needs to include both the formal (and legitimately recognized) as well as the informal communication channels.

Elite Concentration of Power Resources

The fifth contextual dimension is the elite concentration of power resources. This area includes tangible resources like votes, dollars and capital equipment; relationships and access; position; and knowledge and expertise. As former Oregon Governor Barbara Roberts was fond of reminding her students: "Leadership requires putting yourself out on a limb. When you do, you need to know who has the saw and who has the net" (Governor Barbara Roberts, 2002). Sizing up leadership opportunities requires constant attention to gathering this kind of contextual intelligence. The focus of attention within this factor is on the concentration of power resources in an elite group.

Contextual Intelligence Foresight and Discernment

We often can see the train coming down the track and we have enough warning to start to think about what to do in dealing with the train. But what happens when we can't see or hear the train that is coming too fast to allow us to take action? These are the kinds of wicked challenges that occur more frequently and for which special leadership foresight is needed. We can assemble this foresight by listing the key CI factors affecting your potential leadership initiative and seeking to describe their degree of significance depending on your leadership opportunities' context. Based on the information we collect from this probing, we can rate each of the five CI key factors as high, medium or low. This scoring information can be carried forward into the Smart Power Tool (Tool 9) and used to help decide how best to persuade others to join in our leadership journey.

Concluding Thoughts on the Contextual Intelligence (CI) Discernment Tool

The EMERGE CI Discernment Tool assists leaders to concurrently see the whole and the parts of one's leadership opportunity from where we sit—to stand on the balcony watching while also performing on the stage below. In using this tool, public leaders can become proficient in the fifth EMERGE practice of "Discern Emergent Patterns in a Dynamic Situation as a Basis for Persuasion." This information is essential for deepening our Smart Power in relation with followers and stakeholders, which is the focus of Tool 9 in Chapter 11.

Tool 6: Continuous Leadership Learning

> By three methods we may learn wisdom: First, by reflection, which is noblest; Second, by imitation, which is easiest; and third by experience, which is bitterest.
>
> Confucius (quoted in Montapert, 1986)

Public leaders operating in the "new normal" will always be challenged by the limits of their understanding and experience when working with complex and dynamic leadership challenges and opportunities. Success therefore requires continuous and intentional learning. Leaders are responsible for identifying and facilitating their own learning needs, for supporting the learning of others, and for facilitating learning in their leadership team and at the organizational level. This mindful continuous learning is the foundation of prudential judgment, a quality unique to public service leadership that we discuss in our concluding Chapter 12.

Continuous learning is best viewed as a generative process, which has three key requirements. First, it requires knowing what the learning needs are of a given leadership opportunity. Before you suit up to head down the rapids or rope up to make a climbing ascent, you need to know what knowledge and skills are necessary to be successful. Rapids that are rated as a 5.0 require a far different set of knowledge, equipment and practical skills than a 2.0 outing. Once you have this information, you can then take the second step of surrounding yourself with the right combination of team members and deciding what additional learning is necessary before launching your leadership expedition. Finally, you need to build in opportunities for continuous reassessment of what knowledge and skills are required to match the changing nature of the leadership challenge over the course of the journey. In the sections that follow we will elaborate more fully on these three dimensions of the continuous group and organizational learning cycle. This process is also referred to as reflective practice.

The Continuous Leadership Learning Cycle

Reflective practice was first popularized by Argyris and Schon (1974). Their research emphasizes the importance of accessing the knowledge that is acquired over time through the repetitive experience of practice. It is the kind of knowledge that surgeons, carpenters, architects, social workers, planners, public administrators and leaders acquire by paying close attention to the small and large things that make them better through time. Argyris and Schon call this practical knowledge "theory in action." Experienced practitioners develop a theory in action that encapsulates the subtle understanding of what it takes, for example, to design the right building for the setting, or for surgeons to apply their techniques to perfectly fit a new situation they have never quite encountered before. This capacity entails more than simply good judgment; it requires the disciplined habit of reflective practice based on theory in action.

One of the goals of helping leaders become better at what they do is to elicit this theory in action and to make it consciously accessible to oneself and others. This bringing to consciousness opens up access to various kinds of tacit knowledge that are acquired through practical experience and are often essential to success (see our concluding chapter for a more detailed discussion of this topic). Once this knowledge is brought to consciousness and consistently applied, it becomes possible for the practitioner to become "reflective in practice" and thus an agent of generative self-improvement and prudential judgment.

Reflective practice is not easy, especially since it requires leaders to step back from the daily grind of administrative work to ask a variety of questions such as: Where are we headed? What are we to do? What ends should we be serving? How are they defined? What means were used in the past? Who should be involved? What failures as well as successes have occurred? How can we improve upon what the organization is doing? The habit of reflective practice is especially important in large complex organizations which can create pathological cultures and propensities for "groupthink."

The EMERGE approach encourages public leaders to embrace a mindset of continuous learning. To facilitate this, we outline the essential steps in the recursive and continuous learning process in Exhibit 9.11, and also provide the supporting tool on the online EMERGE Public Leadership Performance Platform.

There are five stages of the learning cycle in Exhibit 9.11. It starts by identifying the learning needs associated with a given leadership challenge. This is a reflective mirroring process, where the knowledge and skills required to address a given leadership challenge are examined in the light of the capabilities of the individuals who will comprise the leadership team. This is where our strengths-based approach to leadership becomes important and sets the stage for the second phase of the learning cycle.

Investing in learning to successfully take advantage of a leadership opportunity is a collective process of using individual strengths in the service of a common end. In Chapter 2 we discussed the value of a strengths-based approach to acquiring this knowledge and mutual understanding. For example, individuals who are strong on analytic approaches to problem-solving need to have team members who are good at attending to the emotional needs of the group. Based on research (Evans, 2015), those high in emotional intelligence are likely to have a higher tolerance for uncertainty and ambiguity than those who are mainly analytically driven. The needs of a given leadership challenge determine what the actual mix of individual strengths should be in order successfully to "size up" leadership challenges and opportunities.

The third stage of the continuous learning cycle consists of performing in practice. It is the continuous experience of practice that further hones your understanding and enables you to make the kind of judgments that distinguish ordinary surgeons, architects and social workers from those who excel at their craft. The extraordinary leaders have the ability to read the subtle factors in the context at hand, like an accomplished white-water kayaker, to successfully ride the turbulence that surrounds them.

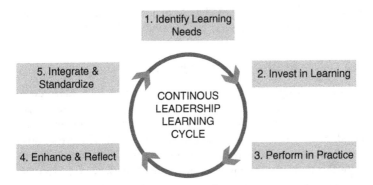

Exhibit 9.11 Tool 6: Continuous Leadership Learning

The fourth stage is where you formally take time out to reflect on the lessons you learned from riding the previous waves of turbulence. This reflective practice stage makes it possible to discover the theory in action. Once this theory is brought to consciousness, it can then serve as the basis for the fifth stage of the learning cycle, integration and standardization. This final stage is the point at which the theory in action becomes an "espoused theory." This espoused theory is reflected in the new norms, processes and structures that have been incorporated into the leadership environment as a result of the reflective practice learning in stage four.

We will carry forward our discussion of the importance of continuous learning in our discussion of prudential judgment in our concluding chapter. There we will argue that without intentionally structured continuous learning, public service leaders cannot build the unique virtue of prudential judgment, which distinguishes public service leaders from leaders in other domains. We draw from the recent neuroscience of the brain to show how we can use this understanding to improve our use of reflective practice to generate greater discernment, creativity and innovation.

Continuous Learning Strategies for "Checking" Your Hunches: "Don't Assume There Is Ever Only One 'Right' Answer"

Complex and chaotic conditions are characterized by high degrees of indeterminacy (i.e., lack of causal certainty) which means that leaders can never be quite certain that they have sized up what is going on accurately. As a consequence, leaders need to use various strategies to check their hunches throughout the continuous learning cycle. A leader should never assume there is only one right answer to a given situation. There are famous examples where assumptions made about facts, the motivation of actors, policy principles, legality, organizational capacity, etc., turned out to be fatally wrong. In navigating this indeterminacy, like white-water kayakers, you need to at least avoid a clearly wrong path, even though the one chosen may not have been the best. In the sections that follow, we review five strategies that can be used to check your hunches and fuel the need for continuous learning.

Getting Others to Assist in Sizing up Leadership Opportunities

One of the recurring themes in our discussion of what it takes to successfully "size up" what is going on is the importance of getting multiple perspectives, much like the "all-seeing eye." Exhibit 9.12 depicts the all-seeing eye that is displayed on the reverse side of the United States Seal. The eye stands above looking down, back and beyond an unfinished work in progress "to create a more perfect union" (in this case an unfinished pyramid). That is what public service leaders do and the all-seeing eye is what makes their work possible. In a system of democratic governance, the all-seeing eye is often the

Exhibit 9.12 The All-Seeing Eye
Source: https://boldlions.files.wordpress.com/2014/01/allseeingeyeondollarbill.jpg

demos who must take ownership of leadership efforts to create a more perfect union. In this section, we draw upon the research regarding the best strategies for enlisting the support of followers in the sizing up process. Without their involvement and ultimate ownership of the definition of a challenge, leaders become ineffective moralizers and doomsday prophesiers, reliant only on the instruments of hard power to get traction in dealing with challenges. As one of our insightful graduate students has observed:

> the conceptual genius of ... tools is not that they help us do anything we couldn't have done already, but that they help us do it in a way where outsiders (anyone who is not inside our brain) can participate ... The public sector question is how to keep outsiders engaged in what's going on behind closed doors. Whether you're trying to open those doors to let innovation breath, get a unified vision for your project team, our just present information publicly, tools present less risk than opportunity.
>
> Chambers (2014)

For our discussion of how to get followers to take ownership of leadership challenges and opportunities, we rely on the extensive research conducted by Benjamin Lichtenstein and his colleagues (Lichtenstein and Plowman, 2009; Hazy, Goldstein, and Lichtenstein, 2007; Lichtenstein, Uhl-Bien, Marion, and Orton, 2007). The authors conclude that the trick to being a good leader in an environment of continuous change is to construct the network of formal and informal space among and between potential followers so that the system as a whole encourages individuals to generate new ideas, freely engage in dialogical exchanges across bureaucratic and legal boundaries and to take collective ownership for addressing challenges (Lichtenstein, Uhl-Bien et al., 2007, 5). Lichtenstein and his colleagues identify the following four sequential leadership strategies for getting followers to engage creatively in helping to "size up" challenges:

1   **"Stir the Pot."** Open up discussions across organizational boundaries both vertically and horizontally. This can be accomplished by using a variety of techniques, including large group discussion methods, fish-bowl gatherings and dialogical approaches that are democratic, interactive and multidirectional. This first phase is intended to get participants to recognize that there is a challenge that needs collective attention. It requires that leaders prevent followers from avoiding issues that need to be addressed and which the leader can't get done on their own. Even if they could, it would not create the buy-in that leaders need to undertake collective action, which in the public sector usually requires a coalescence of unity of vison with shared polity values.

2   **Facilitate "Skunk Works" by Encouraging Dissent and Diversity.** Apple Computers became famous for the way in which it incentivized innovation and the generation of novel ideas in the workplace. Their approach became known as "Skunk Works" because it emphasized the power of small groups of people working together in unconventional ways to come up with new ideas. Like skunks, a small group can create a lot of change quickly with the right kind of "stinking good" idea! There are a variety of structured techniques to mimic Skunk Works activity in the workplace. One well-known technique is called ritual dissent. This technique utilizes a workshop design that creates parallel teams to work on the same problem in a large group meeting environment. Each team appoints a spokesperson who moves from that team's table to another team's table. The spokesperson presents the first group's conclusions while the second group listens in silence. The spokesperson then turns around to face away from the second team, which rips into the presentation, no holds barred, while the spokesperson listens quietly. Each team's spokesperson visits other tables in turn. By the end of the session, all the ideas have been well dissected and honed. Taking turns listening in silence helps everyone understand the value of listening carefully, speaking openly, and not taking criticism personally.

3   **"Don't Let the Pot Boil Over:" Set Barriers to Dissent and Idea Generation.** The risk of stirring the pot and encouraging a large diverse group to participate in sizing up a challenge or identifying potential leadership opportunities is that the process becomes a "Tower of Babel" or worse, an unguided missile of dissent. For these reasons it is

important for leaders to set limits to what is relevant to the dialogical group sizing up process. Lichtenstein and Plowman (2009) give the example of the founders of eBay who created a framing structure to their Skunk Works activities by establishing a simple set of rules: pay on time, deliver merchandise quickly and provide full disclosure on the condition of the merchandise. The process of sizing up can be structured so that participants police themselves by rating one another on the quality of their behavior with respect to the norms established for the dialogical process. Setting boundaries is a common practice for those who facilitate public participation and engagement processes (see especially, International Association of Public Participation, 2004).

4   **"Use Honey to Attract Bees:" Stimulate Attractors.** Lichtenstein and his research associates discovered that the group process for making sense out of emergent conditions reaches a point when ideas begin to resonate with small groups of people at first and then gain momentum with an enlarging circle of followers. They call this stage of the process the attractor phase because, like honey to a bee, it gives structure and coherence to the process of making sense out of muddles. Again, Lichtenstein and his colleagues use eBay as an example. From the beginning eBay used experimental honey probes to see what it would attract, like selling a car, selling baseball cards, selling old wine bottles, etc. If the honey attracts bees, then it is a good sign the process is moving in a constructive direction and doing so with self-organizing structure and coherence.

5   **"Keep Your Focus on the Well-Being of the Hive": Manage Starting Conditions and Monitor for Emergence.** Not everyone in an organizational setting can, nor should, be engaged in emergent sizing up. You don't want everyone on the bridge, when the captain of the ship is trying to change the direction of a large oil tanker that is about to hit a reef. You need most of the crew below deck "stoking the furnace," not on the bridge trying to decide what directional change can and should be made

We do not have a research study for concluding how many followers need to be engaged in the leadership sizing up process, but we do know from our experience and a review of the Gallup study discussed in earlier in this chapter that followers have a choice in whether or not to follow (Fairholm, 2013). They also have a continuing need for "stability and security" and on-going feeding of their sense of devotion. These conditions become increasingly at risk in periods of dynamic emergence. Part of sizing up, then, is being able to keep the organization focused on those challenges that are time-sensitive and complicated, while working selectively with others to see the sources of calm in a sea of turbulence. Leaders need to authentically model a sense of calm and security for followers even while navigating through the white water. Modeling this sense of calm becomes

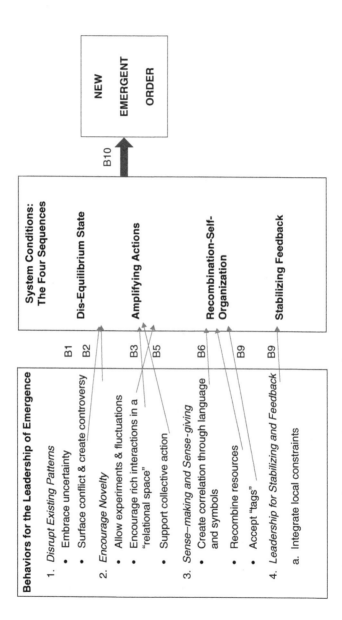

Exhibit 9.13 Leadership Stages and Strategies for Creating Change

easier as you expand your tolerance for ambiguity. As one becomes more tolerant of white-water turbulence, one also becomes more calm and confident that a safe way forward will be possible. So, in sizing up emergence, leaders need to be on the lookout for simple and tame landscapes (or patterns and routines) in the midst of dynamic complexity.

We summarize our discussion of leadership behaviors to elicit participation by followers in the sizing up process with a pictorial representation of Lichtenstein and Plowman's (2009, 621) findings in Exhibit 9.13. A new emergent order comes into existence when leaders: 1) facilitate the creation of disequilibrium; 2) encourage experimentation and novelty; 3) use their sense-making skills to amplify and encourage changes that seem realistic and possible to implement; and 4) transform the changes into a new set of stabilizing organizational protocols.

Conclusion

This chapter has presented an initial framework for EMERGE leadership that public sector leaders can use from where they sit to identify leadership challenges and turn them into opportunities. Our hope is that this framework enables public servants at all levels to see themselves as potential leaders who feel empowered to take leadership initiative to improve the world around them. In order for this to occur, those who have the potential to lead from where they sit have to develop a different mindset from the typical managerial framework that assumes people and organizations can "do better, faster" by simply re-engineering the structures and processes of the organization. While much good has and will continue to be done by organizational re-engineering, we believe these approaches are not well suited to deal with wicked challenges. Progress on this front requires a different mindset, one that assumes there may not be any right answer but a continuous series of "next best answers." Our goal is not just to provide leaders with tools they can use but to give them a sense of what emergence *feels like* from where they sit. This chapter has only focused on the sizing up task leaders face. Leaders also have to take action, an issue we address in Chapter 11 of this volume.

Notes

1 The EMERGE Public Leadership Platform tools and materials described in this chapter and Chapter 11 are available online at www.pdx.edu/cps/NewPublicLeadershipBook.
2 "Know thyself" was written on the forecourt of the Temple of Apollo at Delphi. Legend tells that the seven sages of ancient Greece, philosophers, statesmen and law-givers, who laid the foundation for Western culture, gathered in Delphi to inscribe "know thyself" at the entry to its sacred oracle.
3 This assessment instrument can be found at: www.tech.purdue.edu/ols/courses/ols386/crispo/changereadinesstest.doc

Part III
Taking Leadership Action

Master Case: The Case of the Vision Action Network

This case describes how mythical Cascadia County responded to the adverse consequences created by New Public Management's success in getting public-sector organizations to "run like a business." Administrative leaders used a value-driven community planning process to create a shared vision of the future. By relying on a combination of hard power and soft power, administrative leaders altered the boundaries of responsibility for the co-production of the common good by public, nonprofit and business community partners.

The Adverse Consequences of Being Mission-Driven

Spurred by calls to "reinvent government" and "run government like a business," many agencies over the past few decades have embraced the notion of a business plan as a vehicle to articulate their specific and unique values, mission and strategies. Instead of navigating the wide end of the funnel, where the risk of mission creep and inefficiency is considerable, agencies have migrated to the narrow end, where they can winnow down the field of play and focus on select community priorities and service areas. In Cascadia County a population explosion over a 30-year period challenged the capacity of the organization to respond to the growing demands for social services. During the initial years of the unprecedented growth, voters rejected short-term operating levies, introducing chaos and uncertainty as pink slips and service reductions were contemplated and often implemented. The lack of voter support created an aura of uncertainty for service recipients, partners and employees, not the sort of foundation on which to effectively serve a community or run an organization. With the adoption of a business plan, the county and other local agencies were green-lighted to focus on a shorter list of priority services with a shared understanding that this strategy would result in certain things not getting done, even if they were important to the well-being of the community. Policy-makers and the public were generally supportive of these winnowing efforts because in many communities the demand for services far outstripped the ability to fund them; and while the request to expand services occurred among some sections of the community, by and large voters favored focusing on core and priority services.

From 1970 to 1995, the population of Cascadia County more than doubled, creating huge pressure on public safety, fire, roads, sewers and other infrastructure services. The growth was expected to continue. The percentage of people over 55 was projected to grow from approximately 16 percent in 1990 to 26 percent of the total in 2020. During the same period, the percentage of younger adults (ages 20–54) was expected to decrease from 54 percent to 46 percent of the total population. The relative percentage of Hispanic residents increased significantly from 1990–2000, rising from 4.6 percent to 11.2 percent of the total population and was expected to grow by 200 percent by 2020. One in 15 county residents (and nearly one in ten children) lived below the poverty line.

This data challenged the accepted stereotype of the county. As the home of the state's high-tech industry, the citizens of the county had enjoyed the benefits of good jobs and high levels of service. The community was viewed as relatively homogeneous, middle-class and professional. But other, less-visible issues threatened the quality of life: mental illness, homelessness, hunger, lack of living alternatives for seniors and the disabled, and limited access to affordable health care. The relative affluence of the county obscured the fact that so many residents (1 in 15) lived below the poverty line. The envisioning process provided an opportunity to confront the citizens with this demographic information and its social-service implications for the community.

Building a Civic Infrastructure

Faced with increasingly constrained resources and a growing gap between the rich and the poor, county administrators with strong support from elected officials initiated a community capacity-building process, called Vision West. The goal was to identify community priorities and resources that could be mobilized to address these priorities. Most such processes begin with a strategic planning or a strategic envisioning process and they end with the identification of the central issues of concern to the citizens. But since the purpose of the Vision West process was to create community-wide ownership, and to identify resources that could be leveraged from the private, public and nonprofit sectors to address the issues, the county leaders emphasized the importance of following up with problem-solving teams organized around each set of issues. These teams held meetings to develop an in-depth survey of the more difficult challenges and most promising opportunities in their respective areas of responsibility. Each team was charged with producing an issue paper that included the following: 1) an overview of the trends and conditions pertaining to that issue, 2) specific issues and strategies identified by the issue team, and 3) a short list of key recommendations that participants felt were significant and could be implemented in the next couple of years. The issue papers were made electronically accessible on the Vision West Planning website. The goal was to have the issue papers serve as a starting point for increasing awareness of these issues, and to use the papers to inform a variety of public, private and nonprofit plans and initiatives.

A final step in the process involved the faith community. The Cascadia staff knew early on that it was important to involve the religious community in crafting a county-wide approach in dealing with the emerging complexity of social needs. The churches provide an untold amount of formal and informal social service to the citizens of the county. They have the loyalty and confidence of the citizens, and they provide connective linkages to the citizenry that are not available through other county, business or nonprofit service providers.

How was this support and network of potential trust among religious organizations to be enlisted in the service of the larger needs of the county? The county staff decided to use the same model they had followed in their other outreach efforts: contact the key opinion leaders of the faith community who are most likely to be supportive of the county efforts; build relationships of personal trust; and then call a more formal meeting to set forth the agenda and ask for the participation of faith-based organizations. This model produced surprising results. Not only did the faith community respond with great enthusiasm, its members expressed both surprise and gratitude that county officials would expend the effort to do what they had never done on their own. For the first time in the history of Cascadia County, the church leaders began meeting to discuss how they could contribute to the community-building efforts undertaken by the county leaders. What kind of social services were they each providing? Which groups were falling through the cracks? How might they pool and coordinate their efforts? These were the kinds of questions generated in the meetings.

The experience of working together for the first time was so productive and exhilarating that a core group of faith leaders decided to form the Inter-Religious Network, which would operate under the umbrella of the larger Vision West Planning Process. This new organization is a collection of Christian, Jewish, Muslim and other faith traditions, brought together to achieve the following goals:

- Provide a forum for ongoing relationship-building, information sharing, inter-religious dialogue and community problem-solving;

- Develop sustainable relationships with other community leaders and participate in efforts to identify, discuss and mobilize around concerns of mutual interest;
- Provide a network of faith leaders that can be accessed easily and efficiently;
- Create settings where new and innovative expressions of community leadership by faith-based organizations or individuals may be freely offered;
- Provide opportunities for group information-sharing programs and other activities.

The creation of the Inter-Religious Network represented the final link in a long chain of events that led to the creation of an entirely new organization to implement and sustain the work of the Vision West process.

Building a Civic Infrastructure

In 2002 the Vision Action Network (VAN) was created in response to the social service needs of the county. VAN was formed as a private nonprofit agency to be a catalyst, incubator and facilitator for resulting collaborative efforts to improve life for people throughout Cascadia County.

A critical step in the formation of VAN was the creation of a 16-member Board of Directors made up of a diverse group of community leaders from education, social services, healthcare, business, government and the faith community. With its unique perspective on community issues and needs, the VAN Board began its collaborative effort to leverage the resources from the various sectors to improve the lives of its citizens. This effort is about nurturing a spirit of partnership that will leverage and build upon existing good works (see Vision Action Network, http://visionactionnetwork.org/content/view/22/60/)

The county wanted to reach out to representatives from all sectors of the community, ranging from migrant farm workers to corporate executives, from the homeless to homebuilders, and from the mentally and physically ill to the healthy and vibrant. The idea was to invite individuals and organizations to represent both their self-interests and what they perceived as the community's interests.

Their credibility and network relationships of Board members provided another springboard for developing even stronger relationships and additional partnerships.

Through the Inter-Religious Action Network and/or the one-on-one work with the county and other partners, the various members of the faith community have become active collaborators in undertaking the following activities:

- partnering with Cascadia County and other not-for-profits to expand inclement weather shelters throughout the county;
- combining and expanding food pantries and clothing closets;
- developing housing units to assist alcohol- and drug-addicted residents, including those in government-sponsored programs;
- advocating for the homeless and raising resources for the Community Housing Fund;
- providing services and support to the alcohol and drug addicted;
- focusing on diversity and human rights.

Institutionalizing Success

Not wanting to leave the collaborative infrastructure to chance, Cascadia County formed a not-for-profit agency to serve as a catalyst, incubator, facilitator and champion. VAN was incorporated with the mission to "promote and support community-based problem solving through relationship building, planning and implementation processes that coordinate and optimize public, private and individual actions and resources" (Vision Action Network of Washington County, 2013). Cascadia County provided administrative, legal and financial support to the incorporation process and the initial organizational development efforts. This included the preparation of bylaws, budget, policies, procedures and marketing materials. In 2002, the Board hired an executive director. For the first time, the effort had a vocal champion who was not a county employee.

Cascadia County transferred the leadership reins to a 16-member Board of Directors. This group represented leadership from all sectors, including education, social services, health care, business, government and the faith community. It was tasked with providing the vision, enthusiasm and fuel to keep value-added collaboration alive and well.

VAN utilized the eight issue papers that emerged from the Vision West process as a starting point to identify opportunities for immediate successes. To the frustration of some, the effort was focused on incremental changes over time and participation of the willing, not on big flashy initiatives. The approach was based on collaborative dialogue, problem-solving and mobilization. It was not quick, it was not easy, and it certainly did not produce the "big bang" revolution that some had hoped for. It was, however, a viable method to enhance services and capacity where it otherwise would not exist. According to the lead administrator responsible for creating VAN:

> the county never envisioned the effort as revolutionary, but more aptly, saw it as transformative ... The general community could see the collaborative solutions that were created, but many did not understand or appreciate the important role VAN played in the

building process. Because of this relative invisibility, the commitment from VAN leadership became more became more and more crucial to maintaining the momentum of the movement.

Bohn (2014, 150)

Case Analysis

The creation of the Vision Action Network touches on a variety of themes central to Part III of this book, in addition to reinforcing themes we have already discussed in Part II. Faced with the long-term decline of the "administrative state," county leaders realized that the "new normal" required them to rethink what was possible. In doing so, they lead with the values that were most important to the community. They created a process that facilitated ownership of both the values and the challenges faced by the community by an enlarging the circle of groups in the community that had never thought together about a common future that they could co-produce together.

The Vision Action Network came into existence because two key administrators believed that public servants have an obligation to be more than passive and instrumental caretakers of policy choices made by elected officials. They took the initiative in creating an agenda to meet the needs of the growing number of weak and powerless members of the community. They did not draw a bright-line distinction between the public, private and nonprofit sectors. In reaching out across boundaries to create a new third-party institution, they exercised what we describe in Chapter 4 as polity leadership. Polity leaders undertake risks. There were no examples to follow and there were high degrees of uncertainty about both the process and the outcome. First, there was a complex array of stakeholders operating under separate and independent sources of authority; these stakeholders measured their success by different criteria. Second, participants in the process were asked to create a vision for the future based on data that did not correspond to their current experience. It was hard for many to believe that beneath the patina of economic prosperity lay a large and growing core of residents who were poor and in need of a wide variety of social services not currently available. Third, there was the need to create support for the agenda with elected officials, and to sustain this support over several election cycles.

After successfully undertaking the risk of launching and managing a civic engagement process that cut across sectoral boundaries and produced a shared vision for the future, the administrators subjected themselves to potential criticism on a variety of fronts. For example, if the Vision Action Network became the functional equivalent of a single supplier—a Wall-Mart for the provision of social services to the community—then the jurisdiction would have given up its authority for balancing the competing needs for efficiency, effectiveness, equity, responsiveness and due process considerations. The administrative champions of the Vision West Planning Process spent endless hours pondering how to avoid the worst-case scenario, where a new entity is created that becomes the 800-pound gorilla in the room, has little accountability and places demands on the political system that result in the breakdown of a working political consensus in the community. To avoid this, the administrators took several precautionary steps to preserve their role as a Democratic Balancewheel (see Chapter 5):

- They preserved the jurisdiction's authority over the social service agenda and the county budget to support it.
- They resisted using the creation of the Vision Action Network as an excuse to reduce the county's share of funding, and they succeeded in getting this principle memorialized into the county's agreement by elected officials to support the future operations of the Vision Action Network.
- They worked hard to establish the financial independence of the Vision Action Network and set a certain time when the county would no longer provide financial support.
- They made certain that social service groups with special needs could continue to seek funding through the county and would not be tied to any kind of monopolistic role of the Vision Action Network.

In undertaking their initiative, the two lead administrators used all of the roles identified with the public service leadership traditions that have become deeply embedded in the history and practice of public administration (Chapter 6). They used their technical analytic competence to provide participants with trustworthy and reliable information, to manage the processes of engagement efficiently and effectively, and to produce promised results on time and within budget. But this alone was insufficient. The entire process rested on a foundation of engagement that built trust with critical opinion leaders and stakeholders. To prevent this generation of support from becoming a simple process of coalition-building among elites, administrative leaders expanded the process to obtain ownership by groups not normally a part of the process. In addition to relying on rational planning and civic engagement, administrative leaders were extremely entrepreneurial in the way they went about defining the problem and seeking solutions. They were energetic, creative and innovative—in short, all of the things we associate with "running government like a business." Finally, they were mindful of their interest-balancing role in bringing interests to the table that would not otherwise have been represented without proactive engagement from county leaders. To accomplish this, administrators reached out to organize and involve stakeholders that were previously not an active part of the political process. In short, the creation of the Vision Action Network required administrators to draw on the legacy of our administrative traditions: balancing competing interests, cultivating civic governance, taking entrepreneurial leadership, maintaining accountability for efficient and effective results, and being responsive to the dominant interests in the community without sacrificing the needs and access of those who have no voice.

Public service leadership requires leaders to "size up" the constellation of contending forces at play in the community and to assess the range of plausible approaches for engaging citizens and officials in developing institutional responses. This process entails considerable art as well as science. Tacit knowledge and astute judgment of stakeholders, circumstances and organizational capacity must be linked to systematic analysis. It requires thinking strategically about creating a commonly shared vision; reaching out across public-, private- and nonprofit-sector boundaries to build support for that vision; and transforming it into institutional forms that can endure after the individual agents of change have left the scene. In the United States, such efforts must be conducted in ways that maintain democratic accountability, preserve the role responsibilities of elected officials and ensure some measure of responsiveness to citizens of the community. Career public servants lead at the center of these efforts and serve as democratic stewards in balancing the tensions among our traditions of governance.

10 Leading in Communities from Where We Sit

Power, Authority, Networks and Conciliatory Practices

> We live in a world where no one is "in charge." No one organization or institution has the legitimacy, power, authority, or intelligence to act alone on important public issues and still make substantial headway against the problems that threaten us all. No one is in charge when it comes to the greenhouse effect, AIDS, homelessness, the federal deficit, declining inner cities, drug abuse, domestic violence, or a host of other public problems. Many organizations or institutions are involved, affected, or have a partial responsibility to act ... As a result, we live in a "shared-power" world. If we are to survive and prosper, and if our children and grandchildren—and their children and grandchildren—are to enjoy the benefits of our ability to make the world better, we must find ways to think and act more effectively in a shared-power world.
>
> Barbara C. Crosby and John M. Bryson (2005, xi)

Crosby and Bryson remind us that even the most severe regimes of military authority are not in charge. They do not have the power, authority and resources to address the most challenging problems that face the modern nation state. The conditions that create a "shared-power" world are also the same conditions that inhibit us from engaging in collective action for the common good. We live in increasingly fragmented communities where it is becoming more difficult for citizens to share a common sense of public purpose and to feel that they have authorship over their local collective destiny. This condition is fueled by a combination of factors. Power in policy-making, regulation and delivery of services is dispersed and fragmented among multiple actors. Our communities have become a place to reside rather than a place to live. Gated and bedroom communities have sprouted up as an alternative to "neighborhoods." The growth of technology, double-income families and a highly mobile workforce has added choices and reduced time and motivation for investment in community (Putnam, 2000).

But the irony is that these very forces of disaggregation have spawned countervailing community movements to "think globally, but act locally." These movements are illustrated by the Master Cases for Parts II (The Mt. Hood Stewardship Plan) and III (Vision Action Network) and find expression in thousands of local community initiatives across the United States that deal with issues of racism, homelessness, food security, housing, mental illness, watershed health, etc. This chapter is devoted to helping you undertake leadership on these kinds of issues in a community setting. Our discussion will focus on: 1) ways of thinking about community; 2) creating power and authority for community leadership; 3) leading in different kinds of network governance systems; 4) leading inter-jurisdictional initiatives; and 5) conciliatory leadership practices.

Ways of Thinking About Community

To begin our discussion, we return to Chapter 3 where we introduced image theory as a starting point for undertaking leadership within organizational settings. The kind of leadership we exercise within our organizations and in our communities is a function of our image of what framework is most suited for the challenge at hand. Does the machine, social organism, institutional or polity image work best when leading within an organizational setting? What about images that help us think through the kind of leadership that is appropriate within our community settings? To answer this question, we introduce three images of community that are drawn from community research over the last 50 years: community as pluralist interests, community as elites and community as regime.

Community as Pluralist Interests

Until the 1950s there were few studies of how American local communities were organized and how they went about decision-making. In the absence of empirical research, popular belief defaulted to the long-held view set forth by Alexis de Tocqueville in his classic description in *Democracy in America* (2000/1835). The spirit of American individualism and the opportunity to exercise free choice produced a plethora of voluntary community associations. De Tocqueville observed that instead of relying on government, Americans at the local community level use associations "to found seminaries, to build inns, to raise churches, to distribute books, to send missionaries to the antipodes ... to create hospitals, prisons, schools" (De Tocqueville, 2000/1835, 182, 489 passim). He was so impressed by the vibrancy of voluntary associations, religious sects and organized acts of self-help that he was moved to conclude that:

in democratic countries the science of association is the mother science; the progress of all the others depends on the progress if that one... In order that men remain civilized or become so, the art of associating must be developed and perfected among them in the same ratio as equality of conditions increases.

De Tocqueville (2000/1835, 492)

This vision creates a remarkably different standard for measuring the success of public-service leaders than the traditional dual pillars of creating good management systems and facilitating democratic participation by citizens (Denhardt and Denhardt, 2015).

De Tocqueville viewed the formation of associations as a necessary antidote to the balkanizing forces of the pursuit of economic well-being. Although done for reasons of self-interest, the formation of local associations created a habit of "civic-mindedness" and introduced the importance of a communitarian perspective. Because this communitarian impulse emanated from the enlightened pursuit of one's own self-interest, de Tocqueville dubbed this republican virtue of civic engagement "self-interest rightly understood," to distinguish it from the older aristocratic tradition that considered the virtue of public service an end in itself. The principle of "enlightened self-interest" tempered the stark view that the local community interest is simply the product of the pursuit of multiple individual self-interests. The strong commitment to individualism by American citizens necessarily entails a concern for issues affecting the larger well-being of their community.

De Tocqueville's popular view that Americans have a self-interest in community well-being is supported by community surveys where citizens continually express a desire to live in communities with a real sense of identity and commitment to a larger common good. For example, when asked where they would like to live, most choose vibrant communities that work—where schools function, where potholes are filled, where the perception of a high quality of life exists, where public services are effective and efficient, where people are known and respected, and where the public, private and nonprofit institutions join in fashioning community identity and spirit (Hummon, 1992; Milligan, 1998; Manzo and Devine-Wright, 2013; Kemmis, 1990; cf Bellah, Madsen, Swindler Sullivan, and Tipton, 1996/1985).

Our own experience often confirms the image of community as a quilt of "pluralist interests." People join advocacy groups, professional associations, labor unions and political action groups that target highly specific measures, and then they search for political candidates who support them. In many instances, these groups will faithfully carry an individual's views into the political arena and effectively advocate for his or her interests.

But this interest-group image does not always lead to productive community outcomes. The interest group model of community often produces disaggregated interests that profoundly disagree with each other, not only among groups of people, but within each group as well. Groups easily splinter into a flurry of single-minded commitments and passions. When this occurs, leaders are faced with the condition of hyperpluralism, where coalitions of interests are exceedingly difficult to bring together for broader collective purposes. For example, a diverse array of special local interests may be able to coalesce around a narrow issue of how best to deal with the homeless, gang violence, excessive use of force by the police, citing of a recycling facility or a "safe bicycle" transportation plan, but not be able to obtain the consent of the larger political community. Furthermore, rather than people sorting out what they care about most and affirming it through civic engagement, well-organized and sometimes well-financed interest groups step into their place, speaking for them as professional representatives. Often these groups and the decision-making process are dominated by professionally trained technocrats (Putnam, 2000, 49-52; Knoke 1981). As a result of this group-oriented and professionally dominated approach to public affairs, the interest-based metaphor of community gives way to the metaphor of community as power elites.

Community as Power Elites

The pluralist model of community was seriously called into question by a flush of community power studies triggered by the work of sociologist Lloyd Hunter in the early 1950s. Hunter's study of decision-making in Atlanta, Georgia, emphasized the importance of viewing communities as a network of social and economic elites (Hunter, 2017/1953). Hunter's work spawned more than 300 local community power and decision-making studies over the next 30 years (Hawley and Svara, 1972; Domhoff and Ballard, 1968; Wirt, 1971). These power structure theorists rejected the pluralists who argued that community groups are mainly an artifact of the free-market place and the exercise of rational preferences of individuals who voluntarily form organizations and associations where they live and work. The decision-making process in local communities, they argued, is largely controlled by a combination of economic and professional elites.

In his 1961 study of New Haven, Connecticut, Robert Dahl challenged the "power elite" theorists with his argument that governing elites change with the issue (Dahl, 1958). For example, the professional and economic elites that coalesce to form a majority on urban development will not be the same coalition that forms on issues dealing with housing for the poor, developing a park, proposing a new tax or building new infrastructure for schools. Each issue requires the need to rebuild a winning coalition, thus giving rise to Dahl's theory of "polyarchy democracy," a variation on the traditional model of interest-group pluralism.

The quarrel between the pluralists and the elite theorists at the local community level has not been resolved (Gilbert, 1971). But the debate has produced some important concepts for leadership success, which we incorporate into our EMERGE Leadership Framework in Chapter 11. The pluralist emphasis on interest group advocacy has left us with a leadership lexicon of "stakeholder analysis," "interest-based negotiation" and "interest-group" advocacy. The metaphor of community as elites has left us with a leadership lexicon of "positional authority," "reputational authority," "soft power" and informal networks. Another important concept that emerged from the study of local elites and community decision-making is "non-decision-making," the idea that the status quos is maintained by the refusal to take action or to make proactive decisions (Bachrach and Baratz, 1970). For those wishing to initiate community leadership it may mean exploring the reasons for non-decisions. If it is a fear of creating new constituency groups that compete for scarce resources or threatening those in power, community leaders may need to explore pilot projects that demonstrate that additional community resources can be leveraged without creating conflict or competition. This is the story of the Mt. Hood Stewardship and Vision Action Network Maser Cases for Parts II and III, respectively.

Community as Regime

Treating communities as reducible to one thing, whether it be the pluralist model of interest groups or the elitist model of ruling oligarchs, has given way to the idea that communities are a product of "overlapping and intersecting sociospatial networks of power" (Mann, 1986, 1).[1] Using interconnected networks as a frame for understanding the whole regime has become a dominant approach to the study of power and authority in local communities. There are several characteristics of the "regime" metaphor that have important implications for leadership. These implications are a consequence of taking a holistic approach to an understanding of power and authority in local decision-making.

The Importance of Informal Structures of Power and Authority—"Power With" V. "Power Over"

The regime metaphor calls attention to the complex networks of civil society, business, nonprofit and more formal governmental organizations that occupy the community landscape. The actors in these overlapping networks may not often be intentional agents pursuing self-defining interests; instead, they may be motivated by the kind of relational interests that are characteristic of families and clans. Rather than advance their self-interest, they may at times simply want to be "good" community, neighborhood or network members. This focus on relationship-building emphasizes the processes of attraction between potential coalition partners and how these processes affect policy aspirations rather than placing undue emphasis on who prevails in conflicts or who is positioned to suppress potential issues. When we view politics as a zero-sum game of openly clashing preferences, we tend to miss or underestimate the importance of the varying degrees of attraction of political actors to one another. As they come together, one constellation of attractions may foreclose others. Attraction stems partly from the objectives that players can achieve by combining efforts, but other considerations come into play as well, including common attachment to place, overlapping personal and family relationships, shared experiences, common history, etc.

The network characteristics of regimes pay attention to these relational dimensions and to the opportunities they provide to exercise "power with" network partners. These may be more important than the opportunities to exercise "power over" network partners. The study of community power is ultimately about understanding how competition and attraction toward cooperation interact. Competition is easier to observe through the immediate actions of individuals and organizations. In contrast, attraction toward cooperation is embedded in and reinforced through relationships, some of which may simply be taken as a given. Political innovation is partly about altering relationships by developing new channels of awareness and attraction in order to create new possibilities.

The Limited Access and Effectiveness of Official Decision-Making Structures

The regime metaphor highlights the obligation of leaders who occupy formal positions of power to focus on the well-being of the community taken as a whole. It is often the case that local officials make decisions without much involvement or fanfare from members of the local community. There may be exceptions to "business as usual," but for the most part the 89,500 local governments in the United States make decisions under the radar screen without a whole lot of community involvement or visibility. More often than not, elected officials take this as a sign that they are doing a good job in governing, but this mistakes "good government" for "good governing." The regime metaphor's holistic focus discourages elected officials from taking too much solace from the absence of interest group involvement. Just because the pluralist model may result in an absence of controversy or control by a small, cohesive elite, it does not mean that the political process is open and widely inclusive.

The regime focus provides for a deeper level of analysis that goes beyond the question of how informal network relations affect the formal exercise of power and of local community decision-making. The informal pattern of social and political community relationships that are in place norm expectations, constrain behavior and limit possibilities. These patterns may well be the real problem that needs fixing, as is often the case with institutional racism and other forms of identity discrimination. Changing the formal institutions of political decision-making may be a start, but these efforts will fall short of expectations without changing the underlying pattern of social relationships. Working through well-established relationships is much easier than bringing about fundamental change in these relationships. The regime metaphor thus highlights potential changes that may need to be made in the underlying social relationships within a community as a necessary step toward reconstructing governing arrangements to achieve a more equitable alignment of informal social power with formal political power.

Constrained Power and Authority

While the regime metaphor is useful in framing community leadership, it also can be misleading. Unlike nation states, communities are much more constrained in their capacity to maneuver and control external forces. Communities are not autonomous, free-forming entities. They are shaped by history, legal authority, context, the position of the locality within a larger region, economic possibilities, revenue discretion and opportunities, and a host of other internal and external constraints. Knowing these constraints and making them clear to followers is an important leadership responsibility. This knowledge includes the significant actors, what they think and why they think the way they do. Our discussion of these actors in Chapter 4 is a start, but it needs to be supplemented by the detailed knowledge of the specific actors that are potentially part of any collective action initiative, an issue we deal with in more detail in Chapter 11.

Power and Authority in Communities

Our discussion of community power and authority to this point has not been very precise in distinguishing between the two concepts or in discussing their inter-relationship. This is intentional and due to our regime-centered and relationship-based approach in exercising leadership at the community level. Now we wish to draw some distinctions that are important for all three community metaphors in using power and authority to undertake collective action.

Power: Its Forms and Types

Power is generally understood as the ability to get others to do what you want. American sociologists John French and Bertram Raven (1959) published a now classic article that identified the following five sources of power for accomplishing this goal: legitimate, expert, referent, coercive and reward power. **Legitimate power** comes from the legally authorized role a person has within an organization's hierarchy. This is often referred to as positional power and is defined by job descriptions and the rules and regulations that create policies/programs and structures the exercise of administrative discretion at various levels of the organizational hierarchy. Often this legitimate power coincides with the power that comes from substantive knowledge of the issue at hand, or **expert power.** Possessing high levels of expertise is often a stepping stone to promotion, but expert power often exists separately from one's positional power. We all have colleagues in our work setting who are valued for their problem-solving and other skills that may not be part of their positional power.

But what happens when legitimate power and expert power do not align, or worse, are in conflict? For example, an elected office holder may have been elevated by the voters to a position of power, but possess no particular substantive expertise. In fact, the lack of expertise may be perceived by the voters as an advantage that can be used to temper the excessive privilege of "inside experts." When this tension between expert power and legal power becomes an organizational issue, it can result in a prolonged period of readjustment as those utilizing each source of power work through a manageable rapprochement. The Trump administration has seen this tension play out on a daily basis.

Referent power is derived from interpersonal relationships that a person cultivates and maintains with other people within and outside the work setting. These relationships are held together by a multitude of forces including charisma, resource interdependence, respect, trust access to others, experience and other kinds of assets that decision-makers value. At times, this referent power can become **coercive power,** a form of influence that relies on threats, punishments or sanctions. Coercive power is grounded in a person's ability to punish, fire or reprimand another individual. Coercive power helps control the behavior of employees by ensuring that they adhere to the organization's policies and norms.

Coercive power stands on a different footing than **reward power,** which takes advantage of the desire of human beings to feel a sense of value and appreciation for the work that they do. Herzberg (1964) has helped us understand that rewards in the work place are not of a "whole cloth." The reward factors that remove sources of employee dissatisfaction in the workplace are different and independent from the reward factors that produce positive worker motivation. As a consequence, leaders must learn to attend to both sets of characteristics and not assume that an increase in satisfaction leads directly to an increase in motivation.

In addition to knowing how to use the types of power discussed above, leaders need to be mindful of the "power settings" within which they are acting (Pansardi, 2012; Tjosvold, 1985). For example, having the "power to" do something is a different setting than one that focuses on having "power over" others. Still different is the power setting that emphasizes "having power with" others. These three power settings can exist at the individual, group, organizational or community levels. At the individual level, you may exercise a combination of your positional, referent or expertise power. You can extend this source of power into a group setting. But as we discussed in Chapter 2, groups require task and social facilitation knowledge and skills. One's technical expertise, positional or referential power may not be effective within a group unless it is deemed relevant to facilitating the socially interactive work of the group. At the organizational level, your positional, reward and punishment powers may carry you a long way toward achieving your leadership goals, but these sources of power began rapidly to diminish when leading at the community level, where formal power becomes more dispersed and gets further confounded by multiple centers of informal power that overlap with layers of both formal and informal power.

We are not well served in thinking about power at the community level by using the models of power that have been developed to help us understand power within organizational settings. The reasons have to do with our argument in Chapter 3 that communities are socially constructed through time and are not subject to the kind of "planned change" assumptions and rational models that we use to build our capital infrastructure, plan the expansion of our cities and suburbs, and drive economic development. The categories of analysis that come to the forefront in thinking about power and change within community settings are terms like norms, culture, civic infrastructure, civic capacity, self-efficacy, a developed sense of community authorship, and visible, invisible and hidden power. These are all concepts that are part of "thinking anthropologically." For this reason the literature on community and international development provide us with a more useful set of lenses and conceptual tools for thinking about the sources of community power and the conditions necessary for identifying and developing this power into collective action. For example, the work of McKnight and Kretzmann (1993) on inner-city urban development in poor neighborhoods emphasizes focusing on the assets of a community, the strengths in the existing social structure that conventional planners won't likely see because of their preoccupation with filling the deficits as these are benchmarked against existing standards of what "a good transportation infrastructure," "green city," "livable community" etc. should look like. Their asset-based approach to understanding community power turns the traditional urban planning model on its head by looking for the residual gold that lies hidden from view.

Duncan Green adopts a similar strategy in his discussion of international community development in *How to Make Change Happen* (2016). He observes that poor rural communities are complex systems of power that include invisible, visible and hidden power. Rather than using the classic organizational categories of power developed by French and Raven, Green (2016, 33) suggests the following framework for thinking about power at the community level:

- **Power within:** personal self-confidence and a sense of rights and entitlement.
- **Power with:** collective power, through organization, solidarity and joint action.
- **Power to:** effective choice, the capability to decide actions and carry them out.
- **Power over:** the power of hierarchy and domination through class, economic, military, bureaucratic and oligarchic instruments of control.

Green treats power within a community setting as socially constructed rather than as choices among tactical alternatives. Power is an integrated social construct created by norms, faith, culture and relationships of trust that are the product of complicated combinations of shared interests, personal experiences, friendships and love of place. These relationships become the source of third-party power, what has come to be described as "soft power."

Joseph Nye (2004) first introduced the concept of soft power to describe the use of tactics by nation states that rely on persuasion and cooptation rather than coercion to extract compliance from partners. Over time the phrase has been broadened to describe leadership approaches that rely on persuading followers through a combination of emotional appeals, as well as third-party actors making the case for why it is desirable for others to "get on board the train" (Nye, 2004; Kramer, 2006; Harvey, Heames, and Richey, 2006). Soft power can consist of legal authority, financial resources, political influence and legitimacy within the community. For example, you may not have the official authority as a social service housing counselor to do much about drug use by some of your clients. But you may have good working relationships with those who do have extensive political and legal authority, including the police, the district attorney and powerful community groups motivated to do something about the problem where your clients live. The thing to remember about soft power is that you are relying on strategies that persuade and educate those whose support your need. To quote a famous 6th century Chinese scholar, Lao-tsu (630 BC), "A leader is best when people barely know he exists, not so good when people obey and acclaim him; worst when they despise him" (quoted in Nye, 2004, 1).

Each of our metaphors for community leadership highlights different combinations of power. "Community as pluralist interests" views power as residing in group interests. The interplay of these multiple power centers produces mutual compromise and adjustments. Sometimes this negotiation process occurs informally prior to the emergence of issues that become objects of public debate, and sometimes it occurs as part of the formal processes of official decision-making. But, in all cases, the interest-based model assumes that participants have points of view that are capable of compromise and that power is widely dispersed with the potential for a kind of market-place adjustment. Unlike value-based conflicts, competing interests can be shifted in one direction or another without participants feeling that their core moral identity as a group or individual has been compromised by the adjustment process. This is why conflicts that are cast in moral terms are so difficult to resolve and why "power over" seldom gives way to "power with" (Haidt, 2012; Benjamin, 1990, Chaps 1-2).

The metaphor of community as power elite assumes that power is intentionally held and controlled by key dominant interests, usually the economic elite, to permanently control its vested interests. The informal power that elites exercise is used to control the formal power structure and decision-making processes. Under this model, power is viewed as a zero-sum gain where there can't be winners without losers.

The metaphor of community as regime views power as distributed in networks of overlapping relationships that have been constructed through time. They are not as easy to change as the interests of individuals and groups in the interest group model, but they do not have the oppressive characteristics associated with the "power elite" model. Network and relational power in the polity model are tied to a different set of ends than in either the interest group or power elite models. The ends of power in the polity model are more focused on the future well-being of existing network relationships and how these affect the larger well-being of the community (Heclo, 2011; Selznick, 1993). Scholars are increasingly describing these as "public value networks" because of the close nexus between network relationships and the well-being of the community (O'Flynn, 2007; Agranoff, 2007; Stoker, 2006). The Mt. Hood Forest Stewardship and the Vision Action Network Master Cases for Parts II and III of this volume provide illustrations of what public value networks look like in practice. In these types of networks, it is often difficult to separate power from authority.

Authority

Authority is the right given to leaders to exercise their formal and informal power. This right includes making decisions, giving orders to others, enlisting others to achieve common objectives, and generally being viewed by followers as having the right to engage in these leadership activities even though the followers may not agree with them. This right most often comes from the law and its many derivations within our bureaucratic structures of authority (review our discussion of the various sources of legal authority in Chapter 5, especially Exhibit 5.2). But this definition oversimplifies the complexity of authority, which is socially constructed through time (review our discussion in Chapter 2 of the social construction and interpretive approach to leadership). This process of social construction often creates authority, which is only formally recognized by the law later (Selznick, 1992). We see this frequently occurring with Supreme Court decisions. For example, courts have affirmed changes in the standards of legal liability for products that are harmful because of changed conditions and practices in the commercial world (Levi, 1949). They have constructed new rights, such as the right to paid counsel, the right to abortion, the right to equality, etc. because of the authority of new socially constructed standards of justice, fairness and what constitutes a right. Let us illustrate the significance of this notion for each of our three metaphors of community leadership.

Sometimes authority in the interest-based metaphor is created by the joint agreement among interest groups on "the right thing" for leaders to do. There are numerous instances where interest groups reach agreement that is treated by elected officials as having authority. For example, legislators can't figure out a way to deal with the pollution problem created by field burning, so they turn the problem over to the parties to negotiate a solution with the implicit promise that they will legally reify the decision if the parties can reach agreement (Morgan, 1984). This idea has been officially recognized in negotiated and hybrid rule-making, which are legal processes for creating rules through a process of negotiation. There is an explicit recognition that if the parties reach agreement it will be treated as having the formal authority of law with the subsequent *pro forma imprimatur* of officialdom.

The idea that authority resides outside the formal law and rests in socially constructed agreements in society does not sit well with the official and formal view in the United States that only law creates authority. But it is an unavoidable tension that leaders accept and live with if they are going to be successful in taking leadership action as agents of the community. In the power elite model of community, it is the informal authority that is more important than the formal legal authority; the latter is only window-dressing for the former. The relationship between formal and informal authority is more complicated with the regime metaphor of community. In the regime model, long-standing social institutions in small communities like the local school, public safety department, social service clubs, churches or library may have acquired significant governing authority that both constrains leaders and gives them authority to take leadership action. In larger communities the informal structures of network authority are more complicated, perhaps fragmented and multiple, thus giving leaders more space for taking leadership action outside of and independent of these structures of community authority. The lines between authority and power in these settings are often very hard to draw, requiring community leadership to have a special set of leadership skills that go beyond those needed to lead at the individual, group and organizational levels.

Different Types of Polity Networks and Their Leadership Implications[2]

Leading at the community level requires an understanding of networks, both the different kinds of networks and the leadership practices needed to be successful in varying settings. Four major types of polity networks have been identified in the literature: informal, participant-governed, lead organization and network administrative organization. These are summarized in Exhibit 10.1 with a list of their accompanying traits or characteristics. In the sections that follow we briefly summarize each network type and discuss the kinds of leadership qualities needed to work successfully in each kind of network.

Informal Networks

Informal networks are *ad hoc* arrangements among organizational entities that do not bind member organizations by formal means (Isett, Mergel, LeRoux, Mischen, and Rethemeyer, 2011). These networks may be new and emergent or situational in response to an event, incident or political need. They are decentralized and highly reliant on interpersonal trust-based relationships. Their transitory nature gives them an unstable presence in the community. Informal networks are effective for information-sharing, capacity-building, problem-solving and service delivery. They are commonly used in emergency incidents that require a command structure with shared information among coordinated units, such as fire suppression, disaster rescue and searches (Goldsmith and Eggers, 2004, 69). They are common in the governance and management of large watersheds (Imperial, 2005). Informal networks are also common in the incipient stages of political advocacy, as

Exhibit 10.1   Network Structure Archetypes

Trait	Informal-Spontaneous	Participant-Governed	Lead Organization	Network Admin. Org.
Centrality	Decentralized	Decentralized	Centralized broker(s)	One centralized external broker
Relative Stability	Unstable or transitory	Stable	Stable	Stable
Trust-based Relationships	High use	High use	Medium to low use	Medium
Process-based Relationships	Low use	Low to medium use	High use	High Use
Citation	Isett et al., 2011; Imperial, 2005	Provan and Kenis, 2008; Isett et al., 2011	Provan and Kenis, 2008; Isett et al., 2011	Provan and Kenis, 2008; Isett et al., 2011

was the case in the 1980s with the environmental movement and in the 2000s with the organic foods movement.

The type of leadership needed when operating in informal networks is idiosyncratic to the perceived needs and interests of those who are serving as the lead representatives of the participating organizations. While these representatives are presumably reliable stewards of their organizational interests, this cannot be assumed or easily knowable in the early stages of collaboration. As a result, organizational leaders need to rely on a strategy of developing personal trust with the leader of each member organization in hopes that this trust can be transferred in ways that lead to inter-organizational trust. How a leader undertakes this complicated transference of trust is an issue of great significance, but something we know too little about. What we do know is that it requires a very deliberate and self-conscious effort by an organizational leader to separate their personal views from their organizational role and to make the organizational point of view they represent the center of all informational personal contacts and more formal negotiations (Robinson, 2004, Larsen, 2014)

Most informal networks possess a relatively low or undeveloped sense of the network as an independent entity (e.g. Provan and Milward, 2001). This lack of formal identity makes the application of formal procedures difficult. A further concern is that adoption of formal procedures might hinder network responsiveness and flexibility, and members may be resistant to adopting more formal procedures. Deci-sion-making in the informal-spontaneous network is decentralized and strongly interpersonal in nature, requiring well-developed leadership competencies at the interpersonal and small-group levels of interaction. Group-based decision-making operating in a fluid environment with few rules is the norm.

Participant-Governed Networks

A participant-governed network is one that the members form them-selves (Provan and Kenis, 2008, 234). This type of network has no separate governance entity and the power in the network may be decentralized with the network members having relatively equal power. Decisions are made collectively by the network membership, and all members are highly committed to the network's goals. Network members typically have a high degree of trust between and among each other. Network governance may consist of a combination of formal regularly scheduled meetings of organization representatives and informal discussions among members.

Some participant-governed networks that have been in existence for long periods of time have developed the capacity and trust within the community to undertake initiatives that look to be the product of a network administration organization. For example, an inter-faith coun-cil of churches, synagogues, mosques and temples might become a network to advocate for social service programs and funding at the state capitol (see the formation of Inter-Religious Council Network in the Vision Action Network Master Case for Part III). The network may have been in operation for decades, and the member organizations well known with long track records in the community. The network mem-bers can raise philanthropic funds based on a longstanding presence and member reputation.

Participant-governed networks require a high degree of participation and commitment by all or a large subset of members. As much as the participant-governed networks are recognized as building community capacity, they may be inappropriate in some situations. The inefficien-cies of shared governance may inhibit network responsiveness. The shared, self-governance of participant-governed networks is most effec-tive for small, non-complex networks (Provan and Kenis, 2008, 238). A more permanent presence and a higher level of stability distinguish the participant-governed network from the informal network. Examples may include networks devoted to such broad-ranging issues as home-lessness, teen pregnancy, latch-key school children, summer soccer leagues, etc. Leadership in such settings includes all of the competencies we have mentioned in our discussion of informal networks in the previous section but includes additional competencies.

Some of the leadership implications for a participant-governed network are obvious, but some are maybe less obvious. First, network members rely heavily on dialogic and negotiation processes to conduct their business. Consider, for example, getting the resources to undertake joint business together. This requires adopting a budget and overseeing its execution. Member organizations need to negotiate their respective contributions to support network operations. In addition, they need to adopt protocols for balancing the budget, regular reporting and annual auditing. Finally, the participant members have to be mindful of the impact of their decisions on network members who may have less resources, inefficient operations or poor representation. To prevent anti-competitive behaviors, the network collective must negotiate adjustments in a manner to ensure business competition and fair procedures among its nonprofit and for-profit members.

A second set of leadership competencies consists of an understanding of organizational frameworks, strategies and techniques (see Chapter 3). Since organizationally significant work has to be carried out, leaders in a participant-governed network need an understanding of what it takes to get this work done. This includes a combination of small work-group strategies where the tools for successful task performance (i.e., project management, strategic goal setting, etc.) and the interpersonal social tools for successful group performance (i.e., achieving and maintaining group consensus, participant motivation, individual performance and evaluation, etc.) are integrated.

Third, leaders need an understanding or a vision of what kind of organizational structure and processes are ultimately needed to realize the success of the network. While this kind of knowledge may be considered premature, in fact, it is essential for laying the groundwork for long-term success. For example, if you want to organize the various community groups committed to programs and policies dealing with the homeless, you need both an understanding of the organizational possibilities that are consistent with the realization of this vision, and alignment with the motivations of the various participant groups and organizations.

Finally, the core leaders need to have an understanding of what is politically possible, given the "wiring," both formal and informal, within the local community. This wiring includes the formal structures and processes of authority for making political decisions and allocating scarce resources (see previous sections on the forms and structures of governance). It also includes the informal wiring of the exercise of soft power, brokering relationships, strategies for building interpersonal and organizational trust and exercising both formal and informal power within the community setting.

Lead Organization-Governed Networks

A lead organization-governed network is concentrated around a core organization that takes the role of network leader. Usually, the mission and goals of the network closely align with those of the lead organization, and, in fact, the network itself may have been spawned by the leadership initiative of the lead organization (Goldsmith and Eggers, 2004, 76–81). For these reasons, a lead organization network can be a more effective provider of resources and policy (Provan and Kenis, 2008, 235) than the informal and participant-governed networks discussed in the previous two sections. Through the lead organization the network often has access to clients, financial resources and capacities such as strategic policy development and operational execution. When this occurs, it adds needed stability and continuity to the network through the leadership, staff and budget support provided by the governing entity (Provan and Lemaire, 2012, 645). These advantages, however, can produce disadvantages, especially if the lead agency holds the ultimate authority for program execution by controlling grants and governmental funding, performance and the accomplishment of outcomes. Such control can impair the flexible responsiveness for which a network was originally established (Goldsmith and Eggers, 2004, 31).

Frequently, a governmental entity serves as the lead organization, as is illustrated by the Mt. Hood Stewardship Master Case in Part II. As this case illustrates, decisions are brokered by the lead organization. The degree of trust among network members may be relatively low, but the dominating presence of the lead organization gives the network stability and legitimacy. The lead organization works to facilitate the performance of the other network members. The role of lead organization may emerge from the network membership, or the lead organization may be designated by external donors, procurement contracts or intergovernmental agreements.

There are some important leadership implications for the lead-organization network model. The most obvious is the need for the lead organization to avoid "throwing its weight around" by having a robust and respectful understanding of the role and function of participant members (see the first section of this chapter). While everyone needs to be treated equally, it is also very problematic and ultimately fatal for the lead organization to treat all participants as though they possess the same motivations, purposes, vision and strategies for achieving the public good. Treating everyone as equal, but importantly different, requires some careful leadership tightrope walking.

Second, lead organizations need to think strategically and institutionally (see the second section of this chapter). Successful achievement of the collective goals of the network is not a short-term undertaking, but requires strategically designed and implemented plans of execution. This requires a very high level of organizational leadership competence (see Chapter 2).

Third, lead organization networks need to be willing to play a combination of balancing roles: being the tough cop v. nice cop; capacity builder v. rule enforcer; budget constrainer v. budget empowerer; power broker v. power enforcer, etc.

A final set of leadership competencies is needed, especially when the lead organization is a governmental entity. Such actors operate with the legal presumption that they can exercise no power or make any fiduciary promises without explicit legal authority. Such authority can come from one of the following four sources (Larsen, 2014):

1   **Legislative Directive:** Charge to action and constraint created by the mission of particular agencies at various levels of government expressed through organic or authorizing legislation and further constrained by other laws, as well as appropriations/funding containing both operating funds and direction;

2   **Executive Directive:** Charge to action and constraint by the executive branch or administration, including the body of policy and regulation at various levels of government;

3   **Judicial Directive:** Charge to action and constraint by judicial system in their role of interpreting regime mandates, laws and policies at various levels of government;

4   **Duty to Citizens:**

   (a)   Serve citizens as directed through agency mission as modulated by laws, policy, regulation and court decisions,

   (b)   Engage citizens in participation in decision making as outlined in various laws, regulation and policy,

   (c)   Serve as an interface between citizens and their government within the mission area of their agency.

This authority framework of legal accountability means that the agents of a governmental entity, whether in a lead organization role or serving as a network member, must be abundantly clear and transparent about the scope and limits of their agential discretion. If this is not the case, other participants in the network need to press the issue. Without doing so, participants may assume that more power, resources and other forms of support can be provided by the governing entity than is legally possible, thus contributing to misaligned expectations.

Network Administrative Organization

Networks administered by a network administrative organization (NAO) have a centralized structure. The NAO, however, is a separate organization not engaged in network service delivery, and the NAO serves solely as an administrator, planner and broker for the network (Provan and Kenis, 2008, 236). The NAO may be a government or for-profit organization, but often is a nonprofit organization. The NAO may have a very small executive staff, but it typically has a board of directors that draws wide representation from the network membership. NAO-led networks often blend broad member representation with developed administrative procedures and practices. As with the lead-organization type, the NAO-led type network can tolerate a relatively low level of trust between network members (Provan and Kenis, 2008, 238). The Vision Action Network Master Case in Paryt III, council of government-type organizations and many trade associations fall under this type of network organization.

Establishment of a NAO reflects an awareness of the network as an independent entity and communicates the stability and legitimacy of the network to external partners and the larger community. This allows the network to develop stability and longevity, and to develop a track record of performance and accountability. Revenue for this type of organization may include dues from the member organizations, tax revenues, government grants and philanthropic donations. The NAO takes on the budgeting tasks of strategy and process planning, revenue forecasting, budget development and budget adoption by a board. Budget adoption may be further ratified in formal procedures by the full network. The NAO further executes the budget and is responsible for performance, as well as financial reporting and audits. The budgeting procedures of the NAO stand for the entire network. The internal procedures of member organizations are largely unnecessary in this network type.

The leadership implications for an NAO include all of the characteristics discussed above in the section on lead organization, but they also include all of the leadership competencies associated with managing an organization discussed in Chapter 3: creating the right organizational structure to carry out personnel, budgeting, management information system (MIS), contracting, purchasing and other functions; matching the right talent with the right tasks; correctly tracking changes in the external environment; and adjusting the mission and operational capacity of the organization to accommodate these external changes. These combinations of leadership challenges create a particularly difficult and complex performance bar. Leading NAOs can be one of the most difficult public service leadership challenges there is.

Summary Conclusions on Leading in Networks

The type and structure of networks becomes an important factor affecting how a local government participates in, behaves in and contributes to its networks. Governmental organizations have highly prescriptive accountability requirements, especially when dealing with the rights of privacy, open meeting laws, purchasing, contracting and budgeting issues. Knowing when these formalized legal approaches are absolutely required and when they are not is very important for operating within network settings. From our discussion of network types in the above sections, it is clear that the rule-based system of accountability heavily favored by governing agencies may be required and be effective for network members for internal organizational use, but may be seen as counterproductive as network level procedures for informal and participant-governed networks. In these networks, dialogue and trust-based relations provide the foundation for network governance. High-trust networks fit the archetype image of New Public Governance (NPG, see Chapter 7 for a more extended discussion of this issue). In this image, authority and power in the network are decentralized as member organizations are involved as equals in co-governance and co-management of the network and its performance.

As we have demonstrated, networks responsible for substantial resources and extensive program service delivery ultimately must demonstrate stability and trustworthiness in order to generate revenues. Network legitimacy is critical to reassuring taxpayers, customers who pay fees and charges for service, and philanthropic donors. To generate a robust network that can effectively administer complex programs and that can gain external legitimacy, network governance and management must transition to a more formal, procedure-based approach. The lead organization and the NAO led network forms reflect this more formal configuration. The NAO-led networks often formalize member representation and governance, and also formalize administrative functions including budgeting, financial reporting and performance measurement. Lead-organizations and NAO-led networks always benefit from trust-based relationships between members, but formal procedures are necessary to execute high levels of administration. Lead organizations and NAO-led networks break with the ideal of the dialogic NPG model.

In keeping with our institutional approach to governance, it is useful to remind ourselves that effective participation and governance of a community network must take into account its purpose and its political, social, historic and administrative context. Many networks were intentionally designed to meet specific service delivery needs, but other networks emerged in response to other needs, including political advocacy, leveraging capacity and resources, and local idiosyncratic factors. Local government administrators and other network leaders must diagnose the context, structure and membership of their networks in order to gain effective performance and external legitimacy.

How to Pick Good Network Partners[3]

In the previous section we have identified the predominant network types and some of the leadership implications for operating successfully within each kind of network. As important as this body of literature is, as a whole it does not provide public service leaders with the kind of information needed to choose good network partners. As local governments, civic groups and nonprofit organizations in the United States increasingly rely on complex networks of partners to extend their reach and to increase their flexibility in responding to complex problems and issues, what makes a good partner is a question that needs answering. In this section, we will summarize the limited research that seeks to answer this question.

An important threshold issue in picking good network partners is the outcomes the partners wish to achieve, for example, building community, delivering services or enhancing individual organizational success. In Exhibit 10.2 we present a "civic infrastructure model" developed by Margaret Banyan (Banyan, 2014) that is intended to help us pick good network partners. The network model focuses attention on the larger community-serving and civic-transforming outcomes of the member organizations, thus reminding us that all networks do not exist to serve the overall community good (Provan and Milward, 2001). The benefit of the civic infrastructure model is that it facilitates systematic study of the differences in the community-capacity potential of individual organizations.

Banyan measures the community capacity potential of organizations by two dimensions: the extent to which an organization possess a desire to be part of the larger societal decision-making process (Frumkin, 2002; Knutsen, 2012; Johansen and LeRoux, 2013), and the organization's relationship to its members (Selznick, 1992; Brainard and Siplon, 2004). These two dimensions are summarized in Exhibit 10.3, along with the four prototype organizations that are produced by converting these dimensions into a two-by-two matrix. In the paragraphs that follow we elaborate more fully on each of these dimensions and the accompanying prototype organizations.

The Engagement Dimension

The "engagement in societal decision-making" dimension captures the relative desire of an organization to interact within the larger sociopolitical environment. This dimension is important to the civic infrastructure process because it helps to explain the motivation for organizational participation. At one end of the engagement continuum are organizations that are active in expressing group interests and values in the larger political environment. Expressive action may take many forms and be

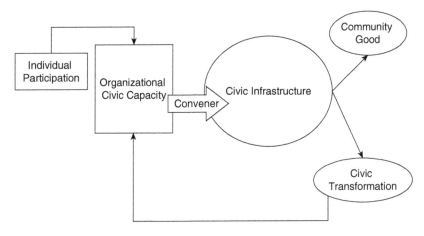

Exhibit 10.2 Civic Infrastructure Model

more or less partisan (Frumkin, 2002; Knutsen, 2012). This also includes both large and small actions such as articulating, "views on issues of public concern, whether they are speaking on behalf of a small group of interested parties or seeking to represent a broader conception of the public good" (Frumkin, 2002, 62). The expressive end of the continuum is distinguished by the extent to which the organization is engaged in the political/policy environment as a means to advance policy concerns.

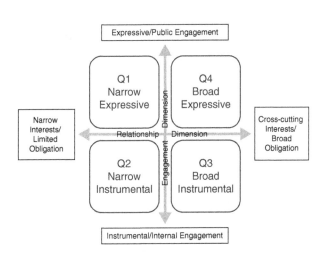

Exhibit 10.3 Characteristics and Types of Network Partners

Organizational activities that are not explicitly intended to have a policy or political outcome are at the other end of the engagement dimension. At this end of the spectrum are activities that may be focused on direct service or enhancing the instrumental good of the organization. While these activities may include interaction with government, they are primarily focused on meeting instrumental internal needs rather than expressing values. These internal needs may be those that generate organizational resources, advance competitiveness or maintain efficiency (Brainard and Siplon, 2004). Frumkin (2002) argues that the instrumental end of the spectrum more adequately describes the activities of nonprofits whose primary purpose is human service provision to a specific target population, such as those that provide job training, homeless shelters or childcare.

Exhibit 10.3 places each end of the dimension on a vertical axis. The vertical line represents the range of engagement from expressive to instrumental. From the perspective of a civic infrastructure, engagement by a nonprofit that primarily delivers services (e.g., food bank, homeless shelter, hospice care) is instrumental. These types of organizations are quite different from those engaged in policy advocacy (Mosley, 2011). For example, the American Association for Retired Persons and the National Rifle Association stand at the opposite end of the continuum from human service providers because they are wholly engaged in advocating for favorable policies consistent with their interests.

The Membership Relationship Dimension

The second dimension that can help leaders assess the potential partnership capacity of community organizations is the relationship of the organization to its members. The relationship dimension focuses our attention on an organization's primary constituency. This dimension helps to explain the extent to which an organization defines its constituency as narrowly or broadly focused. Exhibit 10.3 represents these dimensions on a horizontal axis.

At the right of the horizontal axis in Exhibit 10.3 are organizations that define the relationship to their constituency broadly. These organizations often define their members as including the community as a whole. Due in part to their broad relationship with members, their decision-making processes are porous in that they allow for an adaptable and shared co-construction of interests (Selznick, 1992; Banyan, 2004; Brainard and Siplon, 2004). Selznick (1992) defines these kinds of organizations as institutions. As institutions, goals become deeply embedded with the community, moral agency develops and the organization plays a role in balancing competing interests within the larger community. Due to the deep integration and co-constructed meaning with the larger community, these organizations view their interests broadly, cutting across sectors and issue areas.

On the other end of the spectrum are organizations that have a narrow view of membership that is based on a legal, formal or financial definition. In these organizations, obligation to members is limited to material or purposive benefits such as information, goods or services (Brainard and Siplon, 2004). As a result, organizational interests are narrow and determined by experts, rather than through the participation of members (Brainard and Siplon, 2004). Selznick (1992) argues that this was the outcome of modernized corporations, which disassociated community responsibility from legal membership and in the process justified organizational autonomy. Others argue that this process of community disassociation results from financial pressures that have led to a loss of autonomy, increased bureaucratization and professionalization, and the adaptation of missions to attract funding (Smith and Lipsky, 1993; Frumkin, 2002).

Using the Two Dimensions to Create an Assessment Framework

Banyan uses the engagement and membership relations dimensions to create an assessment framework that results in four types of organizational prototypes in Exhibit 10.3. Quadrant 1 (Q1) represents those organizations that have narrow interests and do not represent a broad community, but nevertheless advocate for favorable policy outcomes. Q1 describes a typical interest group advocacy approach, describing organizations like 527 committees,[4] membership-based advocacy nonprofits or business associations. These kinds of organizations are quite common at the local, state and national levels of government. Child and Grønbjerg (2007) found that nearly one-quarter of nonprofit organizations in Indiana engaged in advocacy. Q1 organizations work to advance favorable policy decisions at the local level and convey material benefits to a narrowly defined constituency.

The second quadrant (Q2) represents those organizations that have narrowly defined interests and obligations and are not primarily engaged in advocacy or expressing values to the broader society. While these organizations may engage with public agencies, organizations in Q2 do so only as a way to enhance their internal organizational health, direct services or funding. In this way, their obligation to members is limited to a narrowly defined constituency. Similar to Q1, these organizations do not necessarily recognize cross-cutting community interests. Mutual- or membership-benefit organizations may fall into this category, as well as nonprofit contractors that engage in direct service to a well-defined set of customers. For example, Ride Connection coordinates and provides transportation services to a legally defined elderly and disabled population. It does not explicitly engage in a policy advocacy role on behalf of its members with the goal of altering community level policies or practices. While Ride Connection has an extensive list of community partners, the focus of its interaction with other organizations is on coordinating, planning and funding to advance the core mission of transportation options (Ride Connection, 2013).

The third quadrant (Q3) is represented by organizations that may have broadly defined interests but do not generally express them within the larger societal arena. These organizations generally do not engage in advocacy, but, as in Q2, may have some interaction with government. These organizations view their membership as involving broad cross-cutting interests and related to a larger community. This is reflected in their mission to respond to the general needs of communities, not promote a narrow range of interests. Depending on their unique attributes, neighborhood organizations, mutual aid societies, churches or private foundations may fall into this category. For example, community foundations are commonly devoted to the broad goal of "strengthening our community." They focus on supporting nonprofit organizations in the community, rather than delivering services or advocating for community interests in the larger political arena. A community foundation's relationship with other organizations is focused on generating philanthropic donations and supporting area nonprofits.

The distinguishing feature of the fourth quadrant (Q4) is that these organizations define their membership and obligations to the community broadly and advocate their values within the larger political arena. These features mean that the organization reflects the interests of a broadly defined constituency and is active within a larger public environment. These organizations may include a wide variety of nonprofit organizations, such as neighborhood associations, watershed councils or churches. What distinguishes organizations in Q4 is their explicit commitment to the betterment of the larger community. Q4 organizations have an explicit mission commitment to work with multiple stakeholder interests in a public policy environment that spans a broad spectrum of cross-cutting community activities in the spirit of "better together" (Putnam and Feldstein, 2003).

The immediate and obvious implication of the framework represented in Exhibit 10.3 is that some organizations are not wired in a way that makes it easy for them to engage in a civic infrastructure. Organizations in Q4 are the most likely partners. They have an expressed interest in engaging the larger political environment as well as view their relationship to constituents in a broadly focused and cross-cutting manner. An advantage of engaging organizations from Q4 is that they may be better prepared to sustain the civic infrastructure over time due to their existing involvement in both the socio-political and community arenas. Simply, they may be the low-hanging organizational fruit.

One of the issues raised by the civic capacity assessment framework in Exhibit 10.3 is the dynamic nature of the civic infrastructure that can inspire organizational change as a result of engagement or time. For example, a key activity in a civic infrastructure is the co-identification of community problems. Through the engagement process, participating organizations may adapt their narrow goals to a broader understanding of community obligation. This was clearly exemplified in the VAN Master Case for Part III of this text where the Living Hope Fellowship of churches incorporated the civic infrastructure's goals into its own ten-year strategic plan and began to participate in the policy arena (Banyan, 2003). Living Hope Fellowship moved from a Q2 to Q4 organization.

For public managers, initial attempts to engage the civic infrastructure might begin with a careful analysis of the range of organizational motivations and relationships within the community. It may be that movement among all of the quadrants is possible, given the appropriate interventions. Considering intervention strategies may be essential to building a diverse, healthy and sustained civic infrastructure. Where a particular organization may not be ready for engagement today, it may be that sustained connections are all that are necessary. The range of possible interventions may also include dialog on the mutual benefits of participation or identifying a champion for involvement in the organization.

Equally important is a strategy that removes the barriers to sustained engagement in the civic infrastructure. For example, Frumkin (2002) argued that in order for collaboration to occur between government and nonprofits, there must be equal power among the sectors. In other words, the development of a non-hierarchical network may be essential. Other research has shown that nonprofit funding is a core barrier to advocacy or expression of interests. Government funding sets up competition among nonprofit participants and establishes a power differential (Mosley, 2011). Further, in their study of the extent of nonprofit political advocacy, Child and Grønbjerg (2007) found that those organizations that received a majority of their funding from government sources decreased their advocacy by nearly 70 percent.

Additional barriers to moving organizations towards Q4 may be conflicts over fundamental values of the organization relative to the overall community good. Some organizations simply have core religious or moral values that do not lend themselves to broader community efforts (Frumkin, 2002). For example, Knutsen (2012) found that several Canadian-Chinese organizations provide help for members to negotiate conflicting expectations of ethnicity and nationality and still others provide support to Chinese family social needs. These member-serving organizations may or may not find value in broad-based community efforts.

Leading Inter-Jurisdictional Initiatives

America's fragmented local government landscape necessitates cooperation across jurisdictional boundaries. Local intergovernmental agreements (IGAs) are the common instrument used to memorialize this cooperation. IGAs summarize the mutual roles and responsibilities of governmental jurisdictions in agreeing to provide a common service (fire, police, water, etc.), engage in joint problem-solving (i.e., annexation, land-using planning, facilities siting, etc.), or to share functions (i.e., purchasing, fleet management, payroll, etc.). Most jurisdictions have dozens of these IGAs and, in fact, may not have a master list of all of the ones in existence. These kinds of agreements are not usually problematic from a leadership point of view. Most are legal documents for which there are templates that have been reviewed by lawyers. They are executed by professionals with little public process.

The agreements that pose leadership challenges are those that are highly complicated (i.e., building an inter-jurisdictional light rail system —see Chapter 8, Exhibit 8.1) or those that are hotly contested by citizens (i.e., building a new bridge that a portion of the community does not want). An example of both is the creation of green space that requires taking land from multiple jurisdictions and private land owners to create a green necklace park (see Chapter 9). These kinds of intersectoral collaboration initiatives require an abundance of conciliatory practice skills.

Leadership and Conciliatory Practices

Leading at the community level requires a set of conciliatory leadership practices that build trust across boundaries—organizational, jurisdictional, racial, urban–rural, ethnic, religious and, more generally, issues that create moral divisions within the community. The following sections provide an abbreviated summary of some of the essential tools we have used for carrying out community leadership roles in these kinds of conflictual settings. The tools are drawn from several bodies of literature, including conflict-management, community development, interest-based negotiation and values-based problem-solving. The tools are organized around the central questions that conciliatory practices are intended to answer. In Chapter 11 we continue our discussion of conciliatory practices for taking leadership action. Our particular focus in Chapter 11 is on strategies for convening and sustaining coalitions of stakeholders to address wicked challenges. But the principles of conciliatory practice are also applicable in more tame leadership settings. We just need to remember that conciliatory practices were designed especially to facilitate agreement when traditional stakeholder and interest-group brokering strategies are not sufficient to obtain and sustain collective agreement. For an elaboration of these practices, along with a template for their use, see the online EMERGE Leadership Platform.

How Do You Choose Whom to Involve?

This is an exercise in stakeholder analysis, which raises important questions that affect the design as well as outcome of the process. Typical questions used to conduct such an analysis are listed below (also see Miller, Shinn, and Bentley, 1994, Chapter 6):

- Who shares authority in the decision setting?
- Who shares power and capacity (with or without authority) to get the job done in the affected setting?
- What jurisdictions are involved with the policy issue, problem or setting?
- Who will be saddled with significant aspects of implementation if an agreement is reached?
- Who is the group allegedly representing?
- What key values are at stake, and what groups are most sensitive to them?
- Who will be affected by the outcomes of the process?
- Which groups or individuals have historically been left out of the process, but should be involved?

This exercise should be carried out by an initial group staffed with people who are sensitive to those who may oppose outcomes from the collaborative effort, or who may be disenfranchised by it and lacking a voice. No group should be excluded from the eventual collaboration on principle; this helps ensure that the collaborative process passes appropriate "publicity" and "participatory" tests. In addition, as the process unfolds, it is important to assess who, or which parties, will be critical to holding the agreement together through the subsequent implementation phase. This may not be obvious at the start of the process.

Finally, in conducting stakeholder analysis, it is often useful to construct a stakeholder map. The map's design can help visualize the array of stakeholders by the intensity of their power, their direct v. indirect relation to the process and desired outcomes, their degree or interest, their access to resources, their relation to the initial leading group, and/or their organizational identities. Such maps also help participants visualize the pattern of institutional relationships that define their community or policy subsystem. There is no single best way to design such maps, and a collaborative group may end up constructing more than one for different purposes. Two common designs for such maps include concentric rings with a core group or organization at the center, with other stakeholders arrayed at different levels around the core; and a networked array or constellation with no core group or organization. More elaborate stakeholder charts and diagrams are offered in the literature (cf. Crosby and Bryson, 2005, 83–84, 203–05, 262, 283), but we think work groups should tailor such visual aids in their own way and strive for a balance between simplicity in visual presentation and comprehensiveness in order to preserve their usefulness.

How Do You Manage Conflicting Values?

Conciliatory practices entail keeping track of value differences that participants care about. This is a leadership task of the highest order. First, those who wish to lead must reflect on and articulate what matters most to them in the collaborative process. Second, they must understand and promote respect for what other participants really care about—what draws them into the collaborative process (Crosby and Bryson, 2005, 37–42). Through use of group facilitation techniques such as periodic brainstorming, nominal-group and values clarification exercises, leaders must keep track of emerging values as they are discovered in the process. Many participants will prioritize criteria differently. Conciliating practices do not disregard these differences; rather, they promote respect and inclusion for them. Exhibit 10.4 illustrates a framework developed by the Rural Resource Management team (Miller, Shinn, and Bentley, 1994) for tracking multiple interests and values.

As the decision process moves forward, participants may say, "I cannot support that alternative because ..." Such statements often articulate meanings not adequately captured in enumerated criteria. Exploring and reflecting upon these meanings contributes to a richer understanding of relevant values, and thereby enhances the "problem structuring" phase of the process. The way a group defines its values affects the definition of the problems or issues the group wishes to act upon, and thereby focuses the group on particular kinds of decision outcomes (Stone, 2001). This aspect of conciliatory practice is usually untidy and open-ended, often provoking suggestions about reweighing criteria and offering new alternatives or variations of existing alternatives.

A task-oriented leader may see these efforts as distractions from the "real" work of decision-making—as "politics" in a negative or irrational sense. This is often a mistake, because it presumes that such leaders have already adequately defined the problem, and that they really do not care to listen and cultivate dialog through which broader commitments and consensus may be built. Moreover, it is common to discover new values or see new alternatives that had not manifested themselves in participants' minds in earlier stages. In the process, people with varied interests may discover a truth greater than either party carried in to the debate, or at least identify one that each party finds worth holding in common. This is what civil discourse is all about. Keeping track of values thus offers a way for seemingly disparate individuals and groups to find and articulate common ground upon which some consensus and decision becomes feasible. The results may not be optimal in the traditional managerial or economic sense, but they are likely more politically palatable and sustainable.

How Do You Keep Everyone Committed to the Process?

Drawing in affected stakeholders and keeping track of values are necessary functions for sustaining and facilitating group interaction and commitment. The players must continually perceive an interest in staying in the game and believe that the process is, on balance, fair and equitable. Ensuring this involves looking for opportunities to reframe or modify alternatives and make concessions that satisfy the priorities of multiple groups. This can be achieved in part through a "rolling alternative" strategy. It is similar to the negotiation strategy of writing umbrella statements or statements that capture the interests of contending parties, such as business and environmental groups in regulatory contexts (cf. Fisher, Ury, and Patton, 2002). Keeping track of what the players care about also enables leaders to identify potential agreements or political solutions to apparent conflicts. For example, it may be possible to identify trades sequenced across time—business concessions (immediate timber harvests) at one point, and environmental concessions at another (land exchanges that enhance conservation).

Conciliatory practices yield varying levels of agreement on specific issues, ranging from no agreement to complete consensus. An important aspect of such practices includes recording patterns of agreement and

Exhibit 10.4 Decision-Making Framework

	Alternative A	Alternative B	Alternative C
Criteria 1			
Criteria 2			
Criteria 3			

Source: Based on Miller, Shinn, and Bentley (1994)

disagreement. For example, an ad hoc stakeholder advisory group recently presented a management plan to the Oregon Fish and Wildlife Commission. They had developed the plan through a collaborative process that did not come to complete consensus on the preferred alternative. The group decided that they had gone as far as they could on the issues, and that the plan preferred by most group members should go forward as the recommendation of the group. The preferred plan was then improperly characterized in public as representing complete agreement by the advisory group, rather than as a plan with substantial agreement and some dissent. The political backlash that ensued could have been forestalled by recording and presenting the nature of both the agreement and the disagreement. Those who disagree must be given their due. Recognizing the dissenting parties helps sustain their commitment to the process and reinforces the idea that the process provides opportunities to revisit issues subsequently. This helps build trust in the integrity of the process, and thereby raises the level of civic capacity.

Another aspect of sustaining commitment and healthy group dynamics means taking the complexities of public problems and the reality of multiple leaders seriously. Leaders must know their own limitations as well as their strengths and seek out other leaders who can compensate for the weaknesses. In some situations, at least, the leader must learn to become a good follower—sometimes referred to as leading from behind (Cohen, 2011). Furthermore, the ablest leaders may not be the best persons to serve as facilitators of group deliberations. Nor may a leader with the most expertise on a subject be the right person to represent a group during deliberative and coalition-building phases. Rather, such leaders may be more effective playing supportive or advisory roles. In many institutional contexts, it is common to hear people say that it's not what you know, but who you know that matters. Such statements invoke ethical relationships defined by status rather than by expertise or ability. Such status may be formal or informal, and it may confer considerable influence, authoritative opinion and credibility. It is critical that leaders identify and involve group members who possess such status, and, when appropriate, defer to them as leaders in their own right.

How to Manage Decision Making in Conciliatory Processes?

In public contexts, arranging the steps necessary for conciliatory decision-making and implementation can be extraordinarily complicated. The multiple, overlapping jurisdictions involved in the process all have their own procedures, requiring multiple sets of meetings and forms of official ratification. At state and federal levels, administrative procedure acts dictate notice of proposed rules and widely varying procedures for conducting hearings and adjudicating disputes. Limits may also exist on the degree to which public officials can delegate authority. This often conditions the circumstances for when and how to include others, and can easily stymie consensus-building dynamics. Local or community-based decision processes are generally more fluid, but are hardly bereft of their own procedures, rituals and structures. In fact, the lack of standard procedural rules and the proliferation of special districts amidst county, city and town governments makes the coordination of decision-making even more difficult. The differences in urban and rural governance also present challenges. Rural governance activity is usually much more informal, downplaying (or even ignoring) formal legal standards and professional norms in favor of community ties that include friendships, clans, religious affiliations, fraternal clubs and so forth.

The complexities of decision-making steps in a shared-power world can make specialized tracking and coordination a necessity. It may require establishment of a coordinating body with the expertise, and perhaps with some authority of its own, to effectively manage such processes. In Oregon, the establishment of Oregon Solutions (www. orsolutions.org/) provides a robust example. The Oregon Solutions approach to problem-solving arose from the commitment of Oregon governor John Kitzhaber to address the challenges of finding community-based solutions to a range of problems. Oregon Solutions uses a community governance system that has the following elements: a community-defined problem or opportunity; a governor's designation of the project and appointment of a community convener; creation of a solutions team of federal, state, local or other government entities, businesses, nonprofits and key citizens; development of an integrated solution; and a declaration of cooperation and commitment signed by the resulting solutions team. Oregon Solutions staff members facilitate projects addressing dozens of public problems, ranging from transportation planning disputes to alternative energy and job training initiatives.

Conclusion

Conciliatory leadership practices are likely to grow in importance as the forces of balkanization continue to erode our motivation and capacity to think and act as members of a common community. In our discussion of "drivers of change" in Chapter 7, there are more factors on the horizon that erode community than serve as coalescing forces of unity. Demographic and ethnic shifts, generational differences, fiscal constraints, growing ideological divides, expansion of "gated communities", declines in civility and civic capacity, growth in income inequality, the forces of globalization and informational and internet individualism all place a premium on leadership practices that can bridge various kinds of divides. While technical issues like global warming, population growth and environmental limits to economic growth will surely test our traditional leadership practices grounded in professional and technical expertise, our future will depend increasingly on leaders who can develop the practices to create morally viable democratic communities that can take collective action.

Notes

1 Michael Mann used the simple idea interconnected networks to explain the development of the modern world from Ancient Greece through the rise of modern nation states (Mann, 1993). These networks are *ideological, economic, military* and *political*—the IEMP model for short. While each of the four categories in Mann's IEMP model may not be equally relevant to the local community level, the notion of multiple overlapping networks is at the heart of viewing "community as regime."

2 We wish to thank Routledge for permission to draw from previously published work for this section (Morgan and Cook in Morgan et al., 2014).

3 We wish to thank Routledge for permission to draw from previously published work for this section. Margaret Banyan (2004b, 2014).

4 A political group organized under section 527 of the IRS code that may accept and spend unlimited amounts of money on election activities so long as they are not spent on broadcast ads run in the last 30 days before a primary or 60 days before a general election in which a clearly identified candidate is referred to and a relevant electorate is targeted.

11 EMERGE Leadership[1]
"Taking Action" to Realize the Vision

Political action occurs in a public space of appearance in which the "innumerable, conflicting wills and intentions" of different people make the achievement of goals unlikely.

Arendt (1958, 120)

[I]n order for a principle to render action politically great, it must not only relate to the public realm we share in common but must also sustain our continued engagement in [the] realm. In addition to inspiring us to act, principles such as virtue and solidarity have what I want to call a "(re)generative" quality such that they reinforce the vitality of the public realm in which they operate.

Cane (2015, 67)

Do your alloted work but renounce its fruit. Be detached and work. Have no desire for reward and work.

Mahatma Gandhi (quoted in Dhinman, 2015)

For us is the life of action, of strenuous performance of duty; let us live in the harness, striving mightily; let us rather run the risk of wearing out than rusting out.

Theodore Roosevelt (1898)

Collective action by its nature is strenuous, mercurial, uncertain and often goes in directions that are novel and even potentially dangerous to the common good. We can't assume that just having good intentions and plans will produce good actions. Collective action is a different kind of leadership activity altogether from the process of "sizing up" leadership challenges and opportunities discussed in Chapter 9. While the latter can inform the former, it cannot control or predict its outcome. Those who feel the compulsion for collective action often find themselves floating on uncertain waters, frustrated by all of the legal, bureaucratic, organizational, political and institutional forces that serve as constraints to action and the lack of predictable control over those whose participation is essential to success. This frustration is well founded, and even intentional. Modern "rule of law systems," like the United States, have deliberately contrived organizational, political and legal systems to channel and tame the uncertain, unpredictable and potentially dangerous directions that unguided collective actions can take.

In Chapter 9 we introduced EMERGE as a "Performing Stage for Prudential Judgement" whereby leaders and followers mix and match the use of 12 core tools as they move toward collective action for the public good (see Exhibit 11.1). In this chapter we introduce another dimension to the EMERGE approach, that of leadership "repertoires" for taking collective action. Repertoires aid leaders and followers in selecting and applying the tools successfully in conditions of emergence. This introductory section is followed by a more detailed discussion of specific leadership tools and practices for taking action. Our goal is to inspire and arm public leaders with the confidence and competence to view the opportunities and barriers around them as necessary tethers that can anchor and leverage their leadership initiatives and align strategic action with organizational and program

THE PERFORMING STAGE FOR PRUDENTIAL JUDGMENT:
EMERGE as a Multifaceted Recursive Process Employing Leader-Follower Tools

VISION

Prudential Judgment Performing Stage

SIZING-UP Tools
6. Continuous Leadership Learning
5. Contextual Intelligence Discernment
4. Leadership System Framing
3. Leadership Opportunity Identification
2. Leadership Challenge Definition
1. Readiness for Leadership Assessment

TAKING-ACTION Tools
12. Strengthen Prudential Judgement
11. Guide Organizational Innovation
10. Convene Stakeholder Coalitions
9. Persuade with Smart Power
8. Inspire Vision with Moral Grounding
7. Model with Relational Trust

Individual-Interpersonal
Team-Unit
Organization-Within & Between
Community-Societal

Exhibit 11.1 The Performing Stage for Prudential Judgment

goals as well as with the polity's laws, processes and values (see Chapters 4, 5 and 6).

Leadership Repertoires for Taking Action in Conditions of Emergence

Emergence requires making sense out of muddles, which necessitates serious intellectual work. Leaders facing emergence are like good pitchers, electricians, doctors and lawyers; they possess the synthetic capacity to integrate what is going on around them into new structures of meaning that alter both theory and practice. Our perspective here is grounded in Ashby's (1957) law of requisite variety which holds that "only variety can beat variety." We argue that leaders will not be able to deal successfully with conditions of emergence if they use a single repertoire based only on one theory or practice. The inherent complexity and dynamic nature of wicked challenges (see Chapter 8) requires leaders and followers to embrace a variety of sizing up, taking action and reflective practice repertoires to address the challenges.

The discursive leadership process of sizing up and taking action in conditions of emergence is at the same time analytic and synthetic. On the one hand, leading requires mastery of the science of decision-making, systems thinking and other analytic aids that enable the whole to be broken down into its relevant parts, as explained in Chapter 9. On the other hand, this analytic undertaking is not sufficient for those who lead, especially in emergent conditions. The parts have to be reassembled into new repertoires of performance that create and sustain agreement for ethically appropriate collective action. This synthetic endeavor—embedded in reflective practice—is developed through experience over time, and is more of an art than a science. However, there are tools that can be used to begin the synthetic meaning-making process as well as to continually refuel the leadership-generation process throughout the various stages of leadership work.

Upon retirement one of the greatest hockey players of all time, Wayne Gretzky, was asked by a reporter what he thought accounted for his success. He replied, "I don't know. All I ever did was skate to where the puck was going to go." How do leaders develop repertoires like Wayne Gretzky's sixth sense of knowing what action is needed to take him to where the puck is going to go? In this section we review the literature to abstract the key leadership repertoires that provide at least some answers to this difficult Wayne Gretzky question (Rittel and Webber, 1973; Bohn, 2014; Termeer, Dewulf, Breeman, and Stiller, 2015). Our conclusion from a review of the leadership literature, research and decades of conducting training programs is that public leaders need to arm themselves with a rich repertoire of "sixth sense practices," especially when dealing with emergent and turbulent conditions. Like Wayne Gretzky, they need to be able to mix and match these repertoires appropriately in order to make successful contributions to the public good. Our experience and review of the leadership literatures surfaces the following four core leader repertoires, which we will elaborate more fully in the sections to follow:

1 Responsive
2 Reflective
3 Resilient
4 Regenerative

The Responsiveness Repertoire

Responsiveness involves acting in a manner that is aligned with contextually specific needs and demands as they change over time. In public realms where polity values are constantly in play, responsiveness includes and is informed by prudence, or the ability to know and do the "right thing" given the practical complexities of the moment. Nonaka describes prudence as "the ability to grasp the essence of particular situations/things; the ability to recognize the constantly changing situation correctly, and quickly sense what lies behind phenomena to envision the future and decide on the action to be taken" (Nonaka, 2010; see EMERGE Tool 12 below and the concluding chapter for a more extensive discussion of prudence).

Many argue that leaders have responsibility for building the quality of prudence into organizations through the creation of structures and processes that produce a continuously learning organization (Argyris, 1999; Senge, 1990). An interesting application of this principle is the efforts undertaken by the Project Management Institute to build flexibility into its certification requirements for project management. You now can become a Project Management Institute Agile Certified Practitioner (PMI-ACP). The Institute distinguishes the previous PMI certificate from their new Agile certificate based on the following principles that are tied to the need for flexibility and the need to simultaneously manage multiple standards for measuring success (Project Management Institute, 2012):

- Agile principles and practices seek to manage change through flexibility, adaptation and direct communication. They are suited to projects which require a nimble response to change and continual communication to citizens/clients/stakeholders/customers.
- The principles guiding the older PMI certificate, often referred to simply as "waterfall," are sequential and phase-driven. Each stage of a project must be planned and completed before further work can progress on the next stage. This approach is suited to projects

where little to no change in requirements is expected, and where requirements are clear and well-understood by all team members.

- Agile principles and practices can be adapted to suit organizations that follow waterfall principles and practices. Agile and waterfall principles and practices are not mutually exclusive—some organizations apply elements of both principles and practices. However, it is important to know that not all organizations and settings lend themselves to agile principles and practices.

The new PMI Agile certification recognizes that leading in conditions of emergence requires a particular kind of responsiveness and adaptability; it needs leaders who are "agile." This new agility is different from the "structured flexibility" processes that are commonly used in complicated contexts (see Brinkerhoff and Ingle, 1989). Structured flexibility starts with a fully developed purpose and an end goal product is fully defined with knowable levels of risk. Situational flexibility is built into the structured flexibility approach, but it is in the service of a predetermined objective. Agile flexibility is different. It starts with goal uncertainty or indeterminacy and is designed to provide short bursts (or "sprints") of searching activity. The outputs of sprints are then shared with stakeholders in order to get feedback that is subsequently folded into the next sprint. Agile projects are proactively designed to focus on these mid-course feedback and correction opportunities that are part of a much longer and sometimes unknown iterative process of meaning-making, challenge-finding and solution-seeking.

Agility requires leaders who are forward-looking. They lean into the wind, standing on their toes, rather than sitting back on their heels waiting to decide which way the winds are blowing. Kouzes and Posner (2017) identify forward-looking as the second most admired trait of a leader. Forward-looking leaders are constantly scanning the strategic context and actively listening for changes at and across social levels that may affect them. They maintain a fast pace, and they believe it is possible to create shorter decision/service provision/review cycles. Emergence leaders are also agile in the sense that they are continuously probing for strategic information. An example is in the software development field, an industry that uses a highly iterative development process. In this industry, leaders build sprints (or probes) into their development work. Sprints are short cycles of development to produce bite-size deliverables that cumulatively result in robust outcomes that may not be exactly what participants had in mind at the start of the process.

To be forward-looking requires leaders to possess a heightened sensitivity to outside forces and to both the short- and long-term needs of others, oneself, the organization and the larger community that leaders serve. This sensitivity fosters vigilant responsiveness and a searching awareness of opportunities for change, almost like a continuously rotating air traffic control radar system. Agile leaders are characterized by an open mind-edness to future possibilities. They are tuned into the multiple sources of influence and authority needed to "size up" what is going on as well as what is needed to craft strategies for collective action that can be sustained through time. Tool 5 in Chapter 9, Contextual Intelligence (CI) Discern-ment, introduces leaders to several key contextual dimensions of a leader-ship opportunity that can assist them in developing their practice of looking forward, what we call foresight.

Finally, responsiveness with prudence and agility includes an under-standing of the need for reciprocity between leaders and followers, between the existing needs of the organization and the future needs of the community, and between the drivers of change and the realities of the contingent organizational setting. In short, agility requires indivi-duals who are comfortable with their public service role responsibilities, while all of the time looking for opportunities to redefine these respon-sibilities within the scope of their discretion to make collective pro-cesses, systems and outcomes better.

The Reflective Practice Repertoire

Responsiveness with prudence recognizes the need for agility to adapt to changes through time. It is not sufficient that leaders know the right thing to do in the circumstances of the moment. They must constantly ask whether what they did yesterday, last week, last month, last year is still applicable today. Being attuned to change through time is part of what is also called reflective practice in the literature. It assumes the capacity for constant improvement by capturing the lessons learned and turning those lessons into new insights that can facilitate adjustment to change. Review our discussion of the Continuous Learning Cycle in Chapter 9, especially Exhibit 9.11.

The reflective practice repertoire also requires getting comfortable living in the past, the present and the future. Richard Hames (2007) calls this condition the "extended now." The "now" requires that we extend our thinking and action backward into the past in order to understand the antecedents of change and their implications for the meaning of what is going on now. It also requires that we extend forward into the future in order to understand how the manifestations of previous antecedents can be used to facilitate future change. For example, a Parks Department can't change the current fee system without first understanding why and how that system was created in the first place. Once this is known, the decision-makers need to extend this information forward into the future so that it does not serve as a barrier, and better yet, can be used to facilitate the desired change. In our discussion of institutional legacy in Chapter 6, we provided an extensive discussion of what this institu-tional legacy looks like from the perspective of the American public service tradition and how it can be used for building legitimacy for change from where we sit.

Emergence is not a condition that is comfortable for individuals who prefer clarity and low levels of ambiguity, conflict and paradoxical points of view. In fact, emergence is exactly the opposite, requiring individuals who get intellectually, emotionally and physically energized when operating in paradoxical settings. The Transformative Innovation Policy Consortium (TIPC, a research council to study innovation) in Norway has recently characterized the paradoxical space of emergence as "We are between 'the no longer and the not yet'" (Transformative Innovation Policy Consortium, 2017). Jim Collins, author of the best-selling management book *From Good to Great* (2001), discovered that not many private sector companies were able to make the transition from good to great, but those that did all had leaders who lived the paradox between absolute dedication to an optimistic vision of what was possible, even when the current reality was not providing any evidence for their optimism. Collins called this the Stockdale paradox in honor of James Stockdale, the fabled American navy officer who survived years of torture in North Vietnamese prisons. Collins observed that Stockdale had an unwavering belief that he would survive and an equally unrelenting vigilance about the everyday realities of his captivity (Westley, Zimmerman, and Patton, 2006).

We agree with the authors of *Getting to Maybe* that emergence leaders must fully embrace the Stockdale paradox when taking action in conditions of emergence. They should be:

> fiercely visionary and hopeful even while determinedly grounding their actions in the cold haven of daily reality testing. For them, hell is not failing; hell is delusion. Hell is kidding yourself about what's going on, for therein are the seeds of failure sown.
>
> Westley, Zimmerman, and Patton (2006, 176)

It is through this crucible of paradoxical and dialectical reasoning that emergence leaders are born (Kurtz and Snowden, 2003). They continuously probe the periphery of their public sector position to develop, reflect on and redevelop contextual intelligence that will be useful in identifying worthy challenges and shared opportunities where collective public leadership action can make a difference. But what separates emergence behavior from emergence leaders is the capacity to hold your optimistic vision about a "better together," even in the coldest and darkest days of winter in Nome, Alaska.

Finally, as we discussed in Chapter 9, sizing up leadership opportunities requires leaders who can steadfastly focus on the success factors and not get distracted, consumed or disillusioned by all of the reasons for failure. The same applies when taking leadership action. Constantly probing for the small lights of hope in the darkest of days requires that you focus your attention, as did Stockdale, on the success factors that surround you. If you are constantly dwelling on the failure factors associated with leadership action, you will often fail to take any action at all. Sometimes taking wrong action is essential to discovering the path to right action, much like explorers charting virgin territory.

The Resilience Repertoire

Over the last 25 years, and especially over the last five, resiliency has become a growing factor of importance for scholars studying leadership success. In a 2013 *Harvard Business Review* article, a respected long-time scholar on organizations, Rosebeth Moss Kanter, observed that if "Surprises Are the New Normal; Resilience Is the New Skill." Kanter defines resiliency as "the ability to recover from fumbles or outright mistakes and bounce back" (Kanter, 2017, 1). This idea of resilience has shown up in practice fields as different as emergency management, military training, business management, social sustainability, public administration and leadership development. In physical design terms, architectural design for earthquake-prone settings has shifted from increasing structural rigidity to engineering in flexibility—buildings designed to sway in earthquakes. Similarly in flood risk reduction, design now includes "green" structures as well as "hard" structures where the goal is not to "control" flooding but rather create conditions where the effects can be accommodated by the river system. Similarly, psychological researchers are using "resiliency theory" to look at how well individuals are prepared to respond to a range of challenges from unemployment to crises like assault, trauma or acute illness. Social work schools, business schools and public administration programs are teaching courses focused on resilience. And the field of sustainability has incorporated resilience of social, economic and ecological systems as a core concept. Resilience is being applied at all levels of analysis—the individual, group or team, organizations, and at the community, policy and social levels. Developing the capacity for resilience is central to our argument that public service leaders are increasingly being required to take action where directions and outcomes are uncertain and where surprises are common. Often the difference between those who are and are not successful is their repertoire for resilience, which needs to be developed at the individual, group, organizational and community levels.

Starting with the individual level, we notice wide variation in the capacity for resilience. For example, in the aftermath of traumatic events, some individuals are devastated, some are muddling through and others are making the best of a tough situation. Why are there such differences? Of course, part of the answer is often found in differences in the individual level of external support structures and systems and the degree of eternal environmental stress. But it is also the case that some people approach life with hope despite devastating losses. Resilient individuals typically have a positive self-image, a realistic understanding of their own strengths and weaknesses, and the ability to capitalize on emergent positive trends in challenging situations. Experience also matters. Expedition leaders feel stress differently than their clients. Individuals with experience, practice and a history of being able to solve problems (decide, plan and execute) for themselves are more resilient. Another finding relates to optimism or a hopefulness about life that balances near- and long-term goals in ways that see changes, road blocks or barriers as "steps along the way" or "challenges" rather than the end of the journey (Segerstrom and Nes, 2006). But excessive optimism can result in an underestimation of the risks associated with various activities and conditions (Weinstein, 1989; Weinstein and Klein, 1996). Those who underestimate risk also take less action. For example, Weinstein, Lyons, Sandman, and Cuite (1998) found that those who underestimated the risk of radon in their homes were less likely than others to engage in risk-detection and risk-reduction behaviors. Self-control and social control (i.e., being able to manage impulses and feelings) is also positively related to resiliency. Being able to build and maintain strong, close relationships and having good communication skills are typically associated with resilience (Henderson, 1999).

To summarize, several things stand out regarding the development of resiliency at the individual level. One is self-care: work-life balance, keeping mind and body healthy, and taking time for one's own needs. Another is a strong sense of coherence, which enables individuals to view events in ways that are comprehensible, manageable and meaningful. This ability to give meaning to particular events in the context of a larger whole helps sustain a leader's sense of positive moral agency. Those with a coherent view of the whole can more easily envision "putting their shoulder to the rail" and rallying the support of others to make a difference, despite lots of negative odds. Knowing yourself, leading from strengths, developing individual level competencies, leading from where you sit and self-care are all parts of improving individual resilience and leadership.

At the group or team level, leading practitioners and theorists alike point out that resilient teams have common goals uniting them along with significant diversity among members. This makes the team strong, creative and adaptable when things don't go as planned, and helps the team attend to both the social side as well as the task side of working in teams and small groups (Bassett-Jones, 2005; Milliken and Martins, 1996; Østergaard, Timmermans, and Kristinsson, 2011; also see discussion of diversity in Chapter 12). Resilient teams need to be working in more than one way toward common goals so that there is always a "plan B." This underscores one of our EMERGE maxims that "everybody leads and everybody follows; and everybody learns to lead and learns to follow."

At the organizational level, resiliency has become more than just about adaptability and flexibility to survive unanticipated and uncertain changes in the external environment. While these values remain important, resiliency has also come to mean building the kind of capacity that allows the organization to thrive and become better despite what happens in the external environment (Sitkin, Sutcliffe, and Schroeder, 1994; Lichtenstein and Plowman, 2009). There are some paradoxes that emerge from this kind of thinking. For example, leaders at the organizational level need to be working on more than one time cycle and have a plan for betting on small as well as large outcomes. These multiple strategies help an organization respond when one path is closed as other pathways are present. Simultaneously being focused in a single-minded way on achieving a goal while embracing multiple goals, diverse approaches and workplace diversity might feel and look paradoxical. Another paradox arises from the need for resilient organizations to deliberately build in redundancy. This defies the organizational mantra to increase efficiency. While efficiency is important, a system tightly focused on efficiency is fragile—the opposite of resilient. In the public sector, where competing values are almost always in play, redundancy provides checks against partisan sets of values that may marginalize competing values that are often necessary for preserving ordered liberty (see the Balancewheel discussion, Exhibit 5.5 in Chapter 5).

At the community or society level, resiliency is directly related to the civic capacity of the community. Communities high in social capital, or those that possess a broad base of competencies among its citizens and a history of collective joint action, are resilient (Shinn, 1999; Adger, 2003; Robinson, Allen, Walker, Barker, Sulimani, and VanderVeen, 2011). Urban planners, disaster and emergency mangers, crisis managers and community developers, social workers and educators are all interested in what makes communities resilient. They are also interested in more complex relationships among concepts of resilient communities and community health and responses to change. The importance of resiliency, both as a practice and a theory, has been accelerated by recent natural disasters (i.e., hurricanes Katrina, Harvey, Ima and Maria and earthquakes, flooding, fires, mudslides, etc.) as leaders try to understand why some individuals, communities and organizations "bounce back" and others do not. Similar questions arise in ecological systems as well.

Resiliency at the individual, group, organizational and community levels is influenced by a complex interplay of factors that leaders need to better understand in order to use their leadership opportunities to build resiliency as well as take advantage of its presence to undertake leadership action.

The Regenerative Repertoire

It is noteworthy that the leadership literature over the last decade (most of which is written from a private-sector perspective) has replaced a focus on leaders with a much greater emphasis on followers (see especially Kouzes and Posner, 2017; Hames, 2007, Chapter 3; Fairholm, 2013). Leaders can't accomplish much without committed followers whose support is essential for creating new initiatives and laying the foundations within the leadership setting (whether it be the group, organizational or community level) to enable the initiative to last. This is especially the case for public-sector leadership where multiple structures of authority and accountability systems often create barriers that require collaborative approaches with those over whom leaders have no formal authority.

But building capacity is important not simply because leaders need individual followers, organizational support and the buy-in from community partners to accomplish their personal agenda. Capacity is also needed to address problems that may not be part of a leader's personal agenda at the moment. Building capacity becomes social capital, a future civic infrastructure that can facilitate collective action to advance the common good on issues that are not yet known. The Vision Action Network and the Mt. Hood Stewardship Master Cases for Parts II and III of this text illustrate this point. The leaders did not fully know what results their capacity-building initiatives would achieve or how they would play out over time. This is one of the things that makes public-sector leadership uniquely different than the private sector, where voluntary collective action with those outside the organizational walls violates most of the core principles of our competitive market economy. Not only is capacity-building outside the walls of the organization often bad for business, it may result in charges of collusion and other anticompetitive practices by the regulatory arm of government.

Leadership Tools and Practices for Taking Action in Conditions of Emergence

In previous chapters we mainly focused on the "what" of leadership (i.e., leaders take responsibility for making meaning and creating direction) and the "why" of leadership (i.e., leadership is a relational quality that requires action to be tethered to the laws, institutions and community values). The tools and practices presented in this chapter focus on "how" to take leadership action (as opposed to how to "size up" leadership opportunities, the focus of Chapter 9). The tools align especially well with our polity leadership focus, which requires taking action where there are high levels of indeterminacy and where there is a need to build authority and legitimacy by mobilizing power for collective action in a highly fragmented social and political landscape.

As with most all clinical practice, public administrators need to generate new tools and adapt existing practices to deal with new conditions. This is part of what it means to rely on your reflective repertoire to learn from action. This learning includes adding and adapting tools to improve our clinical practice. Think of the tools discussed in this chapter as the minimum essentials, similar to the kind of tools recommended for the first-time backpacker who needs to be equipped to go off trail, beyond established official pathways. The tools that follow are for public leaders wishing to take action on challenges that are not simple and where it is necessary to build agreement among those who do not see the world in the same way or feel the same way about what others see.

While the taking action tools in Exhibit 11.2 are discussed sequentially, in keeping with our view of the discursive nature of leadership, taking action occurs on a performance stage that is dynamic and cyclical in nature. Like sizing up challenges and opportunities discussed in Chapter 9, taking action is both a discursive and iterative process. As a discursive process, taking action involves talk with others about how to integrate data, analysis, argument and strongly held opinions of others with your personal intuition and foresight. Taking action is also iterative because of the need to revisit what has been decided in an earlier phase of the action process in the light of new learnings. This discursive and iterative activity has been referred to in recent leadership literature as a process of "building the bridge as you walk on it" (Quinn, 2004).

Tool 7: Model with Relational Trust

> Respect, integrity, and honesty are the outcomes of strong relationships built on trust.
>
> Rath and Conchie (2008, 85)

The EMERGE leadership process we propose for acting on wicked challenges requires strong bonds of trust to hold diverse actors together within and across jurisdictional levels and scales of action. Trust is multilayered and multifaceted. It can comprise interpersonal behavior; confidence in the reliability, competence and expected performance of organizations, and a common bond and sense of goodwill toward a group or organizational cause. Our discussion in this section will focus on the dyadic relationship between leaders and followers working collaboratively within and across organizational boundaries on common EMERGE leadership initiatives (Gassaway and Ingle, 2013). Developing a strong sense of mutual trust in these settings enables the individuals in the relationship to overcome setbacks, set aside fear of ulterior motives when compromise is necessary, and speed up the pace of collective action.

For purposes of our writing here, we take for granted that relational trust between dyads facilitates the transfer of trust from individuals to the teams, organizations and institutions whom they represent and in whose name they act. But we also know this is not always true. In reviewing the literature on trust we have discovered a paucity of studies that would help us understand how to best leverage the transfer of

Exhibit 11.2 Leadership Stage Dimension: Taking Leadership Action

Performance Stage Dimension: Taking Leadership Action

Leadership Practices	*EMERGE Leadership Tools and Descriptions*
Practice Seven: Model Trusting Relationships with Leadership Team Members and Others	**7: Model with Relational Trust** This tool enables leaders, through a process of open dialogue, to model a high level of relational trust with leadership team members and relevant stakeholders with the intent of growing and nurturing transformational trust throughout the leadership initiative.
Practice Eight: Inspire a Shared and Moral Vision/Values Related to a Leadership Initiative	**8: Inspire Vision with Moral Grounding** This tool embeds a shared vision and shares inspiration with moral grounding into the initial vision and values associated with a leadership initiative so that the vision and values become "alive" in everyday public action.
Practice Nine: Use Contextual Intelligence to Develop and Act with a Smart Power Strategy	**9: Persuade with Smart Power** This tool enables leaders to make use of the emergent patterns discerned from the Contextual Intelligence (CI) Tool in developing and acting with a responsive "smart power strategy"—one that represents the "smartest" balance of hard and soft power—or persuading others to engage in a leadership journey.
Practice Ten: Convene and Nurture a Coalition to Realize the Vision	**10: Convene Stakeholder Coalitions** This tool empowers leaders in collaboration with their leadership team to convene and institutionalize a robust network of organizational followers and external stakeholders to realize the common good embedded in the leadership initiative's shared vision.
Practice Eleven: Pioneer Breakthrough Innovation in the Public Arena	**11: Guide Organizational Innovation** When a leadership initiative involves a "pioneering effort" in an organizational context, this tool guides leaders "in blazing a breakthrough trail" with a high level of confidence that one is not taking the wrong braid of the river which endangers the public good.
Practice Twelve: Intentionally Strengthen Prudential Judgment through Reflective Practice	**12: Strengthen Prudential Judgment** This tool provides leaders with a systematic approach to reflective practice—encompassing open dialogue, generative learning and ethical decision-making—with the intent of strengthening prudential judgment.

mutual trust from the individual level to the agencies and organizations they represent (Covey, 2006; Gassaway and Ingle, 2013). This is an important gap in the research that needs to be filled if we are going to be maximally successful in co-producing solutions to wicked challenges. But we do know from research that generalized high levels of trust support social networks by lowering the transaction costs (time, effort, behaviors dictated by formal rules) required of parties to negotiate, reach agreements and execute cooperative interorganizational relationships (Fukuyama, 1995; Zaheer, McEvily, and Perrone, 1998).

Leader–follower relationships flourish when the highest level of trust, e.g., transformational trust, is present (Dirks and Ferrin, 2002; Joseph and Winston, 2005; Webber, 2002). With the good of the whole as the motivating force, a relationship driven by trust is characterized by its synergistic and self-generating energy. An environment of transparency and authenticity, including demonstration of personal vulnerability and free-exchange of information without inhibition, enables participants to feel safe expressing their views without feeling inadequate or threatened by others (Brown, 2012). When this environment exists, participants strive towards a communal relationship in which they are eager to help one another and increase cooperation without generating feelings of indebtedness. Under these circumstances leaders and followers are willing to take on expanded roles, cooperate and go the extra mile for the common good because they see the underlying meaning in what they do and their contribution to the larger group initiative (Haidt, 2012, 236–40).

Trust is made possible by sharing a clearly articulated vision embedded with shared values (see EMERGE Tools 1 and 3). Once in place this shared vision becomes a binding force that aligns leaders and followers and provides a sense of community. This shared vision enables both leaders and followers to take personal risks and subjugate their own needs for that of the vision. In the best of circumstances, this creates a foundation for mutual responsibility and moral accountability to the group in which each member does more than their assigned role through active engagement.

The Model with Relational Trust Tool in Exhibit 11.3 enables leaders, through a process of open dialogue, to model a high level of relational trust with leadership team members and relevant stakeholders with the intent of growing and nurturing transformational trust throughout the leadership initiative. By "model," we mean consistently display, through a dialogic interaction between a leader and others, the seven key elements associated with transformational trust. These are at the core of the Model with Relational Trust Tool in the EMERGE Public Leadership Performance Platform.

The Model with Relational Trust Tool serves as a guide for leaders in assessing whether or not each of their relationships with followers and other leaders has reached a sufficiently high level of trust to ensure the

Exhibit 11.3 Tool 7: Model with Relational Trust

Names of Relationship Members:

Transformational Trust Elements in Relationships	Step 1. Degree Trust Elements Operate in the Relationship			Step 2. Priority Trust Enhancement Actions for Reflection and Dialogue in the Relationship
	Low	*Med*	*High*	
1 Clearly understands their respective actions, roles and responsibilities.				
2 Feels morally responsible for helping each other achieve a shared vision for the leadership opportunity.				
3 Displays a high confidence in each other and forgives short-term breaches of trust irrespective of position or title.				
4 Actively seeks help from each other without generating feelings of indebtedness.				
5 Freely and transparently exchanges information between each other without inhibition.				
6 Shows a high involvement in the leadership opportunity, subjugating some personal needs for the greater good of the shared vision.				
7 Creates positive energy within the relationship that is both synergistic and self-generating.				
Step 3. Trust Commitments				

Source: Developed by M. Ingle, CPS/PSU.

success of a commonly shared leadership initiative (Gassaway and Ingle, 2013). The tool can be used by both leaders and followers when first forming the leadership team, and as each follower/stakeholder is added to the leadership team or coalition (see Tools 4 and 10). Building and sustaining trust is an iterative process, requiring trust to be maintained within each relationship on a regular and on-going basis. The tool allows a leader to undertake an assessment of trust along each of the seven trust elements and also provides a list of potential actions to follow in nurturing and enhancing trust levels.

Leaders should not infer that by default a dyadic relationship starts from a state of distrust (the feeling that another's intentions and motives are not sincere; that they have ulterior motives), but rather, may start anywhere along the continuum from distrust through unconditional or transformational trust. Trust is fragile and requires work to nurture and enhance over time (Covey, 2006). Through the use of the Model with Relational Trust Tool, public leaders should be able to continuously and consistently perform the seventh key leadership practice of "Model Trusting Relationships with the Leadership Team and Others."

Tool 8: Inspire Vision with Moral Grounding

> It's easier to put a jigsaw puzzle together if you can see the picture on the box cover.
>
> Kouzes and Posner (1995, 111)

The visible manifestation that a leadership team has succeeded in generating shared agreement for action is the development of an initial shared vision and values for your leadership opportunity (see discussion of vision in Tools 3 and 4 in Chapter 9). The generation of these products provide participants with a visible manifestation of their collective success (for more information and assistance in developing these vision statements, see especially McNamara, 2017). Examples of this are provided by the Master Cases for Parts II and III of this volume. Both the Mt. Hood Stewardship case and the Vision Action Network case illustrate the need to bring multiple community stakeholders together to build shared agreement around a common future and a strategy of action.

For purposes of our discussion here, we take as a given that you and your leadership team have created a vision in Tool 3, and have explored the alignment of your public values in Tools 1 and 4. In taking action, the leadership team will want to embed within the initial agreements on the vision and values a deeper meaning, and extend the shared agreements to the larger organization and leadership coalition. How does the team deepen the commitment of those who have participated in the initial envisioning process and expand the shared agreements to those who need to join the leadership initiative but have not yet been at the table? How do you create ownership throughout the larger leadership system (as explained in Tool 4 of Chapter 9) for a shared vision with aligned public values? In the sections that follow, we discuss the EMERGE "inspirational strategy" along with the Inspire Vision with Moral Grounding Tool for accomplishing this goal.

In EMERGE, inspiration differs for individuals, e.g., leaders and followers, and for teams and organizations. At the individual level, inspiration is the continual discovery and articulation of connections between your own visions and values and the vision and values embedded in a specific leadership initiative. Individual inspiration and commitment is high when this alignment is strong. At the team or organizational level, inspiration is derived from the discovery and articulation of shared connections across groups within the organizational culture (as discussed in Chapter 9, Tool 4). Inspiration at both the individual and organizational level is critical to transforming shared vision and values into real-life everyday leadership outcomes. Individuals may have both shared and different values and intentions. They respond to different driving forces and are tempted to behave in ways that are inconsistent with a vision and set of values, e.g., uphold the status quo, protect one's turf, etc. So, individuals and organizations need to share an inspirational sense of vision and values to guide everyday actions and decisions. An inspirational vision serves two vital leadership functions: it describes where we are heading (like the destination on a road map) and it is a "powerful attractor" (serving to pull leaders and followers toward a more desirable future).

As a destination, an inspirational vision, when embedded within polity values, serves as a source of public service motivation (PSM). Research has consistently shown that public servants possess higher levels of PSM than their private-sector counterparts (Perry, Hondeghem, and Wise, 2010; Christensen, Paarlberg, and Perry, 2017). They are motivated by public service out of a sense of duty to the common good, the desire to meet the needs of others, the chance to have an impact on public policy, and the opportunity to improve their communities. These motivational sparks that cut across generational differences need to be kept in mind in developing inspirational support for organizational vision and values for public service participants and stakeholders.

In the context of wicked challenges, the attractor function of an inspirational vision is extremely powerful. The vision sets a bounded space for attractive action that provides unlimited possibilities within.

Seeing a vision as an attractor rather than a set of constraints that sets limits to collective action is a distinction that matters. When inspiration is present, individuals (whether leaders or followers) see the creative opportunities within their boundaries and choose to take action that makes a positive change. When inspiration drives action, it creates four positive outcomes:

- Personal Commitment, a heartfelt conviction to embrace vision and values;
- Personal Ownership, assertion of personal buy-in to the vision and values;
- Personal Performance, individuals perform with the intent of creating values-based outcomes;

- Shared Vision and Values, people involved in the leadership initiative share common ground and work together to accomplish shared outcomes.

A sense of personal commitment, for example the state of being bound emotionally and/or rationally to a course of action, is the foundation for inspiration. When individuals are committed to vision and values, they see connections between themselves and others, they then feel personal ownership for the vision and values, and they have a desire to live the commitment in real life.

The Vision and Values with Moral Grounding Tool is intended to generate shared inspiration and infuse that inspiration with moral grounding that is captured by the vision and values statement produced by leaders and followers. The tool does this by creating a venue for capturing the polity values that you deem important for living in alignment with your vision. Related to both your vision and polity values is the tangible legacy that you and others wish to leave as a reflection of your public service engagement and contribution. This tool is graphically illustrated in Exhibit 11.4. Both leaders and followers can use this tool to generate a commonly shared commitment to the vision and values of a given leadership context. The tool consists of four sets of leadership activities: Display Belief and

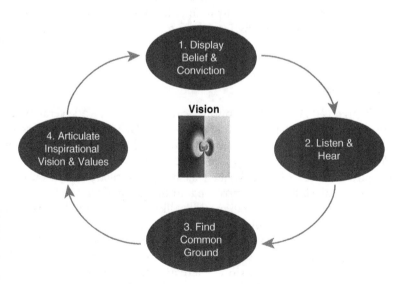

INSPIRATION CYCLE

Exhibit 11.4 Tool 8: Vision and Values with Moral Grounding
Source: Developed by M. Ingle, CPS/PSU with graphics by Tâm Ngô.

Conviction, Listen and Hear, Find Common Ground, and Articulate the Inspirational Vision and Values. As a result of learning more about this tool, and using it on a real-time leadership initiative of your choosing, the EMERGE leader will be able to perform the eighth practice of "Inspire a Shared and Moral Vision/Values related to a Leadership Initiative."

Tool 9: Persuade with Smart Power

> Leadership is a power relationship between leaders and followers, but as we saw earlier, power depends on context.
>
> Nye (2008, 85)

Public service leaders have various types of power available to them for undertaking effective and morally grounded leadership action. They can exercise their formal power (i.e., legal, policy, budget, personal) along with their informal or soft power of influence, persuasion and third-party influence. In Chapter 9 we reviewed the formal and informal types of power as part of sizing-up of your leadership opportunities using Contextual Intelligence (CI) (see especially Exhibit 9.10). In this chapter, we focus on how leaders can balance their hard and soft power to maximize their persuasion with followers and stakeholders. This balancing is often counterintuitive, especially in the context of wicked challenges. So, success needs to flow from a deep understanding of one's own leadership strengths along with the various types of power that are potentially available within your unique leadership system. We discuss how this can best be done by introducing the EMERGE Persuade with Smart Power Tool.

Types of Power

Joseph Nye (2004) divides a public leader's power into several types beginning with hard power and soft power. Hard power consists of your formal position authority and the larger legal framework within which this position authority operates. There are three sub-types of hard-power skills (often described as being transactional in nature): organizational skills like controlling information flows and reward/sanction systems, Machiavellian skills like bullying and bargaining, and coalition creating skills.

Soft power consists of the various forms of your personal power. There are personal soft-power skills that consist of your emotional IQ, communication skills and vision. There are other soft-power skills that have to do with your ability to mobilize through third-party intervention and influence. This third-party power can consist of legal authority, financial resources, political influence and legitimacy within the community. For example, you may not have the official authority as a social service housing counselor to do much about drug use by some of your clients. But you may have good working relationships with those who do have extensive political and legal authority, including the police, the district attorney and powerful community groups motivated to do something about the problem where your clients live. This network approach to taking leadership initiative is an issue we addressed in Chapter 10 in our discussion of creating community and authority in a power-shared world.

Soft power was first introduced by Nye to describe the use of tactics by nation states that rely on persuasion and cooptation rather than coercion to extract compliance from partners. Over time the phrase has been broadened to describe leadership approaches that rely on persuading followers through a combination of emotional appeals and third-party actors to make the case for why it is desirable for others to "get on board the train" (Nye, 2004; Kramer, 2006; Harvey, Heames, and Richey, 2006). The thing to remember about soft power is that you are relying on strategies that persuade and educate those whose support you need. To quote a famous 6th century Chinese scholar, Lao-tsu (630 BC), "A leader is best when people barely know he exists, not so good when people obey and acclaim him; worst when they despise him" (quoted in Nye, 2008, 1).

Nye introduces a third type of power, smart power, to address the question of "what balance of hard and soft power is most pursuasive to followers in a specific leadership context?"

> The moral of the story ... is not that hard or soft power is better, or that an inspirational or a transactional style is the answer, but that it is important to understand how to combine these power resources and leadership styles in different contexts.
>
> Nye (2008, 84)

Nye argues that leaders need a "smart power skillset" defined as the "ability to understand context so that hard and soft power can be successfully combined into a smart power strategy" (Nye, 2008, 84)

EMERGE "Persuade with Smart Power" Tool

The purpose of the Persuade with Smart Power Tool is to assist leaders in developing the most suitable balance of hard and soft power (i.e. smart power) for progressing towards one's vision through effective and ethical persuasion. This tool enables leaders to make use of the emergent patterns discerned from the Contextual Intelligence (CI) Assessment Tool from Chapter 9 to develop and act with a responsive smart power strategy that represents the smartest balance of hard and soft power for persuading others to engage in a leadership journey. The tool includes decision criteria that leaders employ to align the five foresight dimensions gained in the CI Assessment Tool with the most appropriate and persuasive types of power and should be used when a leader would like to enlist the support of others to act for the common good. President Trump's efforts to deal with North Korea are an example of when smart power becomes important. Understanding the contextual nuances in a given situation, including the historical antecedents of a given event, can help inform the combinations of hard and soft power that are needed and the timing of their use. In the absence of using smart power, leaders can blunder and appear to look reckless, foolish and uninformed.

The Persuade with Smart Power Tool is summarized in Exhibit 11.5. Applying this tool in the context of your real-time leadership initiative will enhance your leadership performance, especially when facing wicked challenges.

Tool 10: Convening Stakeholder Coalitions

> Hope is like a path in the countryside. Originally, there is nothing—but as people walk this way again and again, a path appears.
>
> Lu Xun (cited in Leys, 1986, 223)

The multifaceted and dynamic nature of leadership opportunities born of wicked challenges usually requires assistance from a networked coalition comprised of individuals, groups and organizations that share an interest in undertaking common action to address the challenge (Ashby, 1957). The network becomes the fulcrum for expanding access to additional human, financial and physical resources that add diversity, build support and trust, and increase their leverage and capacity to successfully implement a leadership initiative (Granovetter, 1973, 1985; Woolcock, 2001).

The EMERGE Convene Stakeholder Coalitions Tool empowers leaders and their leadership team to convene and institutionalize a robust network of organizational followers and external stakeholders to realize the common good embedded in the leadership initiative's shared vision. This tool is illustrated in Exhibit 11.6.

The leadership team is at the center of the networked coalition and is comprised of a leader and followers that work together to realize the vision. Extending out from each person in the leadership team are branches (i.e. relationships) to stakeholder groups. These branches are established once those in the leadership team determine who among them has the strongest relationships and most persuasive smart power strategy with the stakeholders; these individuals convene the various stakeholder groups.

Leadership Opportunity:

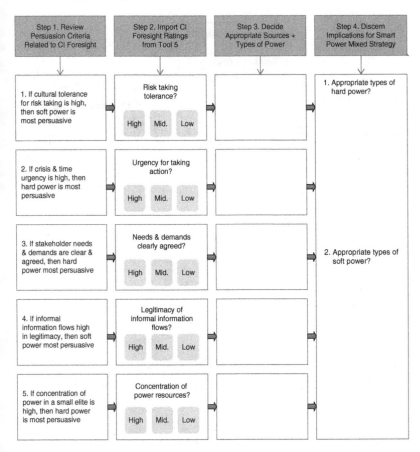

Exhibit 11.5 Tool 9: Persuade with Smart Power

The Convene Stakeholder Coalitions Tool utilizes three steps: 1) Identify Stakeholders and Conveners; 2) Support Followers as Stakeholder Group Conveners; and 3) Convene Stakeholder Groups. These steps are illustrated and described in Exhibit 11.7.

One of our discoveries through applying this tool in many different leadership initiatives over the last few years is that public leaders gain an appreciation of the important role that the for-profit, civil society, non-profit and government organizations play in achieving the common good. Within the context of specific leadership initiative coalitions, the work of these stakeholder organizations is sometimes done cooperatively and sometimes in competition. But in all cases, the values and structures of authority used to accomplish good work by each of the stakeholders are usually

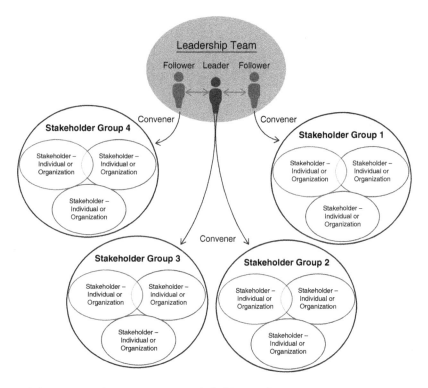

Exhibit 11.6 Tool 10: Convening Stakeholder Coalitions
Source: Developed by M. Ingle, CPS/PSU with graphics by Tâm Ngô.

different, along with the values served by their respective processes and structures of authority. For these reasons, it is important for leaders-as-coalition-conveners to know how the role of each stakeholder can be engaged (or buffered, if negative) to successfully realize their leadership initiative. As one participant in this process observed:

> Wherever I sit in the public, private, civic or non-profit sectors, my ethical framework will adapt to advance the common good. Although the public sector is uniquely responsible for and accountable to citizens, in today's ever-changing shared-power world that is becoming increasingly more complex, interconnected and interdependent, the common good will be advanced through a collaborative networked governance approach that involves multiple actors across sectors applying multiple ethical frameworks; the key is knowing how to partner and who to partner with.
>
> Fogue (2015, 15)

Convening Coalitions Tool Steps

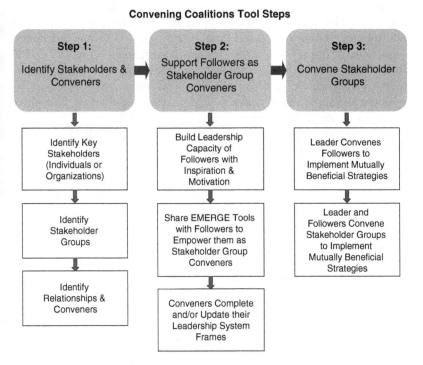

Exhibit 11.7 Convening Coalitions Tool Steps

As a result of using the Convening Stakeholder Coalitions Tool in the dynamic context of real leadership initiatives, you will, as an EMERGE leader, be able to perform the tenth practice of "Convene and Nurture a Coalition to Realize the Vision."

Tool 11: Guide Organizational Innovation

> If you want your system to move toward greater health and strength, you can shift your interactions to change the similarities, differences, or connections that influence patterns toward greater adaptability.
>
> Eoyang and Holladay (2013, 45)

Our argument in Chapters 7 and 9 is that public sector innovation is imperative in the context of wicked challenges. Public service leaders increasingly need to be armed with a new mindset and toolbox that prepares them to deal with 4.0 Industrial Revolution challenges (Schwab, 2017). Public leaders have both a substantive and moral imperative to create "breakthrough innovations"—the kind that Nikhil Sahni and colleagues at Harvard show can concurrently 1) lower costs, 2) increase accessibility, 3) improve services (quality) now and 4) continue to improve services in the future (sustainably) (Sahni, Wessel, and Christensen, 2013). Important to the EMERGE approach, breakthrough innovations are also necessary elements of each of the four leadership repertoires, notably responsiveness, reflection, resilience and regeneration, that we introduced at the beginning of this chapter.

Public service breakthrough innovation (PSBI) is possible in the public sector as demonstrated by several recent case-based reports (Sahni et al., 2013; Napier, Dang, and Vuong, 2012). Public innovation has been an important part of the public service tradition in America, starting with the founding and continuing through each of the major historical periods of development we reviewed in Chapter 6. However, breakthrough innovation is neither easy nor certain in the public sector. Unlike the private sector where innovation is driven by market forces, PSBI in the public sector operates without some of the natural advantages of the private sector: there are few competitive forces, incentives are diffuse and the public sector lacks high degrees of autonomy and discretion due to constitutionally derived public laws, regulations and bureaucratic procedures (often viewed as "red tape;" see Davis and Ingle, 2013).

Recently, innovation in the public sector has begun to receive considerable research attention (Serrat, 2017; Bekker, Victor, and Steijn, 2011). While the concept of breakthrough innovation has been explored along with several conceptual frameworks, very little attention has been given to the process of actually "leading innovation" in an organizational setting. While public leaders can readily attend a seminar on the meaning or enabling conditions of breakthrough innovation, there is almost no guidance to date on the actions necessary for facilitating the public breakthrough innovation dynamic.

The online EMERGE Public Leadership Performance Platform provides a tool for guiding organizational innovation. When a leadership initiative involves a pioneering effort in an organizational context, the Guide Organizational Innovation Tool helps leaders blaze a breakthrough trail with a high level of confidence that one is not taking the wrong braid of the river and endangering the public good. This tool has been especially designed to deal with leadership initiatives characterized by the new normal (Chapter 7) and wicked challenges (Chapter 9).

The Guide Organizational Innovation Tool walks leaders through a detailed six-step process: 1) Form a Team of "Positive Deviants" Around a Leadership Opportunity; 2) Apply the Organizational Innovation Readiness Assessment; 3) Expand on Inspirational Vision for Your Innovation Initiative; 4) Incentivize First Steps with Organizational Persuasive Methods; 5) Institutionalize Innovation and Feedback Loops; and 6) Scale Innovation to Other Slices of the Organization. These steps rely heavily on the concepts of "positive deviants" and "persuasive technology" (the integrated application of computers and persuasion) to lead the breakthrough innovation process (Pascale, Sternin, and Sternin, 2010). The tool and its six steps are graphically displayed in Exhibit 11.8.

We have beta-tested this tool both domestically and internationally, and it consistently produces the following benefits:

- Provides a mechanism for augmenting leadership practice associated with the fostering of public service breakthrough innovations;
- Enables leaders to identify opportunities for breakthrough innovation from where we sit;
- Assists public service leaders in applying a new leadership practice to better serve the public good both now and in the future.

Learning the details of the Guide Organizational Innovation Tool, and experimenting with its use in the context of wicked challenge leadership initiatives, will allow public leaders to perform the eleventh EMERGE practice of "Pioneer Breakthrough Innovation in the Public Arena."

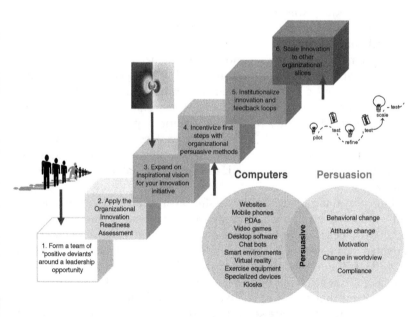

Exhibit 11.8 Tool 11 : Guide Organizational Innovation
Source: Developed by M. Ingle, CPS/PSU with graphics by Tâm Ngô.

Tool 12: Strengthen Prudential Judgment

> What I know for sure is doing the right thing in public service is the
> hardest thing a person can ever do.
>
> Tom Hickman (2014, 10)

A core premise of our EMERGE approach is that sizing up and taking
action on the public service performance stage in wicked contexts are
fraught with turbulence and uncertainty. One needs to approach the
stage with a mindset of small wins. A series of small steps through time
provides learning opportunities where the knowledge that is accumulated and stored builds an ever-larger reservoir that can be drawn upon
for future use. In the next chapter we discuss in greater detail the
neuroscience of the brain that makes the storage and recovery of this
information possible. An important ingredient in this process is enhancing one's capacity to view a challenge from different perspectives. As
Termeer, Dewulf, Breeman, and Stiller (2015, 702) note, "wicked
problems require not only alternative action strategies but also alternative ways of observing and enabling." We run the risk of converting
our knowledge into a kind of "muscle memory", where we begin to
rely on the trained responses of the past to deal with the present.
While this may be good for mastering fly-casting, golfing and white-
water kayaking, where mastery depends on embedding our competence into our muscle memory, in sizing-up and taking action in a
wicked challenge environment, muscle memory is our enemy. We need
innovation and creativity, not muscle memory. This distinction
between what is needed for mastery and what is needed for creativity
and innovation is not well recognized in our current body of leadership research and training. We call this competence to distinguish
what is needed in different sets of conditions prudential judgment. It
serves a "control board" function that enables us to switch from the
routine to the non-routine, from the simple and complicated to the
complex, from chaos to routinization and normalcy, from mastery to
innovation.

Our prevailing models of leadership assume a process where leaders
rally followers around a commonly shared vision and empower them to
take ownership of both the vision and action needed to address a
targeted challenge. While this kind of leadership is embraced by the
EMERGE framework, it sits alongside the prudential judgment model
which focuses attention on the unique combination of circumstances in
the moment that enable us to take action that is both morally justifiable
and successful. There are several "prudential judgement control-board"
characteristics of leading in conditions of emergence that open up
leadership opportunities to a much wider range of possibilities throughout every level of public and nonprofit organizations:

1 **Knowing Strengths and Matching with Contextual Needs.** Knowing the strengths of others and putting these strengths to the highest and best use in the situation at hand will become increasingly important to leadership success. This includes building and maintaining high-performing work groups and organizations that match the unit's capacity with the nature of a given set of challenges. It also includes building community support so that leadership initiatives enjoy the trust of the citizens and clients they serve.

2 **Multitasking Different Challenges Simultaneously.** A second "control-board" function of leadership is the ability to work simultaneously on multiple challenges that may be in different stages of emergence. The nature and priority of a given leadership challenge is frequently characterized by high degrees of fluidity that require trial-and-error, challenge-reduction and problem-solving techniques. One of the chief tasks of a leader is to interpret the "noise" surrounding a given challenge and organize its dimensions into prioritized actionable paths forward. We use the word "paths" to emphasize that a given challenge may necessitate undertaking a mix of initiatives over time, some of which treat the challenge narrowly with a short-term focus, and others that take a more long-term set of actions that confront both the cause-effect uncertainty and the value trade-offs. The literature refers to this kind of flexibility as agile leadership (Ryan and Ali, 2013). An example might be the installation of traffic-sensitive lights at intersections while building a new subway system. The language of pathways also captures the tentative or contingent nature of any given course of action, which will likely require reconsideration as new information and circumstances arise.

3 **Openness to the Next Best Idea.** In a world of the normal and simple challenges (see Exhibit 8.2 in Chapter 8), success often depends on sticking to what has proven to work in the past. But in an emergent world of the new normal, leaders need to think beyond the taken-for-granted. What we have in mind here is illustrated by the Vision Action Network, the Mt. Hood Stewardship and the Medler School System Master Cases in this book. All of these cases illustrate the inadequacy of relying solely on traditional approaches and practices and the need to think and act outside the box.

4 **Heightened Ability to Embrace Surprises.** We have painted a leadership landscape from where we sit that is filled with a combination of the routine and the unusual. But something as seemingly routine as a local road maintenance project can quickly trigger a movement to "stop urban sprawl." Or a port dredging project to enhance the commercial viability of a local community can become an international issue involving the control of "invasive species." A seemingly

typical economic development project to assist a local glass manufacturing business can quickly get transformed into a "clean air" and public health issue as a result of harmful pollutants emitted during the manufacturing process.

The need for, and importance of, prudent judgement is nicely illustrated by our discusssion at the end of Chapter 8 of Major General Michael K. Nagata's challenge of designing a U.S. strategy for fighting the Islamic State of Iraq and the Levant (ISIL). As Major Nagata observed, "We do not understand the movement, and until we do, we are not going to defeat it" (Schmitt 2014). To summarize, prudential judgement is the elusive capacity that enables leaders to do the ethically right thing by matching leadership actions with the needs of the contextual setting, multitasking, being open to the next best answer and responding well in the face of surprises. Through constant dialogue between the leadership team and key stakeholders, the Prudential Judgment Strategic Navigation Tool in Exhibit 11.9 provides leaders with a systematic eight-step approach for strengthening their prudential judgment: 1) Framing; 2) Focusing; 3) Patterning; 4) Perceiving; 5) Consequences; 6) Schema; 7) Effecting; and 8) Coevolving.

Conclusion

In Chapter 9 when we first introduced the EMERGE Public Leadership Performance Platform to address wicked challenges, we noted that the tools associated with this platform are intended to complement a variety of other leadership and management tools and practices for helping public servants lead across a variety of challenge types, ranging from the tame to those that are crises. The tools we have presented in Chapters 9 and 11 have been specifically designed to empower leaders with 12 new additive practices that can help them identify and take action in contexts that are in flux, i.e., wicked challenges. To summarize, the new EMERGE leadership practices are:
   Performance Stage Dimension: Sizing Up Leadership Challenges and Opportunities

1 Develop Awareness of Your Readiness for Public Leadership
2 Know the Nature of a Wicked Leadership Challenge
3 Identify a Practical Leadership Opportunity that Addresses a Wicked Challenge
4 Frame the Key Dimensions of the Multifaceted Leadership Opportunity as a Complex and Dynamic System
5 Discern Emergent Patterns in a Dynamic Situation as the Basis for Persuasion
6 Embrace a Mindset of Continuous Leadership Learning

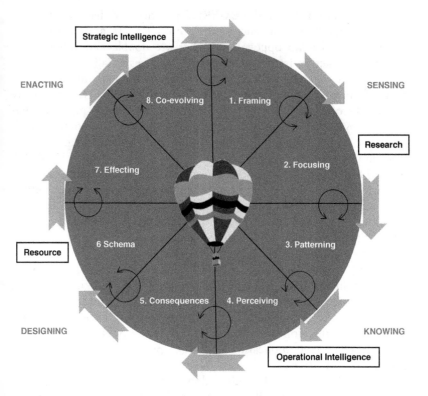

Exhibit 11.9 Tool 12: Strengthen Judgment Navigation
Source: Developed by M. Ingle, CPS/PSU with graphics by Tâm Ngô.

Performance Stage Dimension: Taking Leadership Action

7 Model Trusting Relationships with Leadership Team Members and Others
8 Inspire a Shared and Moral Vision/Values Related to a Leadership Initiative
9 Use Contextual Intelligence to Develop and Act with a Smart Power Strategy
10 Convene and Nurture a Coalition to Realize the Shared Vision
11 Pioneer Breakthrough Innovation in the Public Arena
12 Intentionally Strengthen Prudential Judgment through Reflective Practice

Our experience in introducing new normal public service leaders to these EMERGE practices in a wide variety of domestic and global settings leaves us with several conclusions.

First, when armed with the EMERGE practices, we have witnessed a heightened level of confidence among both leaders and followers in identifying leadership opportunities that are doable and valuable for taking public action from where we sit. This is especially the case with many middle- and lower-level public officials who do not possess a strong feeling of "self-efficacy" and "everyday creativity." The mere availability of these new tools, and their accompanying practices, has been empowering and confidence-building for many of the officials with whom we have worked both in the United States and abroad.

Second, although every public official exposed to the EMERGE Public Leadership Performance Platform is different, most of the officials who have applied some or all of the tools to one of their public-sector challenges leaves believing that the learned EMERGE practices (and not always the same ones) have value in their workplace, and believe that they will be able to use the practice to their organization's advantage in the future. For example, many officials appreciate the availability of the Leadership System Framing graphic (Exhibit 9.7) as a way of integrating the major dimensions (e.g., looking forward, looking backward, looking outward and looking inward) of their leader's role. Others believe they have gained new insight into their ability to mobilize followers in the service of the public good through the more systematic application of "smart power" persuasion in their day-to-day work tasks.

A third insight is that through understanding and applying the tools, many officials actually find that they are being transformed as public leaders. In the extended course of learning the tools, applying them in various contexts and interacting with colleagues in different sectors, these officials come away with new ways of thinking and new practices related to their roles as public leaders. For example, one of our executive master's degree students recently observed toward the end of his EMERGE learning journey that "What I know for sure is that doing the right thing in public service is the hardest thing a person can ever do." What he did not say, but has shared with us, is that doing the right thing is also the most rewarding thing one can do as a public servant. This discovery for some comes not through experience and reading the other chapters in this book, but in understanding and using the EMERGE tools in Chapters 9 and 11. That is why we have strongly encouraged our readers to apply the tools and repertoires by using the online EMERGE Leadership Performance Platform to complete the exercises using real-time public challenges.

A fourth insight comes from colleagues who have examined the EMERGE approach in some depth, and offered some comparisons with other popular leadership approaches. For example, in comparison with the Kouzes and Posner's classic work *The Leadership Challenge* (2017), EMERGE incorporates their five major "practices" and ten "commitments." However, EMERGE differs by the additive focus it provides leaders in these specific EMERGE practice areas:

#1: Develop Awareness of One's Readiness for Public Leadership
#2: Know the Nature of a Wicked Leadership Challenge
#4: Frame the Key Dimensions of the Multifaceted Leadership Opportunity
#5: Discern Patterns in a Dynamic Situation as the Basis for Persuasion
#9: Use Contextual Intelligence to Develop and Act with Smart Power Strategy
#12: Intentionally Strengthen Prudential Judgement through Reflective Practice

There is a final observation on the use of the EMERGE Public Leadership Performance Platform that deserves attention. Many public officials we work with in our leadership development programs and public consultancies at the local, state and global levels have a somewhat different take on the EMERGE tools. Even when they find one or more of the tools valuable, they long for a deeper understanding about when and how to make the best use of the Platform as a whole. They are searching, we believe, for the elusive yet critical leadership practice of "Strengthen Prudential Judgment with Reflective Practice," as discussed in EMERGE Tool 12. In other words, how can the tools be integrated into practical repertoires for emergence that result in the right decisions at the right time, both technically and morally? We address this question in the final chapter.

Note

1 The EMERGE Public Leadership Platform Tools and materials described in this chapter and Chapter 9 are available online at www.pdx.edu/cps/NewPublicLeadershipBook.

Part IV

Building, Retaining and Renewing Public Trust Through Time

Master Case: The Medler Public School System: A Case in Two Scenarios

This is a story of a quasi-fictional organizational challenge of maintaining the trust of citizens through time. What is needed to keep this trust is not static. It changes as the external socio-economic forces, expectations of stakeholders and internal needs of the organization alter the criteria for measuring what counts for the performance success of public entities. Sizing up what is needed from where you sit requires an abundance of prudential judgment at every level of the organization, starting with those working on the front line of service delivery, to supervisors, managers, department heads and those who have strategic leadership responsibility at the apex of public organizations.

The case can be used to complete the exercises in the EMERGE Public Leadership Performance Platform featured in Chapters 9 and 11. The case also provides a practical illustration of the principles of power, authority and conciliatory practice discussed in Chapter 10. Like most examples of leadership within institutional settings, success is a collective effort that requires the knowledge, skills and prudential judgment to lead both vertically and horizontally. It requires a thorough knowable of institutional history and the ability to use that history through time to build trust within the larger community. For these reasons, institutional leadership is not a one-time or one-person occurrence; it is a series of successive opportunities in collaboration with internal and external stakeholders to advance the achievement of the organization mission.

Background

There is nothing more precious to American communities than their local schools. The original Northwest Ordinance of 1787 provided that section 16 of each township be reserved for a public school, thus guaranteeing that local schools would have a revenue stream and the community schoolhouses would be centrally located for all children (Souder and Fairfax, 1996). Schools that are controlled by local citizens have been a cornerstone of American democratic governance since the very beginning of the republic. While school districts have declined by nearly 80 percent over the last 50 years through consolidations (U.S. Census Bureau, 2002, 2007), over 90 percent of the school districts in the United States are still operated independently from other units of government (e.g., sates, counties, cities, towns and boroughs).

Maintaining the confidence and trust of citizens in their local school system is a necessity but an increasingly difficult challenge. Nearly half of the revenue for K-12 education is provided by local sources, mainly the property tax (43.7 percent), with the states providing 48.3 percent and the remainder provided by grants from the federal government (8.1 percent) (U.S. Department of Education, National Center for Education Statistics, 2011). Independent school districts (those not dependent on city or county governments) derive nearly 96 percent of their revenues from property taxes, thus relying more heavily on property taxation than any other type of local government (Fisher, 1997, 320). At the same time, nearly half of the total property tax dollars collected in the United States are used to finance public elementary and secondary education.

> School funding and property taxation are so interconnected that those who are concerned about school finance find themselves examining the role of the property tax, and those who are interested in property taxation inevitably find they need to consider how schools are funded.
>
> Kenyon (2007, 4)

The close nexus between property taxes and school performance has resulted in a national debate over how the state and federal government should use their increasingly limited dollars to support school funding. There is a "growing consensus within the school finance community that state aid should be used to improve student outcomes and that more school aid per pupil should be provided to disadvantaged children than to privileged ones" (Kenyon, 2007, 2).

Case Description for Scenario I: 2004

Against the backdrop of the on-going state and national debate over school funding and student performance, the leaders of the Medler School system have been faced with their own decades-long challenge of addressing declining student enrollments in a manner that would maintain the trust and confidence of taxpayers and parents. Medler is the largest school district in the state with a total enrollment of 48,300 students, 109 schools, 3,600 teachers and a total staff of 6,800 employees. This also makes Medler the third largest governmental entity in the state. The budget totals $968 million, consisting of $570 million in discretionary general fund support, with the balance consisting of U.S. and State Department of Education funding (mostly for target populations) and non-discretionary grants. The federal and state funds are required to be spent for limited and specific purposes. The seven elected members of the school board, who are chosen for a four-year term and serve part-time without compensation, face some significant financial challenges. Three of the seven members of the school board are up for re-election in May—just about the time the budget is required to be formally approved by the board. A number of factors increase the challenges that the board and district faces:

- The district is facing a $58 million shortfall as a result of the expiration of two local option levies and decline in enrollments. School-age population has been on the decline from a high of 80,000 students in 1984 to a current level of 48,000 students. The population is expected to continue declining to a low of 44,000 students by 2020, largely due to increasing costs of housing and a lower birth rate among urban dwellers. Each decline of 1,000 students results in a loss of $5 million in state funding.

- A recent study of Medler's facilities concluded that the district has approximately 33 percent more capacity than the national average for similarly sized districts. In addition, the district's buildings average 62 years of age, compared to the national average of 42. The district spends about 40 percent less on maintenance than other districts of its size.

- Because of a stagnant economy and growing costs of building and managing prisons to accommodate "mandatory sentencing" requirements, the state has been unable to provide K-12 schools with the funding necessary to keep up with cost increases. Based on current state budget projections and current enrollments, Medler expects to receive $15 million less money next year from the state.

- Health care costs have increased an average of 10 percent per year for the past three years and are expected to continue increasing at that level for the next three years. Health care is negotiated as part of the bargaining process with four separate unions. The teachers union worked for ten days free last year to prevent closing schools early in order to balance the budget. In the past, teachers were given health care benefits in lieu of salary increases, which has resulted in teachers in the district being "below market" on pay, but "above market" on health care benefits.

- Nearly 85 percent of parents in the Medler District send their children to public schools, one of the highest rates in the nation for an urban school district. However, only 26 percent of the electorate has children in schools.

- The voters of the state successfully used the initiative process to pass a constitutional amendment which requires that local tax measures obtain a "double majority." This means that a tax measure passes only when a majority of the voters from the last presidential election show up at the polls to vote, and the measure receives a majority of those voting. In the last special election, supporters spent $800,000 on a campaign that succeeded in passing the measure by 56.5 percent with 50.3 percent voting. There is concern that with the large influx of young and new voters since the last election, it will not be possible to meet the double majority requirement when the special levy expires in 2009.

This combination of circumstances presents the board with some daunting choices. They have just hired a nationally renowned superintendent who has launched a series of educational reforms to close the achievement gap between high- and low-performing students. For the first time in seven years, the district staff, teachers and the larger community are enthusiastic about the direction the district is moving. The Board wants to find a way of dealing with its serious fiscal and budgetary challenges in a manner that continues to build the confidence of the community in their schools and in the leadership of the district. This will be difficult to accomplish in the light of the estimated $54 million shortfall—about 12 percent of the general fund budget. This is equivalent to closing the schools for 50 days or laying off 750 teachers.

Case Discussion: Tough Choices

Board members are split on the strategy they should follow. Some favor a "revenue-centered" approach, which emphasizes the importance of filling the various gaps in the district's revenue stream. Others point out the growing citizen hostility to increased taxation and emphasize the importance of a "budget-centered" strategy, which focuses on cutting costs, especially those that will result in permanent long-term savings. The superintendent is worried that the board's decision will be largely framed by a money-centered dialogue that will lose sight of the priority she has been giving to equity and improved performance by students who are disproportionately poor and members of Medler's various minority communities. To build support for her agenda, the superintendent has been working hard to build the trust of parents, teachers and the larger community of engaged stakeholders. To assist in crafting a recommendation to the board, the superintendent decides to create an executive team representing the critical perspectives that need to be taken into account. Each member of the executive team serves as a team leader responsible for collecting information at every level of the organization. The structure and purpose of the advisory team is reflected in Exhibit IV.1. The team leader for each cell in Column 1 has been charged with forming an advisory group, using the assessment matrix and evaluating the importance of a given goal/value on a one to seven scale. Each team leader is responsible for creating a process for completing this activity.

Assume that you have been asked to be a member of one of these assessment teams. How would you rank the priority importance of the various goals/values? After receiving the information from the above assessment process the superintendent and her senior leadership team crafted a set of school closure and K-8 reconfigurations that would advance her reform agenda while also saving the district annual operating expenses. Even with her proposed school reform recommendations, the board will have to adopt additional budget and revenue strategies to balance the budget. The superintendent presented the board with a summary list of 15 strategies in Exhibit IV.2 that her staff had analyzed. There were two school reform strategies, seven budget saving strategies and six revenue producing strategies. Based on this list, what combinations of options would you choose and why?

Case Discussion for Scenario 2: Additional Tough Choices

Ten years later in 2014 Medler found itself facing a new set of conditions that required a reconsideration of its previous policies, strategies and practices. The population research center at the local university, which annually provides enrollment projections for the district and all of its individual schools, projected a long-term growth in the student population, perhaps increasing from a low of 45,083 students in 2013 to 55,000 or even 60,000 students by 2030. The leadership challenge throughout the organization required a switch from a mindset of managing for decline to managing for growth. How do you suddenly move from a decade-long experience of "losing" 17 teachers and two 500-student elementary schools, each and every year, to a period of growth and expansion? District leadership at every level of the organization was required to re-think its assumptions.

The existing superintendent was first appointed to central district leadership in 2003 by the former superintendent. Prior to that she had been the principal of a special focus option school for low-performing students. She has always been a strong advocate of greater equity in the district's effort to improve student performance. She is seeking to find ways of taking advantage of the projected growth in enrollments to advance this agenda, especially through changes in the district's student transfer and school boundary policies. But she is unsure of exactly how

Exhibit IV.1 Priority Scaling (rated on a 1-low to 7-high scale) for Addressing Declining School Enrollments

Perspectives	Goals and Values					
	Efficient use of facilities	Maximize # of classroom teachers	More resources for low-performing students	Diverse curricular choices (i.e., art, music, honors courses, PE, etc.)	Strong neighborhood schools	Improved student performance	Improved equity
Teachers						
Principals						
Facilities Department						
Office of Community Partnerships						
Office of Student Performance						
Equity Office						
Unions						
Office of Business Relations						
District Transfer and Boundary Office						

Exhibit IV.2 Options for Budget Balancing and School Reform

School Reform Strategies

Strategy	Advantages	Disadvantages
1 Reconfigure 7–9 K-6 elementary schools to K-8 configurations	1 Based on research K-8 configurations increase the performance of low-income and minority students 2 Would allow the closing of two middle schools, saving $300,000 per year per school on an on-going basis 3 Would provide for alternative revenue stream for buildings & real estate	1 Would raise issues of equity by targeting low-income schools and neighborhoods, resulting in higher income neighborhoods with traditional middle schools and lower income neighborhoods with a disproportionate number of K-8 configurations 2 Would reduce the number of electives available to students in the upper grade levels of K-8 configurations
2 Close 6–8 elementary schools that are below 400 students and do not have demographic conditions to grow	1 Would result in saving $300,000 per year per school on an on-going basis 2 Would provide for alternative revenue stream for buildings & real estate	1 Will raise concerns regarding the district's strong commitment to neighborhood schools 2 Will be opposed by those championing "small school" learning communities 3 Will anger parents who may move their children to private and charter schools

Budget Cutting Strategies

Strategy	Advantages	Disadvantages
1 Reduce the school year by 50 days	1 Will achieve the budget target 2 Will visibly demonstrate the seriousness of the problem	1 Will seriously compromise the educational mission of the district 2 Will undermine confidence of business, parents and elected officials in the public school system 3 Will be opposed by the teachers union, which favors a higher student faculty ratio than lower pay for teachers 4 Won't do anything to provide a long-term solution

(Continued)

Exhibit IV.2 (Cont.)

Budget Cutting Strategies

Strategy	Advantages	Disadvantages
2 Increase the student faculty ratio from 30:1 to 35:1	1 Will achieve the budget target 2 Will visibly demonstrate the seriousness of the problem	1 Will result in laying off 750 teachers 2 Will undermine the momentum to close the "achievement gap" 3 Will anger parents who may move their children to private and charter schools
3 Undertake "hard-line" negotiations with unions to reduce health care benefits	1 Estimated savings of $8–12 million annual costs 2 Additional steps still necessary to balance the budget	1 Would engulf the community in a bitter battle with unions 2 Would require some off-setting salary increases to make teachers "market competitive" 3 Would likely undermine long-term efforts to build a collaborative relationship with union partners, which is important for carrying out the superintendent and Board's educational reform agenda
4 Contract-out services	1 Estimated savings of $10 million per year on a permanent basis 2 Would not be sufficient to balance the budget	1 Would engulf the community in a bitter battle with unions 2 Would detract attention away from positive focus on the educational mission of the district
5 Establish an outcome-based school performance system, with the goal of closing schools that do not meet criteria	1 Estimated savings of $400–600 thousand per year for each school closed 2 Would demonstrate "good faith" effort that leadership is committed to dealing with long-term problems	1 Would engulf the parents in a bitter struggle to "save" their schools 2 Would likely result in closure of schools in poorer neighborhoods where scores tend to be lower, and because the parent constituents in wealthier neighborhoods wield significant organization and power to resist such measures 3 Would not be sufficient to balance the budget

Strategy	Advantages	Disadvantages
6 Require all organizational units to take a 10% cut in expenses	1 Would be viewed as "fair" 2 Would be easiest to implement	1 Would result in major inequities, particularly at the school-site level 2 Formula could not be applied to about half of the budget, which is funded by dedicated funds 3 Would require major reductions in teaching staff
7 Create a priority ranking system and continue making cuts to balance the budget	1 Would meet expectation of making thoughtful and rational decisions	1 Would take extensive time 2 Would produce conflict 3 Would eliminate existing discretion of principals and site councils to prioritize

Revenue-Based Strategies

Strategy	Advantages	Disadvantages
1 Ask local voters for additional supplementary support through some kind of tax increase	1 Will provide a longer-term solution 2 Can earmark funding for specific purposes to demonstrate accountability to voters	1 Key pollsters argue this is high risk and unlikely to succeed without parents suffering from the consequences of cuts 2 Will require costly and time-consuming campaign 3 Will not address the capital needs of district or declining school enrollments 4 Will not address declining enrollments
2 Lobby the governor and legislature for more adequate funding of schools	1 Will locate responsibility where it legally resides 2 Will allow district to build coalition with other stakeholders throughout the state	1 Likely to be only partially successful in the light of the large state budget shortfall 2 Will not address declining enrollments 3 Won't address the capital needs of district, which have to be locally funded
3 Seek legislative support for dedicating a	1 Potentially could add $15 million annually in new state revenue to the Medler District	

(*Continued*)

Exhibit IV.2 (Cont.)

Revenue-Based Strategies

Strategy	Advantages	Disadvantages
portion of state lottery revenue to education	2 Allows the district to ride the coattails of a private initiative of parents and school lobbyists supporting this solution	1 Will compete with business owners and social service providers who are lobbying for a larger share of lottery revenue 2 Won't address need for district to deal with declining enrollments 3 Won't address the capital needs of district, which have to be locally funded
4 Seek a loan against the district's investment in the State Retirement System, which has generated more income than is necessary to fund projected retirements	1 Could potentially generate $50 million one a one-time basis 2 Avoids the immediate need for a special election to renew the income tax surcharge	1 Uncertain outcome, since issue has never been raised before 2 Won't address need for district to deal with declining enrollments 3 Won't address the capital needs of district, which have to be locally funded 4 Won't address long-term funding needs
5 Convert some school programs to a fee-based system	1 Provides a long-term revenue enhancement 2 Could free up as much as $5 million in existing revenue annually, and generate another $2–3 million in new revenue from the fees	1 Can only contribute to reducing the shortfall by a small amount 2 Creates some inequities for students from low-income families
6 Expand school foundation (501c3) funding for select programs	1 Could provide as much as $10 million annually 2 Increased flexibility in use of funds 3 More buy-in from the community	1 Takes teacher/staff time away from the classroom and from routine administrative work to do development work 2 Funding stream highly variable 3 Donors want more direct influence over targeted programs

to accomplish her goal, so she hires a local university consulting group to undertake a district-wide assessment of what should be done and how.

Consulting Study Findings and Recommendations

After a three-month study that included 14 focus group interviews with a wide group of teachers, community stakeholders, teachers, administrators and members of the business community, the consulting group reported the following findings and recommendations.

Findings

The consultant group assessed the community assets, liabilities and the capacity of the organization to undertake leadership initiative to change past policies and practices.

Liabilities. The consulting group concluded that Medler's strategy for dealing with declining enrollments and reduced budgets had undermined trust and confidence among communities of color and those who wanted a greater emphasis on equity. This loss of trust was based on some cold hard facts. More than 70 percent of the enrollment decline had occurred within just three of Medler's then-nine "High School Clusters." Schools within the north/northeast cluster lost 2,015 of those students during this period. The two high schools in the southeast cluster lost 1,536 students. In its effort to deal with this long period of decline, Medler relied on the following four strategies.

- **School closures.** In 2003–2004 the board closed six elementary schools, most of which occurred in the low-income neighborhoods. In 2012–2013 the board closed two high schools located in these same lower-income/communities of color clusters.
- **Boundary Changes.** In addition to closing schools, Medler frequently changed school boundaries so that the remaining facilities could be used to maximum advantage.
- **School reconfigurations.** In 2003–2004 the board by votes of 4–3 and 5–2 agreed to support a school reform strategy recommended by the superintendent to alter the grade configurations of school programs by eliminating middle schools and converting them to K-8 configurations. These reforms were based on research that showed better performance from low-performing students by allowing them continuity with peers and less-disruptive transitions. During the 2004–2014 decade seven middle school programs (Grades 6–8) were terminated and converted to K-8 programs. By 2014 more than 4,000 6th to 8th graders attended K-8 programs, while about 5,500 still attended Grades 6–8 middle schools. This change was not adopted uniformly across the

district. All seven middle schools closed between 2005 and 2008 were located in middle to low-income neighborhoods. Only one neighborhood K-8 school operated in the more affluent high-income area of the city. This school had only 267 students, making it the smallest neighborhood school in the Medler system and below the 400 "target size" to ensure an appropriate range of educational choices and offerings.

• **Enrollment and Transfer Policies.** A fourth strategy used to balance school enrollments, reduce program budgets and increase class size was to rely on and even expand its long-standing practice of giving parents options outside their assigned neighborhood schools. This strategy resulted in 33 percent of all students attending a school outside their own neighborhood. Some of these were special focus options schools as well as neighborhood schools, most often those with higher student performance records. Student residing in low income neighborhoods used this policy to transfer to higher-performing schools outside their neighborhood, resulting in up to 60 percent of the students within a school boundary attending schools in another part of the district.The consultant report concluded that the majority of school officials and a large and vocal portion of the parent community believe that the district's past practices had exacerbated educational inequities.

Assets. Despite the long period of declining enrollments and shrinking resources (i.e., the district receives $5,500 of state aid for each student enrolled), the consultant report found that there is strong community support and increased involvement from well-organized parent groups.

• **Strong Support of Professional and Middle Class Parent Community.** Many parents – as well as current and past Medler officials and Board members – strongly support the current arrangements and the flexibility and choices they provide students. Some Medler officials even credit this approach during the last decade with helping convince many parents to keep their students in the public school system, rather than opt for private school or other alternatives. Between the 2000 and 2010 censuses, students within the Medler boundaries who were enrolled in non-Medler schools— e.g. private schools and home school options—rose just 2 percent, from 16 percent of the total to 18 percent. And even at 18 percent, Medler still has one of the lowest rates in the U.S. among larger urban school systems. Advocates argue that without such flexibility Medler's school closure situation might have been much worse.

• **Growing District-Wide Parent Support for an Equity Agenda.** The consultants found growing interest among a majority of the superintendent's Advisory Committee on Enrollment and Transfer to increase equity across the district by reducing school option choices for students and making it more difficult for students to transfer out of their neighborhood schools. This strategy is based on demographic data which show that the process of gentrification is increasing diversity within traditional low-income and high-minority neighborhoods. By limiting students from transferring out of low-income schools (which have been as high as 40–60 percent of students), advocates believe that increased student growth can be used to improve the district's equity agenda.

School Capacity. The consulting group concluded that the district did not have sufficient internal clarity and understanding to have a community-wide engagement of the role that school boundary and student transfer policies should play in managing the future growth of the district.

- **Clarifying Role of Boundary and Transfer Policies.** The consulting group identified the following six policy tools that the district uses for balancing school enrollments, only one of which involves boundary changes: Program/School Configuration Tools—program changes, grade configurations; Facilities-Centered Tools—expansion, closure; Boundary-Centered Tools—altering individual school boundaries; and Transfer Tools—limiting transfers. The priorities among these strategies, the rationale for using which combination of strategies when, the criteria for using them, and the way in which Medler will engage the community (if at all) prior to using these strategies was not evident during the group's assessment.
- **Clarify roles of participants.** The report concluded that the district does not have a clearly defined role for staff, stakeholders, central district leaders and principals in making policy changes affecting boundaries and transfers. There have been instances in which some principals openly were involved in supporting and opposing different strategies with parents and prior to any central district office or board process for public engagement.
- **Build infrastructure for community engagement.** The consultants concluded that the district did not have a clearly identified infrastructure and process for engaging the community in a discussion regarding changes in policies governing transfers and school boundaries.

Consultant Report Recommendations

Step I: "Values and Core Principles." Prior to identifying or discussing proposed maps or a long-term framework for future boundary reviews, it is important for Medler to first identify and articulate a set of underlying values, core principles and decision-making criteria against which actual boundaries and related policies will be judged.

Step II: Decision-Making Framework. At the end of Step I—and again, prior to any specific boundary maps or related policies being recommended by Medler officials—the Medler board should formally adopt the framework that will be used to evaluate subsequent proposals on specific boundary lines and a long-term boundary review framework.

Step III: Boundary Maps and Framework Options. Based on the Step II Framework adopted by the board, Medler officials should solicit community input that will result in specific recommendations on boundary-related strategies that are deemed consistent with and designed to help achieve Medler's mission and adopted educational goals.

Step IV: Formal Adoption of New Boundaries and Long-Term Boundary Review Framework. After one or more recommended boundary maps, frameworks and ancillary policies are identified and citizens are provided ample time and opportunity for public input, the Medler board should make final decisions.

Superintendent's Recommendation to the Board

The superintendent is inclined to accept the consultant's report and recommend a four-phased process for creating policies for long-term boundary changes. Before doing so, however, she wants to test the feasibility of Step I by following a process similar to the one that was used for dealing with the major budget problems faced by the board in 2003–2004. As the assistant superintendent who led this internal process, she found it to be informative both in terms of improving the substance of the recommendations but also in testing the willingness and the capacity of the organization to carry through with the recommendations once they were adopted by the board. She created an executive team representing the critical perspectives that need to be taken into account. As in the earlier approach, each member of the executive team serves as a team leader responsible for collecting information at every level of the organization. The structure and purpose of the advisory team is reflected in Exhibit IV.3. The team leader for each cell in Column 1 has been charged with forming an advisory group, using the assessment matrix and evaluating the importance of a given goal/value on a one–seven scale. Each team leader is responsible for creating a process for completing this activity. Assume that you have been asked to be a member of one of these assessment teams, how would you rank the priority importance of the various values, core principles and practices for making boundary changes as the district seeks to find ways of dealing with a long period of slow growth that will crowd existing facilities?

Exhibit IV.3 Values, Core Principles and Practices for Making Boundary Changes (rated on a 1-low to 7-high scale) for Dealing with Overcrowding

Perspectives	*Values, Principles and Practices*						
	Establish school quotas for transfers	*Use lottery to attend non-neighborhood schools*	*Establish maximum physical capacity for all existing schools*	*Increase student curricular choices (i.e., art, music, honors courses, PE, etc.)*	*Limit expansion of school special focus options*	*Increase importance of high-performing neighborhood schools*	*When possible, change boundaries to increase school diversity*	*Use boundary changes in lieu of adding extra capacity*
Teachers							
Principals							
Facilities Department							
Office of Community Partnerships							
Curricular Development Office							

(*Continued*)

Exhibit IV.3 (Cont.)

Perspectives — *Values, Principles and Practices*

Perspectives	Establish school quotas for transfers	Use lottery to attend non-neighborhood schools	Establish maximum physical capacity for all existing schools	Increase student curricular choices (i.e., art, music, honors courses, PE, etc.)	Limit expansion of school special focus options	Increase importance of high-performing neighborhood schools	When possible, change boundaries to increase school diversity	Use boundary changes in lieu of adding extra capacity
Office of Student Performance								
Equity Office								
Unions								
Office of Business Relations								
District Transfer and Boundary Office								

12 Prudential Judgment
The Core Virtue for Leading from Where We Sit

We need phronetic leadership: the ability to grasp the essence of particular situations/things; the ability to recognize the constantly changing situation correctly, and quickly sense what lies behind phenomena to envision the future and decide on the action to be taken. At the basis of such leadership is phronesis.

Nonaka (2010)

To simulate initiative, even at the risk of mistakes, must nowadays never be lost sight of as a task in making the government's services responsible. An official should be as responsible for inaction as for wrong action ... In matters of vital importance the general public is entitled to the views of its permanent servants. Such views may often provide a check against partisan extravagances.

Carl J. Friedrich (1940, 4, 23)

The regulation of [the] various and interfering interests forms the principal task of modern legislation and involves the spirit of party and faction in the necessary and ordinary operations of government.

Hamilton, Madison, and Jay (1961/1787–1789, 79)

In democratic countries the science of association is the mother science; the progress of all the others depends on the progress of that one. Among the laws that rule human societies there is one that seems more precise and clearer than all of the others. In order that men remain civilized or become some, the art of associating must be developed and perfected among them in the same ratio as equality of conditions increase.

Alexis de Tocqueville (2000/1935, 492)

To live together in a world means essentially that a world of things is between those who have it in common, as a table is located between those who sit around it. The world, like everything in between separates and relates men at the same time.

Hannah Arendt (1958, 48)

Taking Stock of Our Public Leadership Legacies: An Exercise in Prudential Judgment

Public service leaders are entering an era where the standards for measuring success have grown ever-more numerous and complex. Each period of reform (see opening epigraphs and Chapter 6) has created a body of principles and practices that have expanded public expectations and the criteria for measuring public service leadership success. Fortunately, this historical legacy has simultaneously increased the repertoire of responses available to our public leaders in building trust and legitimacy in democratic governance. But the increasing "wickedness" of leadership challenges and declining trust in governing institutions is calling into question the adequacy of this historical legacy and repertoire of responses. We have argued that these conditions require the acquisition of a new leadership mindset and an accompanying set of practices that enable us to take initiative from where we sit in an environment characterized by emergent conditions. But arming leaders with new leadership frameworks and practices that are piled on top of existing frameworks adds to the complexity and confusion that impairs our ability to act. A brief summary of the major traditions that comprise current public service leadership practice illustrates this point.

Sometimes leaders need to rely on Populist Era strategies that emphasize responsiveness to majoritarian will. At other times they need to defer to the claims arising from the "politics of place" and invoke the civic republican tradition of the Antifederalists, which leverages the assets of associations in civil society (Sirianni, 2009; Skocpol and Fiorina, 1999; Kemmis, 1990). At other times leaders need to rely on old-fashioned "interest group" political strategies, which emphasize bargaining, negotiation and compromise. And always, public service leaders are expected to carry the problem-solving torch championed by the Progressive Era movement and captured by Carl Friedrich in the opening epigraph. This problem-focused approach places heavy emphasis on deference to professionals who possess the expertise to define problems and craft solutions for political consideration that are supported by appropriate data collection, analysis and evaluation. The unrelenting values of efficiency and effectiveness depend on this torch being re-fueled on occasion, as has been the case with the New Public Management Movement (see Chapter 7).

The rise of New Public Governance, with its emphasis on building collaborative partnerships across organizational, sectoral and jurisdictional boundaries, has further broadened and deepened the criteria for measuring leadership success (see discussion of NPG in Chapter 8 and conciliatory leadership practices in Chapter 10). In addition to running existing administrative systems with high levels of proficiency, our public service leaders are expected to take initiative in providing solutions to governance issues of the kind illustrated in the Master Cases for Parts II, III and IV of this volume. The claims of efficiency and effectiveness now sit alongside the equally important values of citizen responsiveness, protecting rights, honoring the identities and cultural legacies of local communities, and co-producing the public good with multiple community partners through new governance designs.

When we consider together all of the necessary public service role responsibilities described above, we end up with considerable leadership complexity. For example, how do we sort through the repertoire of choices we have as leaders to match the right response with the challenge at hand? How do we develop the ability to weave the collage of multiple and conflicting public values into a commonly shared sense of moral public purpose? How do we simultaneously use multiple leadership models to address different dimensions of a challenge? What do we call such a competency?

Sociologists use the term "salient" to describe select factors or conditions that stand out from others and decisively give meaning to a role within the social setting. Judges and juries use this kind of selective judgment when they decide what facts are most relevant to their legal decision. Aristotle called this capacity of knowing the right thing to do in a given set of circumstances, practical wisdom, or phronesis in Greek. Put simply, phronesis is the capacity to "make sense" out of what is going in your world of practice and action. It is the capacity not only to know what to do, but the ability to do the right thing in the circumstances at hand (Schmidt, 1993). But what is the science that explains prudential judgement? How do we build and hone this competency? What does prudential judgment look like in practice? In chapters 9 and 11 we presented a set of practices. In doing so, we are mindful of the very practical need to make prudential judgment a competency that can be developed by those who sit in positions of leadership opportunity at all levels of public service and in all types of public service organizations. That is why we have devoted so much time in Chapters 9 and 11 to provide the reader with a set of practices and tools for performing with a high sense of agency on the leadership-follower stage. Most of these tools are specifically aimed at cultivating prudential judgment (see especially Tools 2, 4–6, 9–10 and 12).

What is Prudential Judgment?

A practical way of illustrating prudential judgment is to see what it takes to be "good" at a team sport. For example, successful action on the soccer field is informed by a team game plan, but the plan can never script the execution and in many cases it shouldn't. For example, the ability of a person to pass the ball at the right time and in the right place and for the intended receiver to anticipate and control the pass in ways that leverage the next successful move are qualities that cannot be precisely defined or taught. We call it "ball sense." This ball sense is critical to successful action, because action, more so than other kinds of human activity (thinking, laboring, crafting, inventing) is more uncertain, unpredictable and dynamic. It is made even more so by increasing the number of participants. This ball sense operates within a normative framework of acceptable means. There is a clear notion of what constitutes fouls and "dirty play." Both the ends of action and the means to achieve these ends are judged by a moral set of limits. Now that we know what prudential judgment looks like at the individual or group level, what does it look like when expanded to the larger polity level?

Aristotle first used the term phronesis in the *Nichomachean Ethics* (1947/340 BCE) to describe the kind of practical knowledge that leaders need for ruling over others in a shared political community. This kind of practical knowledge is different than ruling over others in a household, an organization, an association or a private company because it requires knowledge of what is best for the political community as a whole (6.51140a25–1140b10). Aristotle describes phronesis as the wisdom to know what is good in general and to make good choices in effectuating these ends in the real world. This practical wisdom has two parts. First, it includes reasoning about moral matters (6.5.1140a24–32; 6.12.1143b23), not just the kind of instrumental reasoning that enables us to match the right means to effectuate a set of ends. Second, phronesis enables us to go beyond moral reasoning in general to understand the right thing to do in the context of the moment. Moral virtues enable us to aim at the right target, prudence enables us to use the right means for the contextual setting (6.12.1144a7–9). Taken together, our moral virtues (doing things for the right reasons), when combined with the right means (doing it the right way), result in actions that are right for the circumstances at hand (doing the right thing) (6.13.1144b20–27).

For purposes of our discussion here, there are three characteristics of phronesis that have special implications for public service leadership. First, phronesis requires *experience*. As Aristotle observed:

> while young men become geometricians and mathematicians and wise in matters like these, it is thought that a young man of practical wisdom cannot be found. The reason is that prudence [phronesis] includes a knowledge of particular facts, and this is derived from experience, which a young man does not possess; for experience is the fruit of years.
>
> Aristotle (1947/340 BCE 6.81142a13–15; 6.7.1141b14–21, 6.8.1142a12–20)

While one can learn the principles of action from books and in the classroom, applying them in the real world to achieve morally virtuous outcomes creates a different kind of knowledge, especially if the knowledge comes from situations that one could not have foreseen. For example, one can know the virtue of being truthful, but being truthful in certain situations might cause pain and offense. Knowing how to be truthful in balance with other considerations and in specific contexts requires experience.

A second characteristic of phronesis is that it involves considerable *forethought and deliberation.* It requires that we be well aware of the context of our actions and that we draw both from our general knowledge, and more especially, our personal experiences of past successes and failures. Context awareness is both outward and inward facing. Outwardly, it requires that we pay close attention to the long-term effects of our contemplated actions both in terms of the practical outcomes and the ethical outcomes on both ourselves and others. Inwardly, it requires that we pay close attention to the internal sets of relationships at the leadership team and organizational levels. Awareness of both the inward- and outward-facing contexts guards against assuming that what was the right thing to do yesterday or in a previous set of similar circumstances will be the right thing to do now. While there may be general principles of human conduct that we can rely upon, phronesis assumes that these principles are "merely true for the most part."

A third characteristic of phronesis is that it can be systematically *acquired and honed* through a regimen of practice, much like a regimen can help build and maintain our physical and emotional well-being. We do not have to depend on the random acquisition of practical experience through time to give us phronesis. We can accelerate the acquisition of prudence, like all other virtues, through systematic incorporation of various exercises and tools into our daily leadership practices. Completing the various exercises in our EMERGE Leadership Platform, especially Tools 6 and 12, helps to facilitate this learning, especially when it is done as a part of reflective practice. By pausing to reflect on the difference between what we think is going on and what is actually occurring in practice, we can gain insight and understanding. But such reflection does not require us to re-examine the moral purposes of our actions, which is essential for the exercise of phronesis.

What Does Prudential Judgment Look Like in Practice?

Prudential judgment is not an abstract idea, but a very practical notion that can be seen around us on a daily basis. We see it exercised by our senior organizational leaders who are trying to manage multiple program missions in the face of contending political factions that want the organization to go in quite different directions (see Mt. Hood Stewardship and the Medler School System Master Cases). We see it in the work of a fellow land-use planner trying to figure out how to manage a variance exception by a resident who wants to build a deck on the front of their house without violating "set-back" requirements that are intended to prevent construction on private property from intruding into the public right-of-way. We see it exercised by a police officer assigned to manage a neighborhood policing program as he struggles on a daily basis to walk the line between empowering neighbors while also protecting the public's safety and guarding the rights of individuals. In all of these instances, public servants are exercising their prudential judgment. Knowing a rule, a set of standard operating procedures, a precedent or the right thing to do in the abstract is insufficient to provide each of the above public leaders with the answer of what to do in the here and now. In all of these instances, there is the need to exercise discretion, the need to work alone and with others in synchronized coordination, the need to know when we should exercise our leadership role and when we should step back and be a self-led follower. These prudential settings provide opportunities to keep and build trust in our democratic institutions of governance. This trust is the product of individual judgments made through time and from where you sit. These individual judgments are a composite of considerations, honed by experience, that result in a political decision that is defended in terms of what is best for the community as a whole. While always debatable, these prudential judgments are rightly viewed as moral decisions, as community-altering decisions and as actions that affect the common good.

Sir Geoffrey Vickers, in his exquisite essay on the *Art of Judgment* (1995/1965), summarizes why prudential judgment is at the heart of what administrators do. It is part of separating causes and effects; it is integral to deciding what values are at stake and what priority should be given to the interplay among them; it is inseparable from the transactional work administrators undertake in carrying out their budgeting, personnel and other instrumental roles. Taken together, these multiple arenas of administrative action require the exercise of judgment and create what Vickers calls an "appreciative system." In their introductory essay for the re-publication of Vickers' 1995/1965 treatise, the editors summarize the following key features of Vickers' system of appreciative judgment (Adams, Catron, Cook, and Vickers, 1995, xxi–xxii):

1   The ability to find pattern in complexity and to shift our choices of pattern according to varying criteria and interests …
2   The artful selectivity in deciding what features of a situation are most important in keeping with shifting interests, values, and concerns …
3   The ability to "read the situation" …
4   The investment of self in the situation at hand.

To illustrate our point that opportunities abound for us to exercise and hone our prudential judgment, we will draw on the four Master Cases accompanying each of the parts of this book. We will highlight the core prudential leadership qualities that are evident in these cases.

Leadership Initiative, Courage and Vision in the Service of the Public Good

Collective action most commonly occurs when initiative is taken by solo public service leaders who step outside or beyond their formal role responsibilities. The Vision Action Network, the Mt. Hood National Forest Strategic Plan and the Medler School redesign initiative came into existence because administrators saw the limitations of doing business as usual. They acted on their sense that "something is not right," "we can't be successful if we continue on this path" and "we can do better." While prepared to accept the consequences for their own organizations, they were not prepared to accept the consequences for their communities. When every person and every organization follow the market-place model of doing a few things well, no one will see or care about the unmet needs of the community. The administrators in the three Master Cases believed that public servants have an obligation to be more than passive and instrumental caretakers of policy choices made by elected officials. They took the initiative to create an agenda that better met the needs of their respective communities. The leaders in the Vision Action Network and Mt. Hood Stewardship Plan did not draw a bright-line distinction between the public, private and nonprofit sectors. As the county leader in the Vision Action case notes, project results were "not reliant on outside investments, legislation or voter approval. They simply happened because someone decided to make them happen" (Bohn, 2014, 149). The Angry Librasry case in Part I poses a very typical problem of prudential judgment for those in first line and middle levels of leadership responsibility.

Prudential Judgment and the Role of Dialogical Competency

In a system of democratic governance where the "voice of the people" plays a decisive role in determining the legitimacy of government processes and outcomes, the art of dialog becomes an integral part of prudential judgment. As described by Don Bohn in the Vision Action Network and Gary Larsen in the Mt. Hood Forest Stewardship Plan, the role of leadership in catalyzing a new public governance capacity-building initiative was highly dialogical. (We introduced several of these dialogical processes in our discussion of "Leadership Tools for Taking Action" in Chapter 11.) Both cases describe an ever-enlarging orbit of conversations that continuously expanded what might be called the "community of care." At various stages of the process leaders helped to redefine and change the possible solutions to the challenge they were seeking to address. For a business owner the initial annoying problem of homeless individuals living in a near-by park gets gradually and continuously redefined as a community resource constraint problem, to a community asset management issue, to a shared conversation about using shared resources to pursue the best options available to advance the common good. The "pristine wilderness" advocate's annoyance at the high-pitched sound of snowmobilers is gradually and continuously redefined as a multiple-use perspective emerges; this perspective is transformed still again into a strategic stewardship plan that all of the participants can own. "Your problem" gradually gets changed to "my problem" and eventually to "our problem." And if the process works well, the focus on addressing challenges gets replaced with a focus on finding opportunities to expand the community's total assets. This shifts the initial conversation away from problems altogether, and replaces it with a conversation about our collective engagement and well-being. While the processes in the two Master Cases may have been initiated by a public organization, the process produced collective ownership of a shared community good with a commitment from participants to share new-found responsibility for action. No one person, group or organization participating in each process was the same at the end as they were at the beginning. The dialogic activity was transformative both in terms of the process and substantive outcomes. The Medler School System case illustrates the challenge of creating a sustainable dialogic with the community that incorporates the past as part of the memory bank of those who are key participants in succeeding rounds of problem-solving. Fears and hopes get planted in an earlier period in time that gets carried forward and creates both barriers and existing conditions for future problem-solving initiatives.

Dialogical processes like those illustrated in the Vision Action Network, Mt. Hood Forest Stewardship Plan and the Medler School System are exercises in prudential judgment. It is not enough that participants simply show up to advance their cause, issue or personal interest. If the process is to be successful it must facilitate mutual understanding, mutual engagement and potential for mutual gain. This process cultivates habits of listening, hearing, reflecting on the relationship between ends and means, and connecting abstract notions of what is in the common good to the particular issue at hand. Prudence is developed through, but also plays an important role in, these education-centered processes. Prudence provides both leaders and followers with the ability to understand when the group needs to know more together, and to create strategies for people to learn together about what they have in common.

Prudential Judgment and Leveraging the "New Normal"

The "new normal" we described in Chapter 7 requires leaders who can correctly assess the on-going and changing opportunities in the context at hand. This assessment is also an exercise in prudential judgment. The "new normal" requires making sense out of the network of organizational, social, political, economic and technological interdependencies and forces at work in the environment. Prudential judgment is reflected in the way in which challenges can be redefined as moral callings to improve the public good. As noted by Carl Friedrich in our opening epigraph, "[a]n official should be as responsible for inaction as for wrong action ... In matters of vital importance the general public is entitled to the views of its permanent servants" (Friedrich, 1940, 4, 23).

In the three Master Cases for Parts II–IV the leaders were astutely attuned to the drivers of change within their respective contextual settings. They were also aware of the subtle changes in these contextual settings throughout the network building process, seizing opportunities at each moment in time to advance the collective objectives of their network initiative (see Tool 10 in Chapter 11). Knowing how to read the tea leaves in the external environment is essential for establishing the enabling conditions that will germinate leadership initiatives and supply sufficient support so that they will be able to survive in the world. Prudence plays an important role in this process as leaders try to assess the varying capacities of communities and organizations to engage in collective problem-solving and action in the pursuit of the collective good. As we have come to appreciate more fully, not all communities and organizations have the motivation and capacity to be good partners in community engagement efforts (Banyan, 2003).

In addition to the role of prudence in assessing the contextual setting, leadership challenges and opportunities in the current environment do not appear in neatly bundled packages. And if they do, they have a dynamic quality that can quickly change the definition of the kind of leadership required at any given moment in time. As Chapter 8 illustrates, some leadership challenges are simple, some are complicated, and a few may be truly "wicked." For the latter there is no clear course of action that will resolve the challenge and certainly none that can be taken without resulting in serious adverse consequences. Prudence enables us to have the right mindset that is grounded in experience, gives us the capacity to switch from one leadership reality to another and arms us with the appropriate frames, tools and leadership practices. This can be illustrated by reviewing the changing leadership strategies that were used in the Vision Action, Mt. Hood and Medler School cases.

Part of the challenge in the early stages of the Vision Action Network was to create awareness of the unmet needs of the broader community. This was accomplished by undertaking very traditional analytic work through the collection of socio-economic and demographic data, organizing that data into meaningful categories, and then disseminating the information to various stakeholder groups in the community. But what constitutes meaningful categories of information is in the eye of the beholder, and negotiation with relevant community groups and organizations may be required to see the data from different points of view.

In addition to traditional analytic work, leaders in the three cases spent lots of time building interpersonal trust one person and one organization at a time. These activities began to alter the definition of the challenge from a "changing demographic problem" to an issue of community inclusion and care. As the definition of the problem began to change, so did the nature of the leadership opportunity on the part of administrative leaders. They needed to separate their catalytic roles in the process from their mission roles as participating partners, which required creating many centers of community ownership among the network partners. The ability to adjust your leadership approach to the needs of the setting is the product of prudential judgment.

Prudential Judgment and the Challenge of Role Balancing

Leaders operating in the current environment cannot rely mainly on their formal/positional role responsibilities to initiate, establish and maintain agreements that last. In fact, leading with these formal roles may discourage involvement for some of the participants, especially if their history with the organization has been adversarial. In the three Master Cases for Parts II–IV, the visible public leaders were initially perceived as having extensive formal authority that affected the motivation of stakeholder groups. While this formal authority and the resources it represented commanded respect among some stakeholders, at the same time this formal power and the history of its use in the past actually served as an initial barrier to building interorganizational and intersectoral trust and confidence among other stakeholders. This is a reminder that power dynamics and privilege can drive away major segments of the citizenry. Being self-aware and transparent with your potential community of stakeholders about this issue throughout the engagement process is important to leadership success.

The uneasy tension between the formal role of administrative leaders and their informal trust-building role with followers is exacerbated by the current external public service environment. Even as trust develops over time, public service leaders have to maintain clear boundaries as to where they have discretion and where their accountability requirements under the American rule of law system prevent such discretion. The lead administrators in all three cases had to have a clear understanding of the boundaries of their legal authority in deciding how much and what kind of decision-making to turn over to stakeholder followers in the community. Deciding how and where to draw this line requires leaders who are superbly adept at functioning simultaneously in vertical and horizontal structures of authority. It requires an abundance of prudential wisdom.

The Medler School case, like the Vision Action Network case, illustrates the need for leaders to anticipate the future and make the adjustments in policy and organizational practices that will enable the institution to retain the trust of the community through time. This becomes especially difficult when the community does not share a common history or a consensus on the priority that should be given to a set of values (i.e., efficient use of resources) that unavoidably come at the expense of other equally important values (i.e., justice and equity). In 2003–2004 the Medler superintendent could not downsize the over-built school system without closing schools, which would disproportionately disadvantage the school communities where the decline in enrollments had been the most severe. These were the low-income and minority school communities that had been displaced by gentrification and whose well-being was best served by a district-wide equity agenda, not school closures. Ten years later when declining enrollments were replaced by long-term growth, the superintendent had an opportunity to give greater priority to her equity agenda, especially in the policies and practices governing enrollment and transfer policies. But this could not be accomplished without first rebuilding the trust that had been undermined with key stakeholder during the previous period of school closures and reconfigurations of elementary schools and K-8s. This illustrates the importance of leaders viewing their roles as community statespersons rather than short-term problem-solvers or simply policy-makers. Statespersons also focus on the impact that change will have on maintaining and building trust in the community's governing institutions and processes.

Prudential Judgment and the Challenge of Competing Moral Purposes

What sets prudence apart from reflective practice is that the latter does not require you to question the moral ends of your action. Through reflective practice you can make continuous quality improvements, be extremely innovative and achieve sufficient consensus for collective action (as illustrated by our discussion of Albert Speer in Chapter 5), but this may contribute to dastardly ends. Prudence requires that you constantly ask, "What is the right thing to do?" And in deciding where to look for guidance to do the morally right thing, prudence requires that you pay close attention to the unique moral values that are part of the extended now and which can be used to legitimate the exercise of your discretionary authority (see Chapters 5 and 6).

The School Board Master Case for Part IV illustrates the importance of prudential judgment in sorting through and managing the multiple moral priorities that were in conflict. Dealing with these conflicts is what makes public service leaders different than artists, doctors, lawyers and architects. The latter are engaged in what Aristotle called production, which is a different kind of activity from leadership action: "production has an end other than itself, action cannot; for good action itself is its end" (1947/340 BCE, 6.5.1140b7–8; cf. 2.4.1105a28–34). Aristotle gives the example of an artist whose production is under the guidance of right reason. Art does not imply that you produce it in a virtuous way; its criterion is only that the product is good (e.g. a well-designed and well-constructed chair). By contrast, prudence enables one to draw on the foundational moral principles of the political system and use those principles as part of our leadership activity to guide what is possible and necessary in the world of both particulars and variability. As Joseph Nye reminds us, prudence encompasses and links ethical intent, ethical action and ethical results (Nye, 2008, 111). All of these are necessary parts of prudential judgment.

The Role of Prudential Judgment in Re-Interpreting Moral Purpose: Maintaining Citizen Trust and Legitimacy

An important element of prudence is a deep affection for the polity and the citizens and residents who make it possible for the collective moral action of leaders and followers to co-produce improvements in the common good. This affection is based on a mutual recognition that the polity is essential for protecting the equal rights we all enjoy as citizens. Without the polity and its commitment to liberty and equality under just laws, political life becomes impossible. This affection for the polity and what it stands for requires vigilance in making it relevant to succeeding generations of citizens. Vigilance is not about reifying the past, but using the past to make it morally relevant for the now and for the future. This is prudential work, which requires the on-going re-examination of the moral meaning of the polity so that it retains the trust and legitimacy of citizens through time. Take, for example, the American commitment to diversity.

The American polity was founded on a general belief that diversity and pluralism were a source of strength and creativity, not weakness and vulnerability. As we observed in Chapter 5, this belief set the United States off from previous history, where it was commonly thought that homogeneity of values and beliefs were necessary to maintain community order and stability. But this commitment to equality and diversity was seriously flawed in practice, nearly fatally so, as evidenced by the Civil War. The commitment did not include African Americans, women and Native Americans, other people of color, gender- and sexual-minorities, and other types of diversity relevant to our contemporary treatment of one another equally as citizens.

Over the last two centuries our embrace of diversity has produced ever-greater cultural pluralism, resulting in differing assumptions about the nature of issues affecting the common good. Cultural competence has now become an essential part of phronesis for present-day American public leaders, as was the case for professional competence for 20th century administrative leaders. Followers need to see this prudential wisdom of leaders at work, and leaders need to engage followers in the spirit of what Aristotle called friendship, a mutual and co-dependent process of co-producing the common good.

Neuroscience of the Brain and Prudential Judgment

We draw from recent research on the neuroscience of the brain to illustrate the three dimensions of prudence in Exhibit 12.1. We also illustrate the switching and integrative circuits that enable the parts of the brain responsible for prudential judgment to work as a seamless whole. In the paragraphs and sections that follow, we elaborate more fully on our on-going efforts to reveal the mysterious neurological dimensions of prudential judgment.

Early use of technologies like positron emission tomography (PET), functional magnetic resonance imaging (fMRI) and magnetoencephalography (MEG) produced neural mapping that localized brain function. Based on this mapping, it was initially believed that executive decision-making functions that we associate with prudential judgment reside in the prefrontal lobe, vision in the occipital lobe, sensory in the parietal lobe, motor coordination in the motor and premotor lobes, and so on throughout the brain. But subsequent studies have produced a much more nuanced understanding of how the brain functions (Barrett, 2017). Human functions are not entirely limited to a given portion of the brain. Like the electrical circuits in our house, there are multiple sub-networks of overlapping and interconnected circuits that depend on very high degrees of coordinated action among different parts to perform a given human function. When an electrical outlet is not working in our house, we are not sure where the problem is located until we check each of the interconnected parts of the circuit all the way back to the main electrical stem into our house.

Prudential judgment appears to be the product of four interconnected electrical networks within the brain as illustrated in Exhibit 12.1: the prefrontal cortex, orbital cortex, anterior cingulate and the insula.[1] Together these networks are the primary sources for regulating the mix of mind-wandering creativity, task management and accomplishment, attention switching, meaning-making, moral judgment and integration of the general with the particular. The prefrontal cortex is the home of what has been described as the executive function. It is historically the most recently developed part of the brain and is the most difficult part of the brain to keep engaged for long periods of time. The prefrontal cortex

Prefrontal Cortex (**Executive Function**):
"Doing it the right way."

- Executes plans
- Assessies consequences
- Differentiates good from bad
- Decides right means for ends
- Controls distractions to tasks

Creative Problem-Solving

This is a separate circuit of the brain consisting of its own electrical circuit and not located in a specific area of the brain.

- **Explores hypotheticals**
- **Projects oneself into the future**
- **Imagines new possibilities**
- **Makes creative connections**

Insula and

Anterior Cingulate
"Doing it in the right proportion."

Controls switching between executing and inventing, between task performance and creativity.

Prefrontal Cortex

Orbital Cortex

Orbital Cortex: "Doing the right thing."
Meaning making (i.e., representing primary reinforces like vision & touch)

- Emotional intelligence
- Controls & connects reward & punishment-related behavior

Exhibit 12.1 The Prudential Judgment Wheelhouse
Source: Adapted from Levitin (2014, 42).

controls the capacity to differentiate among conflicting thoughts, determine good from bad, better and best, same and different; assess the future consequences of current activities; determine what is needed to achieve a defined goal and to asses outcomes and expectation based on different courses of action; and to control "antisocial behavior." This executive function of the brain controls understanding, deciding, recalling, memorizing and inhibition (i.e., keeping distractions at bay until task completion). We have labeled this dimension of prudential judgment, "doing it the right way." It ranges from the relatively simple task of getting our academic paper assignments constructed, argued and theoretically supported with the appropriate literature to the more complex task of designing and building a bridge across the Mississippi River. These activities consume enormous amounts of energy and cannot be sustained for long periods of time without rest or shots of glucose, which offer only a short-term solution.

The function of the orbital cortex is not as well understood as the prefrontal cortex, but there is agreement that it plays an important role in meaning-making activities, such as decoding and representing some primary reinforcers (like taste and touch); learning and reversing associations of visual and other stimuli to these primary reinforces; and controlling and correcting reward-related and punishment-related behavior, thus controlling our emotional and moral intelligence. We have labeled this dimension of prudential judgment, "doing the right thing" in Exhibit 12.1. These functions are all essential to personal and organizational learning, but exactly how this learning function interfaces with the executive function in the prefrontal lobe is not yet fully known.

What is better known is that the executive function stands in contrast to the mind-wandering mode where the brain freely associates ideas, explores "what ifs", projects oneself into a set of circumstances or social situations, daydreams, experiences feelings of empathy and otherwise experiences a lack of barriers between senses and concepts. This mind-wandering mode is not located in any specific part of the brain, as is the case with the executive function in the prefrontal cortex. Instead, it is its own network comprised of neurons that are distributed in the brain but connected to one another to form the equivalent of an electrical circuit (Levitin, 2014, 39). We have labeled this network of prudential judgment in Exhibit 12.1, "doing the right thing in the circumstances" of the moment and place. When this network is engaged it shuts down the executive function network and vice versa. This is the brain's way of ensuring maximum performance of specific tasks. But what controls switching between the active mode of task performance and the more passive mode of mind-wandering that can result in creativity and innovation?

Together the insula and the anterior cingulate provide the switching mechanisms that allow us to move back and forth between star-gazing new possibilities and hunkering down with focused attention to complete a given task on time and on budget. It wasn't until 2010 that researchers Vinon Menon and Daniel Levitin discovered that the main switching function between these two quite separate human activities is controlled by the insula (Sridharan, Levitin, and Menon, 2008) but in partnership with the anterior cingulate. This is because the insula has bidirectional connections to the anterior cingulate, which plays a crucial role in initiation, motivation and goal-directed behaviors (Devinsky, Morrell, and Vogt, 1995).

> [The] efficacy of the insula-cingulate network varies from person to person, in some functioning like a well-oiled switch, and in others like a rusty old gate. But switch it does, and if it is called upon to switch too much or too often, we feel tired and a bit dizzy, as though we are see-sawing too rapidly.
>
> Levitin (2014, 43)

What is important for our discussion here regarding leadership development is the way in which the various parts of the brain interact to create meaning. The prefrontal cortex coordinates the comparison of what's in your head (what you know/believe/feel/think) with what's out there in the world (best practices, theory, professional practice, the opinion of others, etc.). Daniel Levitin uses the example of mopping the floor and the metaphor of moving back and forth between being the boss and being the worker to drive home the importance of training the brain through comparative exercises to go beyond being satisfied with just completing instrumental tasks. In mopping a floor,

> [w]e like what we see or we don't, and then we go back to the task, either moving forward again, or backtracking to fix a conceptual or physical mistake ... In situations like this we are functioning as both the boss and the employee ... Planning and doing require separate parts of the brain. To be both a boss and a worker, one needs to form and maintain multiple, hierarchically organized attentional sets and then bounce back and forth between them. It's the central executive in your brain that notices that the floor is dirty. It forms an executive attentional set for "mop the floor" and constructs a worker attentional set to do the actual mopping ... This constant back-and-forth is one of the most metabolism-consuming things that our brain can do.
>
> Levitin (2014, 174–75 passim)

In keeping with the mopping analogy, let's add an additional exercise after the mopping task has been completed and ask the worker/boss to imagine new possibilities for ensuring a clean floor. We are now asking the participant in our exercise to undertake a different kind of mental activity that engages the mind-wandering electrical network of the brain and exercises the rusty connections between the insula and the anterior cingulate. Unless we specify the time devoted to this task of imagining new strategies for ensuring a clean floor, our participant will not know when to stop the exercise, when they have done enough or when they have succeeded in responding to the request. The insula–anterior cingulate connection performs this function.

When the mopping analogy is carried through its various stages of complexity and possibilities for learning, it illustrates why the accumulation of knowledge through experience is important. Like good clinical practice physicians, cabinet makers and seasoned athletes, mopping lots of different kinds of floors builds up a store-house of knowledge that enables the practitioner to recognize patterns, not just focus on a single measure of performance. Both the floor mopper and the medical clinician can combine direct information from the particular setting with "good science" and best practices to "size up" what it all means and determine the next best options. What separates a journeyman from the master craftsman is a large storehouse of experience from which to draw and the capacity to access this experience.

What if we complicate the mopping analogy by adding an element of moral judgment? What if we ask our mopper to participate in a program sponsored by a community nonprofit organization to train people with learning difficulties for employment? Now our floor mopper has to pay attention to the moral relationship he/she has with another individual in addition to the non-moral relationship he/she has with the floor. This requires tapping into the orbital cortex circuit of the brain (see Exhibit 12.1). Recent studies suggest that this circuit is associated with higher levels of moral reasoning (i.e., reasoning that focuses on the needs and interests of others; see especially Fang et al., 2017; Raine and Yang, 2006; also see literature on emotional intelligence, especially Goleman, 1995). Other studies suggest that a higher level of moral reasoning is associated with life experience (see Wallskog, 1992). Taken together these studies suggest with Aristotle that higher levels of moral reasoning are a process of maturation. But lest we become too optimistic about the moral advantages of the aging process, neuroscience research has found that the prefrontal cortex reasoning circuit is often at war with the emotional and cognitive subsystems grounded in different regions of the brain (Greene and Haidt, 2002). This means that leaders can't simply rely on "reason" to create moral agreement. They have to tap into their storehouse of experience and find potential points of common emotional ground to which disputants can relate. This is illustrated by parents who believe that all lesbians are perverts until their daughter announces that she is a lesbian, or declared racists who change their views when they experience interracial marriage within their family. Prudential leadership requires a rich storehouse of experience upon which leaders can draw to tap into the emotional, moral and rationale neuro-circuits of their followers. Since these circuits are all linked, the leadership storehouse needs to be large and continuously expanding.

Leaders' storehouses of knowledge consist of their accumulated memory of places, ideas and social relationships that are deposited in a complex circuitry often referred to as the mind-wandering or low-energy part of the brain. The more we can increase this storehouse, the more potential we have as a leader to make good decisions. This storehouse provides multiple descriptive and moral lenses to filter a given leadership challenge. This is the advantage of having a very broad exposure to multiple disciplines and multicultural experiences. It arms the subject through reading, travel and multiple disciplinary perspectives with a rich array of experiences. As Daniel Levitin (2014, 368) observes in the *Organized Mind*, neuroscience research suggests that "listening to music, looking at art, and watching dance, may lead to two desirable outcomes: increased interpersonal empathy and better executive attention control."

How do We Acquire, Access and Hone Prudential Judgment?

In preparing individuals for leadership, we cannot direct them to a given discipline that stands on the same footing as the disciplines of political science, economics, sociology, psychology, history, cultural anthropology, philosophy and the natural sciences. It is even more striking, yet not surprising, that we do not have an identified field of study that stands on the same footing as the clinical practices of law, medicine, dentistry, occupational and physical therapy, teaching and others. This vacuum was recognized in 2002 with the founding of the first journal devoted to the research and study of leadership education. In the inaugural issue of *The Journal of Leadership Education* (*JOLE*), the editor observed that:

> our journal sits at the nexus of education theory and practice and leadership theory and practice, and from this divide, this mountain pass, there is a need to look 'both ways'. Whether or not leadership education is a discipline of its own is unclear, at least at present. If nothing else, by looking both ways this journal hopes to provide a passageway between two disciplines, enriching both in the process.
> (Gallagher, 2002, ii)

Since the founding of this journal, what have we learned about leadership development and the role of prudential judgment? In our review of more than 300 articles published in the JOLE from 2002 to 2014 there appears to be a general consensus that 1) we can educate everyone for moral leadership; 2) our moral education is a continuous process that is part of life-long learning; 3) moral education requires constant reflection on the values that serve as the ends of human action, not simply the instrumental means; and 4) there are some common enabling conditions for cultivating and enhancing the moral judgment of leaders. But there is not a single article that discusses how to cultivate prudential judgment.

Based on the neuroscience of the brain, we now know what has been assumed for some time by those interested in prudential judgment. The prudential judgement storehouse is built through multiple leadership experiences in different contexts over an extended period of time. There is no substitute for experience, especially experience upon which you reflect and abstract the lessons learned. This is why we have relied so heavily in this monograph on cases, leadership exercises and reflective practice. The leadership practices and tools in Chapters 9 and 11 are especially designed to provide you the experiences needed to increase your capacity for prudential judgment. But having a rich prudential storehouse doesn't do us any good unless we learn how to access it and use it for informed leadership decision-making.

One of the most important things we have learned from neuroscience is that creativity, meaning-making and innovative thinking are located in a different circuit than the one that controls executive decision-making. When the prefrontal cortex is in high gear to perform executive decision-making, it shuts down the part of the brain that is the repository of information needed for creativity, imagination and ethical decision-making. As Albert Einstein observes, this part of the brain may be the most important.

> When I examine myself and my methods of thought, I come to the conclusion that the gift of imagination has meant more to me than any talent for absorbing absolute knowledge ... All great achievements ... must start from intuitive knowledge.
> Einstein (quoted in Calaprice, 2000, 10, 22, 287)

The trick to getting access to this imaginative storehouse is to activate the quiet, mind-wandering part of the brain. As David Rock observes In *Your Brain at Work* (2009, 212):

> people have insights when their brain is in a specific state. Insights happen when people think globally and widely rather than thinking on details. Insights require a quiet brain, meaning there is an overall low level of activity, which helps people notice subtle internal signals.

This low level of activity in the brain is the product of the right chemical balance between norepinephrine, which controls one's interest in a topic, and dopamine, which controls the amount of alertness one has to focus on a given topic. This chemical balance can be self-controlled to some extent. Self-control involves deactivating the prefrontal cortex sufficiently so that new connections are being formed by tapping into the reservoir of experience, ideas, relationships and places that are stored in mind-wandering circuitry of the brain. Therefore, any activities that increase the efficacy of the switching mechanisms controlled by the insula, anterior cingulate and orbital cortex are highly beneficial for cultivating prudential judgment. Training and leadership development programs and activities that move participants back and forth between agency-based exercises, group discussions or case studies, and various kinds of reflective practice exercises provide participants with the experience of what a "flow state" feels like. Our leadership Tool 5, "Contextual Intelligence with Foresight," and our leadership Tool 11, "Leading Innovation," are designed to help you create a space between your repertoire of experience and its relevant application to the challenge at hand. This state is described in the neuroscience literature as a neurochemical condition where a flow of new ideas is coming into the prefrontal cortex that energizes task completion and where the executor is so immersed in the leadership experience that time seems to stand still (Rock, 2009, 68–69; Levitin, 2014, 203–208).

In short, while you can't get more prudential judgment by reading more books or working harder, you can facilitate the capacity for its exercise. You can build in time to step back from the completion of specific tasks (which engage the executive function of the brain) and ask how these tasks connect to your personal experience, to a larger body of theory or professional practice and to ethical principles of right action. Stepping back engages the mind-wandering part of the brain, which is the storehouse for thinking about new possibilities, alternative futures and different ways of responding to shared challenges. You are exercising what Levitin characterizes as the "rusty" network of neurological connections. You can think of "stepping back" as adding some WD-40 lubricant to the complex neurological connections that comprise the prudential wheelhouse in the brain. But in doing so, we need to remind ourselves that training the brain is not simply about the development of clear thinking, but more importantly, it is about learning how to think, act, and feel together with others in ways that spark collective action for the common good.

In Exhibit 12.2 we present a graphic summary of the role of prudential judgment in sparking collective action for the common good. Leaders are required to bring together two worlds into a single integrated whole. There is first the world of complex social interdependence, which has grown ever-more fragmented, unpredictable, unknowable and filled with value conflicts. There is the second world that we inhabit as stewards of the public trust. This world has a logic of its own that is knit together by legal

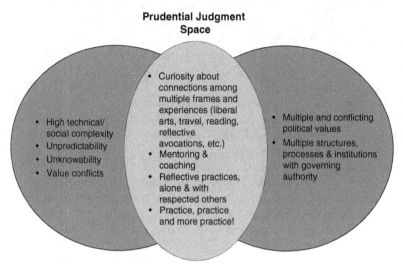

Socially Complex Interdependence   Ethical Principles of the Political System

Prudential Judgment
Space

- High technical/
  social complexity
- Unpredictability
- Unknowability
- Value conflicts

- Curiosity about
  connections among
  multiple frames and
  experiences (liberal
  arts, travel, reading,
  reflective
  avocations, etc.)
- Mentoring &
  coaching
- Reflective practices,
  alone & with
  respected others
- Practice, practice
  and more practice!

- Multiple and conflicting
  political values
- Multiple structures,
  processes & institutions
  with governing
  authority

Exhibit 12.2 Prudential Judgment Space

structures, processes, values and institutions that hold and carry values through time. Prudential judgment is the space in between that integrates these two overlapping worlds into organic leadership initiatives intended to advance the common good.

Conclusion

American democracy unavoidably depends on ground-level leadership initiatives by career public servants from where they sit. This is the space where leadership action is most visible to citizens, where it matters most in terms of services that add up to a difference that counts, and where democratic governance takes on real meaning as an active and on-going process of renewal between citizens and their leaders. The American political tradition is fortunate to have a rich and contested set of democratic values and institutions that enable each generation of leaders at all levels of government to draw upon these traditions to renew trust and legitimacy in democratic institutions (see Chapters 5–6). These traditions are kept alive only when they are contested from within and challenged from without, when they embody what Alastair MacIntyre called "continuities in conflict" (McIntyre, 1981, 206). This continuous process of conflict and renewal requires public servants who are prepared to lead from where they sit. Doing so is the work of community statesman, who must ultimately rely on their prudential wisdom.

Our goal in writing this book has been to inspire career public servants to use their discretion and to trust their prudential judgment to advance the public good from where they sit. This has always been a daunting task because citizens are of mixed minds on what the public good requires. With the rise of more wicked challenges and decline of trust in government, our call to action is even more daunting. While not easy, our call is really quite "old school." We are urging a return to viewing administrative leaders as stewards of the commons (Morgan, 1994; Morgan and Cook, 2014). This stewardship role may be different than elected officials and judges, but it is equally important statesmanship and state-building work. As we argued in Chapter 7, this role is characteristic of the pre-classic period of public administration that is most closely associated with the founding of the American republic. During this period, President George Washington consciously recruited members of his administrative leadership team based on their 1) competence in building a governance system; 2) their sensitivity to the needs and values of local citizens; 3) their ability to increase the reputation and trust in the larger political system; and 4) their ability to create and maintain a shared sense of common values and purpose. In short, the work of administrative leaders was not seen as simply being instrumental and loyal but as being an integral part of shaping the meaning, value and legitimacy of the political order itself. This kind of leadership is political, constitutive and value-centered (Hames, 2007; Fairholm, 2013, 2004).

Viewed from this broader perspective, administrators are what Herbert Storing calls "closet statesmen ... who are carried beyond immediate practical issues by a need to understand the deeper ground on which they rest" (Storing, 1964, 152–54; also see Morgan, Kirwan, Rohr, Rosenbloom, and Schaefer, 2010, for a further discussion of this phrase coined by Herbert Storing). As closet statesman, administrators need to be firmly planted in the political soil of the various communities they serve. The unique values, history, institutions and structures of authority of these various communities shape the nature of leadership challenges and the possibilities for successful collective action (Morgan et al., 2010). Knowing this history and assessing its applicability to the present, making sense out of what is going on, enlisting citizens in this sense-making activity, and taking action, all require an abundance of prudential judgment.

Prudential judgment is the decisive virtue that separates public administrators from others who are considered great at what they do. Our "halls of fame" are filled with the names of famous people who have been honored for their achievements, but we have no "halls of fame" that honor those skilled in prudential wisdom. This is because prudential judgment is an integral part of the ordinary work of government. It is the distinctive skill that comes from rolling up your sleeves and actively participating in the facilitation of the common good. This is what makes public service leadership unique, challenging and especially rewarding. Most important of all, it is what enables civilizations to survive and future generations to thrive.

Note

1 Our discussion here is draw from Levitin (2012, especially 40–44 and 174–76).

Bibliography

Acton, Lord. 1887. "Letter to Bishop Mandell Creighton," April 3, 1887. Acton Institute, A. Lord Acton quote archive. www.acton.org/research/lord-acton-quote-archive, accessed February 16, 2015

Adamonir, John. 2010. *Strategic Leadership: How to Think and Plan Strategically and Provide Direction*. London, UK: Kogan Page Publishers.

Adams, Guy, Bayard Catron, and Scott D.N. Cook. 1995. "Forward to the Centenary Edition." In Geoffrey Vickers (Ed.), *The Art of Judgment: A Study of Policy Making*, Newbury Park, CA: Sage.

Adams, Guy B. and Danny L. Balfour. 2004. *Unmasking Administrative Evil*. 3rd ed. Armonk, NY: M.E. Sharpe.

Adger, W. Neil. 2003. "Social Capital, Collective Action, and Adaptation to Climate Change." *Economic Geography*, 79(4): 387–404.

Agranoff, Robert. 2007. *Managing Within Networks: Adding Value to Public Organizations*. Washington, DC: Georgetown University Press.

Ajemian, Robert. 1987. "Where Is the Real George Bush?" *Time*. January26.

Alford, John. 2002. "Defining the Client in the Public Sector: A Social Exchange Perspective." *Public Administration Review*, 62(3): 337–46.

Allen, Stuart, Denise Wickwar, Fred Clark, Robert Potts, and Stephanie Snyder. 2009. *Values, Beliefs, and Attitudes: Technical Guide for Forest Service Land and Resource Management, Planning, and Decision Making*. PNW-GTR-788. Portland, OR: USDA Forest Service, PNW Research Station.

Allison, Graham T. 1971. *The Essence of Decision: Explaining the Cuban Missile Crisis*. New York, NY: HarperCollins.

American Psychological Association. 2018. "Ethical Principles of Psychologists and Code of Conduct." www.apa.org/ethics/code/index.aspx, accessed June 5, 2018.

Ammons, David N. and William C. Rivenbark. 2008. "Factors Influencing the Use of Performance Data to Improve Municipal Services: Evidence from the North Carolina Benchmarking Project." *Public Administration Review*, 68(2): 304–18.

Appleby, Paul H. 1952. *Morality and Administration in Democratic Government*. Baton Rouge, LA: Louisiana State University Press.

Arendt, Hannah. 1958. *The Human Condition*. Chicago, IL: University of Chicago Press.

Argyris, Chris. 1964. *Integrating the Individual and the Organization*. New York, NY: Wiley.

Argyris, Chris. 1999. *On Organizational Learning*. Boston, MA: Blackwell Publishers Inc.

Argyris, Chris and Donald A. Schon. 1974. *Theory in Practice: Increasing Professional Effectiveness*. San Francisco, CA: Jossey-Bass.

Aristotle. C. 1947/340 BCE. *Nichomachean Ethics*. Trans by H. Rackham, Loeb Library. ed. Cambridge, MA: Harvard University Press.

Ashby, W. Ross. 1957. *An Introduction to Cybernetics*. London, UK: Chapman and Hall.

Bachrach, Peter and Morton S. Baratz. 1970. *Power and Poverty: Theory and Practice*. Oxford, UK: Oxford University Press.

Baer, Markus, Greg R. Oldham, and Anne Cummings. 2003. "Rewarding Creativity: When does it really matter?" *The Leadership Quarterly*, 14(4): 569–86.

Banyan, Margaret. 2003. "Civic Infrastructure, Organizational Civic Capacity and Service Learning: A Community Capacity-Building Model (Doctoral dissertation, Portland State University, 2003)." *Dissertation Abstracts International*, 1: 281.

Banyan, Margaret. 2004. "Wiring Organizations for Community Governance: Characteristics of High Organizational Citizenship." *Administrative Theory and Praxis*, 26(3): 325–44.

Banyan, Margaret. 2014. "Civic Capacity Assessment Framework." In Douglas F. Morgan and Brian J. Cook (Eds), *New Public Governance: A Regime-Centered Perspective*. Armonk, NY: M.E. Sharpe.

Bao, Guoxian, Xuejun Wang, Gary Larsen, and Douglas F. Morgan. 2013. "Beyond New Public Governance: A Value-Based Global Framework for Performance Management, Governance and Leadership." *Administration and Society*, 45(4): 443–67.

Barkan, Joanne. 2013. "Plutocrats at Work: How Big Philanthropy Undermines Democracy." *Social Research: An International Quarterly*, 80(2): 635–52.

Barnard, Chester I. 1938. *Functions of the Executive*. Cambridge, MA: Harvard University Press.

Barrett, Lisa Feldman. 2017. *How Emotions Are Made*. New York, NY: Houghton Mifflin Harcourt.

Barron, David J. 1999. "The Promise of Cooley's City: Traces of Local Constitutionalism." *University of Pennsylvania Law Review*, 147(January)3: 487–611.

Bassett-Jones, Nigel. 2005. "The Paradox of Diversity Management, Creativity and Innovation." *Creativity & Innovation Management*, 14(2): 169–75.

Batie, Sandra S. 2008. "Wicked Problems and Applied Economics." *American Journal of Agricultural Economics*, 90(5): 1176–91.

Bay, Austin. 2011. *Ataturk: Lessons in Leadership from the Greatest General of the Ottoman Empire*. New York, NY: Palgrave Macmillan.

Becker, Howard S., Blanche Geer, Everett Hughes, and Anselm L. Strauss. 1961. *The Boys in White: Student Culture in Medical School*. Chicago, IL: University of Chicago Press.

Bekkers, Victor, Jurian Edelenbos, and Bram Steijn. 2011. "An Innovative Public Sector? Embarking on the Innovation Journey." In Bekkers, Victor, Jurian Edelenbos, and Bram Steijn (Eds), *Innovation in the Public Sector*. New York, NY: Palgrave Macmillan.

Bellah, Robert N., William M. Richard Madsen, Ann Swindler Sullivan, and Steven Tipton.1996/1985. *Habits of the Heart: Individualism and Commitment in American Life*. Berkeley, CA: University of California Press.

Benjamin, Martin. 1990. *Splitting the Difference: Compromise and Integrity in Ethics and Politics.* Lawrence, KS: University Press of Kansas.

Bennett, Lance W. 2012. "The Personalization of Politics: Political Identity, Social Media, and Changing Patterns of Participation." *The Annals of the American Academy of Political and Social Science,* 644(1): 20–39.

Berger, Peter and Thomas K. Luckmann. 1967. *The Social Construction of Reality.* Gardem City, NY: Doubleday Anchor.

Berger, Peter L. and Richard. J. Neuhaus. 1996. "To Empower People: From State to Civil Society." In M. Novak (Ed.), *To Empower People.* 2nd ed. Washington, DC: The Free Press.

Berry, Jeffrey M. and David F. Arons. 2003. *A Voice for Nonprofits.* Washington, DC: Brookings Institution.

Blake, Robert R. and Jane S. Mouton. 1964. *The Managerial Grid.* Houston, TX: Gulf.

Blumenthal, Richard. 1969. "The Bureaucracy: Antipoverty and the Community Action Program." In Allen P. Sindler (Ed.), *American Political Institutions and Public Policy.* Boston, MA: Little Brown & Co.

Bohn, Don. 2014. "Civic Infrastructure and Capacity Building: Lessons from the Field." In Douglas Morgan and Brian Cook (Eds.), *New Publicc Governane: A Reime-Centered Perspective.* Armonk, NY: M.E. Sharpe.

Bolman, Lee G. and Terrence E. Deal. 1997. *Reframing Organizations: Artistry, Choice, and Leadership.* 2d ed. San Francisco, CA: Jossey-Bass.

Bornstein, David. 2007. *How to Change the World: Social Entrepreneurs and the Power of New Ideas.* Cambridge, UK: Oxford University Press.

Bosman, Julie. 2015. "Iowans Question G.O.P Talk on Immigration," *New York Times,* September 4.

Boston Globe. 2014. "What Went Wrong with the Big Dig?" November 14, 2014. Boston, MA: *The Boston Globe.*

Box, Richard C. 1998. *Citizen Governance: Leading American Communities into the 21st Century.* Thousand Oaks, CA: Sage Publications.

Boyatzis, Richard E. 1982. *The Competent Manager: A Model for Effective Performance.* Hoboken, NJ: John Wiley.

Boyne, George A. 2002. "Public and Private Management: What's the Difference." *Journal of Management Studies,* 39(January)1: 97–122.

Boyte, Harry, Benjamin Barber, and Will Marshall. 1994. *Civic Declaration.* https://digitalcommons.unomaha.edu/cgi/viewcontent.cgi?referer=https://search.yahoo.com/&httpsredir=1&article=1016&context=slceciviceng, accessed June 10, 2018.

Bradberry, Travis and Jean Greaves. 2012. *Leadership 2.0.* San Diego, CA: TalentSmart.

Brainard, Lori A. and Patricia D. Siplon. 2004. "Toward Nonprofit Organization Reform in the Voluntary Spirit: Lessons from the Internet." *Nonprofit and Voluntary Sector Quarterly,* 33(3): 435–57.

Bridges, William and Susan Bridges. 2016. *Managing Transitions: Making the Most of Change.* 4th ed. Boston, MA: Da Capo Press.

Bright, Leonard. 2003. "An Empirical Investigation of the Intrinsic Reward Preferences of Washington County Oregon Employees." PhD dissertation, Portland State University.

Bright, Leonard. 2013. "Where Does Public Service Motivation Count the Most in Government Work Environments? A Preliminary Empirical Investigation and Hypotheses." *Public Personnel Management*, 42(1): 5–26.

Brinkerhoff, Derek W. and Marcus Ingle. 1989. "Integrating Blueprint and Process: A Structured Flexibility Approach to Developmental Management." *Public Administration and Development*, 9(5): 487–503.

Brinkley, Alan, Nelson W. Polsby, and Kathleen M. Sullivan. 1997. *New Federalist Papers: Essays in Defense of the Constitution.* New York, NY: W.W. Norton & Company.

Milward, H. Brinton and Keith Provan. 2000. "Governing the Hollow State." *Journal of Public Administration Research and Theory*, 10(2): 359–79.

Brookes, Stephen. 2008. "Responding to the New Public Leadership Challenge." Paper presented at the Herbert Simon 2nd Annual Conference, April, Manchester, UK.

Brookes, Stephen, and Keith Grint. 2010. *The New Public Leadership Challenge.* New York, NY: Palgrave Macmillan.

Brooks, David. 2012. *The Social Animal: The Hidden Sources of Love, Character, and Achievement.* New York, NY: Random House.

Brooks, David. 2013. "Thinking for the Future." December 14. *New York Times.* www.nytimes.com/2013/12/10/opinion/brooks-thinking-for-the-future.html, accessed February 13, 2015

Brown, Berne. 2012. *The Power of Vulnerability: Teachings of Authenticity, Connection and Courage.* Cambridge, MA: Audible.

Brown v. Board of Education of Topeka, 347 U.S. 483 (1954).

Brown, Valerie A., John A. Harris, and Jacquelin Y. Russell. 2010. *Tackling Wicked Problems: Through the Transdisciplinary Imagination.* London, UK: Routledge.

Burke, John. 1988. *Bureaucratic Responsibility.* Baltimore, MD: Johns Hopkins University Press.

Burns, James MacGregor. 2012/1978. *Leadership.* New York: NY: Open Road Media.

Burns, Nancy. 1994. *The Formation of American Local Government: Private Values in Public Institutions.* New York, NY: Oxford University Press.

Calaprice, Alice (Ed). 2000. *The Expanded Quotable Einstein.* Princeton, NJ: Princeton University Press.

Cane, Lucy. 2015. "Hannah Arendt on the Principles of Political Action". *European Journal of Political Theory*, 14 (1): 55–75.

Caprio, G., Jr, 2009. "Financial Regulation in a Changing World." Center for Development Economics. CDE Working Papers Series. Williams College.

Carnegie, Andrew. 1962/1889. "Wealth." In Edward C. Kirkland (Ed.), *The Gospel of Wealth and Other Timely Essays.* Cambridge, MA: Harvard University Press.

Carney, Eliza Newlin. 2017. "Trumps Assault on the 'Administrative State.'" *The American Prospect.* http://prospect.org/article/trump's-assault-'administrative-state, accessed June 10, 2018.

Carroll, Archie B. 1999. "Corporate Social Responsibility: Evolution of a Definitional Construct." *Business and Society*, 38(3): 268–95.

Carver, John. 1990. *Boards That Make a Difference: A New Design for Leadership in Nonprofit and Public Organizations.* 2nd ed. San Francisco, CA: Jossey-Bass.

Chan, Joseph, To-ch'ŏl Sin, and Melissa S. Williams (Eds). 2016. *East Asian Perspectives on Political Legitimacy: Bridging the Empirical-Normative Divide.* Cambridge, UK: Cambridge University Press.

Chaleff, Ira. 2003. *The Courageous Follower: Standing Up to and For our Leaders.* 2nd ed. San Francisco, CA: Berrett-Koehler.

Chambers, Chris. 2014. "A Meditation on the Value of Tools." Final posting for Masters of Public Administration PA 558 course. Spring term. Portland State University.

Child, Curtis D. and Kirsten A. Grønbjerg. 2007. "Nonprofit Advocacy Organizations: Their Characteristics and Activities." *Social Science Quarterly,* 88(1): 259–81.

Christensen, Robert K., Laurie Paarlberg, and James L. Perry. 2017. "Public Service Motivation Research: Lessons for Practice." *Public Administration Review,* 77(July/August)4: 529–41.

Citizens United v. Federal Election Commission, 558 U.S. 50 (2010).

Civic Practices Network. 2013. "Cvil Society." www.sustainable.org/creating-community/civic-engagement/532-civic-practices-network-cpn, accessed June 10, 2018.

Clean Water Services. 2017. "About US." www.cleanwaterservices.org/about-us/, accessed July, 2017.

Clinton v Cedar Rapids. 24 Iowa 455 (1868).

Cognitive Edge. 2007. "Ritual Dissent/Assent." http://newtechusa.net/wp-content/uploads/2012/02/RitualDissentMethodDocument.pdf, accessed June 6, 2014.

Cohen, Jean and Andrew Arato. 1992. *Civil Society and Political Theory.* Cambridge, MA: MIT Press.

Cohen, Michael D., James G. March, and Johan P. Olsen. 1972. "A Garbage Can Model of Organizational Choice." *Administrative Science Quarterly,* 17: 1–25.

Cohen, Roger. 2011. "Leading from Behind." *The New York Times,* October 31.

Conklin, Jeff. 2005.*Dialogue Mapping: Building Shared Understanding of Wicked Problems.* Hoboken, NJ: John Wiley & Sons.

Conley, John M. and Cynthia A. Williams. 2005–2006. "Engage, Embed, and Embellish: Theory Versus Practice in the Corporate Social Responsibility Movement." *Journal of Corporate Leadership,* 31(Fall)1: 1–38.

Cook, Brian J. 2007. *Democracy and Administration: Woodrow Wilson's Ideas and the Challenges of Public Management.* Baltimore, MD: Johns Hopkins University Press.

Cook, Brian J. 2014. *Bureaucracy and Self Government: Reconsidering the Role of Public Administration in American Politics.* 2nd ed. Baltimore, MD: Johns Hopkins University Press.

Cooley, Thomas M. 1878. *A Treatise on the Constitutional Limitations Which Rest Upon the Legislative Power of the States of the American Union.* 4th ed. Boston, MA: Little Brown & Co.

Cooper, Phillip J. 2003. *Governing by Contract: Challenges and Opportunities for Public Managers.* Washington, DC: CQ Press.

Cooper, Phillip J. 2005. "George Bush, Edgar Allan Poe, and the Use and Abuse of Presidential Signing Statements." *Presidential Studies Quarterly*, 35(3): 515–32.

Cooper, Phillip J. 2007. *Public Law and Public Administration*. 4th edition. Belmont, CA: Wadsworth Publishing.

Cooper, Phillip J. 2009. *The War Against Regulation: From Jimmy Carter to George W. Bush*. Lawrence, KS: University Press of Kansas.

Cooper, Phillip J. 2014/2002. *By Order of the President: The Use and Abuse of Executive Direct Action*. Lawrence, KS: University Press of Kansas.

Cooper, Phillip J. 2018. *Policy Tools in Policy Design*. Irvine, CA: Melvin and Leigh.

Cooper, Terry. 2004. *An Ethic of C itizenship for Public Administration*. Englewood Cliffs, NJ: Prentice Hall.

Couto, Richard A. 1999. *Making Democracy Work Better: Mediating Structures, Social Capital, and the Democratic Prospect*. Chapel Hill, NC: University of North Carolina Press.

Covey, Steven M. 2004. *The Seven Habits of Highly Effective People*. Bel Air, CA: Touchstone Press.

Covey, Steven M. 2005. *The 8th Habit: From Effectiveness to Greatness*. New York, NY: Free Press.

Covey, Steven M. 2006. *The Speed of Trust*. Washington, DC: Free Press.

Shinn, Craig.W. 1999. "Civic Capacity: Theory, Research and Practice." *Administrative Theory and Praxis*, 21 (March)1: 103–19.

Croly, Herbert. 1964. *The Promise of American Life*. New York, NY: Capricorn.

Crosby, Barbara C. 2010. "Leading in a Shared-Power World of 2010." *Public Administration Review*, 70(s1): s69–s77.

Crosby, Barbara C. and John M. Bryson. 2005. *Leadership for the Common Good: Tackling Public Problems in a Shared-Power World*. 2nd ed. San Francisco, CA: Jossey-Bass Publishers.

Cyert, Richard M. and James G. March. 1963. *A Behavioral Theory of the Firm*. Englewood Cliffs, NJ: Prentice Hall.

Daft, Richard. 1984. "Toward a Model of Organizations as Interpretation Systems." *Academy of Management Review*, 9(2): 284–95.

Daft, Richard. 1992. *Organization Theory and Design*. 4th ed. New York, NY: West.

Dahl, Robert A. 1958. "A Critique of the Ruling Elite Model." *American Political Science Review*, 52 (June): 463–69.

Dahl, Robert A. 1964. *Who Governs? Democracy and Power in an American City*. New Haven, CT: Yale University Press.

Darwin, Charles. 1859. *On the Origin of Species by Means of Natural Selection, or the Preservation of Favoured Races in the Struggle for Life*. London, UK: John Murray.

Davis, Chris and Marcus Ingle. 2013. "Bridging EMERGE Leadership and Breakthrough Innovation in Public Service: Assessment of Compatibility and Sufficiency, and a New EMERGE Tool." Presented at the Third International Conference on Public Performance and Leadership, Waseda University, Tokyo, Japan, September 14.

Davis, Nickolas and Richard Samans. 2017. World Economic Forum. Annual Meeting, Geneva Switzerland, June 22. www.weforum.org/agenda/2017/06/toward-a-human-centered-model-of-economic-growth, accessed June 10, 2018.

De Tocqueville, Alexis. 2000/1835. *Democracy in America.* Trans. and Eds Harvey Mansfield and Della Winthrop. Chicago, IL: University of Chicago Press.

Denhardt, Janet V. and Robert B. Denhardt. 2015. *The New Public Service: Serving, Not Steering.* 4th ed. London, UK: Routledge.

DePree, Max. 2008. *Leadership Jazz.* Revised ed. New York, NY: Doubleday.

Devinsky, Orrin, Martha J. Morrell, and Brent A. Vogt. 1995. "Contributions of Anterior Cingulate Cortex to Behavior." *Brain,* 118(1): 279–306.

Dhinman, Satinder. 2015. *Gandhi and Leadership: New Horizons in Exemplary Leadership.* New York, NY: Palgrave Macmillan.

Diamond, Jared. 2011. *Collapse: How Societies Choose to Fail or Succeed.* Revised ed. New York, NY: Penguin Books.

Diamond, Martin. 1979. "Ethics and Politics: The American Way." In Robert Goldwin (Ed.), *The Moral Foundations of the American Republic.* 2nd ed. Charlottesville, VA: University of Virginia Press.

Diamond, Martin, Winston Mills Fisk, and Herbert Garfinkel. 1966. The *Democratic Republic: An Introduction to American National Government.* Chicago, IL: Rand McNally.

DiMaggio, Paul and Walter Powell. 1983. "The Iron Cage Revisited: Institutional Isomorphism and Collective Rationality in Organizational Fields." *American Sociological Review,* 48(2): 147–60.

Dionne. E. J. 2016. *Why the Right Went Wrong. Conservatism: From Goldwater to Trump and Beyond.* New York, NY: Simon and Schuster.

Dionne. E. J., Norman J. Ornstein, and Thomas E. Mann. 2017. *One Nation After Trump.* New York, NY: St. Martin's Press.

Dirks, Kurt T. and Donald L. Ferrin. 2002. "Trust in Leadership: Meta-analytic Findings and Implications for Research and Practice." *Journal of Applied Psychology,* 87(4): 611–28.

Dobel, Patrick. 2002. *Public Integrity.* Baltimore, MD: John Hopkins University Press.

Dolan v. Tigard, 512 U.S. 687(1994).

Domhoff, G. William and Hoyt B. Ballard (Eds). 1968. *C. Wright Mills and the Power Elite.* Boston, MA: Beacon.

Douglas, Mary. 1986. *How Institutions Think.* Syracuse, NY: Syracuse University Press.

Dror, Yehezkel. 2005. *The Capacity to Govern: A Report to the Club of Rome.* New York, NY: Taylor & Francis.

Drucker, Peter F. 2001. *The Essential Drucker.* New York, NY: HarperCollins.

Dunsire, Andrew. 1979. *Control in a Bureaucracy.* New York, NY: St. Martin's.

Eberly, Don E. (Ed.). 1994. *Building a Community of Citizens: Civil Society in the 21st Century.* Lanham, MD: University Press of America and the Commonwealth Foundation for Public Policy Alternatives.

Edelman, Murray. 1964. *The Symbolic Uses of Politics.* Urban, IL: University of Illinois Press.

Ehrenhalt, Samuel M. 1999. *Government Employment Report 6.* Washington, DC: U.S. Government Printing Office.

Elkin, Stephen and Karol Edward Soltan (Eds). 1993. *A New Constitutionalism: Designing Political Institutions for a Good Society.* Chicago, IL: University of Chicago Press.

Elliot, Jonathan (Ed.). 1891/1836. *Debates in the Several State Conventions on the Adoption of the Federal Constitution, as Recommended by the General Convention at Philadelphia in 1787.* Five volumes. Washington, DC: Lippincott.

Emery, Fred. 1959. *Characteristics of Socio-Technical Systems.* Travistock Document 527. London, UK: Travistock.

Emery, Fred and Eric Trist. 1965. "The Causal Texture of Organizational Environments." *Human Relations,* 18(1): 21–32.

Ennis, Sharon R., Merarys Ríos-Vargas, and Nora G. Albert. 2011. "The Hispanic Population: 2010." *2010 Census Briefs,* May. www.census.gov/prod/cen2010/briefs/c2010br-04.pdf, accessed June 10, 2018.

Eoyang, Glenda H. and Royce J. Holladay. 2013. *Adaptive Action: Leveraging Uncertainty in Your Organization.* Stanford, CA: Stanford University Press.

Etzioni, Amitai. 1975. *A Comparative Analysis of Complex Organizations.* New York, NY: Free Press.

Evans, Dylan. 2015. *Risk Intelligence: How to Live with Uncertainty.* New York, NY: Free Press.

Evans, Sara and Harry Boyte. 1992. *Free Spaces: The Sources of Democratic Change in America.* Chicago, IL: University of Chicago Press.

Fadzil, Hanim Faoudziah and Harranto Nyoto. 2011. "Fiscal Decentralization after Implementation of Local Government Autonomy in Indonesia." *World Review of Business Research,* 1(2): 51–70.

Fairholm, Matthew R. 2004. "Different Perspectives on the Practice of Leadership." *Public Administration Review,* 64(September/October)5: 577–90.

Fairholm, Matthew R. 2013. *Putting Your Values to Work: Becoming the Leader Others Want to Follow.* Westport, CN: Praeger.

Fang, Zhuo, Wi Hoon Jung, Marc Korczykowski, Liiuan Luo, Kristin Prehn, Shua Xu, John A Detre, Joseph W. Kable, Diana C. Robertson, and Hengyi Rao. 2017. "Post-Conventional Moral Reasoning is Associated with Increased Ventral Striatal Activity at Rest and During Task." *Scientific Reports,* 7, Article number: 7105.

Farrel, Pam. 1996. *Woman of Influence: Ten Traits of Those Who Want to Make a Difference.* Downers Grove, IL: Intervarsity.

Fayol, Henri. 1949. *General and Industrial Management.* London, UK: Pitman.

Fiedler, Fred E. 1967. *A Theory of Leadership Effectiveness.* New York, NY: McGraw-Hill.

Fiedler, Fred E. and Joseph E. Garcia. 1987. *New Approaches to Effective Leadership: Cognitive Resources and Organizational Performance.* New York, NY: Wiley.

Field, Jonathan. 2003. *Social Capital.* London, UK: Routledge.

Fisher, Glenn W. 1997. "Some Lessons from the History of the Property Tax." *Assessment Journal,* 4(May/June)3: 40–47.

Fisher, Helen E. 1999. *The First Sex: The Natural Talents of Women and How They Are Changing the World.* New York, NY: Random House.

Fisher, Roger, William L. Ury, and Bruce Patton. 2002. *Getting to Yes: Negotiating Agreement Without Giving.* New York, NY: Penguin.

Flint, Anthony. 2015. "The Years Later, Did the Big Dig Deliver?" *The Boston Globe.* December 29 2015. www.bostonglobe.com/magazine/2015/12/29/years-later-did-big-dig-deliver/tSb8PIMS4QJUETsMpA7SpI/story.html, accessed June 14, 2018.

Floyd, Hunter. 2017/1953. *Community Power Structure*. Chapel Hill, NC: University of North Carolina.

Fogue, Andrea. 2015. "EMPA Professional Development Portfolio." Center for Public Service. Hatfield School of Government. Portland State University.

Follet, Mary Parker. 1926. "The Giving of Orders." In Henry C. Metcalf (Ed.), *Scientific Foundations of Business Administration*,. Baltimore, MD: Williams and Wilkins.

Fox, Charles and Hugh Miller. 1996. *Postmodern Public Administration: Toward Discourse*. Newbury Park, CA: Sage.

French, John RP, Bertram Raven, and D. Cartwright. 1959. "The Bases of Social Power." *Classics of Organization Theory*, 7.

Friedman, Thomas L. 2005. *The World Is Flat: A Brief History of the Twenty-first Century*. New York, NY: Farrar, Straus and Giroux.

Friedman, Thomas L. 2017. *New York Times Op Ed Articles*. June 21. www.nytimes.com/column/thomas-l-friedman, accessed June 10, 2018.

Friedrich, Carl J. 1940. "Public Policy and the Nature of Administrative Responsibility." In In C. J. Friedrich and E. S. Mason (Eds), *Public Policy*. Cambridge, MA: Harvard University Press.

Frumkin, Peter. 2002. *On Being Nonprofit: A Conceptual and Policy Primer*. Cambridge, MA: Harvard University Press.

Fukuyama, Francis. 1995. *Trust: The Social Virtues and the Creation of Prosperity*. New York, NY: Free Press.

Fullan, Michael. 2001. *Leading in a Culture of Change*. San Francisco, CA: Jossey-Bass.

Fulmer, Robert M., Stephen A. Stumpf, and Janet S. Bleak. 2009. "The Strategic Development of High Potential Leaders." *Strategy & Leadership*, 37(3): 17–22.

Gallagher, Tom. 2002. "The Founding of a New Conversation." *Journal of Leadership Education*, 1(1): ii.

Gassaway, David and Marcus Ingle. 2013. "Trust-Building Tool." Center for Public Service. Mark O. Hatfield School of Government. Portland State University.

Gibson, F., C. Shinn, and J. Locklear. 1990. *The Influence of Social Information: The Case of the Job Characteristics Model*. Salt Lake City, UT: Western Academy of Management.

Gilbert, Claire W. 1971. "Communities, Power Structures & Research Bias." *Polity*, 4(2): 218–35.

Glenn, Andrea L. and Adrian Raine. 2009. "The Immoral Brain." In Jan Verplaetse, Jelle de Schrijver, Sven Vanneste, and Johan Braeckman (Eds), *The Moral Brain: Essays on the Evolutionary and Neuroscientific Aspects of Morality*. Dordrecht: Springer.

Gilligan, Carol. 1993. *In a Different Voice: Psychological Theory and Women's Development*. 2d edition. Cambridge, MA: Harvard University Press.

Global Communities Initiative. 2018. "Global Cities Initiative." www.globalcommunities.org/globalcitiesinitiative, accessed June 14, 2018.

Goldsmith, Stephen and William D. Eggers. 2004. *Governing by Network: The New Shape of the Public Sector*. Washington, DC: Brookings.

Goleman, Daniel. 1995. *Emotional Intelligence*. New York, NY, England: Bantam Books, Inc.

Government Innovations Network. 2018. www.innovations.harvard.edu, accessed June 4, 2018.

Granovetter, Mark S. 1973. "The Strength of Weak Ties." *American Journal of Sociology*, 78(6): 1360–80.

Granovetter, Mark S. 1985. "Economic Action and Social Structure: The Problem of Embeddedness." *American Journal of Sociology*, 91(3): 481–510.

Green, Duncan. 2016. *How Change Happens*. http://how-change-happens.com/, accessed January 3, 2018.

Green, Richard T. 1993. "Prudent Constitutionalism: Hamiltonian Lessons for a Responsible Public Administration." *International Journal of Public Administration*, 16(2): 165–86.

Green, Richard T. 2002. "Alexander Hamilton: Founder of the American Public Administration." *Administration and Society*, 34(5): 541–62.

Green, Richard T. 2012. "Plutocracy, Bureaucracy, and the End of Public Trust." *Administration and Society*, 44(1): 109–43.

Green, Richard T. 2014. "Institutional History." In Douglas F. Morgan and Brian J. Cook (Eds), *New Public Governance: A Regime-Centered Perspective*. Armonk, NY: M.E. Sharpe.

Green, Richard T. 2019. *Hamilton's Public Administration*. Tuscaloosa, Alabama: The University of Alabama Press, forthcoming.

Green, Richard and Douglas Morgan. 2014. "Meeting John Rohr's Challenge: Toward a Theory of Regime Values for Local Governance." A paper presented at the ASPA Conference, Washington, DC, March 14–18.

Green, Richard T. and Robert Zinke. 1993. "The Rhetorical Way of Knowing and Public Administration." *Administration & Society*, 25(3): 317–34.

Greenberg, Gary. 1984. "Revolt at Justice." In Amy Gutman and Dennis Thompson (Eds), *Ethics and Politics: Cases and Commentary*. Chicago, IL: Nelson.

Greene, Joshua and Jonathan Haidt. 2002. "How (and Where) Does Moral Judgment Work?" *Trends in Cognitive Sciences*, 6(12): 517–23.

Grint, Keith. 2000. *The Arts of Leadership*. Oxford, UK: Oxford University Press.

Gross, Edward and Amitai Etzioni. 1985. *Organizations in Society*. Upper Saddle River, NJ: Prentice Hall.

Gulick, Luther and Lyndall Urwick (Eds). 1937. *Papers on the Science of Administration*. New York, NY: Institute of Public Administration.

Haidt, Jonathan. 2012. *The Righteous Mind: Why Good People are Divided by Politics and Religion*. New York, NY: Vintage.

Hall, Peter Dobkin. 1992. *Inventing the Nonprofit Sector and Other Essays on Philanthropy, Voluntarism, and Nonprofit Organizations*. Baltimore, MD: The Johns Hopkins University.

Halpern, Daine F. 2009. "Capital Gains." *RSA Journal*, 155(Fall)5539: 10–15.

Hames, Richard D. 2007. *The Five Literacies of Global Leadership: What Authentic Leaders Know and You Need to Find Out*. Thousand Oaks, CA: Jossey-Bass.

Hames, Richard D. 2013. Interview by Rueben van der Laan. November 22. http://rubenvanderlaan.com/2013/11/self-management-invariably-works-better-than-hierarchies-interview-with-richard-hames/, accessed May 26, 2014.

Hamilton, Alexander. 1975/1787-1789. "Letter from Alexander Hamilton to Marquis de Lafayette." January 6, 1799. In Harold C. Syrett (Ed.), *The Papers of Alexander Hamilton*, vol. 22, July 1798 – March 1799. New York, NY: Columbia University Press.

Hamilton, Alexander, James Madison, and John Jay, under pseudonym Publius. 1961/1787–1789. *The Federalist Papers*, Clinton Rossiter (Ed). New York, NY: New American Library.

Hannay, Maureen. 2009. "The Cross-Cultural Leader: The Application of Servant Leadership Theory in the International Context." *Journal of International Business & Cultural Studies*, 1(1): 1–12.

Hardin, Garrett. 1968. "Tragedy of the Commons." *Science*, 62: 1243–48.

Harvard Law Forum. 2016. *Corporate Governance and Financial Disclosure*. Harvard Law School. https://corpgov.law.harvard.edu/2016/09/, accessed September 22 2017.

Harvey, Michael, Joyce Heames, and R. Glenn Richey. 2006. "Bullying: From the Playground to the Boardroom." *Journal of Leadership and Organizational Studies*, 12(4): 1–11.

Hatry, Harry P. 2002. "Performance Measurement: Fashions and Fallacies." *Public Performance and Management Review*, 25(4): 352–58.

Hatry, Harry P. 2010. "Looking into the Crystal Ball: Performance Management over the Next Decade." *Public Administration Review*, 70(S1): s208–s211.

Hawley, Willy and James Svara. 1972. *The Study of Community Power*. Santa Barbara, CA: ABC Clio.

Haynes, Wendy. 2008. "Boston's Big Dig Project: A Cautionary Tale." *Bridgewater Review*, 27(1): 3–7.

Hazy, James K., Jeffrey A. Goldstein, and Benyamin B. Lichtenstein. 2007. *Complex Systems Leadership Theory*. Boston, MA: ISCE Publishing.

Head, Brain W. and John Alford. 2015. "Wicked Problems: Implications for Public Policy and Management." *Administration & Society*, 47(6): 711–39.

Heclo, Hugh. 2008. *On Thinking Institutionally*. Cambridge, UK: Oxford University Press.

Hefetz, Amir and Mildred Warner. 2007. "Beyond the Market vs. Planning Dichotomy: Understanding Privatisation and Its Reverse in US Cities." *Local Government Studies*, 33(4): 555–72.

Heifetz, Ronald. 1994. *Leadership Without Easy Answers*. Cambridge, MA: Harvard University Press.

Heifetz, Ronald, and Marty Linsky. 2017. *Leadership on the Line, With a New Preface: Staying Alive Through the Dangers of Change*. Cambridge, MA: Harvard Business Press.

Heifetz, Ronald, Alexander Grashow, and Marty Linsky. 2009. *The Practice of Adaptive Leadership: Tools and Tactics for Changing Your Organization and the World*. Boston, MA: Harvard Business Review Press.

Held, David. 2004. *Global Covenant: The Social Democratic Alternative to the Washington Consensus*. Cambridge, UK: Polity Press.

Helgesen, Sally. 1990. *The Female Advantage: Women's Ways of Leadership*. New York and Toronto: Doubleday Currency.

Henderson, Nan. 1999. "Preface." In Nan Henderson, Bonnie Benard, and Nancy Sharp-Light (Eds.), *Resiliency In Action: Practical Ideas for Overcoming Risks and Building Strengths in Youth, Families, & Communities*. San Diego, CA: Resiliency in Action, Inc.

Henderson, Rebecca, Ranjay Gulati, and Michael Tushman (Eds). 2016. *Leading Sustainable Change: An Organizational Perspective.* Oxford: OUP.

Hersey, Paul. 1977. *The Management of Organizational Behavior.* 3rd ed. Upper Saddle River, NJ: Prentice Hall.

Hersey, Paul and Blanchard, Kenneth. H. 1977. *Organizational Change Through Effective Leadership.* Englewood Cliffs, NJ: Prentice Hall.

Hersey, Paul and Blanchard, Kenneth. H. 1981. "So You Want to Know Your Leadership Style?" *Training and Development Journal,* 35(6): 34–54.

Hersey, Paul, Kenneth Blanchard, and Dewey Johnson. 2001. *Management of Organizational Behavior.* Upper Saddle River, NJ: Prentice Hall.

Hersh, Seymour M. 2004. *Chain of Command: The Road from 9/11 to Abu Ghraib.* New York, NY: HarperCollins.

Herzberg, Frederick. 1964. "The Motivation-Hygiene Concept and Problems of Manpower." *Personnel Administrator,* 27(January-February): 3–7.

Hickman, Tom. 2014. "EMPA Professional Development Portfolio." Center for Public Service. Hatfield School of Government. Portland State University.

Hirschman, Albert O. 1977. *The Passions and the Interests: Political Arguments for Capitalism Before Its Triumph.* Princeton, NJ: Princeton University Press.

Hirschman, Albert O. 1981. *Essays in Trespassing: Economics to Politics and Beyond.* Cambridge, UK: Cambridge University Press.

Hobbs, Frank and Nicole Stoops. 2002. "Demographic Trends in the 20th Century Census 2000," Special Report. U.S. Census Bureau, November. www.census.gov/prod/2002pubs/censr-4.pdf, accessed October 18, 2007.

Home Building & Loan Association v. Blaisdell, 290 U.S. 398, (1934).

Hood, Christopher. 1991. "A Public Management for All Seasons." *Public Administration,* 69(spring): 3–19.

Horowitz, Donald. 1977. *The Courts and Social Policy.* Washington, DC: Brookings Institution Press.

Horrigan, John. B. and Lee Rainie. 2015. *Americans' Views on Open Government Data.* Pew Research Center. April 21. www.pewinternet.org/2015/04/21/open-government-data/, accessed May 8, 2015.

House, Robert J. 1971. "A Path-Goal Theory of Leader Effectiveness." *Administrative Science Quarterly,* 16(3): 321–28.

House, Robert J. 1996. "Path-Goal Theory of Leadership: Lessons, Legacy, and a Reformulated Theory." *Leadership Quarterly,* 7(3): 323–52.

House, Robert J. and Ram N. Aditya. 1997. "The Social Scientific Study of Leadership: Quo Vadis?." *Journal of Management,* 23(3): 409–65.

House, Robert J. and T.R. Mitchell. 1974. "Path-Goal Theory of Leadership." *Journal of Contemporary Business,* 3(autumn): 81–97.

Hughes, Richard L., Katherine M Beatty, and David Dinwoodie. 2014. *Becoming a Strategic Leader: Your Role in Your Organization's Enduring Success.* 2nd ed. Thousand Oaks, CA: Jossey Bass.

Hult, Karen M. and Charles Walcott. 1990. *Governing Public Organizations: Politics, Structures, and Institutional Design.* Pacific Grove, CA: Brooks/Cole.

Human Systems Dynamic Institute. n.d. "Attractor Patterns." www.wiki.hsdinstitute.org/attractor_patterns, accessed June 7, 2018.

Humes, Karen R., Nicholas A. Jones, and Roberto R. Ramirez. 2011. "Overview of Race and Hispanic Origin: 2010." In *2010 Census Brief, March.*

Washington, DC: U.S. Census Bureau. www.census.gov/prod/cen2010/briefs/c2010br-02.pdf, accessed June 4, 2012.

Hummon, David M. 1992. *Place Attachment.* Boston, MA: Springer.

Hunter, Floyd. 2017/1953. *Community Power Structure: AStudy of Decision Makers.* Chapel Hill, NC: UNC Press Books.

Imperial, Mark. 2005. "Using Collaboration as a Governance Strategy." *Administration & Society*, 37(July)3: 281–320.

International Association of Public Participation. 2004. "IA2P Public Participation Toolkit." http://c.ymcdn.com/sites/www.iap2.org/resource/resmgr/imported/toolbox.pdf, accessed June 5, 2014.

International City County Management Association. 2006. *Municipal Form of Government, 2006 Trends in Structure, Responsibility, and Composition.* Washington, DC: ICMA. https://icma.org/sites/default/files/664_fog2006web.pdf, accessed December 29, 2017.

Isett, Kimberley R., Ines A. Mergel, Kelly LeRoux, Pamela A. Mischen, and R. Karl Rethemeyer. 2011. "Networks in Public Administration Scholarship: Understanding Where We Are and Where We Need to Go." *Journal of Public Administration Research and Theory*, 21(supplement no. 1 (January)): i157–i173.

Iyengar, Shanto and Douglas Kinder. 2012. *News that Matters.* Chicago, IL: University of Chicago.

Jaffa, Harry V. 1959. *The Crisis of the House Divided: An Interpretation of the Lincoln-Douglas Debates.* Garden, NY: Doubleday and Co.

Janac, Felicia, Jason Evjen, Ryan Edge, and Nichole Lasich. 2012. "The New Normal. Now What?" MPA student class project presentation for Dr. Marcus Ingle. Portland State University, June.

Jantsch, Erich. 1975. *Design for Evolution: Self-Organization and Planning in the Life of Human Systems.* New York, NY: George Braziller.

Jennings, Eugene Emerson. 1961. "The Anatomy of Leadership." *Management of Personnel Quarterly*, 1(1): 2–10.

Johansen, Morgen and Kelly LeRoux. 2013. "Managerial Networking in Non-profit Organizations: The Impact of Networking on Organizational and Advocacy Effectiveness." *Public Administration Review*, 73(2): 355–63.

Johnson, Donald Bruce and Kirk H. Porter. 1973. *National Party Platforms, 1840–1972.* Urbana, IL: University of Illinois Press.

Johnson, Steven. 2002. "The Transformation of Civic Institutions and Practicves in Portland, Oregon, 1960–1999." Doctoral Dissertation. Portland State University.

Johnson, Steven Reed. 2001. *Emergence.* New York, NY: Scribner.

Jones, James H. 1993. *Bad Blood.* New York, NY: Free Press.

Jørgensen, Torben Beck and Barry Bozeman. 2007. "Public Values: An Inventory." *Administration & Society*, 39(3): 354–81.

Joseph, Errol E. and Bruce Winston. 2005. "A Correlation of Servant Leadership, Leader Trust, and Organizational Trust." *Leadership & Organization Development Journal*, 26(1): 6–22.

Jowell, Jeffrey. 1975. *Law and Bureaucracy: Administrative Discretion and the Limits of Legal Action.* Port Washington, NY: Denellen.

Judge, Timothy A., Joyce E. Bono, Remus Ilies, and Megan W. Gerhardt. 2002. "Personality and Leadership: A Qualitative and Quantitative Review." *Journal of Applied Psychology*, 87(4): 765.

Kanter, Rosebeth Moss. 2017. "Surprises are the New Normal; Resilience is the New Skill." *Harvard Business Review*, July 17.

Karl, Barry. 1987. "The American Bureaucrat: A History of Sheep in Wolves' Clothing." *Public Administration Review*, 47(1): 26–34.

Kaufman, Herbert. 1960. *The Forest Ranger*. Baltimore, MD: Johns Hopkins University Press.

Kauffman, S.A. 1993. *The Origins of Order: Self-Organization and Selection in Evolution*. New York, NY: Oxford University Press.

Kelly, Rita M. 1998. "An Inclusive Democratic Polity, Representative Bureaucracies, and the New Public Management." *Public Administration Review*, 58(3): 201–08.

Kemmis, Daniel. 1990. *Community and the Politics of Place*. Norman, OK: University of Oklahoma Press.

Kendi, Ibram X. 2016. *Stamped from the Beginning: The Definitive History of Racist Ideas in America*. New York, NY: Nation Books.

Kenyon, Daphne. 2007. "The Property Tax-School Funding Dilemma." The Lincoln Institute of Land and Policy. Cambridge, MA, www.lincolninst.edu/pubs/1308_The-Property-Tax-School-Funding-Dilemma, accessed June 14, 2018.

Keohane, George. 2013. *Social Entrepreneurship for the 21ˢᵗ Century: Innovation Across the Nonprofit, Private and Public Sectors*. New York: NY: McGraw Hill.

Keohane, Robert O., and Joseph S. Nye. 1987. "Power and Interdependence Revisited." *International Organization*, 41(4): 725–53.

Keohane, Robert O. and Joseph S. Nye, Jr. 2000. "Governance in a Globalizing World," www.pols.boun.edu.tr/uploads%5Cfiles%5C1095.pdf, accessed February 14, 2015.

Kirkpatrick, Shelley A. and Edwin A. Locke. 1991. "Leadership: Do Traits Matter?" *Academy of Management Executive*, 5(2): 48–60.

Knoke, David. 1981. "Commitment and Detachment in Voluntary Associations." *American Sociological Review*, 46(2): 141–58.

Knutsen, Wenjue Lu. 2012. "Adapted Institutional Logics of Contemporary Nonprofit Organizations." *Administration and Society*, 44(8): 985–1013.

Kochhar, Rakesh. 2012. "Labor Force Growth Slows, Hispanic Share Grows." Pew Social and Demographic Trends, Pew Research Center, February 13.

Koliba, Christopher, Jack Meek, and Asim Zia. 2011. *Governance Networks in Public Administration and Public Policy*. Boca Raton, FL: CRS Press/Taylor Francis Group.

Kotter, John P. 1996. *Leading Change*. Boston, MA: Harvard Business School Press.

Kotter, John. 2012. *Leading Change*. Boston, MA: Harvard Business Review Press.

Kotter, John. 2014. *Accelerate: Building Strategic Agility for a Faster-Moving World*. Boston, MA: Harvard Business Review Press.

Kouzes, James and Barry Posner. 2017. *The Leadership Challenge: How to Make Extraordinary Things Happen in Organizations*. 6th Ed. Hoboken, NJ: John Wiley & Sons, Inc.

Kramer, Roderick. 2006. "The Great Intimidators." *Harvard Business Review*, February, 90.

Kretzmann, John and John P. McKnight. 1996. "Assets-based Community Development." *National Civic Review*, 85(4): 23–29.

Kuhn, Thomas. 1977. *The Essential Tension: Selected Studies in Scientific Tradition and Change.* Revised Edition. Chicagon, IL: University of Chicago Press.

Kurtz, Cynthia F. and David J. Snowden. 2003. "The New Dynamics of Strategy: Sense-making in a complex and complicated world." *IBM Systems Journal*, 42(3): 462–83.

Lane, Larry. 1988. "Individualism and Public Administration: The Implications of American Habits of the Heart." *Administration and Society*, 20(May)1: 3–45.

Larsen, Gary L. 2008. "Emerging Governance at the Edge of Constrained Federalism: Public Administrators at the Frontier of Democracy". Doctorate of Philosophy, Portland State University, Portland, Oregon. http://gradworks.umi.com/33/43/3343771.html, accessed July 14, 2010.

Larsen, Gary L. 2014. "Forging Vertical and Horizontal Integration in Public Administration Leadership and Management: Theory and Case Study." In Douglas Morgan and Brian Cook (Eds.), *New Public Governance: A Regime Perspective.* Armonk, NY: M.E. Sharpe.

Larsen, Gary.L., Robert Lynn, David Kapaldo, and John Fedkiw. 1990. *Analysis of an Emerging Timber Supply Disruption.* (FS-460). Washington D.C.: USDA Forest Service.

Lauria, Mickey (Ed). 1997. *Reconstructing Urban Regime Theory: Regulating Local Government in a Global Economy.* Thousand Oaks, CA: Sage.

Lelea, Margareta Amy, Guyo Malicha Roba, Anja Christinck, and Brigitte Kaufmann. 2015. "All Relevant Stakeholders: A Literature Review of Stakeholder Analysis to Support Inclusivity of Innovation Processes in Farming and Food Systems." In *12th European IFSA Symposium.*

Leo, Christopher. 1998. "Regional Growth Management Regime: The Case of Portland, Oregon." *Journal of Urban Affairs*, 20(4): 363–94.

LeRoux, Kelly (Ed.). 2007. *Service Contracting: A Local Government Guide.* 2nd ed. Washington, DC: ICMA Press.

LeRoux, Kelly, Paul W. Brandenburger, and Sanjay K. Pandey. 2010. "Interlocal Services Cooperation in U.S. Cities: A Social Network Explanation." *Public Administration Review*, 70(March/April)2: 268–78.

LeRoux, Kelly and Jered B. Carr. 2007. "Explaining Local Government Cooperation on Public Works: Evidence from Michigan." *Public Works Management & Policy*, 12(1): 344–58.

Levi, Edward. 1949. *An Introduction to Legal Reasoning.* Chicago, IL: University of Chicago Press.

Levine, Charles. 1984. "Citizenship and Service Delivery: The Promise of Coproduction." *Public Administration Review*, 44(March): 178–87.

Levitin, Daniel. 2014. *The Organized Mind: Thinking Straight in the Age of Information Overload.* Hialeah, FL: Dutton Press.

Leys, Simon. 1986. *The Burning Forest: Essays on Chinese Culture and Politics.* New York, NY: Holt, Rinehart, and Winston.

Leys, Wayne. 1943. "Ethics and Administrative Discretion." *Public Administration Review*, 3(winter)1: 10–23.

Lichtenstein, Benyamin B. and Donde Ashmos Plowman. 2009. "The Leadership of Emergence: A Complex Systems Leadership Theory of Emergence at Successive Organizational Levels." *The Leadership Quarterly*, 20(4): 617–30.

Lichtenstein, Benyamin B., Mary Uhl-Bien, Russ Marion, Anson Seers, James Douglas Orton, and Craig Schreiber. 2006. "Complexity Leadership Theory: An Interactive Perspective on Leading in Complex Adaptive Systems." *Emergence: Complexity and Organization*, 8(4): 2–12.

Lindblom, Charles. 1959. "The Science of Muddling Through." *Public Administration Review*, 19(2): 79–85.

Lindblom, Charles. 1965. *The Intelligence of Democracy: Decision-Making Through Mutual Adjustment*. New York, NY: Free Press.

Lowi, Theodore. 1979. *The End of Liberalism: The Second Republic of the United States*, 2nd ed. New York, NY: Norton.

Luke, Jeffrey S. 1998. *Catalytic Leadership: Strategies for an Interconnected World*. San Francisco, CA: Jossey-Bass.

Lynn, Lawrence. Jr. 1998. "The New Public Management: How to Transform a Theme into a Legacy." *Public Administration Review*, 58(3): 231–37.

MacIntyre, Alasdair. 1984. *After Virtue*. 2d ed. Notre Dame, IN: Notre Dame University Press.

Mackenzie, Dana and Jennifer Tzar. 2002. "The Science of Surprise." *Discover Magazine*, February 1. http://discovermagazine.com/2002/feb/featsurprise, accessed May 29, 2014.

Magis, Kristen, Marcus Ingle and Ngo Huy Duc. 2014. "EMERGE: Public Leadership for Sustainable Development." In Douglas F. Morgan and Brian J. Cook (Eds), *New Public Governance: A Regime-Centered Perspective*. Armonk, NY: M.E. Sharpe.

Malloch, Kathy, and Tim Porter-O'Grady. 2009. *The Quantum Leader: Applications for the New World of Work*. Burlington, MA: Jones & Bartlett Learning.

Mango, Andrew. 2000. *Atatürk*. Woodstock, NY: Overlook Press.

Mann, Michael. 1986. *The Sources of Social Power: A History of Power from the Beginning to A.D. 1760*. Vol. 1. New York, NY: Cambridge University Press.

Manzo, Lynne C. and Patrick Devine-Wright (Eds). 2013. *Place Attachment*. London, UK: Routledge.

Marbach, Peter and Janet Cook. 2005. *Mount Hood, The Heart of Oregon*. Berkley, CA: Graphic Arts Books.

Marche, Sunny and James McNiven. 2003. "E-Government and E-Governance: The Future Isn't What It Used To Be." *Canadian Journal of Administrative Sciences*, 20(March)1: 1–95.

Marken, Joanne. 2013. "Plutocrats at Work: How Big Philanthropy Undermines Democracy." *Dissent*. www.dissentmagazine.org/article/plutocrats-at-work-how-big-philanthropy-undermines-democracy, accessed May 2, 2015.

Mayo, Elton. 1933. *The Human Problems of an Industrial Civilization*. New York, NY: Macmillan.

McCullough, Thomas E. 1991. *The Moral Imagination and Public Life*. Chatham, NJ: Chatham House.

McGrandle, Jocelyn and Frank Ohemeng. 2017. "The Conundrum of Absenteeism in the Canadian Public Service: A Wicked Problem Perspective." *Canadian Public Administration*, 66(June)2: 215–40.

McGregor, Douglas. 1960. *The Human Side of Enterprise*. New York, NY: McGraw-Hill.

McGregor, Eugene B. Jr. and Richard Sundeen. 1984. "The Great Paradox of Democratic Citizenship and Public Personnel Administration." *Public*

Administration Review, 44(March)Special Issue: Citizenship and Public Administration: 126–35.

McKnight, John and John Kretzmann. 1993. *Building Communities from the Inside Out: A Path Toward Finding and Mobilizing a Community's Assets*. Chicago, IL: ACTA Publications.

McNamara, Carter. 2017. "Basics of Developing Mission and Value Statements." Free Management Library. https://managementhelp.org/strategicplan ning/mission-vision-values.htm, accessed January 2, 2018.

Meade, Edward J. 1991. "Foundations and the Public Schools: An Impressionistic Retrospective, 1960–1990." *The Phi Delta Kappan*, 73(Oct.)2: K1–K12.

Merton, Robert K. 1940. "Bureaucratic Structure and Personality." *Social Forces*, 18(4): 560–68.

Meyer, William Jay. 1975. "Political Ethics and Political Authority." *Ethics*, 86(1): 61–69.

Micheli, Pietro and Neely, Andy. 2010. "Performance Measurement in the Public Sector in England: Searching for the Golden Thread." *Public Administration Review*, 70(4), 591–600.

Milkis, Sidney. 1993. *The President and the Parties: The Transformation of the American Party System since the New Deal*. New York, NY: Oxford University Press.

Miller, Sandra, Craig Shinn and William. Bentley. 1994. *Rural Resource Management: Problem Solving for the Long Run*. Ames, IA: Iowa State University Press.

Milligan, Melinda J. 1998. "Interactional Past and Potential: The Social Construction of Place Attachment."*Symbolic interaction*, 21(1): 1–33.

Milliken, Francis and Luis Martins. 1996. "Searching for Common Threads: Understanding the Multiple Effects of Diversity in Organizational Groups." *Academy of Management Review*, 21(2): 402–33.

Mintzberg, Henry. 1979. *The Structure of Organizations*. Englewood Cliffs, NJ: Prentice Hall.

Mintzberg, Henry. 1983. *Structure in Fives: Designing Effective Organizations*. Upper Saddle River, NJ: Prentice Hall.

Mishel, Lawrence, Jared Bernstein, and Sylvia Allegretto. 2005. *The State of Working America, 2004–2005*. Ithaca, NY: Cornell University Press.

Missouri River Railroad v. Lewis, 101 U.S. 22 (1879).

Moe, Ronald and Kevin Kosar. 2005. *The Quasi-Government: Hybrid Organizations with Both Government and Private Sector Legal Characteristics*. Washington, DC: Congressional Research Service.

Moe, Ronald C. and Robert S. Gilmour. 1995. "Rediscovering Principles of Public Administration: The Neglected Foundation of Public Law." *Public Administration Review*, 55(2): 135–46.

Moe, Terry. 1994. "Integrating Politics and Organizations: Positive Theory and Public Administration." *Journal of Public Administration Research and Theory*, 4(1): 17–25.

Mogren, Eric T. 2011. "Governance in the United States Columbia River Basin: an Historical Analysis." PhD dissertation, Portland State University

Montapert, Alfred. 1986. *Words of Wisdom to Live By*. Los Angeles, CA: Borden Publishing.

Montjoy, Robert S. and Douglas J. Watson. 1995. "A Case for Reinterpreted Dichotomy of Politics and Administration as a Professional Standard in

Council-Manager Government." *Public Administration Review*, 55(3): 231–39.

Moore, Mark. 1994. "Public Value as the Focus of Strategy." *Australian Journal of Public Administration*, 53(3): 296–303.

Moore, Mark. 1995. *Creating Public Value: Strategic Management in Government*. Cambridge, MA: Harvard University Press.

Morgan, Douglas. 1984. "Private Policy in Search of Public Authority: EPA and Field Burning in the Willamette Valley." Paper presented at the Western Political Science Association, Sacramento, California, April.

Morgan, Douglas F. and Brian J. Cook. 2014. *New Public Governance: A Regime-Centered Perspective*. Armonk, NY: M.E. Sharpe.

Morgan, Douglas. F. and Henry D. Kass. 1993. "The American Odyssey of the Career Public Service: The Ethical Crises of Role Reversal." In H. George Frederickson (Ed.), *Ethics and Public Administration*. Armonk, NY: M.E. Sharpe, Inc.

Morgan, Douglas and John Rohr. 1986. "Traditional Responses to American Administrative Discretion." In Douglas H. Shumavon and H. Kenneth Hibbeln (Eds), *Administrative Discretion and Public Policy Implementation*. Westport, CT: Praeger.

Morgan, Douglas, Kelly G. Bacon, Ron Bunch, Charles D. Cameron, and Robert Deis. 1996. "What Middle Managers Do in Local Government: Stewardship of the Public Trust and Limits of Reinventing Government." *Public Administration Review*, 56(4): 359–66.

Morgan, Douglas F., Kent A. Kirwan, John A. Rohr, David H. Rosenbloom, and David Lewis Schaefer. 2010. "Recovering, Restoring, and Renewing the Foundations of American Public Administration: The Contributions of Herbert J. Storing." *Public Administration Review*, 70(4): 621–33.

Morgan, Douglas F., Richard Green, Craig W. Shinn, and Kent S. Robinson. 2013/2008. *Foundations of Public Service*. Armonk, NY: M.E. Sharpe.

Morgan, Douglas F., Craig W. Shinn and Brian J. Cook. 2014. "Epilogue." In Douglas F. Morgan and Brian J. Cook (Eds), *New Public Governance: A Regime-Centered Perspective*. Armonk, NY: M.E. Sharpe.

Morgan, Douglas, Kent Robinson, Dennis Strachota, and James Hough. 2014. *Budgeting for Local Governments and Communities*. Armonk, NY: M.E. Sharpe.

Morgan, Douglas, Kent Robinson, Dennis Strachota, and James Hough. 2015. *Budgeting for Local Governments and Communities*. Armonk, NY: M.E. Sharpe.

Morgan, Gareth. 2006/1986. *Images of Organizations*. Thousand Oaks, CA: Sage.

Mosley, Jennifer E. 2011. "Institutionalization, Privatization, and Political Opportunity: What Tactical Choices Reveal About the Policy Advocacy of Human Service Nonprofits." *Nonprofit and Voluntary Sector Quarterly*, 40(3): 435–57.

Moynihan, Donald P. and Sanjay K. Pandey. 2005. "Testing How Management Matters in an Era of Government by Performance Management." *Journal of Public Administration Research and Theory*, 15(3): 421–39.

Muramatsu, Michio, Farrukh Iqbal, and Ikuo Kume (Eds). 2001. *Local Government Development in Post-war Japan*. Oxford, UK: Oxford University Press.

Myantt, Phusyn. 2007. "Personal discussion with Dr. Ingle on Ph.D. dissertation." March.

Nagourney, Adam, Jack Healy, and Nelson L. Schwartz. 2015. "California Drought Tests History of Endless Growth." *New York Times*. April 4. www. nytimes.com/2015/04/05/us/california-drought-tests-history-of-endless-growth.html, accessed December 28, 2017.

Napier, Nancy K., Dang Le Nguyen Vu, and Quan Hoang Vuong. 2012. "It Takes Two to Tango: Entrepreneurship and Creativity in Troubled Times – Vietnam 2012." https://scholar.google.com/scholar?hl=en≈sdt=0% 2C38&q=Dang+and+Napier++%E2%80%9CIt+takes+two+to+tango%3A +Entrepreneurship+and+creativity+in+troubled+times+%E2%80%93+Viet nam+2012%E2%80%9D.+Sociology+Study%2C+2%289%29%3A+662% E2%80%93674.&btnG=, accessed January 3, 2018.

National Civic League. 1996. *Survey of Forms of Government*. Washington, DC: Natiopnal Civic League.

National Council of State Governments. 2010. "2010–2011 Policies for the Jurisdiction of the Budgets and Revenue Committee." State-Federal Relations and Standing Committees, Budget and Revenue Standing Committee. www. ncsl.org/default.aspx?TabID=773&tabs=855,20,632#855, accessed August 8, 2011.

National Council of State Governments. 2017. *Mandate Monitor*. www.ncsl.org/ ncsl-in-dc/standing-committees/budgets-and-revenue/mandate-monitor-over view.aspx, accessed October 18, 2017.

Neustadt, Richard E. and Ernest R. May. 1986. *Thinking in Time: The Uses of History for Decision Makers*. New York, NY: Free Press.

Nishishiba, Masami, Margaret Banyan, and Douglas Morgan. 2012. "Looking Back on the Founding: Civic Engagement Traditions in the United States." In Hindy Lauer Schachter and Kaifeng Yang (Eds), *The State of Citizen Participation in America*. New York, NY: Information Age Publishing.

Nishishiba, Masami, Marcus Ingle, Hisao Tsukamoto, and Mari Kobayashi. 2006. *Project Management Toolkit: A Strategic Framework for New Local Governance*. (In Japanese and English). Tokyo, Japan: The Tokyo Foundation.

Nonaka, Ikujiro. 2010. "Cultivating Leaders with Practical Wisdom: Scrum and Ba Building." www.slideshare.net/hiranabe/agilejapan2010-keynote-by-iku jiro-nonaka-phronetic-leadership, accessed December 28, 2017.

Norden, Eric. 1971. "Interview with Albert Speer." *Playboy*, 18(June)6: 69–96, 168, 190–203.

Nye, Joseph. 2004. "Soft Power and American Foreign Policy." *Political Science Quarterly*, 119(2): 255–70.

Nye, Joseph. 2008. *The Powers to Lead*. London, UK: Oxford University Press.

O'Dowd, and Jerome T. Barrett. 2005. *Interest-Based Bargaining: A User's Guide*. CreateSpace Independent Publishing Platform. Toronto, Canada: Tranfford Publishing.

O'Flynn, Janine. 2007. "From New Public Management to Public Value: Paradigm Change and Managerial Implications." *The Australian Journal of Public Administration*, 66(3): 353–56.

O'Leary, Rosemary. 2006. *The Ethics of Dissent: Managing Guerrilla Government*. Washington, DC: CQ Press.

O'Reilly, Charles A. III and Michael L. Tushman. 2013. "Organizational Ambidexterity: Past, Present and Future." *SSRM Electronic Journal*, 27(4). www.

hbs.edu/faculty/Publication%20Files/O%27Reilly%20and%20Tushman%20AMP%20Ms%20051413_c66b0c53-5fcd-46d5-aa16-943eab6aa4a1.pdf, accessed December 28, 2017.

O'Toole, Laurence. 1997. "Treating Networks Seriously: Practical and Research Based Agendas in Public Administration". *Public Administration Review*, 57(1): 45–52.

OECD (Organization for Economic Co-operation and Development). 2003. *Managing Decentralisation: A New Role for Labour Market Policy*. Local Economic and Employment Development (Program). Paris, France: OECD Publishing.

Okun, Arthur. 1975. *Equality and Efficiency: The Big Tradeoff*. Washington, DC: Brookings Institution.

Olivier, Serrat. 2017. *Innovation in the Public Sector. Knowledge Solutions: Tools, Methods, and Approaches to Drive Organizational Performance*. Singapore: Springer Press.

Olsen, Johan. P. 2001. "Grabage Cans: New Institutionalism and the Study of Politics." *American Political Science Review*, 95(01): 191–98.

OMB (Office of Management and Budget). 2002. *The President's Management Agenda*. www.whitehouse.gov/omb/budget/fy2002/mgmt.pdf, accessed April 10, 2013.

Omnibus Public Land Management Act of 2009, Pub. L. No. 111-11, Subtitle C–Mt. Hood Wilderness, Oregon, § 1201–1207, 123 Stat. 992 (2009).

Oregon Biodiversity Information Center. 2012. *Rare, Threatened, and Endangered Species of Oregon*. Portland State University. http://orbic.pdx.edu/rte-species.html, accessed April 4, 2013.

Osborne, David and Ted Gaebler. 1993. *Reinventing Government*. New York, NY: Plume.

Osborne, David and Peter Hutchinson. 2004. *The Price of Government: Getting the Results We Need in an Age of Permanent Fiscal Crisis*. New York, NY: Basic Books.

Osborne, Stephen P. 2008. *The Third Sector in Europe: Prospects and Challenges*. London, UK: Routledge.

Osborne, Stephen (Ed.). 2010. *The New Public Governance? Emerging Perspectives on the Theory and Practice of Public Governance*. London, UK: Routledge.

Østergaard, Christian R., Bram Timmermans, and Kari Kristinsson. 2011. "Does a Different View Create Something New? The Effect of Employee Diversity on Innovation." *Research Policy*, 40(3): 500–09.

Ott, J. Steven. 1989. *The Organizational Culture Perspective*. Chicago, IL: Dorsey.

Ozawa, Connie (Ed.). 2005. *The Portland Edge: Challenges and Successes in Growing Communities*. Washington, DC: Island Press.

Page, Scott E. 2007. "Making the Difference: Applying a logic of diversity." *Academy of Management Perspectives*, 21: 6–20.

Page, Scott E. 2010. *Diversity and Complexity*. Princeton, NJ: Princeton University Press.

Pansardi, Pamela. 2012. "Power to and Power Over: Two Distinct Concepts." *Journal of Political Power*, 5(April)1: 73–9.

Pascale, Richard, Jerry Sternin, and Monique Sternin. 2010. *The Power of Positive Deviance*. Boston, MA: Harvard Business School Publishing.

People ex rel. Le Roy v. Hurlbut, 24 Michigan. 44, 107–08 (1871) (Cooley, J. concurring).

Perrow, Charles. 1986. *Complex Organizations: A Critical Essay.* New York, NY: McGraw-Hill.

Perry, James L. and Annie Hondeghem. 2008. *Motivation in Public Management.* Oxford, UK: Oxford University Press..

Perry, James L. and Lois Recascino Wise. 1990. "The Motivational Bases of Public Service." *Public Administration Review*, 50(May): 367–73.

Perry, James, Annie Hondeghem, and Lois Wise. 2010. "Revisiting the Motivational Bases of Public Service: Twenty Years of Research and an Agenda for the Future." *Public Administration Review*, 70(5): 681–90.

Peter, Laurence J. 1982. *Peter's Almanac.* New York, NY: William Morrow.

Peters, B. Guy, Jon Pierre, and Desmond S. King. 2005. "The Politics of Path Dependency: Political Conflict in Historical Institutionalism." *The Journal of Politics*, 67(4): 1275–300.

Peters, Thomas J. and Robert H. Waterman, Jr. 1982. *In Search of Excellence.* New York, NY: Harper & Row.

Pew Research Center. 2016. "Social Media Update." November 11. www. pewinternet.org/2016/11/11/social-media-update-2016/, accessed November 10, 2017.

Pew Research Center. 2017. "10 demographic trends that are shaping the U.S. and the world." March 30. www.pewresearch.org/fact-tank/2016/03/31/10-demographic-trends-that-are-shaping-the-u-s-and-the-world, accessed October 18, 2017.

Picone, Guido and Fernardo Tesson. 2006. *Rational Choice and Deliberation: A Theory of Discourse Failure.* Cambridge, UK: Cambridge University Press.

Pirsig, Robert. 2006. *Zen and the Art of Motorcycle Maintenance.* New York, NY: Harper Torch.

Pope, Alexander. 1871. *Essay on Man.* Gloucestershire, England: Clarendon Press.

Powell, Walter W. and Paul J. DiMaggio. 1991. *The New Institutionalism in Organizational Analysis.* Chicago, IL: University of Chicago Press.

Prior, Markus. 2005. "News vs. Entertainment: How Increasing Media Choice Widens Gaps in Political Knowledge and Turnout." *American Journal of Political Science*, 49(3): 577–92.

Pritchett, C. Herman. 1968. *The American Constitution.* 2d ed. New York: McGraw-Hill.

Project Management Institute. 2012. "Frequently Asked Questions: What is Agile?" www.pmi.org/~/media/Files/PDF/Agile/Agile%20Certification% 20Integrated%20Services%20FAQ%20IT%202011-001%200%20_External %20Version_.ashx, accessed June 1, 2014.

Provan Keith G. and Robin H. Lemaire. 2012. "Core Concepts and Key Ideas for Understanding Public Sector Organizational Networks: Using Research to Inform Scholarship and Practice." *Public Administration Review*, 72(Sept/ Oct)5: 638–48.

Provan, Keith and H. Brinton Milward. 2001. "Do Networks really Work? A Framework for Evaluating Public-Sector Organizational Networks." *Public Administration Review*, 61(4): 414–23.

Provan, Keith G. and Patrick Kenis. 2008. "Modes of Network Governance: Structure, Management and Effectiveness." *Journal of Public Administration Research and Theory*, 18(2): 229–52.

Putnam, Robert. D. 2000. *Bowling Alone: The Collapse and Revival of American Community*. New York, NY: Simon & Schuster.

Putnam, Robert D. and Lewis M. Feldstein, with Don Cohen. 2003. *Better Together: Restoring the American Community*. New York, NY: Simon and Schuster.

Quinn, Robert E. 2004. *Building the Bridge As You Walk on It: Strategies for Leading Change*. San Francisco, CA: Jossey-Bass.

Raine, Adrian and Yaling Yang. 2006. "Neural Foundations to Moral Reasoning and Antisocial Behavior." *Social Cognitive and Affective Neuroscience*, 1(3): 203–13.

Rainey, Hal. 2014. *Understanding and Managing Public Organizations*. 5th ed. San Francisco, CA: Jossey-Bass.

Rath, Tom and Barry Conchie. 2017/2008. *Strengths Based Leadership*. New York, NY: Gallup press.

Rebuilding Civil Society. 1995. "A Symposium." *The New Democrat*, 7(March-April): 2.

Reddin, William. 1970. *Managerial Effectiveness*. New York, NY: McGraw-Hill.

Regan, Helen B. and Gwen H. Brooks. 1995. *Out of Women's Experience: Creating Relational Leadership*. Thousand Oaks, CA: Corwin.

Reich, Robert. 1992. *The Work of Nations: Preparing Ourselves for 21st Century Capitalism*. New York, NY: Vintage.

Reid, Elizabeth. 1999. "Nonprofit Advocacy and Political Participation." In E.C. Eugene (Ed.), *Nonprofits and Government: Collaboration and Conflict*. Washington, DC: Urban Institute Press.

Richardson, James D (Ed.). 1899. *A Compilation of the Messages and Papers of the Presidents*. Vol. 2. Washington, DC: U.S. Government Printing Office.

Ride Connection. 2013. "Ride Connection: Giving the Gift of Mobility." www. rideconnection.org/Ride/home.aspx, accessed May 26, 2017.

Rijs, Jacob. 1890. *How the Other Half Lives*. New York, NY: Charles Scribner and Sons.

Riordon, William L. 1963. *Plunkitt of Tammany Hall*. New York, NY: E.P. Dutton.

Risen, James. 2015. "American Psychological Association Bolstered C.I.A. Torture Program, Report Says". *New York Times*, April 30. www.nytimes.com/2015/05/01/us/report-says-american-psychological-association-collaborated-on-torture-justification.html, accessed June 6, 2018.

Rittel, Horst W.J. and Melvin M. Webber. 1973. "Dilemmas in a General Theory of Planning." *Policy Sciences*, 4(2): 155–69.

Roberts, Barbara. 2002. "Presentation to Legacy Leadership Program Participants." September 2002, Hatfield School of Government, Portland, Oregon.

Robinson, Alexandra, Angela D. Allen, Dana M. Walker, Derek W.M. Barker, Foday Sulimani, and Zach VanderVeen. 2011. *Research on Civic Capacity: An Analysis of Kettering Literature and Related Scholarship*. Washington, DC: Kettering Foundation.

410   *Bibliography*

Robinson, Kent. 2004. "The Contribution of Social Trust and Reliance to Administrative Process." PhD diss., February. Source DAI/A 65-10, Publication No. 3150620. http://gradworks.umi.com/31/50/3150620.html.

Robinson, Kent S. and Douglas F. Morgan. 2014. "Local Government as Polity Leadership: Implications for New Public Governance." In Douglas F. Morgan and Brian J. Cook (Eds), *New Public Governance: A Regime-Centered Approach*. Armonk, NY: M.E. Sharpe, Inc.

Rock, David. 2009. *Your Brain at Work*. New York, NY: Harper.

Rodriguez, Richard. 2003. *Brown: The Last Discovery of America*. East Rutherford, NJ: Penguin.

Roe v. Wade, 410 U.S. 113 (1973).

Roethlisberger, Frank J. and William J. Dickson. 1939. *Management and the Worker*. Cambridge, MA: Harvard University Press.

Rohr, John A. 1981. "Financial Disclosures: Power in Search of Policy." *Public Personnel Management*, 10: 29–40.

Rohr, John A. 1989. *Ethics for Bureaucrats: An Essay on Law and Values*. 2nd ed. New York, NY: Marcel-Dekker.

Rohr, John A. 1995. *Founding Republics in France and America: A Study in Constitutional Governance*. Lawrence, KA: University Press of Kansas.

Roosevelt, Theodore. 1898. "Address at the Opening of the Gubernatorial Campaign. New York City, October 5." In *Theodore Roosevelt: Letters and Speeches* (Louis Achinincloss, Ed.) 1st edition (2004). Library of America.

Rosenau, James N. 1998. "Governance and Democracy in a Globalizing World." In Daniele Archibugi, David Held, and Martin Kohler (Eds), *Reimagining Political Community*. Stanford, CA: Stanford University Press.

Rosenbloom, David H. 2003. *Administrative Law for Public Managers*. Boulder, CO: Westview Press.

Rosenbloom, David H. and Robert S. Kravchuk. 2005. *Public Administration: Understanding Management, Politics, and Law in the Public Sector*. 6th ed. Boston, MA: McGraw Hill.

Rosenthal, Cindy Simon. 1998. *When Women Lead: Integrative Leadership in State Legislatures*. New York, NY: Oxford University Press.

Ryan, Kathrine and Abed Ali. 2013. *The New Government Leader: Mobilizing Agile Public Leadership in Disruptive Times*. West Lake, TX: Deloitte University Press.

Sahni, Nikhil, Maxwell Wessel, and Clayton Christensen. 2013. "Unleashing Breakthrough Innovation in Government." *Stanford Social Innovation Review*, 3(summer). www.ssireview.org/articles/entry/unleashing_breakthrough_innovation_in_government, accessed April 16, 2014.

Salamon, Lester. 1999. *America's Nonprofit Sector: A Primer*. 2nd ed. New York, NY: The Foundation Center.

Salamon, Lester. 2002. *The Tools of Government: A Guide to the New Governance*. New York, NY: Oxford University Press.

Salamon, Lester. 2012. *The State of Nonprofit America*. 2nd ed. Washington, DC: Brookings Institution Press.

Sandy River Basin Partners. 2007. *The Wild Legacy of the Sandy River Basin*. www.sandyriverbasinpartners.org, accessed April 10, 2013.

Sanger, Mary Bryna. 2008. "From Measurement to Management: Breaking through the Barriers to State and Local Performance." *Public Administration Review*, 68(S1): s70–s85.

Sathe, Vijay. 1985. *Culture and Related Corporate Realities*. Homewood, IL: Richard D. Irwin.

Saulny, Susan. 2011. "Census Data Presents Rise in Multiracial Population of Youths." *New York Times*, March 24, A3.

Saxena, Kul Bhushan Chandra. 2005. "Towards Excellence in E-governance." *International Journal of Public Sector Management*, 18(6): 498–513.

Sayre, Wallace. 1958. "Reminiscences of Wallace Stanley Sayre: Lecture." New York, NY: Columbia University.

Schambra, William. 1995. "By The People: The Old Values of the New Citizenship." *Policy Review*, 84(2): 101–13.

Scharmer, C. Otto. 2009. *Theory U: Learning from the future as it emerges*. San Francisco, CA: Berrett-Koehler Publishers.

Schein, Edgar H. 1985. *Organizational Culture and Leadership*. San Francisco, CA: Jossey-Bass.

Schein, Edgar H. 1993. *Organizational Culture and Leadership*. 2d ed. San Francisco, CA: Jossey-Bass.

Schmidt, Mary R. 1993. "Grout: Alternative Kinds of Knowledge and Why They are Ignored." *Public Administration Review*, 53(November/December) 6: 525–30.

Schmitt, Eric. 2014. "In Battle to Defang ISIS, U.S. Targets Its Psychology." *New York Times*. December 29. www.nytimes.com/2014/12/29/us/politics/in-battle-to-defang-isis-us-targets-its-psychology-.html, accessed June 13, 2018.

Schwab, Klaus. 2017. *The Fourth Industrial Revolution*. New York, NY: Crown Business.

Schwartz, Barry. 2005. *The Paradox of Choice: Why More Is Less*. New York, NY: Harper Perennial.

Scott, William G. 1992. *Chester I. Barnard and the Guardians of the Managerial State*. Lawrence, KA: University of Kansas Press.

Segerstrom, Suzanne C. and Lise Nes Solberg. 2006. "When Goals Conflict but People Prosper: The Case of Dispositional Optimism." *Journal of Research in Personality*, 40(5): 675–93.

Selznick, Philip. 1949. *TVA and the Grass Roots*. Berkeley, CA: University of California Press.

Selznick, Philip. 1957. *Leadership in Administration: A Sociological Interpretation*. Evanston, IL: Row, Peterson.

Selznick, Philip. 1992. *The Moral Commonwealth: Social Theory and the Promise of Community*. Berkeley, CA: University of California Press.

Sendak, Maurice. 1971. *In the Night Kitchen*. New York, NY: HarperCollins.

Senge, Peter M. 2015/1990. *The Fifth Discipline: The Art and Practice of the Learning Organization*. New York, NY: Doubleday.

Senge, Peter, Hal Hamilton, and John Kania. (2015). "The dawn of system leadership." *Stanford Social Innovation Review*, 13(1): 27–33.

Sergiovanni, Thomas A. and John E. Corbally (Eds). 1984. *Leadership and Organizational Culture*. Urbana, IL: University of Illinois Press.

Shafritz, Jay M. and Albert C. Hyde. 1992. *Classics of Public Administration*. Belmont, CA: Brooks/Cole Publishing Company.

Shair-Rosenfield, Sarah, Liesbet Hooghe, William R. Kenan, and Gary Marks. 2010. "Regional Authority in Indonesia, Malaysia, the Philippines, South Korea and Thailand from 1950 to 2010." Paper presented to the 2012 Annual Meeting of the American Political Science Association. New Orleans, LA.

Shair-Rosenfield, Sarah, Gary Marks, and Liesbet Hooghe.2014. "A Comparative Measure of Decentralization for Southeast Asia." *Journal of East Asian Studies*, 14(1): 85–108.

Shalley, Christina E. and Lucy L. Gilson. 2004. "What Leaders Need to Know: A Review of the Social and Contextual Factors that Can Foster or Hinder Creativity." *The Leadership Quarterly*, 15(1): 33–53.

Simon, Herbert. 1947. *Administrative Behavior: A Study of Decision-Making Processes in Administrative Organization*. New York, NY: Free Press.

Sinclair, Upton. 1906. *The Jungle*. New York, NY: Doubleday, Page.

Singer, Ethan A. and Leland M. Wooton. 1976. "The Triumph and Failure of Albert Speer's Administrative Genius: Implications for Current Management Theory and Practice." *The Journal of Applied Behavioral Science*, 12(1): 79–103.

Sirianni, Carmen. 2009. *Investing in Democracy: Engaging Citizens in Collaborative Governance*. Washington, DC: Brookings Institution Press.

Sitkin, Sim B., Kathleen M. Sutcliffe, and Roger G. Schroeder. 1994. "Distinguishing Control from Learning in Total Quality Management: A Contingency Perspective." *Academy of Management Review*, 19(3): 537–64.

Sivers, Derik. 2015. *First Follower: Leadership Lessons from Dancing Guy*. You Tube, https://video.search.yahoo.com/yhs/search?fr=yhs-pty-pty_weather&h simp=yhs-pty_weather&hspart=pty&p=The+dancing+guy#id=2&vid=b48e f94a51b65739bb2aceaf712c5b40&action=click, accessed June 25, 2015.

Skocpol, Theda. 1997. "The Tocqueville Problem: Civic Engagement in American Democracy." *Social Science History*, 21(4): 455–79.

Skocpol, Theda and Morris P. Fiorina. 1999. *Making Sense of the Civic Engagement Debate.Civic Engagement in American Democracy*. Washington, DC: Brookings Institution Press.

Slaughter-House Cases, 83 U.S. 36 (1873).

Smith, Adam. 2003/1776. *The Wealth of Nations*. London, UK: Stratton and Cadell.

Smith, Gerald E. and Carole A. Huntsman. 1997. "Reframing the Metaphor off the Citizen-Government Relationship: A Value-Centered perspective." *Public Administration Review*, 57(4): 309–18.

Smith, Steven R. and Michael Lipsky. 1993. *Nonprofits for Hire: The Welfare State in the Age of Contracting*. Cambridge, MA: Harvard University Press.

Smith, Steven R. and Judith Smyth. 2010. "The Government Contracting Relationship: Killing the Golden Goose." In Steven Osborne (Ed.), *The New Public Governance? Emerging Perspectives on the Theory and Practice of Public Governance*. London, UK: Routledge.

Snowden, David J. and Marry E. Boone. 2007. "A Leader's Framework for Decision Making." *Harvard Business Review*, 85(11): 68–76.

Souder, Jon A. and Sally K. Fairfax. 1996. *State Trust Lands: History, Management, and Sustainable Use*. Lawrence, KA: University Press of Kansas.

Spencer, Herbert. 1994. *Spencer: Political Writings*. Ed. John Offer. Cambridge, UK: Cambridge University Press.

Sridharan, Devarajan, Daniel J. Levitin, and Vinod Menon. 2008. "A Critical Role for the Right Fronto-insular Cortex in Switching between Central-executive and Default-Mode Networks." *Proceedings of the National Academy of Science*, 105(34): 12569–74.

Steffens, Lincoln. 1904. *The Shame of Cities*. New York, NY: McClure, Philips.

Stepan, Alfred, Juan J. Linz, and Yogendra Yadav. 2011. *Crafting State-Nations: India and Other Multinational Democracies*. Baltimore, MD: Johns Hopkins University Press.

Stever, James A. 1988. *The End of Public Administration: Problems of the Profession in the Post-Progressive Era*. Ferry, NY: Transnational Publishers.

Stever, James A. 1990. "The Dual Image of the Administrator in Progressive Administrative Theory." *Administration & Society*, 22(1): 39–57.

Stivers, Camilla. 2002a. *Gender Images in Public Administration: Legitimacy and the Administrative State*. 2nd ed. Thousand Oaks, CA: Sage.

Stivers, Camela. 2002b. *Bureau Men, Settlement Women: Constructing Public Administration in the Progressive Era*. Lawrence, KS: University of Kansas Press.

Stoker, Gerry. 2006. "Public Value Management: A New Narrative for Networked Governance?" *American Review of Public Administration*, 36(1): 41–57.

Stone, Clarence N. 1989. *Regime Politics: Governing Atlanta*. Lawrence, KA: University Press of Kansas.

Stone, Clarence N. 1993. "Urban Regimes and the Capacity to Govern: A Political Economy Approach." *Journal of Urban Affairs*, 15(1): 1–28.

Stone, Deborah A. 1997. *Policy Paradox: The Art of Political Decision Making*. New York, NY: Norton.

Stone, Deborah A. 2001. *Policy Paradox: The Art of Political Decision Making*. 3rd ed. New York, NY: Norton.

Storing, Herbert. 1964. "Political Parties and the Bureaucracy." In Robert A. Goldwin (Ed.), *Political Parties U.S.A.*. Chicago, IL: Rand McNally.

Storing, Herbert J. 1981a. *The Complete Anti-Federalist*. vols.7 Chicago, IL: University of Chicago Press.

Storing, Herbert J. 1981b. *What the Anti-Federalists Were For: The Political Thought of the Opponents of the Constitution*. Chicago, IL: University of Chicago Press.

Swanson, Guy E. 1970. "Toward Corporate Action: A Reconstruction of Elementary Collective Processes." In T. Shubtani (Ed.), *Human Nature and Collective Behavior: Papers in Honor of Herbert Blumer*. Englewood Cliffs, NJ: Prentice Hall.

Svara, James H. 1985. "Dichotomy and Duality: Reconceptualizing the Relationship between Policy and Administration in Council-Manager Cities." *Public Administration Review*, 45(1): 221–32.

Svara, James H. 1990. *Official Leadership in the City: Patterns of Conflict and Cooperation*. Oxford, UK: Oxford University Press.

Svara, James H. 1991. "City Manager Role: Conflict, Divergence, or Congruence?" *Administration & Society*, 23(2): 227–46.

Svara, James H. 1999. "The Shifting Boundary between Elected Officials and City Managers in Large Council-Manager Cities." *Public Administration Review*, 1(59): 207–27.

Svara, James H. 2006. "Complexity in Political-Administrative Relations and the Limits of the Dichotomy Concept." *Administrative Theory & Praxis*, 28(1): 121–39.

Swindler, William. 1969. *Court and Constitution in the 20th Century: The Old Legality*. New York, NY: Bobbs-Merrill.

Talisse, Robert B. 2009. *Democracy and Moral Conflict*. Cambridge, UK: Cambridge University Press.

Taylor, Frederick. 1911. *The Principles of Scientific Management*. London, UK: Harper (Reprinted, New York: Cosimo Books, 2006).

Taylor, Henry. (1998/1836). *The Statesman*, Eds D.L. Schaefer and R.R. Schaefer. Westport, CT: Praeger.

Taylor, Paul. 2014. *The Next America: Boomers, Millennials, and the Looming Generational Showdown*. New York, NY: Public Affairs.

Temin, Peter. 1969. *The Jacksonian Economy*. New York, NY: Norton.

Termeer, Catrien J., Art Dewulf, Ferard Breeman, and Sabina J. Stiller. 2015. "Governance Capabilities for Dealing Wisely with Wicked Problems." *Administration and Society*, 47(6): 680–710.

Thach, Charles. 1969. *The Creation of the Presidency: 1775–1789*. Baltimore, MD: Johns Hopkins University Press.

Thaler, Richard H. and Cass R. Sunstein. 2009. *Nudge: Improving Decisions about Health, Wealth, and Happiness*. Revised and expanded ed. New York, NY: Penguin Books.

Thompson, James D. 1967. *Organizations in Action*. New York, NY: McGraw-Hill.

Thornton, Paul B. 2010. *Leadership: Off the Wall*. Bloomington, IN: WestBow Press.

Thurmaier, Kurt and Curtis Wood. 2002. "Interlocal Agreements as Overlapping Social Networks: Picket-Fence Regionalism in Metropolitan Kansas City." *Public Administration Review*, 62 5(September/October): 585–98.

Tinker v. Des Moines Independent Community School District, 393 U.S. 503 (1969).

Tjosvold, Dean. 1985. "Power and Social Context in Superior-Subordinate Interaction." *Organizational Behavior and Human Decision Processes*, 35(3): 281–93.

Transformative Innovation Policy Consortium. 2017. "Home." www.transformative-innovation-policy.net/, accessed January 3, 2018.

Trist, Eric L. 1981. "The Evolution of Sociotechnical Systems as a Conceptual Framework for Action Research." In A.H. Van De Ven and W.F. Joyce (Eds), *Perspectives in Organizational Design and Behavior*. New York, NY: Wiley.

U.S. Bureau of Labor Statistics. 2017. "Employment Situation Summary, Table B. Establishment data." www.bls.gov/news.release/empsit.b.htm, accessed December 12, 2017.

U.S. Census Bureau. 2002. *Census of Governments*. Vol. 1, no. 1, Government Operations, Series GCO2(1)-1.

U.S. Census Bureau. 2007. "Statistics about Business Size." www.census.gov/econ/smallbus.html#Nonemployers, accessed December 29, 2017.

U.S. Census Bureau. 2011. "State and Local Government Finance Summary." www2.census.gov/govs/local/summary_report.pdf, accessed December 29, 2017.

U.S. Census Bureau. 2012a. "Census of Governments. Summary of County-Type Areas by Number of Governments and State." Table 2 https://factfinder.census. gov/faces/tableservices/jsf/pages/productview.xhtml?src=bkmk, accessed December 29, 2017.

U.S. Census Bureau. 2012b. "Household Income Inequality within U.S. Counties: 2006–2010." American Community Survey Brief. www.census.gov/prod/ 2012pubs/acsbr10-18.pdf, accessed December 2012.

U.S. Census Bureau. 2018. "Population Projections: Older People Projected to Outnumber Children for First Time in U.S. History." www.census.gov/news room/press-releases/2018/cb18-41-population-projections.html, accessed June 4, 2018.

U.S. Forest Service. 1993. *The Principal Laws Relating to Forest Service Activities.* Washington DC: United States Department of Agriculture.

U.S. Forest Service. 2006. *Mt. Hood National Forest Strategic Stewardship Plan: Weaving Together the Environment, People, and the Economy.* Washington, DC: U.S. Forest Service. www.fs.usda. gov/Internet/FSE_DOCUMENTS/fsbdev3_036319.pdf, accessed April 10, 2013.

U.S. Forest Service. 2007. *The U.S. Forest Service: An Overview.* Washington DC: U.S. Forest Service. www.fs.fed.us/documents/USFS_An_Overview_0106MJS. pdf, accessed April 10, 2013.

U.S. Forest Service. 2008. *Mission, Motto, Vison, and Guiding Principles.* Washington DC: U.S. Forest Service. www.fs.fed.us/aboutus/mission.shtml, accessed April 10, 2013.

U.S. Forest Service. 2013. *Stewardship Contracting Results: Success Stories.* Washington. DC: U.S. Forest Service.

U.S. GAO (U.S Government Accountability Office). 2014. "FEDERAL WORK-FORCE: Recent Trends in Federal Civilian Employment and Compensation," GAO-14-215. January 29.

U.S. Geological Service. 2016. "California Water Science Center." https://ca. water.usgs.gov/california-drought/index.html, accessed January 3, 2018.

U.S. Government Revenue. 2010. www.usgovernmentrevenue.com/year rev2010_0.html, accessed June 4, 2018.

U.S. NASA (National Astronautic and Space Administration). 2003. *Report of Columbia Accident Investigation Board.* Washington, DC: Government Printing Office.

U.S. President's Committee on Administrative Management. 1937. *Report with Special Studies* (also known as the Brownlow Report). Washington, DC: U.S. President's Committee on Administrative Management.

Uhl-Bien, Mary, Russ Marion, and Bill McKelvey. 2007. "Complexity Leadership Theory: Shifting Leadership from the Industrial Age to the Information Era." *The Leadership Quarterly*, 18(4): 298–318.

The Unfunded Mandates Information and Transparency Act. 1995, Pub. L. 104–04.

United Nations. 2006. "Economic and Social Commission for Asia and the Pacific: Local Government in Asia and the Pacific." www.unescap.org/huset/ lgstudy/index.htm, accessed September 18, 2012.

United States Advisory Commission on Intergovernmental Relations. 1987. *The Organization of Local Public Economies.* Washington, DC: ACIR.

United States Advisory Commission on Intergovernmental Relations. 1993. *Local Government Autonomy: Needs for State Constitutional, Statutory, and Judicial Clarification*, A–127. Washington, DC: ACIR.

Van Maanen, John. 1976. "Breaking In: Socialization to Work." In R. Dubin (Ed.), *Handbook of Work, Organization, and Society*. Chicago, IL: Rand McNally.

Van Riper, Paul. 1958. *History of the United States Civil Service*. Evanston, IL: Row, Peterson.

Vance, J. D. 2016. *Hillbilly Elegy*. New York, NY: HarperCollins.

Vaughn, Diane. 1996. *The Challenger Launch Decision: Risky Technology, Culture, and Deviance at NASA*. Chicago, IL: Chicago Press.

Venezuela, Sebastian, Namsu Park, and Kerk F. Kee. 2009. "Is There Social Capital in a Social Network Site? Facebook Use and College Students' Life Satisfaction, Trust, and Participation." *Journal of Computer-Mediated Communication*, 14 (July)4: 875–901.

Vickers, Geoffrey. 1995/1965. *The Art of Judgment: A Study of Policy Making*. Newbury Park, CA: Sage.

Vision Action Network of Washington County. 2013. "Collaborative Solutions for Washington County." http://visionactionnetwork.org/component/option, com_frontpage/Itemid,1/, accessed on April 9, 2017.

Vollmer, Howard M. and Donald L. Mills. 1966. *Professionalization*. Englewood Cliffs, NJ: Prentice Hall.

Vroom, Victor H. and Philip W. Yetton. 1973. *Leadership and Decision Making*. Pittsburgh, PA: University of Pittsburgh Press.

Walker, David. 2000–2009. Presentations of David Walker, Comptroller General. www.gao.gov/cghome/dwbiog.html, accessed February 14, 2015.

Wallskog, Joyce Marie. 1992. "The Relationship Between Life Experiences and Moral Reasoning in College-Educated Women." *Dissertations (1962–2010) Access via Proquest Digital Dissertations*. AAI9306005. http://epublications. marquette.edu/dissertations/AAI9306005, accessed December 27, 2017.

Walzer, Michael. 1973. "Political Action: The Problem of Dirty Hands." *Philosophy and Public Affair*, 2(winter)2: 160–80.

Walzer, Michael. 1992. "The Civil Society Argument." In Chantal Mouffe (Ed.), *Dimensions of Radical Democracy: Pluralism, Citizenship, Community*. London, UK: Verso.

Wanat, John A. 1978. *Introduction to Budgeting*. Scituate, MA: Duxbury Press.

Warner, Mildred E. and Amir Hefetz. 2004. "Pragmatism over Politics: Alternative service delivery in local government, 1992–2002." *The Municipal Year Book 2004*: 8–16.

Weatherford, Jack. 2004. *Genghis Khan and the Making of the Modern World*. New York, NY: Crown.

Webber, Sheila Simsarian. 2002. "Leadership and Trust Facilitating Cross-Functional Team Success." *Journal of Management Development*, 21(3): 201–14.

Weber, Max. 1946/1924. *Max Weber: Essays in Sociology*. Eds. H.H. Gerth and C. Wright Mills. New York, NY: Oxford University Press.

Weber, Max. 1968/1924. *Economy and Society*. Eds. Guenther Roth and Claus Wittich. New York, NY: Bedminster.

Weick, Karl. 1979. *The Social Psychology of Organizing*. 2nd ed. Reading, MA: Addison-Wesley.

Weinstein, Neil D. 1989. "Optimistic Biases about Personal Risks." *Science*, 246: 1232–33.

Weinstein, Neil D. and William Klein. 1996. ""Unrealistic Optimism: Present and Future." *Journal of Social and Clinical Psychology*, 15: 1–8.

Weinstein, Neil D., Judith E. Lyons, Peter M. Sandman, and Cara L. Cuite. 1998. "Experimental Evidence for Stages of Health Behaviour Change: The Precaution Adoption Process Applied to Home Radon Resting." *Health Psychology*, 17(5): 445–53.

Welch, Eric and Wilson Wong. 1998. "Public Administration in a Global Context: Bridging the Gaps of Theory and Practice between Western and Non-Western Nations." *Public Administration Review*, 58(1): 40–49.

Wescott, Clay G. 1999. "Decentralization Policy and Practice in Viet Nam: 1991–2003." In Paul Smoke and Edwardo Gomez (Eds), *Decentralization in Comparative Perspective*. Northampton, MA: Edward Elgar Press.

Westcott, Clay G. 2003. "Hierarchies, Networks and Local Government in Vietnam." *International Public Management Review*, 4(2): 20–40.

Westley, Francis, Brenda Zimmerman, and Michael Q. Patton. 2006. *Getting to Maybe*. Toronto, Canada: Vintage Books.

Wheatley, Margaret. 2000. *Leadership and the New Science*. San Francisco, CA: Berrett-Koehler Publishers.

Whitall, Debra, Craig Thomas, Steve Brink, and Gina Bartlett. 2014. "Interest-Based Deliberative Democracy in Natural Resource Management." In Douglas Morgan and Brian Cook (Eds), *A Regime Approach to New Pubic Governance*. Armonk: NY: M.E. Sharpe.

White, Leonard D. 1951. *The Jeffersonians: A Study in Administrative History, 1801–1829*. New York, NY: Macmillan.

White, Leonard D. 1958. *The Republican Era: A Study in Administrative History, 1869–1901*. New York, NY: Macmillan.

Wholey, Joseph S. and Harry P. Hatry. 1992. "The Case for Performance Monitoring." *Public Administration Review*, 52(6): 604–10.

Whyte, William H., Jr. 1956. *The Organization Man*. Garden City, NY: Doubleday.

Wildavsky, Aaron. 1964. *The Politics of the Budgetary Process*. Boston, MA: Little, Brown.

Wildavsky, Aaron. 1979. *Speaking Truth to Power: The Art and Craft of Policy Analysis*. Boston, MA: Little, Brown, MA..

Wilkerson, Charles. 2006. *Blood Struggle: The Rise of Modern Indian Nations*. New York, NY: W.W. Norton & Company.

Williams, Katherine Y. and Charles A. O'Reilly. 1998. "Demography and Diversity in Organizations: A Review of 40 Years of Research." *Research in Organizational Behavior*, 20: 77–140.

Wilson, Gerald L. 2002. *Groups in Context: Leadership and Participation in Small Groups*. 6th ed. New York, NY: McGraw-Hill.

Wilson, Woodrow. 1992/1887. "The Study of Public Administration." In Jay Shafritz and Albert C. Hyde (Eds), *Classics of Public Administration*. 3rd ed. Belmont, CA: Brooks/Cole. 1996. Originally published in *Political Science Quarterly* 2 (June 1887): 197–222.

Wirt, Frederick M. (Ed). 1971. *Future Directions in Community Power Research: A Colloquium*. Berkeley, CA: University of California, Institute of Governmental Studies.

Woolcock, Michael. 2001. "The Place of Social Capital in Understanding Social and Economic Outcomes." *Canadian Journal of Policy Research*, 2(1): 1–17.

World Bank, Socialist Republic of Vietnam. 2013. *Assessment of Financing Framework for Municipal Infrastructure in Vietnam*. Washington, DC: World Bank.

Wright, Robert. 1995. *The Moral Animal: Why We Are, the Way We Are: The New Science of Evolutionary Psychology*. New York, NY: Vintage.

Yaffee, Steven Lewis. 1994. *The Wisdom of the Spotted Owl: Policy Lessons for a New Century*. Washington, DC: Island.

Yang, Kaifeng and Mark Holzer 2006. "The Performance-Trust Link: Implications for Performance Measurement." *Public Administration Review*, 66(1): 114–26.

Yukl, Gary A. 1981. *Leadership in Organizations*. Englewood Cliffs, NJ: Prentice Hall.

Yukl, Gary. 2012. "Effective Leadership Behavior: What We Know and What Questions Need More Attention." *Academy of Management*, 26 (November) 4: 66–85.

Zaheer, Akbar, Bill McEvily, and Vincenzo Perrone. 1998. "Does Trust Matter? Exploring the effects of interorganizational and interpersonal trust on performance." *Organization Science*, 9(2): 141–59.

Zimmermann, Arthur and Claudia Maennling. 2007. "Muti-Stakeholder Management: Tools for Stakeholder Analysis: 10 Building Blocks for Designing Participatory Systems of Cooperation." Deutsche Gesellschaft für Technische Zusammenarbeit (GTZ) GmbH Postfach: 5180: 65726, Bonn.

Zinn, Howard. 2015/2005. *A People's History of the United States*. Reissue edition. New York: NY: Harper Perennial Modern Classics.

Index

424 *Index*

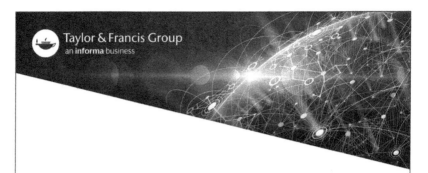